THEODORE ROOSEVELT
AND
THE MAKING OF
AMERICAN
LEADERSHIP

JON A. KNOKEY

Skyhorse Publishing

Skyhorse Publishing books may be purchased in bulk at special discounts for sales promotion, corporate gifts, fund-raising, or educational purposes. Special editions can also be created to specifications. For details, contact the Special Sales Department, Skyhorse Publishing, 307 West 36th Street, 11th Floor, New York, NY 10018 or info@skyhorsepublishing.com.

Skyhorse® and Skyhorse Publishing® are registered trademarks of Skyhorse Publishing, Inc.®, a Delaware corporation. Visit our website at www.skyhorsepublishing.com.

10 9 8 7 6 5 4 3 2 1

Library of Congress Cataloging-in-Publication Data is available on file.

Cover design by Tom Lau
Cover image courtesy of the Theodore Roosevelt Collection, Houghton Library, Harvard University

Print ISBN: 978-1-63450-356-3
Ebook ISBN: 978-1-5107-0130-4

Printed in the United States of America

For Meghan
My wife, my dearest friend

If I have anything at all resembling genius, it is in the gift for leadership . . . To tell the truth, I like to believe that, by what I have accomplished without great gifts, I may be a source of encouragement to Americans.

— Theodore Roosevelt

Contents

Preface

———————————————◇

Union Square, New York City. April 25th, 1865

At two o'clock in the afternoon, the casket was loaded onto a wagon pulled by sixteen horses. The box was six feet six inches in length and lined with lead. A small plate had been bolted to the outside:

ABRAHAM LINCOLN, SIXTEENTH PRESIDENT OF THE
UNITED STATES,
BORN FEB, 12 1809, DIED APRIL 15, 1865[1]

Eleven days had passed since John Wilkes Booth fired a bullet from a .44 caliber Derringer and further devastated a nation already divided by civil war. The joy from the recent armistice between Ulysses S. Grant and Robert E. Lee had been obliterated by murder. Just days after the most terrible of wars had ended, America had now lost her president in a final crescendo of senseless violence.

The funeral procession—retracing the route that had brought president-elect Lincoln into a house already divided—treaded solemnly through the streets of New York City. It was the city's turn to mourn and ask the Almighty for strength. It was their time to honor the man who gave the last full measure of devotion so that their nation might live. It was fitting and proper that thousands of citizens lined the streets. A light rain drizzled, church bells rang, Americans wept openly.

The clouds above were heavy and deep. Lampposts and homes were draped in large black shrouds. Black horses, cloaked in black cloth, pulled the black canopied hearse past mourners dressed in dark frock coats and holding black umbrellas.[2] Behind the casket limped the Invalid Brigade, a column of wounded and deformed soldiers.

In the mass of people, homemade signs and banners were visible: "GOD'S NOBLEST WORK, AN HONEST MAN, OUR CHIEF HAS FALLEN."[3] The poet Walt Whitman, tortured by the event, would turn to poetry to grieve:

> *O Captain! my Captain! rise up and hear the bells;*
> *Rise up—for you the flag is flung—for you the bugle trills;*
> *For you bouquets and ribboned wreaths—for you the shores a-crowd-*
> *ing;*
> *For you they call, the swaying mass, their eager faces turning;*
> *   Here Captain! dear father!*
> *   This arm beneath your head;*
> *   It is some dream that on the deck,*
> *   You've fallen cold and dead.*

As Abraham Lincoln's cortege made its way into Union Square, a photographer captured an iconic scene. Two young boys—six-year-old Theodore and his younger brother, Elliott—peer out of the second story window of the mansion owned by their grandfather, Cornelius Van Schaack Roosevelt.[4] Alongside the boys had been little Edith Carow. Not quite four years old, she began to cry at the sight of the disfigured men below. Annoyed, young Theodore shoved his future wife into a back room and locked the door. She never saw the service.

The procession rolled into Union Square where a rabbi, an archbishop and a minister all looked heavenward for answers—perhaps reading the same Bible, perhaps praying to the same God. When prayers were finished, the funeral march continued west to Fifth Avenue before turning north to 34th Street. The procession took one last turn west towards the Hudson River Railway Depot at the corner of 30th Street and 10th Avenue.[5]

At the Railway Depot, a guard of honor placed the coffin back aboard the Lincoln Special, a locomotive with the martyred president's photograph above the cowcatcher. At 4:15 p.m., the train slowly broke from the station. Its next stop was Albany. After that,

Buffalo, Cleveland, Columbus, Indianapolis, Michigan City, Chicago. The 1,654-mile route would eventually take Mr. Lincoln home to Springfield, Illinois. "In the larger cities," a magazine wrote, "the casket would be unloaded and paraded through the streets; in the countryside farmers standing beside their bonfires in the dark and rain would catch only a glimpse of the train as it passed."[6]

As the locomotive charged west, southern cities still smoldered from Sherman's march to the sea. America was shattered, still divided. The country was left to bind up her wounds. All its citizens pondered whether the better angels of its nature would ever again swell the full chorus of the Union.

Thirty-three years later, San Juan Heights, Santiago de Cuba. July 1st, 1898

At about 11:00 a.m. the Spanish bullets began to fall "like the first drops of a rainstorm."[7] The 1st Volunteer Cavalry—known throughout America as Roosevelt's Rough Riders—was trapped in an opening at the bottom of a creek bed, later to be renamed Bloody Bend. Three commanding U.S. officers went down in ten minutes. The wounded lay where they were hit, "men gasped on their backs, like fishes in the bottom of the boat."[8] Soldiers trampled over the dead, desperate to find cover.

The men could not retreat and they could not remain. There was only one option: charge the guns fortified on top of the hill.

Theodore Roosevelt jumped on his horse and rode to the front. One trooper remembers a great distinction. "He didn't say 'Go on'; he said, 'Come on!'"[9] The spirit of the moment seized those still alive. A wild animalistic cheer erupted. One Rough Rider called it "patriotic insanity."[10] A Pawnee Indian, the son of Chief Big Eagle, let out a native war cry.[11]

The patriotic outburst inspired the nearby 9th Cavalry—the African-American Regiment—known throughout America as the Buffalo Soldiers. They sprinted to join the charge.

The united men at the bottom of San Juan Heights now represented all of America: "Aristocrats from the east, cowboys from the west, millionaires, paupers, shyster lawyers, quack doctors, farmers, college professors, miners, adventurers, preachers, prospectors, socialists, journalists, clerks, Mormons, musicians, publicists, Jews, politicians, Gentiles, Mexicans, professed Christians, Indians, West Point graduates, wild men, Ivy League athletes, and thinkers."[12] They were from the North and they were from the South. They were from every part of the Union. They had one leader, Theodore Roosevelt.

Roosevelt was the only man on horseback, an easier target for his men to follow as well for the enemy, who were trained to aim at officers. He was dressed in khaki trousers, a blue flannel shirt, and a brown felt hat; he had tied a blue polka-dot bandana to his head, described as both a "warrior's headdress—and a bull's eye."[13]

"By God, there go our boys up the hill!" someone yelled from the military attaché a mile and a half away. "They can never take it," another moaned. "Never in the world. It is slaughter, absolute slaughter," another cried in horror.[14]

Amidst a shower of enemy bullets, Roosevelt galloped ahead.[15] His blue handkerchief whipped in the wind, as if it were a guidon.[16]

"No man," wrote journalist Richard Harding Davis, "who saw Roosevelt take that ride expected he would finish it alive."[17]

Within minutes, the Americans had seized the hill. The charge proved to be the turning point in the battle that led to victory in the war.

At the top of the hill, the triumphant Americans stood for a picture. Towering above the soldiers was an American flag which, like the men, was ragged and torn by war. Theodore Roosevelt stood in the middle, his head cocked to the side in self-assurance. To his left and right were fighters exhausted from the toil of battle, gritty and resilient.

In a matter of days the picture would make Theodore Roosevelt the most famous man in America. One snap of the camera captured the spirit of the Union and the rise of America into world supremacy. A Rough Rider, who immediately appreciated the historical consequence of the charge, captured the moment:

"The nation had undergone a painful adolescence when brother fought brother in civil war. But it had now grown up. America was conscious of itself as a single country, now ready to accept the responsibility of global leadership."[18]

Theodore Roosevelt considered the charge up San Juan Heights his "crowded hour," referring to Sir Walter Scott's maxim, "one crowded hour of glorious life is worth an age without a name."[19] Within six months of the charge, Theodore would be the governor of New York. Within thirty-two months, vice president of the United States. Within thirty-eight months, president.

But it was not the charge up the hill that put him in the White House. It was his ability to lead those from different backgrounds that made him president of the United States. He knew how to lead the Fifth Avenue clubman of New York as well as the frontiersman from the West. And when he got the opportunity to lead them together, he healed the scars of the Civil War and united a nation around a new vision: America as a superpower.

The story of Theodore Roosevelt's life has been well documented, but I do not think the story of his leadership journey has been told before.

I wrote this book out of curiosity. One afternoon as a graduate student at Harvard, I ventured into the Houghton Library which houses the Theodore Roosevelt Collection of documents, including diaries, speeches, and articles. My aim was not to find material to write a book but rather just to look at something neat and historical.

Wallace Finley Dailey—the curator of the collection—showed me a cart of six leather boxes that contained letters and interview notes from Roosevelt's contemporaries. The documents are hidden historical gems. Some of the first-hand accounts praise Roosevelt, some question his antics, some tell inside jokes, some are song lyrics, some are pointless, and some are obvious embellishments.

I asked Wallace if the documents had been published, and, to my surprise, he answered that most of them remained unpublished. Over the next several months my mind wandered: could these seemingly abstract stories from first-hand witnesses give us insight into how Theodore Roosevelt became a leader of consequence?

As I began to layer these never-before-published stories with Roosevelt's key biographical points, I began to see a pattern in his leadership development.

The documents I use come from an amusing cast of characters that only America could create: elite and wealthy Harvard chaps, reform-minded politicians from New York, tough-as-rawhide cowboys from the Badlands of North Dakota and Montana, and idealistic political reformers from the District of Columbia. Perhaps the greatest leadership insights come from the Rough Riders. We learn from them how Roosevelt embraced diversity and united frontiersmen and Natives from the American interior with Ivy League athletes and aristocrats from the eastern seaboard. Even a century later this story is inspirational.

You will read that none of the accounts considered Roosevelt to be a born leader. You will also notice a profound pattern of character traits that take hold early in his life, but later these traits get tempered by tragedy and introspection as Roosevelt learned how to shape events, interpret people, and humble himself. It is clear that Roosevelt was not born the right person for the times but assiduously cultivated the opportunity to become its spokesman. He learned how to lead the individual, which allowed him to lead the country.

Theodore Roosevelt once said that to understand a president, "the personal equation is always of vital consequence."[20] Theodore's personal equation, influenced by his life experiences, made him the president he would become. In fact, all of his grand achievements as president—the Square Deal economic policies to help the common American, the conservation of natural land, the opening of a global shipping lane in Panama, the creation of a strong U.S. Navy, the exorcism of government corruption, the aggressive action as a "trust buster" to break up corporate monopolies that preyed on consumers—had roots in previous experiences prior to his ascension to the White House. When one focuses on Roosevelt's leadership maturation, it is vividly clear that his impressive accomplishments as president were not original; his pre-presidential years were a harbinger of his actions as the nation's executive.

The story of Theodore Roosevelt's rise to power mirrors America's rise to power. They happened at the same time. Roosevelt was born shortly before the Civil War and lived through the aftermath of seedy reconstructionist policies and corrupt government machinists that profited by keeping the nation divided. You will see Roosevelt navigate an isolationist, politically divided, and war-torn country before eventually leading an entire generation of patriotism-starved Americans into the arena of global leadership. By examining how Roosevelt personally became a leader, we appreciate the making of American power itself.

"Roosevelt is not an American you know," a writer once quipped, "He is America."[21]

It is the duty of future generations to embrace the memory of past leaders. They should appreciate the timeless pattern and learn from their success and failings. Only when the next generation of leaders looks to the past can they prepare for their unknown and unique future. While writing this book on Roosevelt, I was reminded of a stanza from a William Knox poem, "Oh! Why Should the Spirit of Mortal Be Proud?": "For we are the same our fathers have been; / We see the same sights our fathers have seen; / We drink the same stream, and view the same sun, / And run the same course our fathers have run." The words of Theodore Roosevelt's contemporaries echo a reminder to future generations.

This is the story of how one man shaped events, people, and himself to create an authentic American style of leadership that has endured for over a century.

I

FOUNDATION

1. MOTHER AND FATHER, NORTH AND SOUTH

———————————————◇

THE FATHER OF THE TWENTY-SIXTH PRESIDENT OF THE United States, Theodore Roosevelt Sr., nicknamed Thee, was born September 22nd, 1831, the last of five boys to Cornelius Van Schaack Roosevelt. Though Thee would complain of being the "fifth wheel to the coach," he never complained of his birthright into one of the richest families in New York.[1] The Roosevelt lineage, a family of Dutch immigrants, established roots on Manhattan Island in the mid-seventeenth century when Claes Martenszen Van Rosenvelt settled in the colony of New Amsterdam in the year 1649—a full one hundred and eighty-two years before Theodore Senior had been born.[2] The Dutch Roosevelt family motto, Qui Plantavit Curabit—He Who Has Planted Will Preserve—characteristically encapsulated the Roosevelts of New York.[3] For seven generations, the Roosevelts had firmly planted on Manhattan Island, and through perseverance and means they bred many successes: state senators, lawyers, engineers, an alderman, a state supreme court justice, a bank president, a congressman, a district attorney, and an appellate court judge.[4]

But it was Cornelius Van Schaack Roosevelt, a curious looking man with a large head and short red hair, who would become "the family's initial man of fortune, the first Roosevelt millionaire."[5] Cornelius, claiming that "economy is my doctrine at all times," transformed the family business, Roosevelt and Son, from a hardware distributor to a plate glass importer, and wealth soon followed.[6] Cornelius caught his big break when President Andrew Jackson refused to renew the charter of the Second Bank of the United States, which led to the Panic of 1837 and, therefore, widespread deflation. Insulated from the panic, he was able to quickly buy up land on the island of Manhattan at a depressed price. Armed with assets and cash, Cornelius was appointed one of the first directors under a new charter at the Chemical Bank— the core of what would become JPMorgan Chase. This move catapulted his family into the financial elite, where the Roosevelt name became synonymous with Vanderbilt and Astor.[7]

In 1857, another panic solidified the Roosevelt fortune. When nearly every bank in the land suspended payments after a run on the financial institutions, the Chemical Bank continued to pay out in hard gold.[8] Nicknamed "Old Bullion," the Chemical Bank would earn a rock solid reputation as an institute of permanence. It also entrenched the Roosevelts into the upper-echelon of the aristocratic class.[9] Two solid institutions had been born.

In 1868, when an intrusive publication, *The Galaxy*, branded Cornelius as one of "ten bona fide millionaires" in New York, the family responded angrily to the invasion of privacy. However, no one disputed the authenticity of the report.[10]

When the time came to pass Roosevelt and Son onto a son, the Roosevelt that was chosen was James Alfred, the second eldest. It was undoubtedly the right choice. Focused and sharp, James understood business. When Cornelius retired, James was named both senior partner of the Roosevelt holdings and director at Chemical Bank.[11]

When it came to money, Thee could have cared less. Unlike his brother James, Thee has been described as a "miscast" businessman, uninterested in profit and never one who exhibited any real talent at making money. The historical record indicates that Thee's interests were in people, and that he cared for just about everyone. He knew his employees by name and he went to their homes. If a worker was suffering from medical or burial expenses he would reach into his own pocket and then roll up his sleeves and help finish any work around the house.[12] "[Thee is] a dignified, courteous man," an employee at Roosevelt and Son wrote, "who took a lively interest in the welfare of every employee, and was held in affectionate regard by all, from office boy upward."[13] In a time when boatload after boatload of immigrants flooded into New York City and laborers were nothing more than dispensable property, Thee's actions were extraordinary.

By the 1870s, New York City's population had tripled in three decades and was approaching five million.[14] The torrent of new residents sent real estate prices through the roof and wealthy landowners realized returns that doubled their investments annually. While the Astors, Vanderbilts, and Roosevelts got silly rich, the poor faced sensational despair.[15] Intergenerational immigrant families, wholly incapable of paying the inflated rent, were forced to share rooms in overcrowded, filthy tenements and quite literally lived on top of each other, sharing bathrooms, beds, even pillows. In a two mile stretch from Fifth Avenue at Washington Square to 42nd Street, there were roughly four-hundred wealthy families. In contrast, a single block in the immigrant district sheltered seven-hundred families. New York's Fourth Ward had nearly 290,000 citizens per square mile, a density unmatched by any other civilized country.[16] Two distinct worlds prevailed: the few ultra-rich and the mighty poor. At no time and at no place in the history of the United States was the income inequality as pronounced as it was in New York during this era.

The rich lived comfortably uptown, the poor lived in rat infested slums, and the government public safety net was a thing of the future. The immigration problem seemed unsolvable. Murders, street riots, property theft, and gang rapes skyrocketed. Prostitutes roamed the crammed streets. Vice was king. The main culprits of crime were the immigrant poor, who, according to historical police arrests, were responsible for more than three quarters of all serious felonies. Police Chief George Marshall found these "street rats" to be both "degrading and disgusting." New York Mayor Ambrose C. Kingsland criticized the children as "apt pupils in the school of vice, licentiousness, and theft."[17]

The famous English author Charles Dickinson had journeyed to America for inspiration on his work *Martin Chuzzlewit*. Touring New York's Five Points neighborhood in lower Manhattan, Dickinson did not find the land of opportunity; he found filth: "ruined houses, open to the street, whence, through wide gaps in the walls, other ruins loom upon the eye, as though the world of vice and misery had nothing else to show; hideous tenements which take their name from robbery and murder; all that is loathsome, drooping, and decayed is here."[18]

The two worlds that existed in New York affected Thee Roosevelt profoundly. Rather than focusing on growing the family business, he believed that it was his duty—indeed, his calling as a dutiful Christian and a man of means—to dedicate his life to the worthy cause of helping the poor. With James Alfred managing the Roosevelt fortune, Thee was free to pursue the love of his life, philanthropy. He would become the greatest humanitarian New York City has ever known.

Much has been written about President Roosevelt's ability to bridge the differences between the rich and poor, while maintaining harmony in both. This was a trait the boy learned from his father. Theodore Sr. was equally comfortable inspiring the orphans on the street as he was in the ballroom at high-society soirees.

Before his premature death at age forty-six, Theodore Sr. helped found the State Charities Aid Association, the Newsboys' Lodging House, the Young Men's Christian Association [YMCA], the Metropolitan Museum of Art, the American Museum of Natural History, a Training School for Nurses, and the New York Children's Orthopedic Hospital.[19] A man of endless energy, he achieved almost everything he undertook, and he undertook many things.

"I can see him [Thee] now," writes Louisa Lee Schuyler, president of the State Charities Aid Association, "in full evening dress, serving a most generous supper to his newsboys in the Lodging House, and later dashing off to an evening party in Fifth Avenue."[20]

Tall and handsome, Roosevelt Sr. had chestnut hair and a matching beard. His square Dutch jaw and piercing blue eyes gave an impression of strict sternness, a man with perhaps a hidden dark streak. But though his eyes and jaw made him an imposing figure, his personality was passionate and loveable. Almost every surviving record makes reference to his infectious enthusiasm, his desire to do good, and his overabundance of cheer. He also detested inactivity; every minute of every day was devoted towards progress. "Get action!" and "Seize the moment!" were his standard sayings, constantly and consistently reused.[21] In the family, he was affectionately called "Greatheart," a reference to the Puritan warrior in John Bunyan's Christian allegory who was the "guide and protector of wayfaring innocents, fearless leader in life's purposeful journey."[22] This was an exceptionally appropriate title for a man so devoted to family, righteousness, charity, and God.

"Whatever he [Thee] had to do, he did all out," confirms Charles Loring Brace, a friend and fellow pioneer in the field of social work.[23] To give vagabond children a fighting chance at life, Thee established and helped fund the Newsboys' Lodging House. From 1854 until 1877, an astounding 144,263 children would go through the doors of the Lodging House, at an expense of $237,569, or over six million in today's dollars.[24] Roosevelt did much more than just write a check. When Brace asked Thee if he would be willing to preach to the boys "every other Sunday evening at the Lodging House," Thee scoffed, explaining that his "troublesome conscience" would not allow it; "he would be there *every* Sunday."[25]

"His work in the lodging house was not perfunctory; it was not done as a duty," Charles Brace recalled. "He seemed to attract and win the sympathies of every boy in the house. He knew them by name, he knew their histories, and whenever he came there, they would gather round him, and he would question each one as to what he was doing, and give him advice and sympathy and direction."[26] Every Sunday evening, after church, Thee would read and speak to the children, promoting the values of the Roosevelt creed: "patriotism, good citizenship, and manly morality."[27]

Thee's oldest child, Anna, nicknamed Bamie, suffered from a debilitating spinal affliction. She was able to restore her health through expensive orthopedic treatment. Her parents were rich, so she got treatment, and this troubled Thee's conscience. He knew that if his rich friends saw what the new instruments could do for poor handicapped children, then they would be compelled to give money.[28]

So one day, under the guise of a purely social gathering, Thee invited his aristocratic friends over for a party of food and cocktails. When the festivities were well underway, he signaled for attention and then moved towards the door of the grand dining room. With silence prevailing and all eyes on him, he theatrically flung open the door where, surrounding a long table, to the horrible surprise of the aristocratic guests, sat several decrepit, handicapped children. The scene was terrible, ghastly. Some of the children slumped in chairs and others lay on the ground. All were helpless, none could move. On the majestic dining room table lay monstrous steel appliances. These appliances, Thee explained, could help cure the children, if and only if, they had a hospital to fit them to the apparatuses. On cue from her father, Corinne the youngest daughter, began fitting an instrument to one pitifully helpless child.

The guests were shocked, jaws on the ground. The sight of an aristocratic Roosevelt daughter aiding a handicapped poor child, had a deep effect on the guests. Mrs. John Jacob Astor leaned over one fragile child and began to tear up. "Theodore you are right," she sniffled, "these children must be restored and made into active citizens again, and I for one will help you in your work."[29] That night, more than enough money was raised to start the first Orthopedic Hospital in New York, later to be built on East 59th Street.[30]

The news of Thee's philanthropic techniques made many of his wealthy friends fearful of a sudden visit. The running family joke told that when a friend saw Thee approach, they would simply take out their pocketbooks and ask, "How much this time, Theodore?"[31] One wealthy New Yorker, upon hearing that Thee was travelling abroad, quipped that "it would save him at least a thousand dollars."[32]

The future president, Theodore Roosevelt Jr., nicknamed Teedie by the family, idolized his father and grew up emulating him. But for a good portion of his invalid childhood, his mother engaged most of his attention. Teedie would grow up to be much more like her, perhaps more than he ever realized. Certainly the intensity of his demeanor could be traced to her vibrant personality and pulsating emotions.[33] The future president's showmanship and flair for theatrics were undoubtedly her qualities; his quirky mannerisms and maxims were influenced by his mother: "the square deal," "the lunatic fringe," "good to the last drop," "speak softly and carry a big stick," "the bully pulpit," "thumbed over," "my hat is in the ring."[34]

Martha Bulloch, nicknamed Mittie, was the quintessential Southern Belle. Born in 1835 to a wealthy prominent family entrenched in the society of Old Savannah, Georgia, she was remarkably attractive. As full of emotion and fortitude as she was beautiful, Mittie's dark hair, blue eyes, delicate features, and petite waist made her perhaps the most "remarkably beautiful woman" in all of Georgia.[35] Her skin was said to be "the purest and most delicate white, more moonlight white than cream-white."[36] She spoke with a natural flair and loved nothing more than to tell Southern stories overcrowded with idealism and reminiscence. When she spoke of her own childhood in Roswell, her children were left to wonder if their mother had been born in a foreign country.[37]

The Bulloch estate in Roswell, Georgia, was a picturesque manor on a sprawling plantation. Oak, pine, and cypress trees scattered the property and dripped with hanging moss. To the west, the vast estate meandered into a wide valley, presenting a quaint and sloping southern landscape. The crop was cotton. The life was simple. Local tradition still holds that Margaret Mitchell, who wrote about the Bulloch Hall as an Atlanta newspaper reporter in the 1920s, used it as the model for the Tara Plantation in her book *Gone With The Wind.*[38] Whether or not the house was the inspiration for the American classic is still debated, but the similarities between Mittie Bullock and Scarlett O'Hara are too exceptional to discredit. Both women were Southern beauties. Both were children of wealth. Both lived patriarchal lives. Both had families that owned slaves. And both wholly subscribed to the idealism of antebellum virtues.

In 1850, a friend of Theodore Roosevelt Sr., Hilborne West, married Mittie's half-sister Susan Elliott, in Roswell, Georgia, and Thee, then a nineteen-year-old Knickerbocker, wanted to see for himself the charms of the South and its feudal way of life.[39] Upon arrival in Roswell, he was captivated by life on the plantation— the white blossoms on the dogwoods, the azaleas, the rolling plantations, the white-columned manors. But the most beautiful sight was fifteen-year-old Mittie. When it was time for Thee to return to the city, he took Mittie's gold thimble as a keepsake back with him.[40] He left his heart in Roswell.

Though both had been born into wealth, Mittie and Thee's homes were a thousand miles from each other; their families a world apart. The son of a long line of business and civic leaders, Thee represented progress, efficiency, and entrepreneurship. Mittie was the daughter of planters who embodied the slaveholding gentry. But love, as it often does, conquered difference and distance and the couple married at the Bulloch mansion in December of 1853. "Does it not seem strange to think we should have met and become engaged," Mittie wrote Thee, ". . . sometimes when I think of it all I feel as if it were ordered by some higher power."[41]

Not lost on the Roosevelt children was the romantic story of "the Southern girl who went away with her Northern lover," daughter Corinne Roosevelt reminisced. "We children . . . loved nothing better than to make my mother . . . tell us the story of the gay wedding at the old home near Atlanta."[42]

Mittie cherished telling her stories as much as the children loved hearing them. From the start, little Teedie was inundated with heroic tales of courage, stories ripe with his mother's definition of Southern masculinity—stories of men "who love the name of honor more than [they] fear death."[43]

"My earliest training and principles were Southern," Theodore claimed later, referring to Mittie's endless tales of family pride, military struggle, and daring code duellos.[44] It is important to appreciate that Mittie had left Roswell just the decade preceding the notorious Hatfield and McCoy family feud, the violent era in Southern society where the values of family honor, justice, and brutal vengeance were rampant.

The distinguished and high-ranking members in Mittie's family undoubtedly added to her sensationalized stories. The Bulloch family had long been entrenched in Southern military leadership; among her direct ancestors she could count six notable political leaders, including the president of the revolutionary Georgia, the great Archibald Bulloch.[45]

Almost a century before Theodore Jr. was born, Governor Archibald Bulloch established himself as a prominent leader in Southern society and culture. First a member of the Commons House of Georgia and later elected as the president of Georgia, Bulloch was also a member of the 1775 Continental Congress where he won the favor of John Adams, who would praise Bulloch as a man with astute "abilities and fortitude."[46] While Congress was drafting the Declaration of Independence in Philadelphia, Bulloch—who undoubtedly would have been a signer of the document—was forced to return to Georgia to lead the revolutionary uprising in the state.[47] Upon his return home, Bulloch was chosen as president and commander-in-chief of Georgia, and on February 22nd, 1777, when facing the threat of British invasion, he was granted executive power to lead his militia into battle. Just a few hours after the command was given, Bulloch was dead. The cause of his death is a mystery to this day, but rumors of a poisoning persist, perhaps from someone within his inner circle—like Brutus cutting down Julius Caesar.[48] And though the name Archibald Bulloch has for the most part been lost to history, he was considered one of the great American revolutionaries of his era. To his great-great-grandson, he would forever be the model of a patriotic warrior; a man who answered his nation's call and risked his life in the name of honor. To Teedie, it was as if Archibald Bulloch and Julius Caesar were one and the same.[49]

In a poignant scene in *Gone With The Wind*, Scarlett O'Hara refers to the Southern culture prior to the Civil War and wonders if her sprawling plantation home is standing or if it had "gone with the wind which had swept through Georgia."[50] When Mittie was swept away to Manhattan, New York, she forever departed the Southern way of life, never to return. The South as she knew it would forevermore be an irretrievable place made of memories.

In New York, the young Roosevelts settled into a luxurious house on 20th Street, a wedding gift from Cornelius. For Mittie, the hustle of horse carts and sea of humanity was a far cry from the quiet serenity of rolling cotton fields. But she adjusted well. Almost every night the young couple could be found on the circuit of balls and soirees that consumed the social elite. Their life was comfortable and cosmopolitan. They were young, rich, beautiful, and exquisite. They were the new picture of wealth and prestige on the New York scene.[51]

In the fall of 1858, Mittie and Thee were expecting their second child and first boy, Theodore. Across America, the significant issue of slavery was rapidly dividing the country. Nebraska and Kansas had recently bloodied themselves over the immense question of sovereignty and the ongoing dispute of whether all men were indeed created equal. Stephen Douglas, a senator from Illinois, aiming to settle the dispute once and for all, brokered the Kansas-Nebraska Act of 1854, a grand bargain which would allow settlers in those territories to determine whether they were a free state or not. Outraged by the act, a new political party, the Republican Party, was founded with the hell-bent focus of preventing the spread of slavery to the Western states. A tall, gangly, and poorly dressed lawyer from Illinois was chosen by the new party to run for the Illinois senate seat to dethrone Stephen Douglas. Inspired by scripture—Matthew 12:25—Abraham Lincoln announced his candidacy in June of 1858, claiming that he believed "a house divided against itself cannot stand" and that the "government cannot endure, permanently, half-slave and half-free."[52]

In October 1858, Douglas and Lincoln crisscrossed Illinois for seven debates, arguing their views on slavery and sovereignty. The entire nation looked to Illinois with rapt attention. Horace Greeley's *New York Tribune* cheered that Lincoln had turned the race into nothing less than "a contest for the Kingdom of Heaven or the Kingdom of Satan—a contest for advance or retrograde in civilization."[53] It is unknown whether the Roosevelts read the article, but the very pregnant Mittie would have undoubtedly fiercely disapproved. Her husband would have agreed with Greeley.

The last Lincoln-Douglas debate took place on October 15th in Alton, Illinois. Twelve days later, on October 27th, Theodore Roosevelt was born. On election day, November 3rd, Lincoln and the new Republican Party were soundly defeated.[54]

There about the same day, Ulysses S. Grant, a West Point graduate who had been kicked out of the Army due to his severe drinking problem, gave up on his latest failure and sold off his crop and farming equipment.[55]

Just two years and five months later, on April 12th, 1861, at four thirty in the morning, Confederate batteries opened fire upon Fort Sumter in Charleston Harbor, South Carolina. Abraham Lincoln was president, Ulysses S. Grant would be allowed to return to the U.S. army.

The momentous issue of Civil War was fully upon the country. The fault line that divided the Republic ran right through the Roosevelt home.

2. CIVIL WAR

When civil war was declared, the Roosevelt family consisted of a Northern father, a Southern mother, and three children: six-year-old Anna, nicknamed Bamie, two-year-old Theodore, and fourteen-month-old Elliott.[1] Mittie was pregnant with the family's final child Corinne, who was born the week after the First Battle of Lexington.[2] Rounding out the Roosevelt home was a bevy of servants, as well as Mittie's sister, Anna, and mother, Grandma Bulloch, both of whom had left the feudal life in Roswell for New York. As the nation was divided, so too was the Roosevelt home. The Northern man stood alone, a steadfast Lincoln supporter. The three strong-willed Bulloch women, from their vicarious Southern bloodline, were unflinching Confederate sympathizers. The women openly prayed for southern victories and wept over lost battles. It was said that the women of the household, upon hearing the news that Port Royal fell, cried for days.[3] Mrs. Bulloch declared in a letter that she, along with the rest of the South, would "rather be buried in one common grave than ever live under the same government again."[4] It was also rumored, though probably not true, that Mittie hung the Confederate flag outside her window after an early Southern victory.[5]

The fracture in the Roosevelt home was not uncommon for the times. Abraham Lincoln had a Southern wife whose three half-sisters were married to Confederate officers.[6] It was the tension in the Roosevelt home that was peculiar. In a letter, Thee pensively wrote to Mittie that he wished they "sympathized together on this question of so vital moment to our country," before admitting, "I know you cannot understand my feelings, and of course I do not expect it."[7]

The dual allegiance in his household influenced Thee. Though he was twenty-nine years old, healthy, and fit, he decided to not bear arms for the Union cause and hired two stand-in soldiers to fight in his place. This permission slip out of war cost him $300 per soldier, an amount well beyond the means of an ordinary citizen.[8] The practice of hiring a substitute fighter was very common among the wealthy class, as men of means skirted the war. But the double standard instigated intense resentment from the poor, who viewed it as class warfare, quite literally. In the summer of 1863, angry mobs marched through the streets of New York prompting a violent uproar. In what was to become known as the New York Draft Riots, hundreds of skirmishes broke out across the city as the angry citizens shouted insults directly at men like Thee: "Down with the rich men!" and "There goes a three-hundred-dollarman!"[9]

Teedie was almost five years old during the Draft Riots, and the terrifying scene of mobs shouting in the streets and setting fire to property certainly left a bewildering impression.[10]

The Draft Riots, and his father's decision not to fight, would forever haunt Theodore Roosevelt Jr.

According to a memoir written by Anna Roosevelt, Thee, in fact, regretted the decision and "always afterward felt that he had done a very wrong thing in not having put every other feeling aside and joined the absolute fighting forces."[11] But worse, none of the five Roosevelt brothers saw active service in the war, and Teedie, who grew up listening to his mother's stories of Southern military exploits, was forced to reconcile the fact that his father, as well as the rest of the Roosevelt men, were not fighters.[12] Sister Corinne would explain that she "felt strongly that her elder brother's aggressive personal passion for active military service in any national emergency was in part compensation for an unspoken disappointment in his father's course in 1861."[13] Teedie would grow up to believe that military glory would provide him the opportunity to surpass the father he idolized, as well as restore honor to the Roosevelt family name.[14]

Though Thee did not fight as a soldier, he did wholeheartedly engage in aiding the war effort in a civilian capacity. Naturally, he gravitated to a charitable cause.

When the fighting men went off to war there was no system in place for soldiers to send a portion of their military stipend home to their wives and children, where it was sorely needed. "Millions of government dollars were flowing through the pockets of Union soldiers and into the hands of sutlers, who infested military camps, hawking bottles of liquor hidden in loaves of bread," an account reads, "The sutlers charged such exorbitant prices that their customers soon had no money left to send home to their families."[15]

Thee was committed to "right this wrong" and, with two other wealthy New Yorkers, he drafted a bill to create an allotment commission that would enable soldiers to send money home to their needy families, at no additional cost or risk.[16] Thee, always eager to help vulnerable women and children, travelled to Washington, DC to encourage legislators to pass his plan. Politically naive, his efforts were stonewalled, the congressional commission was delayed by what a friend called "the utter inability of Congressmen to understand why anyone should urge a bill from which no one could selfishly secure an advantage."[17]

Undeterred, Thee decided on a "direct approach" and went right to the White House and called on Abraham Lincoln's private secretary, John Hay. "[I] explained my object in a few words and was immediately shown into the next room where the president sat,"[18] Thee wrote to Mittie. President Lincoln liked Thee and his plan, and endorsed both. Of the meeting, Thee recalled that the war-torn president's only enjoyment came when ten-year-old Willie Lincoln entered the room "and the president's expression of face then for the first time softened into a very pleasant smile."[19]

Thee stayed in Washington for three months as his legislation trudged through Congress. He had his correspondence forwarded to the White House and, in short order, he and the president struck up a friendship. But it was Mrs. Lincoln, a Southerner like Mittie, who was most impressed with Thee's charm and tenderness. She took him bonnet shopping and invited him on carriage rides. The first lady also invited the twenty-nine-year-old to a private party at the White House where, according to Thee, "the largest collection of notables there ever gathered in the country" was in attendance.[20]

While the allotment commission was debated on the hill, Thee and White House secretary John Hay, both men in their twenties, became very close friends. They lunched and walked together. On one Sunday, Hay invited Thee to share the presidential pew at the service at St. John's Church. As the two entered the church, Thee took great enjoyment that many onlookers mistook him, with his height and whiskers, to be the president.[21]

John Hay and Thee had begun a friendship that would last a lifetime. Some years later, Thee brought Hay to New York to meet his family. The two men arrived in a torrential rain storm, and the children, waiting eagerly by the window, got a good laugh when Hay tried to open his umbrella and it blew inside-out, "like a dilapidated pinwheel."[22] The children, between laughing fits, rushed to the door to meet the soaking-wet stranger.[23]

"Mittie, I want to present to you a young man, who in the future, I believe, will make his name well known in the United States," Thee boomed as he entered the house. "This is Mr. John Hay, and I wish the children to shake hands with him."[24]

Teedie, a small boy of eleven, shook hands with the stranger, and perhaps wondered how this Hay fellow was going to "make his name well known in the United States."[25] Mr. Hay certainly did not suspect that one day the eleven-year-old would be the president and he would be his secretary of state.[26] Hay was too preoccupied with his broken umbrella.

When the Allotment Commission finally passed into law, Lincoln appointed Thee as one of the three commissioners from the state of New York. Over the next two years, his service to the cause would prove remarkable. He spent months trekking by train, boat, and horseback from muddy army camp to army camp, urging the men to take care of their families back home. In one stretch of over thirty days, he slept in a train car every night. Thee's idea to send money home, which is now standard military practice, was initially a tough sell. At almost every Army camp he was greeted with a gun to his chest and asked to explain why he needed to pass through the secured perimeter.[27]

At just twenty-nine years old, Thee had devised a plan and personally saw to it that it passed congress with President Lincoln's approval. He tirelessly implemented a policy which led to millions of dollars being sent home to wives and children where it was sorely needed. Thee proved leadership and initiative, a crusader's quest to help countless military families. Yet, exceptionally telling, Thee's honorable service was not mentioned at all in his son's autobiography. Instead, Theodore Jr. chose to write about his mother's brother and half-brother, Confederate soldiers who exemplified courage and bravery, men who fought in combat.

James Dunwoodie Bulloch, Mittie's half-brother, and Irvine Bulloch, Mittie's full brother, were both proud of their family's important and distinguished Southern military legacy.[28] When the war came, it was their honor to fight for the Confederate cause. James was dispatched to England to quickly and quietly procure six steam vessels for a million dollars under direct orders from Confederate President Jefferson Davis.[29] The British government, intensely suspicious of any ship building efforts that would aid the belligerent South, was exceptionally wary of James Bulloch's arrival. Under the guise of being a ship builder working for a cotton magnate, James managed to build ship No. 290—the 290th ship built at the Laird Shipyard in Liverpool.[30] "I cannot exaggerate, sir," James confided to a Confederate agent in London, "the caution and tact required to get a ship to sea with even the external experience of a man-of-war."[31]

Bulloch designed the ship—900 tons and 230 feet in length—with the grand plan to leave Liverpool as an innocent commerce cruiser "to be armed later in the Azores."[32] The plan went well until the American Minister to Britain, Charles Francis Adams—grandson of John and Abigail Adams—was tipped off by a secret agent that Bulloch was working for the

Confederacy. Adams confronted the British government with his suspicions, but for five days the Queen's Advocate, perhaps weary of causing an international incident, took no action.[33] The spy games took a dramatic turn when James learned that Adams was conspiring to have him arrested and decided on a daring escape fit for fiction. He decided to steal the unfinished ship in broad daylight.

On the morning of July 29th, 1862 James Bulloch invited a large party of "fashionable ladies and gentlemen" to christen the ship under the guise of a "short trial run and a picnic lunch."[34] The British government, alerted that the ship was leaving the dock, put several officials aboard to ensure that the vessel would not be stolen and "no international wrong" manifested.[35] The vessel had barely left the dock, when a tug boat came alongside *No. 290* and James shepherded all those aboard onto the smaller boat. He then pointed the bow of the *No. 290,* soon to be renamed the *CSS Alabama,* out to sea and into the Civil War. James Bulloch had stolen the ship right under the nose of British authorities, high-treason at its finest. In time, the CSS *Alabama* would prove to be one of the most effective Confederate raiders of the war, destroying fifty-eight vessels valued at over $6 million.[36]

In an ironic twist of history, when the CSS *Alabama* was finally destroyed on June 19th, 1864, off the coast of Cherbourg, France, it was Irvine Bulloch, James's half-brother and the youngest officer on board, who fearlessly fired the last battery as the ship sank under heavy fire from the USS *Kearsarge.*[37] Irvine was rescued by a British yacht and immediately rejoined the Confederate cause on the CSS *Shenandoah,* a raider responsible for sinking numerous commercial and whaling ships. It was the *Shenandoah* that fired the last shot in the Civil War.[38]

Both Bulloch brothers survived the war only to be denied amnesty. Forced into exile in Liverpool, England, the Bulloch uncles became mythological heroes to young Teedie. One uncle had stolen the ship that the other uncle had heroically fired the last shot from as it sank. Their buccaneering adventures on the high seas evidently stirred something deep within the child. However, it is important to remember that Teedie was only six years old when the war ended, much too young to truly appreciate and wholly embrace the events that surrounded him. What actually

stirred the boy's imagination were his mother's dramatic retell-
ings of the Bulloch uncles and their fearless acts.

As Thee trudged from one Army camp to another, Mittie was free
to entertain Theodore with fables of gallantry and Southern manhood. The "heroes" that he was raised on were all on her side; all
of them Southern, masculine, full of vigor.[39] And when these stories were combined with real-life acts of drama, with real members
of the family, the effect on the child was intensified exponentially.

One day, five years after the war had ended, Mittie was sitting
at the breakfast table when she received a peculiar letter. The
children saw the flush leave her face, as she burst into tears. "Oh,"
she cried, "this must be from Irvine!"

> If Mrs. Theodore Roosevelt and Miss Anna Bulloch will
> walk in Central Park up in the Mall [the letter read], at
> 3 o'clock on Thursday afternoon of this week and notice a
> young man standing under the third tree on the left with a
> red handkerchief tied around his throat, it will be of inter-
> est to them.[40]

Irvine Bulloch had been missing for over five years; no one
had heard from him. To Teedie, the mystery letter represented
the epitome of Southern heroism. Somehow Irvine had fought
valiantly to survive the war and now was braving the authorities
again. On the following Thursday, Mittie went to the third tree on
the left where Irvine awaited—no longer a "round-faced boy" but
a "thin, haggard-looking young man."[41] "He had worked his way
over in the steerage of a sailing-vessel under an assumed name,"
sister Corinne recalled.[42]

For a brief hour, the southern siblings reminisced about their
childhood on the plantation before Irvine said goodbye, and vanished back to England, as quietly as he had come. For Teedie, it
was Irvine the great war hero who came and went like a ghost,
who reinforced the romanticism and idealism of his mother's stories. He was a real-life, romantic warrior.

It is interesting to note that Teedie always rooted for the Northern cause, the Roosevelt side. At a young age, it was evident that he compartmentalized the Civil War as good versus evil. But the line was not drawn North and South. His Confederate uncles were heroes fighting for honor and duty; others in the Southern cause were immoral. When Theodore was eleven years old the Roosevelt family went to Liverpool to reunite with the exiled Bulloch brothers. One afternoon, Teedie and brother Elliott encountered the son of Jefferson Davis, the former president of the Confederate States of America. Jefferson Davis, exiled himself, had enrolled his child at the same Waterloo school that Teedie's cousin attended. "We had a nice time," young Teedie wrote in his dairy, "but met Jeff Davises's son and some sharp words ensued."[43] The image of the young patriotic vigilant of justice threatening the son of the exiled president of the Confederacy is certainly entertaining. But it is also very ironic. The Bulloch brothers were off limits. The son of Jefferson Davis was fair game. The skirmish, though juvenile and seemingly inconsequential at the time, certainly illustrates a contradictory definition of right and wrong.

When Theodore grew older he, quite purposefully, never acknowledged his father's incredible efforts during the Civil War. Though Thee exhibited substantial leadership and helped thousands of women and children while personally influencing the president of the United States, he was still no match for the Bulloch uncles and their heroic, albeit rebellious, acts. And almost four decades after Thee's decision to substitute out of the war, Theodore Roosevelt was confronted with an eerily similar situation. In 1898, he was a young rising star in political circles, serving in a civilian capacity as assistant secretary of the navy; a leader providing substantial policy and operational management to his country. Just like Thee had done. But when the Spanish-American War came, Theodore would resign his post and actively seek combat at the front with a rag-tag regiment of Rough Rider volunteers. Faced with a startlingly similar situation, the boy would make the exact opposite decision of the father.

The Civil War was a traumatic event for an entire generation of American children. For Teedie it was full of death, anxiety, and struggle. His grandmother died during the war, his father was absent for the majority of two years, and his mother—a woman never lacking in emotion—incessantly worried for her husband and brothers. Teedie was in no way immune to the substantial emotional tension of a country fully absorbed in war. On the street, he would witness the wounded coming home, the missing limbs, the women weeping for those left behind.

The Civil War accentuated Theodore Roosevelt's dual birthright. For the rest of his life he would embrace the Bulloch lineage of heroic combatants and the Roosevelt heritage of principle and morality.[44] He would claim that ". . . from hearing of the feats performed by my southern forefathers and kinsfolk, and from knowing my father, I felt a great admiration for men who were fearless and who could hold their own in the world, and I had a great desire to be like them."[45]

Theodore coveted this dual allegiance; it made him special, it made him different. His dual birthright allowed him to better understand the Northern and Southern cause, equally and uniformly.

> It has been my very great good fortune to have the right to claim my blood is half Southern and half Northern, and I would deny the right of any man here to feel a greater pride in the deeds of every Southerner than I feel. . . . don't you think I have the ancestral right to claim a proud kinship with those who showed their devotion to duty as they saw the duty, whether they wore the grey or whether they wore the blue? All Americans who are worthy the name feel an equal pride in the valor of those who fought on one side or the other, provided only that each did with all his might and soul and mind his duty as it was given to him to see his duty.[46]

To arrive at an understanding of Theodore Roosevelt's many-sided character, one must first embrace, in the words of his sister, "the combination of personalities and the different strains of blood in those personalities from whom he was descended in summing up the man he was."[47] The intensity and judgment of the old Dutch blood from his Northern father contrasted with the gaiety and love of heroism from the lineage of his Southern mother. He embraced both contrasts seamlessly, almost naturally. And it was this ability—to embrace contradiction among diverse groups of people—that would become, over time, one of his greatest strengths as a leader.

But all that would happen in the future.

In 1865, when the Civil War finally ended, the Roosevelt parents were only mildly relieved. The nation's horror had come to a close, but another horror had no end in sight. Teedie was haunted by a sickness that threatened to pull him from the dawn of a new America.[48]

3. FIGHT TO SURVIVE

WHEN THEODORE ROOSEVELT WAS THREE YEARS OLD, HE SUDdenly awoke one night and could not breathe. Thee rushed to his son's bedside, concerned and bewildered. The pale lamplight illuminated a wretched scene: a fragile child violently heaving for air while his father watched in horror, helpless. The boy, trapped in a ferocious asthmatic fit, was gasping for breath and grasping for life.

Anxious, Thee ordered a servant to the stable to procure a horse and carriage, hoping that a midnight ride would force breath into the boy's struggling lungs.[1] Outside of the home the street was dark and quiet.

Fretful moments passed, the violent sound of wheezing and gulping filled the home. The young boy's body continued to strangle itself; no air went in or out of his lungs. The silence of the night outside was finally broken by the pounding of hooves on the cobblestone streets, announcing the arrival of the carriage. Theodore Sr., embracing his namesake bundled in blankets, rushed outside and leapt aboard. With a crack of the whip the horses were off. Father and son burst into the black of night in pursuit of precious air.

Theodore Roosevelt Jr. suffered from a debilitating form of asthma, and when an attack struck, almost always without warning, his chest would tighten and breathing became strenuous. A high-pitched wheeze followed. The child would try, with all his might, to pull air into his constricted lungs; he coughed, he cried, he thrashed violently. If he could speak, it was in short frantic wheezes.[2] In a matter of seconds the sensation of strangulation or drowning overcame him. Terrified, he fought for air, "tugging, straining, elbows planted on his knees, shoulders hunched high, his head thrown back, eyes popping."[3] His body would begin to convulse violently. There was no telling how long the episode would last, but when it finally did end, Teedie would lay soaked in sweat, quivering and exhausted. Then the psychological trepidation would begin: the boy was relieved that he survived the attack but was forced to accept the harsh reality that another assault was inevitable in the near future.[4]

In the context of contemporary medicine, it is hard to imagine asthma as a debilitating illness. The most severe forms can easily be controlled with medication. But treatment for asthma in the mid-nineteenth century was primitive. There was no relief, nothing was known to open the swollen air passages. And at the request of doctors, and love for their child, Mittie and Thee forced Teedie to swallow magnesia, quinine with iron, and ipecac—a compound used to instigate vomiting.[5] When the medicine did not work, the parents "applied heated mustard plasters to his chest."[6] When the plasters failed, they gave him black coffee, believing that the caffeine would stymie an attack. When that failed, doctors ordered that the child smoke cigars, believing that excessive nicotine would help. "I sat up for 4 successive hours and Papa made me smoke a cigar," reads a diary account.[7]

Water treatment, rest, and long walks were also ordered. In his diary Teedie recounts one morning when he received a chest massage that was so hard "that the blood came out."[8] Who administered the massage is unknown.

At the request of the family doctor, the distraught Roosevelt parents arranged a meeting with Alphonso D. Rockwell, a leading specialist popular for treating "high-strung, excessively refined aristocrats who had inherited neurasthenia from a parent."[9] Teedie was immediately diagnosed with "the handicap of riches," in what was described as a "typical case of excessive upper-class refinement."[10] Rockwell, subscribing to his own theory that the root cause of neurasthenia was the increased modernity of American life, blamed contemporary forces: "steam power, the telegraph, scientific discoveries, the periodical press, and even women's increased intellectual activity—for wearing out the delicate nervous systems of brain workers and other cultured types who were multiplying in an affluent industrial world."[11] His groundbreaking findings were supplemented by a grotesque series of procedures whereby he attached electrical equipment to his "patient's head and the abdomen or feet and sent a charge throughout the body to restore its energy and 'vital force' in order to cure the patient of his 'overcivilization.'"[12] Electric charges would restore a patient's nervous energy, Rockwell knew.

Years later, Dr. Rockwell recalled that Teedie, precocious and curious, "had shown a great deal of curiosity about how the electricity worked."[13] What is not documented is the boy's emotional reaction to such a troubling experiment.

The shock treatment had the same result as the medicines, cigars, coffee, mustard plasters, and massages. Nothing, it seemed, could help the boy.

Death in the Roosevelt household was a constant and unrelenting reality. The asthmatic fits dominated every aspect of Teedie's childhood and each ordeal was a terrifying fight for life. The boy absolutely knew that children died of the affliction and that any attack could kill him.[14] Theodore would bluntly state that "nobody seemed to think I would live," perhaps even referring to himself.[15]

For reasons still unknown, the majority of the asthmatic fits usually took place in the dead of night. And the nights were awful. "Mama came in and then she lay down and I stroked her head and she felt my hands and nearly cried because they were feverish," young Teedie tenderly wrote in his diary.[16] Elsewhere he writes that his gentle mother soothed, petted and "rubbed me with her delicate fingers."[17] Unable to sleep, Teedie developed a form of persistent diarrhea which he termed "cholera morbus,"[18] and began succumbing to re-occurring hallucinations that a werewolf sat on the edge of his bed waiting to kill him. "Don't you see the werewolf?" he bawled to his mother one night, "He is sitting on the foot of my bed now!"[19] The child pointed to nothing, the mother fought back tears.

The werewolf quickly morphed into something worse and Teedie began to nightmare "that the Devil was carrying me away."[20] Well before his tenth birthday Teedie was forced to reconcile that "his deity had a darker side that might be brought to bear on him soon."[21]

The lasting effect of severe asthma is not of the body but of the mind. Once the attack ended, and the ordeal was over, Theodore felt like any normal healthy boy; his body rebounded quickly and life returned to normal. It was the dreadful memories of the attacks that had the lasting implications. The belief that death was always at the doorstep instilled in Theodore the conviction that life on earth was a challenge to merely survive.[22] And it was the battle to stay alive that would forever motivate Roosevelt. He would spend his entire adult life pushing himself to outpace death. "Black care," he claimed, "rarely sits behind a rider whose pace is fast enough."[23]

Another consequence of Teedie's debilitating struggle was that it implicitly bred narcissistic tendencies.[24] While Teedie fought off an attack, the entire Roosevelt house was held hostage, consumed by the crisis. The boy was the center of attention, the one in the middle of the storm, the one everybody cared so dearly about. Everyone—servants, siblings, parents, cousins, friends, doctor after doctor—were all focused on keeping him alive, attending to his every need. Though driven by good intentions, this overprotection could very well have been the root cause of Roosevelt's overpowering sense of entitlement. Roosevelt's daughter, Alice, would later famously quip, that her "father always wanted to be the corpse at every funeral, the bride at every wedding, and the baby at every christening."[25] The man needed to be the center of attention for everything he undertook.

Restricted by his physical limitations, young Teedie became an omnivorous reader.[26] Confined to his sick room, Teedie's outlet for his oversized imagination was the valiant characters in his books—Ivanhoe, Robin Hood, Robinson Crusoe, Natty Bumppo, and Davy Crocket.[27] When reading about courageous characters, Teedie was able to transport his mind far from his physical troubles and into a world of heroic deed and action, and throughout his early childhood he could be found, according to a friend, "sitting in a great arm chair, propped up with pillows, absolutely absorbed in a book while the wildest games were raging around him."[28] Barred from the rough-and-tumble, his favorite place to daydream was in a chair with tassels—"softly upholstered in red velvet"—that seemed to contour perfectly to his weak frame.[29] Quarantined indoors, where he was safe, he was a miscast to others his age:

> His father was troubled about his health [a boyhood acquaintance recalled]. . . . He was not considered strong enough for schoolwork. . . . I did not think there was any- thing great about him. . . . He was very much alone for some years, say from ten to thirteen, because he was not with the boys in their schoolwork or with their heavier sports. He was not strong enough to take part in football or baseball. . . . He had to be at home when other boys were away, and he had to have his fun in his own way.[30]

Weak and undersized physically, Teedie's mind was vigorous. He wanted facts, any facts, and "would get as persistent as a mos- quito on a summer night when he wanted information," a friend recounted.[31] He was sick and nervous much of the time; his par- ents encouraged Teedie to let his imagination run wild, to learn about great leaders, to be distracted from his health. Reading his diary it is evident that a young Theodore Roosevelt knew of no clear line between child's play and reading about great men. In his young scrawl, at the age of nine, he writes:

August 15th
Saturday

> All the morning I played store and "baby." In the afternoon I wrote, read and drew. That afternoon I received a continuence of Washington's life.[32]

On the same day, the boy played children's games before reading a hefty multivolume biography on the country's first president.[33]

Thousands of tomes passed through the sick boy's hands, each igniting his imagination just a bit more than the last. And as he migrated into adolescence he began to take books even more seriously, if possible. "[He] was reading more in a year than most boys read in ten," a friend boasted.[34] "He read sitting down and he read standing up; at times he read standing on only one leg 'like a pelican in the wilderness supporting the other against the thigh of the first and using it as a book-rest.'"[35]

From his readings Theodore procured lessons on life. "All this individual morality," he claimed, ". . . was taught by the books I read at home. . . ."[36] In his autobiography Roosevelt credits his favorite beloved magazine, *Our Young Folks*, as the source of his foundation of principles: "Everything in this magazine instilled the individual virtues, and the necessity of character as the chief factor in any man's success. . . . [No man has] the right stuff, unless he has self-reliance, energy, courage, the power of insisting on his own rights and the sympathy that makes him regardful of the rights of others."[37] Embedded in these "good healthy stories," he would claim, were ample lessons of "manliness, decency, and good conduct."[38]

The most influential of young Theodore's books came from the writings of Captain Thomas Mayne Reid, an Irish-born author who had immigrated to the U.S. in time to fight with Major General Winfield Scott's army as it invaded Mexico in 1846. When Reid's duty to his expat country was over, he moved to New York and began writing about the wonders of the untamed West. Reid's stories—*The Boy Hunters, The Hunter's Feast, The Scalp Hunters,* among others—were expansive and enchanting tales of Wild West adventures. To the boy reader, Reid made it clear that "God was in nature—a force—and nowhere so plainly as beyond the Mississippi."[39]

Unroll the world's map, and look upon the great northern continent of America. Away to the wild West—away towards the setting sun—away beyond many a far meridian. . . . You are looking upon a land . . . still bearing the marks of the

Almighty mold, as upon the morning of creation. A region, whose every object wears the impress of God's magic. His ambient spirit lives in the silent grandeur of its mountains, and speaks in the roar of its mighty rivers. A region redolent of romance—rich in the reality of adventure.[40] [Beginning of *Scalp Hunters*]

Roosevelt so dearly loved Reid's stories that he mentioned them a full five times in his autobiography.[41] It was Captain Reid who introduced the young sickly aristocrat to a Western world where brave men could overcome great odds.[42]

If reading was Theodore's first love, then natural history was a very close second. Mayne Reid had that covered, too. A naturalist observer himself, Reid's stories brought the natural world to life, giving intricate descriptions of flora, animals, and geology, all while using correct zoological names.

About noon, as they were riding through a thicket of the wild sage [*Artemisia tridentata*], a brace of those singular birds, sage cocks or prairie grouse [*Tetrao urophasi*], the largest of all the grouse family, whirred up before the heads of their horses.[43]

"While still a small boy," Theodore Roosevelt explained, "I began to take an interest in natural history. I remember distinctly the first day that I started on my career as a zoologist. I was walking up Broadway, and as I passed the market to which I used sometimes to be sent before breakfast to get strawberries, I suddenly saw a dead seal laid out on a slab of wood. That seal filled me with every possible feeling of romance and adventure. I asked where it was killed, and was informed in the harbor. I had already begun to read some of Mayne Reid's books and other boys' books of adventure, and I felt that this seal brought all these adventures in realistic fashion before me."[44] Immediately, the boy was enthralled: How much did the seal weigh? When was it killed? What killed it? How did it get here? What did it eat? What was its natural habitat?

"The adventure of the seal and the novels of Mayne Reid together strengthened my instinctive interest in natural history," Theodore wrote.[45]

Theodore haunted the market for several days before getting his hands on the dead seal's skull with which he promptly started the Roosevelt Museum of Natural History. The institution, housed in his bedroom, would instantly grow to a large and varied collection of birds, squirrels, ants, beetles, and a seal skull.[46] As if the curator of a real museum, the young boy began to methodically arrange, classify, and index his findings in a notebook entitled "The Natural History on Insects. By Theodore Roosevelt, Jr." In time, the notebook would be filled with thousands of copious descriptions of dragonflies, rodents, snakes, turtles, and whatever else he could find—all entries, of course, "gained by observation."[47] To encourage Teedie's love in natural history, Thee decided to help his son expand the bedroom collection of curiosities and, in the process, helped build the greatest natural history museum the world had ever seen. In the late 1860s, Albert S. Bickmore, the most prominent young naturalist of his day, aspired to create a museum in New York and after a few dead ends, Bickmore was told that one man in particular could make such an idea a reality. He called on Thee. In their first meeting, Thee prophesized to Bickmore: "Professor, New York wants a museum of natural history and it shall have one. . . ."[48]

Thee, a man of his word, organized the fundraising, hosted the meeting where the charter was approved, and helped design the museum layout.[49] With Thee in charge, the American Museum of Natural History opened its doors in 1877 on Central Park West. When President Rutherford B. Hayes came to preview the one-of-a-kind museum, it was Thee who served as the president's personal tour guide. Later, when it came time to unpack the renowned Verraux Collection—over two hundred thousand mounted animals and three thousand birds—Teedie was the only child present to witness the event.[50] In the official records of the museum, it still notes that among its first donations were "a turtle, a bat, a red squirrel skull, several bird eggs, and more from Mr. Theodore Roosevelt, Jr."[51]

Today, the American Museum of Natural History is one of the largest and most celebrated museums in the world, containing over thirty-two million specimens and entertaining over five million visitors annually.[52] To Teedie, the museum was a treasure unlike any other. In modern context, it was as if a son takes a great interest in youth football and the father goes out and buys an NFL team.

Teedie's love for reading and studying natural history, as well as his overactive imagination, did not help him win favor with tougher boys. His narrow world was confined to books, in an aristocratic setting, on a comfy and expensive velvet chair with tassels. Inevitably, when he and his younger brother, Elliot, did confront bullies, it was the athletic and stronger Elliott who served as a bodyguard.[53] For almost all of their childhood, Teedie—consistently frail and ill—was perceived as the younger brother.[54]

As he neared his teenage years, propelled by his curiosity and relentless reading regiment, Teedie's intellectual achievements were at an adult level, but his emotional development was stunted.[55] He had no real friends outside of his family. He was ingenious, aloof, and socially awkward on account of his constant absentmindedness. To the other children in the neighborhood, he appeared preoccupied and distracted, at times wildly introverted and then suddenly loud and bombastic, as if he did not know how to interact with friends.[56] The years of invalidism had shaped his personality: he was self-centered, precocious, opinionated, smart, and intensely dependent on a strict but loving father.[57]

Of his entire childhood, Theodore would frankly admit, "I cannot remember that I did anything that even lifted me up to be average."[58]

He was certainly not a born leader.

4. MAKE THE BODY

By the summer of 1870, Theodore Roosevelt was nearing his twelfth birthday. He was puny, asthmatic, and pig-chested.[1] An owlish looking thing with a thin frame and scrawny legs, he had the appearance of a bookworm; hair perpetually uncombed, squinting eyes that took in minute details of the world around him, shirt untucked, skin pale.[2]

But that summer a significant transformation was afoot. Sister Corinne, an eyewitness to the change, would later explain that for the first time Theodore began to combine "patience, concentration, and determination" with a new paramount emphasis on "physical power and courage." Almost overnight, she claims, Theodore acquired "an ardor for healthfulness," a singular focus on beating his affliction through strenuous activity.[3]

As with many transformational changes, a single catalytic event does not exist. Instead, a serious of events—occurring between the summer of 1870 and the fall of 1872—provided ammunition for the metamorphic change in Theodore Roosevelt. The events included a challenge, a poem, a fight, a billboard, and a death.

Thee's patience had been frayed by the time he summoned his eldest son into his study, and looked his sickly boy in the eye. "Theodore, you have the mind but you have not the body, and without the help of the body, the mind cannot go as far as it should. You must *make* your body. It is hard drudgery to make one's body, but I know you will do it."[4] The pathetically ill child paused a moment, then threw back his head and with a flash of his teeth roared, "I'll make my body."[5]

No doubt this story, influenced by its future implications, is probably exaggerated.

However, family records do indicate that around this time Teedie does immediately begin to rebel against his body's limitations. His outlet was the nearby Wood's Gymnasium, a sports hall reserved for rich children and athletes from nearby Columbia University. He attended daily workouts, flailed against punching bags, pumped dumbbells, hung from horizontal bars, and did sit-ups and push-ups until he could not lift his arms.[6]

The father's challenge was integral to the origin of Theodore Roosevelt's remarkable courage and fighting spirit. It implied to the boy that there was only one way to survive: to make it on your own. According to Corinne, the challenge was the first important promise Theodore made to himself which "eventuated in his being not only the apostle but the exponent of the strenuous life."[7] The life-long obsession of arduous activity had begun.

Watching the intense action was Mittie Roosevelt, who could not have been more pleased. She never missed a session at Wood's Gym. Often the only adult in attendance, the Southern belle in her white silk dress, sat alone on a crude wooden bench cheering the vigorous efforts of her son.[8]

"How many horse-power do you suppose Theodore will have used by the time he gets through with that machine?" she enthusiastically asked a trainer.[9]

To further encourage strenuous activity, Thee, at Mittie's urging, transformed the family's second-floor piazza into an open-air gymnasium complete with a battery of nineteenth-century exercise equipment, including seesaws, swings, weights, barbells.[10]

But for all of his weight lifting, Teedie had little to show to the outside world. Compared to other boys his age, he was still spindly and weak, nervous and timid. After a series of particularly severe asthma attacks, Thee decided to send Teedie to an outdoor boys summer camp on the shore of Moosehead Lake in Maine. Thee had hoped that the mountain air would help Teedie breathe better and, perhaps, the boy might gain a few friends at camp. Thee also thought that Theodore was old enough to go alone, which meant neither his father nor younger brother, Elliot, would be around for protection.

On the last leg of the journey by stagecoach to Moosehead Lake, Teedie was a sitting duck. Two bullies charged up to him, and as he remembered it, "found that I was a foreordained and predestined victim, and industriously proceeded to make life miserable for me."[11] The bullies toyed with the fragile aristocrat like a puppet.

The wound to Teedie's pride was extraordinary. "The worst feature," Roosevelt wrote over forty years later, "was that when I finally tried to fight them I discovered that either one singly could not only handle me with easy contempt, but handle me so as not to hurt me much and yet to prevent my doing any damage whatever in return."[12]

It had not mattered that Teedie had spent an enormous amount of time building up his body in the name of self-sufficiency. He had been manhandled by boys near his own age.

The lopsided fight had a lifelong effect. The chief lesson was that he had been building himself up within the friendly confines of his aristocratic setting. There was a difference between lifting weights with other wealthy kids and scrapping it with the toughs in the Maine woods.[13] The progress he had made weightlifting had been trumped by the harsh reality that he could not take care of himself. Embarrassed, he could have concluded that building his body was a lost cause, his time wasted. After all, up until this point in his life he had only known sickness and defeat. Instead he decided to learn how to fight, so that he "would not again be put in such a helpless position."[14]

The decision to learn to box was one step towards the creation of the aggressive character which would come to dominate the future president's personality.[15] But it cannot be overstated just how much Thee influenced and encouraged his son's activities in every venture. When Teedie was interested in natural history, Thee started a museum. When Teedie wanted to learn how to ride a horse, Thee bought him a pony. When Teedie began working out, Thee built a home gym. When Teedie wanted to box, Thee hired ex-prize fighter, John Long.

"I can see his rooms now [John Long's boxing arena]," Roosevelt Jr. recalled, "with colored pictures of the fights between

Tom Hyer and Yankee Sullivan, and Heenan and Sayers, and other great events in the annals of the squared circle."[16]

Ferociously, the young boy began pelting punching bags, skipping rope, and learning the nuances of boxing: hands up, chin down, pinpoint strike, combination punching, head dodging, bob and weave. A self-proclaimed, "painfully slow and awkward pupil,"[17] Teedie made up for a lack of talent with an insatiable drive. Success soon followed. John Long had structured a series of championship matches for different weight classes with the top prize being a worthless pewter mug.

Half a century later the pewter mug would symbolize one of Roosevelt's most prized accomplishments.[18]

> Neither he [John Long] nor I had any idea that I could do anything, but I was entered in the light-weight contest, in which it happened that I was pitted in succession against a couple of reedy striplings who were even worse than I was. Equally to their surprise and to my own, and to John Long's, I won, and the pewter mug became one of my most prized possessions. I kept it, and alluded to it, and I fear bragged about it, for a number of years. . . .[19]

Teedie, for the first time in his life, had experienced victory. His body had not failed him; he was a winner. "I read an account of a little man who once in a fifth-rate handicap race won a worthless pewter medal and joyed in it ever after," Theodore wrote years later. "Well, as soon as I read that story I felt that little man and I were brothers."[20]

As Teedie amped up his exercising and boxing regimen he still maintained his enormously serious reading schedule. The old epics and the heroes of the wildest adventures were still his inspiration, his gateway to idolizing courageous heroes. In the comfort of his home, safe from the bullies, Teedie continued to devour books and dream of brave men. "Until I was nearly fourteen,"

Roosevelt once wrote about his hero-worshiping, "I let this desire take no more definite shape than day-dreams."[21]

But the recent unbridled charge to change his body coupled with the manhandling incident at Moosehead Lake had stirred something within the child. The combination of these circumstances was no doubt on the boy's mind when he read Robert Browning's poem, *The Flight of the Duchess,* an account of an "over-bred son of a worthy line" who returns home to discover that he is a poser.[22]

> . . .*the pertest little ape*
> *That ever affronted human shape:*
> *Full of his travel, struck at himself. . . .*

> *So, all that the old dukes had been, without knowing it,*
> *This Duke would fain know he was, without being it; . . .*
> *And chief in the chase his neck he perilled*
> *On a lathy horse, all legs and length,*
> *With blood for bone, all speed, no strength.*

As soon as Teedie finished the passage, a visceral reaction took hold. He felt exposed. It was clear that the duke only wanted to "appear to be like" his great ancestors "without making any effort to actually *be* like them."[23]

Teedie's immediate reaction to the poem was obsessive and unwarranted. But then he learned a lesson that would change his life trajectory: rhetoric and dreaming were useless without action. It was one thing to admire past heroes, it was another thing to take action to be like them. From this point forward, as a close friend would later recall, the poem taunted Roosevelt and, as such, Theodore believed that "there was no harm in dreaming, but henceforth he would not be satisfied unless, even while he dreamed, he labored to translate the dream into action."[24]

Roosevelt immediately passed into what he would later describe as "the fellowship of the doers."[25]

For the rest of his life, Theodore would follow the maxim that the leader that really mattered was the doer. In a letter regarding Ulysses S. Grant, Roosevelt stated that it was the duty of future generations to embrace "the great memory" of previous leaders "to serve forever as an example and inspiration." But Theodore warned that "[M]ere lip-loyalty is not loyalty at all . . . the only homage that counts is the homage of deeds, not of words."[26]

Naturally, one of Roosevelt's favorite Bible verses comes from James 1:22, "be ye doers of the world, not hearers only."[27] At his second inaugural address, he took the oath of office with the Bible opened and his hand on the verse.

During the transformational change, Thee continued to encourage his son to get outdoors, and sent him to see Uncle Robert Roosevelt for advice on a shotgun. Armed with his uncle's advice, Teedie requested a French-engineered, 12-gauge, double-barreled Lefaucheux shotgun, one with "a lot of kick" and a "rugged design."[28] Thee, of course, bought one immediately.

Upon receiving the gift, the awkward boy commenced to the woods near Dobbs Ferry to fire away at birds, squirrels, and just about anything else that moved. But again the boy was exposed. He could not hit a thing, but worse, he could not even see what his friends were shooting at.[29] Brother Elliott was shocked that Teedie had been forty feet from a deer and had not even seen it.[30] "It puzzled me to find that my companions seemed to see things to shoot at which I could not see at all," Theodore wrote.[31]

When a friend read aloud an advertisement in huge letters on a distant billboard, Teedie finally realized that something was the matter, "for not only was I unable to read the sign, but I could not even see the letters."[32] Teedie told Thee of the incident and was immediately fitted for spectacles.

The glasses changed his life. While his workout regimen took time to yield results, the effect of the spectacles was immediate and life altering. His range of vision is estimated to have been about ten yards; "everything beyond was a blur."[33] Worse, nobody in the family, including Teedie, had any idea how disabled he truly was.[34] The sick and scrawny child that went through fourteen

years of miserable asthmatic attacks was also unable to see that
entire time.

No two cases of asthma are ever exactly the same, but modern
medical research indicates that a great proportion of asthma
sufferers are children who, for reasons still unknown, grow out
of the affliction as they pass through their teenage years. Theodore Roosevelt fit into this category. As he grew older, the vicious
attacks waned. Though sporadic occurrences persisted throughout his life, the affliction had become non-life-threatening. It is
assumed today that Roosevelt, like most children, simply grew out
of his asthma. But to the impressionable boy it was a different
story. His illness faded shortly after he made a promise to build up
his body and began to exercise. To him, this was no coincidence.
After all, there was no research or medical facts available to prove
otherwise.

The foundation of Roosevelt's legendary courage, the tenacity of his character and the fight in his spirit can be traced back
to his certainty that he beat his asthma. On account of the Roosevelt wealth, the best doctors, medications, and treatments that
the world could offer were available to him. Everything failed.
The child simply knew that he could not be cured through outside help. The only means for survival was courage and the will to
change his circumstance from within.

Furthering this belief was Charles Darwin. The first copies
of *On the Origin of Species by Means of Natural Selection* reached
American ports in 1859, just one year after Teedie was born. By
the 1870s the idea of the survival of the fittest had captured the
nation's attention. As preachers and natural scientists debated
the theory of evolution, Teedie, the invalid natural scientist, listened intently.

Darwin's theory just made sense to Teedie. Organisms competed against each other and lived in a perpetual struggle for
survival. Only the organisms that adapted to their surroundings,

or abolished their own weaknesses, could survive. As Teedie was making his own body, he was proving Darwin right.

As a devout follower of God, Roosevelt had no problem marrying the contradiction between morality and evolution. To Roosevelt, evolutionary development did not undermine the belief that God created man in His image. God and evolution worked together—the spiritual world was filled with endless holy grace and nature was a calloused place where only the fittest could survive. God, in his infinite wisdom, had created a beautiful self-sustaining environment. This idea was as culturally contradictory in the 1870s as it is today. Theodore embraced the contradiction before he became a teenager.

By the end of the summer 1872, Teedie's efforts to remake his body were in full earnest. In the past two years he had been challenged by his father, had begun to exercise, had learned to box, had found an intrinsic drive from a poem, and now, with the help of spectacles, he could see the world around him. But for all of the child's struggles in his early life, there was one thing that would be given to him without any effort: money. And he had lots of it.

In 1871, Grandfather Cornelius Van Schaack Roosevelt died at his home in Oyster Bay, New York. The loss to the Roosevelt family was monumental, as he was the patriarch. When the estate was finally settled, it is believed Cornelius was worth between $3 million to $7 million, inferring that Thee's portion of the wealth was no less than $1 million, more than $20 million in present day dollars.[35]

The Roosevelt fortune enabled Teedie to gain world experiences not available to most children. Thee, ever the adventurist, took the family on two extensive international treks. The latter trip was a one-year voyage across Britain, Europe, North Africa, and the Middle East.

Teedie was enamored with the Arab world of Egypt, the Mediterranean, Alexandria, Syria, Palestine, Jerusalem, and Damascus. "I shall never forget that drive," Teedie wrote about the first time he entered the Eastern domain, "on all sides were screaming Arabs, shouting Dragomen, shrieking donkey boys, and braying donkeys. . . ."[36]

The family spent ample time in the ancient Holy Land and, in classic Roosevelt fashion, not a historic ruin or temple was missed along the way. The children marveled at the Sphinx, stood silent at the Wailing Wall, and were intrigued by the nails in the stones at the Mosque of Omar. Crossing the Jordan River, Teedie was unimpressed—"what we should call a rather small creek in America."[37]

Teedie, who had turned fifteen on the second voyage home across the Atlantic, had an almost unimaginable portfolio of worldly experiences. "He had plumbed the Catacombs and climbed the Great Pyramid"; a historian writes, "slept in a monastery and toured a harem; hunted jackals on horseback; kissed the Pope's hand; stared into a volcano; traced an ancient civilization to its source; and followed the wanderings of Jesus. He had been exposed to much of the world's greatest art and architecture, was conversant in two foreign languages, and felt as much at home in Arab bazaars as at a German kaffeeklatsch, or on the shaven lawns of an English estate."[38]

Though the international experience of new peoples, cultures, and a dissimilar natural world all combined to broaden his worldview, Teedie's formal education had been limited. On account of his asthma, he had been homeschooled his entire childhood. As college neared, Thee hired a distinguished tutor, Arthur Cutler, to manage his son's education and to prepare him for the entrance exams. Cutler did his job. Theodore gained admission into the Harvard class starting the fall of 1876.[39] His formal education would begin at the age of eighteen.

5. HARVARD

———————————————————◇

IN MANY WAYS, HARVARD COLLEGE OF 1876 WAS THE
same rural academic oasis it had been since its founding in 1636.
Standing at the gate, an incoming freshman in 1876 would have
heard the same pacifying noises of 240 years earlier: the clap of the
whip, the clop of the hoof, the neigh of the engine, the squeak of
the wagon wheel, the tinker of horse bells.[1] The streets surrounding the college were only sporadically dotted with cobblestone.
The major throughway, Harvard Street, still had no brick sidewalks. The three mile trek along the Charles River to Boston—
to the financial district, or theaters, or girl shows—was done in
carts, drawn by two horses, and it took just under an hour.[2] In the
spring, the roads were almost impassable on account of the mud.

In the center of the sleepy community of Cambridge was
Harvard Yard, a sweeping campus crisscrossed with gravel paths
and shaded by a canopy of large, indigenous elms.[3] Around the
twenty-five acre commons ran a two-rail granite post fence, a symbol of the exclusivity of America's oldest and most venerated educational institution.[4] Inside the fence, fifteen dissimilar buildings
indicated that the Harvard of 1876 was both very old and very new.
Massachusetts Hall, erected between 1718 and 1720, had been
built half a century prior to the Revolutionary War, and was the
place of education for Founding Fathers John Adams, John Han-
cock, and Samuel Adams. Massachusetts Hall stood stoically, as it
still does today, on the western approach. In contrast, scattered
throughout the Yard, were Thayer, Matthews, and Weld Halls, all
of which had all been built within the previous five years.[5]

At the southern entrance, Grays Hall, finished just thirteen
years prior to Teedie's arrival, became the first building with

water taps in the basement. Residents of other buildings hauled in water from pumps sprinkled around the dormitories.[6]

Just north of Cambridge Street stood the newly erected Memorial Hall, then as it is now, the grandest of all of Harvard's buildings. Finished the year Theodore arrived, the Hall houses a large refectory, a theater, and a nine-thousand square foot great room. It was the symbol of a new stately Harvard as well as a severe reminder of the last great war. The main chamber, covered by a timber roof and stained windows to let in light, still gives a hallowed impression. On its interior walls hang grand marble tablets inscribed with the names of the consecrated dead who fell in their prime to save the Union.

Just outside the Yard, on Boylston Street, was the car barn for the horses. Next to that was Carl's Place, a tavern where teamsters, students, and professors dropped in to complain about one another over a beer. If you were hungry, you went upstairs at Carl's place where there were crude wooden tables and ham sandwiches.[7]

Next to Carl's was the College Pharmacy, where proprietor Horace S. Bartlett advertised "goods at moderate prices," with shelves stocked with "splendid toilet articles, rich cream soda, all mineral waters, Indian clubs, and dumbbells."[8] Bartlett's choicest "toilet articles" had been, as the advertisement claimed, "especially adapted to use of *Our Society*,"[9] an unabashed appeal directed to flatter the fortunate boys of Harvard.

When one in five thousand American's went to college, the 821 Harvard students were indeed the privileged of the privileged.[10] And it was around 1870, the Harvard Crimson would later comment, that the college began "to look like the school it is today—a place of legacy, tradition, old money, and high class."[11]

Prior to his beginning at Harvard, Theodore's eldest sister, Bamie, was sent to Cambridge to procure and decorate his college living arrangements. And they were princely. While other freshmen packed into the dormitories, Theodore took up a room on the second floor of an exquisitely Victorian boarding house on 16 Winthrop Street. The large home came with a spacious living room, a chaise longue, a fur rug in front of a rock fireplace that proudly displayed his bowie knives across the mantel, and several large oak tables showcasing his stuffed birds.[12] His fine living situation came with a servant woman to do his laundry and a manservant to build his fire in the morning and blacken his boots.[13] He wore his mother's comfortable slippers around his new home.

The Harvard graduating class of 1880 was the opposite of diverse. Of the 821 students, everyone was male and everyone was white.[14] But despite the homogeneity, there was a distinct social cleavage. There were the upper-class gentlemen, or the high set—twenty or so boys that came from the richest and most connected families in the Northeast—and then there was the rest of the roster.[15] The gentlemen belonged to the Brahmin Class and, according to a student, "ran the class politics while donning a new tailored suit of clothes for every day of the week."[16] The high-society men, dressed like dandies, stood out in their tightly tailored suits, walking canes, parted hair, and gaudy watches.[17] Teedie was no exception. Accompanying his beaver felt hat and a cutaway coat was a walking stick and thick "English" side-whiskers.[18]

"They owned the class and were snobs," student Harry S. Rand vividly remembered. Rand, a non-gentleman, sat next to Josiah Quincy for four years and recalled that Josiah "did not deign to speak to me once."[19] As for Roosevelt, Rand confirms, "He was right in this group in every way," but at least was, "willing to talk to the others" if the occasion warranted.[20]

"I stand 19th in the class, which began with 230 fellows," Theodore wrote home to Anna, "Only one gentleman stands ahead of me."[21] Evidently the seventeen other non-gentlemen—the common students—did not really matter.

Further exhibiting the instincts of a snob, Teedie investigated the "antecedents" of his classmates to confirm whether they were worthy of his company. "On this very account," he wrote his sister, "I have avoided being very intimate with the New York fellows."[22]

In less than a week at Harvard, Roosevelt and a few other gentlemen decided against eating with the regular students in the cafeteria and took their custom meals at Mrs. Morgan's place on the corner of Story and Mount Auburn Street. The eating club afforded the rich students a reprieve from common food.[23] Members of the eating club, Theodore's first real social connections in life, would continue to be elite, going on to hold impressive professional positions: a prominent New York lawyer, a distinguished teacher of medicine at Harvard Medical School, a judge of the New York Court of Appeals, the president of Massachusetts Gas Company, a vice president of the New York Security and Trust, and a U.S. secretary of state.[24]

Evidence of Theodore's elitism can be seen through his finances; in a single year at Harvard, he spent $761.59 on clothes alone. This was at a time when the American family annual income was around $400.[25] Teedie's own personal financial records show that the American family could have lived for just shy of a decade on what he alone was spending per year on his room and board, private eating club, manservant, laundress, and stable for his horse.[26]

Throughout his first two years of college, his letters and diaries are filled with references to an easy life. His time was consumed with dancing class, theater parties, Sunday drives, and poetry readings.[27]

"He had all the ear-marks of a snob," Roosevelt's philosophy teacher, Professor Palmer stated, "He had plenty of money and moved in the most aristocratic of society."[28] But Professor Palmer clarifies, "he was not a snob, though one not knowing him personally and judging him by appearance only" would never have guessed it.[29]

There is no mistaking that the president who would become the champion of the common man was at first an aristocrat elitist, a young man who not only sought out the company of other rich friends but also was "arrogantly fashionable" in his choice of clothes and expenditures.[30]

But one also gets the sense that Roosevelt was just guilty by association. Before he arrived at Harvard, he had never had any true friends outside of his family. At Harvard, the gentlemen class was a built-in network of boys that provided camaraderie. Never mind that they were the elite of the elitists; they were, above all, friends. For the first time in Theodore's life, he exhibited signs of sociability, albeit awkwardly. As Theodore became more comfortable in his social setting, his personality began to blossom and his classmates no longer knew what to make of him.

A month after Theodore arrived at Harvard, on the night of October 26th, 1876, the quiet streets surrounding Harvard Yard were consumed by a frenzied student rally. It was less than two weeks until the presidential election and the Republican-supporting freshmen were storming the cobblestone sidewalks in support of their man, Rutherford B. Hayes. It was a quintessential college movement with one banner calling for "Free Trade, Free Press, and Free Beer."[31] Under the flickering of torchlights, the young progressives shouted into the night sky, "Hurrah for Hayes and Honest Ways! Hurrah for Hayes and Honest Ways!"[32]

A second story window was suddenly flung open and a Harvard senior stuck his head out, "Hush up, you blooming freshmen!" he barked. Accompanying the insult was a potato that was harmlessly thrown down into the crowd.[33]

The freshmen in the streets below were a little perturbed. One went ballistic.

"I noticed one little man," Albert Bushnell Hart would later recall, "small but firmly knit. He had slammed his torch to the street. His fist quivered like steel springs and swished through the air as if plunging a hole through a mattress. I had never seen a man so angry before."[34]

"Who's that man?" someone asked, pointing to the enraged youngster.

"It's Roosevelt from New York," was the reply.[35]

The Harvard mentality in the late 1870s has been termed the "cult of indifference." The sons of the Northeastern elite were never in a hurry as they nonchalantly sauntered—known as the "Harvard swing"—from class to class. The "Harvard drawl" was said to border "on a yawn."[36] Harvard men purposely met the outside world and its difficulties with a cultivated laid-back insolence.[37] If one applied himself vigorously, he would be deemed an outcast. In *Scribner's Monthly* for July 1876, Horace E. Scudder described that at Harvard, the wise students asked "How may I express myself most dispassionately?" because the "divine fervor of enthusiasm is openly, or by implication, voted a vulgar thing."[38] Class poet George Pellow, summarized the Harvard philosophy in his "Ode to Indifference," read at the Hasty Pudding:

> We deem it narrow-minded to excel.
> We call the man fanatic who applies
> His life to one grand purpose till he dies.
> Enthusiasm sees one side, one fact,
> We try to see all sides, but do not act.
> . . .We long to sit with newspapers unfurled,
> Indifferent spectators of the world.[39]

The chief malefactor of the Harvard indifference was the president, Charles Eliot who, according to one student, "stalked through the yard without a glance to the right or to the left."[40] Indifference permeated throughout the institution, from the president's office, to the faculty lounge, to the lecture room, to the nearby pool hall. The entire community was apathetic.

The senior who threw the potato down from the window at the Hayes demonstration was not against the freshmen's political view per se, but was rather a cultivator of the Harvard culture. The flying potato was a warning to the new class that it was not acceptable to voice a loud opinion or to take a hard stand. The freshmen should be more indifferent, the potato thrower thought.

But indifference was one thing that Theodore Roosevelt was incapable of cultivating. His need for action combined with his inner vitality would simply not allow it. "He puzzled us by his effusive manner," a friend confirms, before qualifying, ". . . in truth, Roosevelt was the most un-Harvard-like man that ever came out of Harvard."[41]

"It was not considered good form to move at more than a walk," a classmate explained, "[but] Roosevelt was always running."[42]

Immediately, Roosevelt's classmates thought him to be peculiar, unrestrained, and senseless, or, as one student put it, "a good deal of a joke."[43]

"He was so enthusiastic," Owen Wister stated, "he was his own limelight, and could not help it: a creature charged with such a voltage as his, became the central presence at once."[44]

Though everybody in the class had a distinct impression of Roosevelt, none of his classmates ever referred to him, even after he became president, as a leader at Harvard. All initial accounts portray him as an oddity, a boy whose personality varied between being outlandishly eccentric when he wanted information from others, and intensely introverted when he wanted information from books.[45]

His power of concentration was intense. Classmate Richard Saltonstall recalled a time when Theodore was sitting in front of his fireplace, buried in a book on scientific German prose, completely unaware that three friends were rough housing and ramming into his chair.[46] The only thing that got Roosevelt to get his nose out of his book was the foul smell of burning boots. So engrossed in his reading, he had caught them on fire.[47]

"Never have I seen or read of a man with such an amazing array of interests," classmate John Woodbury professed. "He used to stop men in the Yard, or call them to him. Then he would block the narrow gravel path and soon make sparks from an argument fly."[48]

The velocity at which Theodore spoke startled others. He seemed to have a speech impediment, bombarding his listeners with a torrent of disconnected words. "When he did speak he spoke rapidly," his philosophy professor recalled, "sort of spluttered as if his thoughts came faster than his mouth could express them—something like water coming out of a thin-necked bottle."[49] Richard Saltonstall would claim that Roosevelt, as a student, never knew how to come to the point of the story.

Classmates often incited Roosevelt into arguments just for the fun of watching his antics; arms flailing as words fought against one another in a surge of activity. When Roosevelt caught on that his classmates were goading him for their enjoyment, the game changed only slightly. Classmate Woodbury fondly remembers that they would still prod Theodore just to watch "him forced to keep quiet by the rush of ideas [of] which he was so full."[50]

Nathanial Southgate Shaler, a professor of paleontology and an advocate of evolution, was an expert in his field and adored by his students. Roosevelt annoyed him. As Shaler gave a lecture one day, Roosevelt assaulted him with questions, interjecting his own opinions on natural history. The gray-bearded teacher, aggravated by Theodore's lack of respect for authority, exploded "Now look here Roosevelt, let *me* talk!" Shaler shouted, "I'm running this course!"[51]

Professor Hill shared Professor Shaler's annoyance towards the overactive pupil, asking Roosevelt in class to "shut up" before telling everyone Theodore did not "know how to write the English language."[52] Roosevelt stormed out of the room and sprinted directly to President Eliot's office so that Eliot would force Professor Hill to make a public apology to Theodore Roosevelt. Luckily, President Eliot was out of town and the matter blew over. But the story highlights an important detail: the rich aristocratic child got his feelings hurt and reacted like a brat, storming off to the president's office just to get an apology.[53]

Throughout his life, and still to this day, Roosevelt's eccentricities have often been called impulsive or rash. Certainly, he had his impetuous moments, especially as a young man. But even at Harvard there were those who recognized his ability to quickly interpret the world around him. "What people describe as impulsive," a classmate clarified after seeing Roosevelt operate over time, was nothing more than "a keen power of drawing information from all sorts of questions quickly and making deductions with such rapidity as to appear to be merely acting on his impulse."[54] The odd freshman was not so much challenging professors and students, as much as he was trying to obtain information quickly and vigorously, the only way he knew how. Never forced to refine his social skills in elementary school, his bombastic and brash manners seemed accusatory. Evidently, his family members never sought to curb his overbearing ways.

At Harvard, Teedie obviously did not feel it necessary to temper his odd idiosyncrasies. He made no effort to comply with the culture of indifference prevalent in Harvard society. Instead he chose to act as he wanted to—odd, verbose, energetic, and active—regardless of the deeply rooted cultural norms that surrounded him. This trend would carry throughout his entire life.

When Teedie went off to college, Thee had strong advice for his son: "Take care of your morals first, your health next, and finally your studies."[55] Teedie followed his father's advice in the order it was given.

To take care of his morals, he attended a Sunday school at a local church where he spoke on his views of Christ and manly morality.[56] A small glimpse of the moral crusader he would become is evident in his thesis paper indicating that, "there can be no question that women should have equal rights with men."[57]

As for the girls of Cambridge, he abstained outright. His moral convictions were a duty to himself and the Roosevelt family name. His father had long since instilled in him that the world of morality was black or white. Nothing lay in between.

The second on Thee's list was health, and though poor eyesight and a slight build kept him from participating in team sports, he was very active on horseback and in the gym: lifting, boxing, vaulting. He was still nowhere near a gifted athlete. "[Roosevelt] had neither health nor muscle," a classmate frankly recalled. "But he had a superabundance of a third quality, vitality, and he seemed to realize that this nervous vitality had been given in order to help him get the other two things."[58]

In a Harvard boxing competition Roosevelt was pitted against a classmate named Hanks, a much more seasoned fighter who, unlike his opponent, had skill and eyesight. From the opening bell, Roosevelt got pummeled. "It was no fight at all," said a classmate, "Hanks had the longer reach and was stronger." But Roosevelt hung tough. "You should have seen the little fellow staggering about, banging the air. Hanks couldn't put him out and Roosevelt wouldn't give up. It wasn't a fight, but, oh, he showed himself a fighter!"[59] When the referee finally stopped the thrasing, Roosevelt's face was bloody, but he was still standing, smiling. "He took punishment with a grin," a friend recalled.[60]

The third on Thee's list of advice was studies, and Teedie, at least when he first arrived in Cambridge, took school seriously. His academic curriculum, as well as his entire life up to this point, was focused on becoming a natural scientist. "It was a veritable museum," a classmate said of Theodore's living arrangements, "with stuffed animals and mounted birds perched on desk and table; and here and there a pair of antlers looked down from the wall . . ."[61] In one corner of the room, Theodore created a makeshift cage to house transient lobsters, snakes, and even an enormous tortoise. The unknowing landlady, Mrs. Richardson, is said to have been scared out of her wits when she stumbled upon a tortoise that had broken free from Theodore's room and slowly roamed the halls.[62] Her panic climaxed when nobody could find where the snakes went.

Natural science was Teedie's calling. His collection of hundreds of animals coupled with his extensive studies of birds and wildlife made him probably the most accomplished eighteen-year-old in the country.[63] After his freshman year, Thee sat down with Theodore to talk about the boy's future. "He told me that if I wished to become a scientific man I could do so," Theodore wrote, but only if "I really intensely desired to do scientific work . . . *if I intended to do the very best work there was in me.*"[64]

"After this conversation," Roosevelt concluded, "I fully intended to make science my life-work."[65] A few days after the father-son talk, Teedie left Harvard to begin his sophomore year, his future seemingly solidified.

In less than six months Theodore Roosevelt Sr. would be dead and Theodore Roosevelt Jr. would, for the first time, question the purpose of his life.

In 1876, President Rutherford B. Hayes was elected on the national reform ticket, and there was no better opportunity for him to prove his reform agenda than to act on the most corrupt institution in America: the Customhouse in New York.[66] "Everything about the Customhouse was mammoth," a historian writes. "If considered as a business operation, it stood in a class by itself, doing an annual dollar volume approximately five times that of the largest business office in the country. The revenues collected exceed those of all the other American ports of entry combined." The power and prestige that came with running the Customhouse was on par with that of a cabinet member.[67]

The problem was that the Customhouse was wholly fraudulent and had been for a while. Politicians and machine bosses used the system to their advantage, both skimming profits off the top as well as placing excessive duties on arbitrary goods. Employees were given job security and financial kickbacks, so long as they enabled the racket. An independent commission looking into the graft "confirmed the worst suspicions of Customhouse corruption, inefficiency, waste, and stupidity."[68]

President Hayes decided to announce his presence with authority and took bold action to remove the head of the Customhouse, Chet Arthur, a sketchy politician who served the New York Republican machine. Hayes wanted a man in charge who embodied integrity, strength, and an "exemplary reputation and a blameless life."[69] Hayes chose Theodore Roosevelt Sr., who at age forty-six, was, according to the *Tribune*, "in the prime of vigorous manhood."[70] Thee—wealthy and charitable, wholly apolitical—was a safe choice for President Hayes. If there ever was a man who could rise above the corruption, it was Thee Roosevelt.

From the end of October through December of 1877, a battle for reform waged between President Hayes and the corrupt wing of his own party. Thee's nomination went to the U.S. Congress where Senator Roscoe Conkling, the New York Republican boss and incessant womanizer known for his "turkey-gobbler strut," fought tooth and nail to keep his man Chet Arthur in charge.[71] Chet was great for business, Conkling told his inner circle.

Conkling first delayed the Senate confirmation before flexing all of his political muscle to have Thee's confirmation rejected by a vote of twenty-five to thirty-one.[72] It was said that Conkling gave the speech of his life, but everyone knew that a seedy deal had been struck. Thee had been a helpless victim of backroom politics at its worse.

The struggle to displace Chet Arthur garnered national attention and Roosevelt Sr. became, albeit briefly, the symbol of what could be right in politics: an honestly pure individual seeking to right a corrupt institution. Chet, or Chester A. Arthur, kept his collectorship post, and three years later—aided by Roscoe Conkling the entire way—was sworn in as the twenty-first president of the United States.

From Harvard, Teedie read of his father's plight in the newspapers and family correspondence, with what he claimed was, "the greatest interest."[73] But he never engaged in any political dialogue or penned any insight into the politics of the day. It seems as if he was interested in his father's happenings simply because it was his father. Teedie, the same boy who would often write page after page of notes on birds, never commented on politics.[74]

On December 16th, the senate formally confirmed the inevitable and Thee was voted down.[75] Two days later Thee collapsed. Doctors diagnosed him with acute peritonitis and urged him to rest. The doctors were wrong. Thee had a malignant fibrous tumor of the bowel that was strangling his intestines. Nobody knew the seriousness of the affliction.[76]

"I am very uneasy about father," Teedie wrote home upon hearing the news of his father's collapse, "Does the Doctor think it is anything serious?"[77] Returning to New York for Christmas a week later, Teedie was upbeat: "Xmas. Father seems much brighter."[78]

But back at Cambridge, on the late afternoon of Saturday, February 9th, Teedie received an urgent summons. He left immediately for the station, catching the overnight train to New York. He arrived on Sunday morning, but he was too late. The flags in New York were already at half-mast.[79] Greatheart was dead.

That night, in his diary, Theodore drew a line down the margin.

My dear Father. Born Sept. 22rd, 1831.

He stopped; he could write no more.[80]
Two days later, he found the strength to continue:

He has just been buried. I shall never forget these terrible three days; the hideous suspense of the ride on; the dull, inert sorrow, during which I felt as I had been stunned, or as if part of my life had been taken away; and the two moments of sharp bitter agony, when I kissed the dear, dead face and realized that he would never again on this earth speak to me or greet me with his loving smile, and then when I heard the sound of the first clod dropping on the coffin holding the one I loved dearest on earth. He looked so calm and sweet. I feel that if it were not for the certainty, that as he himself has so often said, "He is not dead but gone before," I should almost perish. With the help of my God, I will try to lead such a life as he would have wished.[81]

According to cousin Emlen, Thee's premature death had an effect on Theodore that was "stunning."[82] The boy did not just lose a father; he lost his emotional support, his guidance, his direction, his resolve. "He was everything to me," Theodore bawled to everyone.[83]

The son had no idea where to turn, how to act, what to do. He had lived his entire life in a cocoon of dependence on Thee and now, in the immediate absence of his nurturing father, he slipped into anguish so extreme that the family worried of a complete mental breakdown.[84] In the depths of despair, Theodore began to claim that the "aim and purpose of my life had been taken away."[85]

Excerpts from his writings confirm a profound depression had settled on Theodore:

> Every now and then it seems to me like a hideous dream . . . Sometimes when I fully realize my loss I feel as if I should go wild— . . . He was everything to me; father, companion, friend . . . He shared all my joys, and in sharing doubled them, and soothed all the sorrows I ever had . . . It is impossible to tell in words how terribly I miss him . . . Every event of my life is bound up with him; he was as pure and unselfish as he was wise and good . . . Oh Father, Father, how bitterly I miss you, mourn you and long for you.[86]

The writings continue in this vein for over a year.

Soon grief turned to incompetency. Theodore felt inferior and shameful in comparison to the memory of the great man. He saw his father as everything he could never become. "I often feel badly that such a wonderful man as Father should have had a son of so little worth as I," the depressed boy wrote, ". . . I could not help reflecting sadly on how little use I am, or ever shall be in the world, not through lack of perseverance and good intentions, but through sheer inability. I realize more and more every day that I am as much inferior to Father morally and mentally as physically."[87]

Theodore's self-criticisms were obsessive and unwarranted. Just a month prior to his death, Thee had told Theodore that he had "never caused him a moment's pain" and that he was "the dearest of his children to him."[88]

Thee's words had not mattered. "Oh, how little worthy I am of such a Father," Theodore wrote privately, "How I wish I could ever do something to keep up his name."[89]

There is no direct evidence that Theodore attributed his father's political defeat to his immediate death. But Thee had in fact died shortly after a stinging loss. Corrupt politics had taken down a good man, for all to see, and now that good man was dead and unable to fight the moral cause or even defend himself. It was obvious that during the Customhouse debate, Thee exhibited zero political power or influence; he was an honorable and good man but nothing more than a sacrificial figure in the reform battle between President Hayes and the corrupt elements of the New York Republican machine.

So how would the hero-worshipping son remedy the fact that his beloved Greatheart's last act was a failure? How would he respond to his father's public defeat?

As soon as Thee died, his son began obsessively searching for "something to keep up" Thee's good name. It is probably more than coincidence that the son's life ambition included becoming a moral crusader for good government as well as a war hero.[90] Both things at which his father had failed.

Sister Corinne Roosevelt believed that the most powerful lesson that Thee imbued into Theodore was the "sense of duty to be performed, of opportunity to be seized, of high resolve to be squared with practical and effective action. . ."[92]

"Years afterward," Corinne continued, "[when Theodore was] President of the United States, he told me frequently that he never took any serious step or made any vital decision for his country without thinking first what position his father would have taken on the question."[93]

The devotion to the memory of his father and the requirement to live up to his name was a lifelong pursuit. In his study at Sagamore Hill, Roosevelt would hang a large oil portrait of Thee between two smaller portraits of Lincoln and Grant. Thee always kept watch on his son below.[94]

On September 22nd, 1901, Theodore took residence in the White House for the very first time. It would have been his father's seventieth birthday. "I have realized it as I signed various papers all day long, and I feel that it is a good omen," he remarked to his family at dinner that night. "I feel as if my father's hand were on my shoulder," he added, not referring to just that day.[95]

Around the time of Thee's death Teedie was, rather symbolically, signing his name as, "Thee Jr.," "Ted," "Tedo," "Theo," or "Teddy."[96] "He seemed not to know what he should be called," a family historian confirmed.[97] He also did not know what he wanted to do with his life.

As summer came Theodore sought clarity at the familiarity of his childhood refuge, the beaches of Oyster Bay where Thee, as Cornelius Van Shaack had done before him, established a summer residence.[98] But with Thee gone, things were not the same. Teedie immediately launched into a flurry of activity, his vengeful pace a clear indication that he was trying to distract himself from the tragedy. He rode his horse, Lightfoot, so hard—morning, noon, and night—that he all but destroyed the animal.[99] When bothered by a neighbor's dog on a morning ride, he simply drew his gun and killed it—"rolling it over with my revolver neatly as it ran alongside the horse."[100] On a cruise up Long Island Sound he savagely shot his gun at everything from bottles to buoys to fish to trees.[101] A cousin, genuinely worried that Theodore may have gone mad, notified an adult Roosevelt.

In late August, Edith Carow—dubbed the "fifth Roosevelt" because she was homeschooled in the family nursery as a child— came to Oyster Bay and it looked, for a brief moment, as if life was getting better for Theodore. He rowed her across the bay and the couple picked water lilies at Cold Spring Harbor.[102] A young love seemed ready to blossom.

But after a sailing trip the following day, the couple went to a family gathering and "afterwards," he writes in his diary, "Edith and I went up to the summer house."[103] And then something happened, because Edith is not mentioned again for several months—as if she ceased to exist. It is lost to history what actually occurred. Edith and Theodore never spoke of the incident, taking the conversation, or more aptly their fight, to the grave. Even stranger, the gossipy Roosevelt family is stone quiet on the mystery. Did Theodore propose and she reject him? Was she too forward? Did she love someone else? All that is known is that the very intimate relationship was over.

When Theodore got into Harvard, Mr. Cutler, the personal tutor, had assumed his work was finished. But when Cutler heard that Thee died, he knew that his young pupil would be lost. Cutler, an outdoorsman, had hunted the wilds of Aroostook County near Island Falls in Northern Maine and had become friends with a backwoodsman named Bill Sewall.[104] Cutler believed that Sewall, a hunting guide and lumberman, might provide the direction that Theodore so desperately craved.

Seeking an anchor for his troubled mind, Theodore, his two cousins, and friend Will Thomson, took Cutler's advice and boarded an overnight train to Mattawamkeag Station in northern Maine. From the station, the party embarked on a thirty-six mile buckboard journey to Sewall's homestead along the Mattawam-keag River.[105] It was dusk when the aristocrats came upon a clearing along the river where the home stood. The gentlemen were in the middle of nowhere; nothing but desolate forest stretched for miles.

One of the boys pounded on the front door and Sewall, a Viking of a man at six feet tall with a thick red beard, let the boys into his home and into his world. For the next eighteen days the aristocrats became Maine outdoorsmen: thirty mile hiking treks, shooting the rapids in canoes, ascending mountain tops, stalking and killing game, surviving the wild.[106]

The wilderness of Maine—desolate, dark, and deep—was no Manhattan; it was no Harvard. The area around Sewall's home was "lost in the immensity of the wilderness," a commentary writes, "the nearest railroad was a day's ride to the south . . . the few inhabitants relied wholly on themselves for food. Their chief activities were either hunting and lumbering, or a frontier sort of farming in which crops were planted among the stumps of the clearings. Indians were still encountered, and many a white youth, Sewall among them, had learned to build a birch canoe by watching an Indian build one. The life bred its own canniness and self-reliance. It presented the essential features of the first American frontier. . . ."[107]

Bill Sewall was the boss of his own lumber operation and had a crew of tough men working under him.[108] He was self-made, tough, and gritty. Any man who came to leadership in these parts, had to be courageous and competent. Young Theodore was impressed. In the back country he realized that his hunting guide, a common man with no social background or money, embodied the values that he himself coveted.

Years later, when asked why Bill Sewall made such an impression on him, Theodore responded with a question: "How could I be a snob when I admired him so much?"[109] The death of his esteemed father clearly marked a shift in his thinking. He began to shy from his high society classmates and adopt a reverence for men who lived outdoors.

The year before his own death, Roosevelt reflected on the molding experience that took place in the isolated woods of Maine. He wrote an entire book, *My Debt to Maine*, to express his gratitude for Sewall. "I was accepted as part of the household; and the family and friends represented in their lives the kind of Americanism—self-respecting, duty-performing, life-enjoying—which is the most valuable possession that any generation can hand on to the next."[110] Forty years after the encounter, Roosevelt genuinely acknowledged and appreciated the moment he first met the common man.

The night before breaking camp in Maine to head back to Harvard, Theodore realized a contradiction that would come to exemplify his future, "And my life has such absurd contrasts. At one time I live in the height of luxury; and then for a month will undergo really severe toil and hardship—and I enjoy both extremes almost equally."[111]

In his last two years at Harvard, Roosevelt would make two more trips to Maine, one in March and the other in September of 1879.[112] On each trip he would both pursue wild game and search for understanding about the man who worked with his hands for a living.

Theodore went from the wilds of Maine to the sophistication of Harvard to find that he was, all of a sudden, popular. The status may have been sympathy born of the death of his father, or the stigma around his new inheritance, or simply because he was now an upperclassman. Regardless, the uptick in status genuinely surprised him, and in no time his hands were full with what he called "society works"[113]: the theatrical Hasty Pudding Club, the social O.K. Club, the Alpha Delta Phi. He became the editor of the *Harvard Advocate*, and, naturally, the Natural History Society's vice president. But the highest social honor bestowed upon Theodore was his initiation into the Porcellian Club, an exclusive organization formed in 1791 that took in only eight men from each of the junior and senior classes.[114] The club, which consisted of several rooms over a row of stores on Harvard Street—housing a billiards table and massive library—was a place where the select few could embrace the Porcellian motto—*Dum vivimus vivamus*, "While we live, let's live."[115] The mornings consisted of champagne breakfasts while the evenings were filled with suppers of partridge and burgundy, which gave way to smoking, drinking, billiards, and cards.

Though Roosevelt did not drink or smoke he did embrace the effortless lifestyle of a Porcellian. Almost in defiance to the lessons taught by Bill Sewall, he confides to his diary, "I am living a life of most luxurious ease at present. I breakfast in the Club about 10; my horse is there before the door, and I ride off—generally lunching at some friend's house. It is very pleasant—but I do not suppose it would be healthy to continue it too long."[116]

His money allowed this type of luxurious lifestyle. By the fall of his junior year Theodore's inheritance from his father's estate had been settled and he was collecting $8,000 annually.[117] The annual salary of the president of Harvard, Charles Eliot, was only $5,000.[118] The Harvard junior's annual stipend was over twenty times the amount the average American family lived on. Theodore had his own dog cart, his own horse, a lavish living arrangement, and two servants. That autumn he also found love.

On Friday, October 18th, 1878, Theodore and his friend Richard Saltonstall took a buggy to the Saltonstall family mansion in Chestnut Hill, a six mile trip over gently sloping countryside ablaze with the colored leaves of autumn. Theodore was greeted with two huge Victorian mansions perched on a hill. One was the Saltonstall manor and the other belonged to Richard's uncle, George Cabot Lee, a wealthy banker entrenched in the Brahmin class.

When Lee's daughter, Alice Hathaway Lee, welcomed Theodore into the home, it was all over. "As long as I live," Theodore wrote, "I shall never forget how sweetly she looked, and how prettily she greeted me."[119] Alice was a beauty, extraordinarily attractive. Her hair was honey-blonde, her eyes bright blue, her nose upturned, her frame athletic and lean.[120] Called "Sunshine" by her family, all surviving accounts are testaments to her grace and prettiness.[121] Like most in the Brahmin class, she was very educated, a lover of Thackeray, Longfellow, and Wadsworth.[122]

Theodore proposed marriage just six short months later. For reasons unknown, she told him no. No specific record explains why Alice declined Theodore's offer, but what is known is that almost immediately suitors began to circle her like sharks to blood. Determined, Theodore cornered a friend at a Hasty Pudding event and barked loudly for everyone to hear, "See that girl I am going to marry her, she won't have me, but I am going to have her!"[123]

As Alice continued to waffle on the decision to marry, Theodore became increasingly obsessive. He bought a pair of French dueling pistols to scare off any would-be suitors.[124] Tense and angry, one night he punched a drunkard in the teeth, opening a gash on his knuckles.[125]

It got worse. With the dueling pistols displayed for the world to take notice, he got into several more shouting matches, pages from his diary were ripped out, and he began to suffer insomnia. "I went nearly crazy at the mere thought of losing her," he admitted to a family member. "Night after night I have not even gone to bed."[126] Jittery and unable to sleep, he began wandering the streets of Cambridge alone in the dark, complaining of the "tortures of the last four months."[127] Someone sent a telegram to the Roosevelts of New York to alert them of Theodore's unhinged actions. His friends were left to wonder: Did Thee's death and now the rejection from a young love break the young man mentally?

Cousin West Roosevelt was dispatched with urgency to Cambridge to calm Theodore. It is not known if he was able to help.[128]

Finally, in January of 1880, after fifteen months of erratic courtship, Roosevelt—distraught and uneasy—put forth an ultimatum. "I drove over to the Lees determined to make an end of things at last; it was nearly eight months since I had first proposed to her, and I had been nearly crazy during the past year; after much pleading my own sweet, pretty darling consented to be my wife. Oh, how bewitchingly pretty she looked!"[129]

The courtship of Alice proved a tumultuous and quintessential Roosevelt victory, complete with a challenge at the beginning and an intermediate failure that was trumped by an inability to give up on what he desired. The wedding date was set for October 27th, 1880, the groom's twenty-second birthday.

That April, Mittie threw a series of teas and parties in New York to introduce Alice to extended family and friends. James Roosevelt, a distant cousin and wealthy businessman, came down from Hyde Park to attend one of the gatherings. At the party,

James, a fifty-one-year-old widower, met Sarah Delano, a charming aristocrat half his age. Despite the age gap the couple married that October and fifteen months later, Sara would give birth to their only son, Franklin Delano Roosevelt.[130]

Years after graduating Harvard, an ex-classmate, upon reuniting with Roosevelt, looked back in amazement. "The first two years in college we all thought you [Theodore] would be a scientist, and the last two [years] we thought you would probably be a professor of political economy or a historian, but we never had any idea that you would become a practical politician."[131]

Roosevelt, upon hearing his friends' assertion, just shook his head and laughed, "I never did either."[132]

In his first two years at Harvard, Theodore had intended to make his profession as a natural scientist. But immediately after Thee's death that career morphed into a hobby. But it is equally clear that Roosevelt had yet to embrace the career path that would dominate the rest of his life. His class selection is telling; of his twelve elective courses ten were classes in German, Italian, and natural history—subjects in which he was already well versed. The man who would become the nation's foremost historian, author, and leader of political economy, took no more history, literature, or government classes than were required.[133]

Though Roosevelt graduated near the top ten percent of his class, a rank of 21 out of 171, nobody claimed him to be an impressive student. Richard Saltonstall flatly stated that Roosevelt "did not work hard, he had a good time."[134] When asked if Theodore was a good student, President Eliot, who never liked Roosevelt, concluded that "he didn't work hard enough on his studies . . . he never went to the bottom of things, that was characteristic of the man throughout his career."[135] It is known that Theodore refused to take Henry Cabot Lodge's history class because Lodge, a young, up-and-coming professor, marked papers too critically.[136] This is the same Henry Cabot Lodge whom Theodore would team up with in just a few short years to create one of the greatest political alliances in U.S. history.

In many ways, Roosevelt's inability to focus academically was indicative of his outlook on life. The man was perhaps the greatest scholar to ascend to the White House; perhaps the most learned president in U.S. history. But on certain topics, he often chose action over academic understanding, particularly in the matter of economics. As president, Theodore instigated one of the boldest moves in U.S. history by breaking up the trusts and later reorganizing the entire financial system in America. Roosevelt had the vision but no idea how to execute it and formed a committee to propose a strategy for "labor, trust, railways, [and] banks." Harvard's Political Economy professor J. Lawrence Laughlin was appointed chairman.

At the committee's first meeting, Theodore burst into the room, boasting loud for everyone to hear, "That's the man that taught me my economics!" he shouted, waving his finger in the vicinity of Professor Laughlin.

Over the next several minutes, Professor Laughlin laid out the expansive regulatory and economic actions required to forever change the financial system in America. When finished, Roosevelt blasted, "Don't let it start in Congress, let some small banker in Oregon or Florida suggest it!"

Laughlin was perplexed. Where were the questions on his plan, the grilling of the details? This was landmark economic policy; the president should understand its implications.

Laughlin pushed back on Roosevelt to see if the president actually understood the strategy.

"When it comes to finance or compound differentials, I'm all up in the air," was Roosevelt's reply, clearly indicating that he did not understand anything Laughlin had presented.

"That," said the professor, "taken in connection with the statement you just made, that I taught you your Economics, is not a good testimonial to my course or my teaching."

"Say," exclaimed Roosevelt leaning over and slapping Laughlin's knee, "do you know—that was the best course I took in college!"[137]

Roosevelt smiled and then bolted out of the room and that was that.

Shortly after Theodore Roosevelt's death in 1919, a Roosevelt family historian decided to interview several of Theodore's Harvard contemporaries for a hagiographic book on the twenty-sixth president's time in college. The book was to chronicle the making of the man, spotlighting the profound leader Roosevelt had been in college. The historian was shocked by what he found, confiding privately that he "discovered no one who was intimate with him [Theodore] and a few who were sympathetic."[138] All of Theodore Roosevelt's college friends were periphery, not life-long acquaintances. Worse, "most of his classmates simply did not like him."[139]

The historian would try to clarify the contradiction of a student who was selected to the prestigious Porcellian Club but still had no long-lasting friendships from college:

> He made his own world. He could associate most amicably and delightfully with congenial acquaintances; no one loved a good time more than he. But he could also withdraw himself into his own personal world abruptly and completely, leaving his friends vaguely wondering what happened to Theodore. He permitted his friends to go just so far, and no farther. Nothing was said, but suddenly there was a closed door barring the way that led to his inmost being. What was behind that door he reveled to no one. Perhaps he scarcely knew himself.[140]

Equally perplexing was the sheer absence of leadership in Roosevelt's life. From the time of his birth until his twenty-second birthday, he had never led anything. He also did not, in the slightest, impress upon his classmates that he would grow up to be a leader, or even be successful for that matter. "Evidently no one," the historian concluded, "ever imagined that Roosevelt would have a great career."[141]

One professor, stating the obvious, confirmed that Roosevelt, "had not yet come to a head in his development" and that while "many of his contemporaries . . . were college leaders," Theodore was still "in the process of growing, a process that continued after graduation."[142]

But what his Harvard contemporaries could not see was the intrinsic motivation that had ignited Roosevelt's ambitions during his last year at Harvard. Three events took place that foreshadowed his remarkable future.

In his senior year, Theodore began researching the naval activities of the War of 1812 for fun. Inspired by the Bulloch uncles' naval heroics, Roosevelt dug up documents in archives that shed new light on the sixty-eight-year-old war. Armed with unpublished facts, he resolved to write a history of the war and to discover if a career as a historian was a possibility.

When *The Naval War of 1812* was finally published it was so meticulously written that Theodore would instantly become a scholar on naval strategy and nationally recognized as a strong advocate for a new Navy. The Navy thought so much of his work that it was standard issue and put on each of their ships.[143] When the debate over the preparedness of the American Navy was thrust onto the nation's conscience eighteen years after the published date, the book would prove politically significant for Roosevelt. By the time he graduated Harvard he had completed the first two chapters.

The second event took place three months before graduation when Theodore underwent a physical examination with Dr. Dudley Sargeant, the college physician. Though Theodore had been healthy at Harvard—succumbing to only a few asthmatic flare-ups the entire four years—Dr. Sargeant found that Theodore's heart was frighteningly weak, perhaps due to a genetic condition. Dr. Sargeant pleaded with Roosevelt to refrain from running up stairs, to walk, not run from class to class, and to put an end to the trips to the Maine woods starting immediately. It was paramount, according to the doctor, that Theodore "favor his heart by a sedentary lifestyle" or he would die at a very young age.[144]

"Doctor," Roosevelt immediately retorted, "I am going to do all the things you tell me not to do. If I've got to live the sort of life you have described, I don't care how short it is."[145]

Not only did Roosevelt not tell his fiancée, Alice Lee, of the doctor's prognosis but he refused to even acknowledge it in his own diary. Dr. Sargeant's diagnosis is only confirmed by Harvard records later discovered in the old sports hall. In fact, only a few days after the disastrous doctor appointment, Theodore happily wrote, "My career at college has been happier and more successful than that of any man I have ever known."[146]

For the rest of his life, once Theodore made up his mind, he did not hesitate to disregard authoritative elders, even if they were experienced and educated like Dr. Sargeant.

The third and final incident of Roosevelt's intrinsic change took place as graduation was looming. At a committee meeting of the Alpha Delta Phi in Holworthy Hall, he struck up a conversation with classmate William Roscoe Thayer. "Roosevelt and I sat in the window-seat overlooking the College Yard and chatted together in the intervals when business was slack," Thayer recounted. "We discussed what we intended to do after graduation."[147]

"I am going to try to help the cause of better government in New York City," Roosevelt proclaimed to his friend, "I don't know exactly how."[148]

6. FINDING HIS WAY

—————————————————◇

"IT WAS THE DEAREST LITTLE WEDDING," A FAMILY FRIEND PUT to her diary on October 27th, 1880, "Alice looked perfectly lovely and Theodore *so* happy and responded in the most determined and Theodore-like tones."[1] At the Brookline Unitarian Church, on a brilliantly warm afternoon, nineteen-year-old Alice and twenty-two-year-old Theodore married. "Our intense happiness is too sacred to be written about," Theodore wrote in his diary that evening.[2]

Theodore's love for Alice was passionate and fervent. His letters and diary entries are a tender testament of a young man who absolutely adored his wife:

> "Not an hour has passed that I have not thought of her"[3]—"If ever man loved woman I love her"[4]—"My happiness now is almost too great"[5]—"She is too sweet to me in everything"[6]—"I am living in dreamland"[7]—"When I hold her in my arms there is nothing on earth left to wish for . . . If ever a man has been blessed by a Merciful Providence, I am he"[8]

Theodore, ever his father's son, had scheduled a lavish five-month European honeymoon, set for the following spring. After a two-week temporary honeymoon at Oyster Bay, Mr. and Mrs. Theodore Roosevelt, moved into their new home on 6 West Fifty-Seventh Street. The entire Roosevelt clan was on hand to help them move in. Domestic life had begun.

Theodore at once became the head of the family. Now, after church, the family went to his home for supper. He was appointed a trustee for the Orthopedic Hospital and New York Infant Asylum, his father's charities. He even did his best impression of Thee by attending the Newsboy Lodging House every Sunday night and speaking to the underprivileged children. And just as his father and mother had been twenty years earlier, Theodore and Alice were the fashionable couple on the high-society party circuit. Mrs. Astor, the matriarch of the New York Society—"her word was social law"—invited the young Roosevelts to her lavish soirees.[9] There was no higher honor among the social elite in the entire country. In the arena of wealth and privilege, Theodore and Alice were already victors.

While Theodore's nights were reserved for fashionable balls, his days were spent focused on the law. Both activities he seems to have chosen by default; it was what other people expected of him. As for his career, he knew that he no longer wanted to be a natural scientist but that was about the extent of it. Uncle Robert, a lawyer and Democratic congressman, offered Theodore an apprenticeship at Blackstone & Coke in an effort to both help his nephew find his professional calling and to influence the young Roosevelt to become a good Democrat, just like himself.[10] The law, Robert encouraged upon Theodore, would provide a foundation for a career in business, public life, or perhaps literature or publishing. Law was the safe choice.

Just nine days after moving into his new home with Alice, Theodore began classes at Columbia Law, a department that was "little more than a cavernous old house."[11] The school's principal lecture room, perpetually overcrowded with abysmal ventilation, was so affected by the noise from the street that students and professors had to literally shout at one another to communicate. The loud arguing, the intellectual questioning, the constant interrogation of facts suited Theodore well. Contrasting his beginnings at Harvard, and on account of the combative nature of law school, Theodore was viewed as a class "favorite," an "energetic questioner of the lectures," and a student who, according to one professor, "seemed to grasp everything instantly, who made notes rapidly and incessantly."[12] It was also clear that his interest in government had budded; he registered for all the courses in political science, public law, and political history.[13]

Throughout the winter and spring of 1880–1881 it seemed to the outside world that Theodore was destined to be a lawyer. He himself wanted to write. At the close of morning classes he would, secretly and quietly, head off to the Astor Library to sit alone and relive the War of 1812.

Theodore's first two chapters of the *War of 1812*, completed at Harvard were, in his own words, "so dry they would have made [the] dictionary seem light reading by comparison."[14] Though the Bullouch uncles were navy men, he himself had no primary knowledge on the subject nor had he any insight into the "complex nautical vocabulary."[15] Driven by passion and undeterred by his limitations, he set out to write the definitive book on the subject.

When finished, the almost five-hundred-page book was still as dry as a dictionary, but harbored profound, prophetic assertions. Roosevelt's thesis concluded that America's failures in the War of 1812 stemmed from an unprepared government. The best defense, he argued, was a standing navy, not one hastily equipped under duress. To draw lessons from the past, Theodore harshly accused Thomas Jefferson and James Madison, both beloved presidents and American heroes, with "criminal folly" for neglecting "to prepare for the struggle that anyone might see was inevitable."[16] Scathing in its accusations, the text is saved by hordes of data and statistics which proved to be both accurate and visionary.

So what gave the twenty-two-year-old with no naval experience the nerve to claim that two cherished ex-presidents were guilty of criminal folly?

To Roosevelt, it was a matter of courage. "Life had presented Theodore with a bodily challenge; he had met it with a dogged effort. . . ." writes a historian with close ties to the Roosevelt family. "Beyond this, Theodore's own stamina of body, mind, and heart [each having grown from the other in that order] made him naturally combative. When he said in later years that 'aggressive fighting for the right is the noblest sport the world affords,' he was but expressing the essence of his own nature and its imperative need."[17] Theodore would forever scorn the coward, the man who shrank from a challenge.

The significant data that he collected for his book had proven to Roosevelt that Jefferson and Madison were wrong, dead wrong. Backed by facts, he felt it was his duty, his responsibility, to not shrink from the danger of expressing his opinions. Fighting combatively for what he believed to be right, regardless of whom he was fighting, was just a normal function of his personality.[18] Theodore's facts accentuated that Thomas Jefferson had let his country down, so Roosevelt thought nothing of calling Jefferson "perhaps the most incapable executive that ever filled the presidential chair."[19]

Throughout the winter of 1881, it seemed that Theodore was adjusting to life as the head of the Roosevelt family—Thee's old position. He was balancing the social circuit with charitable causes, both a Fifth Avenue dandy at night and a law student during the day; the weekends were for philanthropy. But that winter, Theodore began dabbling in a world filled with chewing tobacco, cigar smoke, coarse stories, liquor, gambling, and seedy characters.

He entered the domain of New York City politics.

The Twenty-first District Republican Association met at Morton Hall, a barn-like room over a saloon on Fifty-Ninth Street. It was a dive, nothing more than a two thousand square foot warehouse with crude floorboards and exposed columns. "Its furniture," Theodore remembered, "was of the canonical kind: dingy benches, spittoons, a dais at one end with a table and chair and a stout pitcher for iced water, and on the walls pictures of General Grant, and of [Governor] Levi P. Morton, to whose generosity we owed the room."[20]

Theodore's political career began on February 14th, 1881. The only evidence is a simple diary entry: "Political meeting; then Patriarch's Ball."[21] It seems that he had stopped by Morton Hall on his way to an aristocratic Valentine's Day soiree later that night. Theodore's political start, rather fittingly, began with a contradiction: he was dressed in a cocktail suit that cost more than the average man's monthly earnings—a wealthy outsider to the working man's union.

Theodore's class, the aristocrats, usually came about politics the respectable way. A man of society would first become a lawyer or business success for a number of years and then buy a Senate seat later in life. The rich nobles, especially the young rich, did not associate with the club, and once word leaked that Theodore was spending time at Morton Hall, a few elder society men— lawyers, businessmen, Thee's friends—tried to talk some sense into the boy. "[They] told me that politics were 'low,'" Roosevelt remembered, "that the organizations were not controlled by 'gentlemen'; that I would find them run by saloon-keepers, horse-car conductors, and the like, and not by men with any of whom I would come in contact outside; and, moreover, they assured me that the men I met would be rough and brutal and unpleasant to deal with."[22]

"For a young man of Roosevelt's position," a classmate remembered, "to desire to take up politics seemed to his friends almost comic."[23] But Theodore was curious and persistent, not at all intimidated. If the political men "proved too hard-bit for me" he later wrote, "I supposed I would have to quit."[24] Until then he would see what they knew. He was challenged to give it a shot, or, as he put it, "hold my own in the rough and tumble."[25]

Perhaps to appease the elders of his own family, Theodore invited Cousin Emlen to accompany him to the club. "I went with him into Morton Hall," Emlen recalled," but I did not relish the personnel of the organization . . . they were crooked for the most part."[26] Emlen promptly quit the political meetings and focused his career on investment banking for Roosevelt & Son.

"[Theodore] joined the political workers," Emlen recalled. "[T]hey didn't really care for him [but] he fought his way into their ranks."[27]

Morton Hall's members were a tight knit social club of political men. "I had to break into the organization," Theodore recalled, ". . . I insisted on taking part in all the discussions. Some of them sneered at my black coat and a tall hat. But I made them understand that I should come dressed as I chose . . . Then after the discussion I used to play poker and smoke with them."[28] Theodore's intent was to lessen "the defective moral quality of being a stranger," while learning how he might navigate the New York political machine.[29]

From February until the end of April, when he and Alice left for their honeymoon, Theodore attended a handful of meetings at Morton Hall. He gave one impromptu speech, but it was not noteworthy, and his time in the club impressed upon no one that he even desired a political career. He just listened and made it known that he was curious about what was happening in the dimly lit, smoke-filled chamber.

Years later, Roosevelt would claim that he chose the Republican Party "because a young man of my bringing up and convictions could join only the Republican Party."[30] An odd assertion considering he was surrounded by Democrats: the Hyde Park Roosevelts; his in-laws, the Lees; and his uncle, Robert Roosevelt, a congressman.[31] Family legend holds that Uncle Rob was surprised and saddened that his favorite nephew went Republican.

"Uncle Rob, I'm going to join the Republican Party," Theodore is credited with saying.

"What's that?" came the response.

"Yes, I'm going to get some of those good offices you ought to have had but which your party didn't have the sense to give you," was the confident boy's reply.[32]

In May of 1881, Theodore and Alice embarked on a five-month-long European honeymoon that was nothing short of magnificent. The itinerary was remarkable: "A week in Paris, dining deliciously, and exploring the caverns of the Louvre; five days in a Venetian palace, with evening rides through the "water streets," and balcony breakfasts shared with pigeons; an afternoon spent under the "immense, cool, vaulted arches" of Milan Cathedral, four days in the marbled splendor of the Villa d'Este on Lake Como; then north in a rented carriage for a tour of the Alps."[33]

In early July, the couple settled into Bormio at the Northern edge of the Italian high country, where their merriment was interrupted by news reports from America that President James A. Garfield had been shot.[34] Theodore, from his quaint Alpine retreat, anxiously read the Italian newspaper accounts that told of Garfield arriving at the Sixth Street Station of the Baltimore and Potomac Railroad on the morning of July 2nd and getting gunned down from behind by a disgruntled federal office-seeker, Charles J. Guiteau. After shooting the President, the deranged Guiteau repeatedly shouted that he was a "Stalwart of the Stalwarts! I did it and I want to be arrested! Arthur is President now!"[35]

The Stalwarts, a large faction in the Republican Party led by Roscoe Conkling, had been in favor of political machine and spoils system-style patronage, which had thrived under the early Reconstruction efforts and President Grant's administration. The Stalwarts' in-party political opponent, the Half-Breeds, favored civil service reform and a merit system, which had been supported under Grant's more reformist successor, President Hayes. The Half-Breeds were the rank and file and the Stalwarts were the machine men who controlled the politics. The two factions were both vying to lead the GOP into the future and therefore resorted to increasingly corrupt measures. The country was distinctly polarized.

Guiteau, a lunatic, felt that President Garfield should have given him an ambassadorship to Paris on account of two meaningless speeches that he had made during Garfield's campaign, and, feeling slighted, he took the president's life. Indicative of the political climate at that time, American sentiment blamed the murder, not on Guiteau the person, but on the bitter partisanship fight and corrupt politics of the Republican Party.

On July 5th, the young Roosevelt put to his diary, "Just heard of Garfield's assassination; frightful calamity for America."[36]

After a day of introspection, from his lofty suite high in the alps of northern Italy, he revealed, "this means work in the future for all men who wish their country well."[37]

Not lost on Theodore was the fact that President Garfield's successor was Chester A. Arthur, the very man that Thee was supposed to replace in the Customhouse. The idea that Thee's rival was now heading to the White House no doubt sent the young man's precocious mind racing. Would Arthur's presidency lead to uninterrupted poltical corruption? If Thee had survived could he have become president? Should men of conviction and character even get into politics?

The honeymooners returned to America on October 2nd, 1881, walking off the gangway of the trans-Atlantic *Britannic* to "all of both families."[38] Within a week Theodore had started up classes again at Columbia Law, and within eighty days, the publishers had his final draft of the *Naval War.* But to the complete surprise to everyone, even to himself, in five weeks time, he would be the newly elected New York State assemblyman from the twenty-first district.

On October 17th, 1881, Theodore listed his priorities in his diary, "Am working fairly hard at my law, hard at politics, and hardest of all at my book."[39] He may have lied to himself on the first activity; by the end of the month he had abandoned the study of law for the rest of his life. He would claim that "doubtless chiefly through my own fault, some of the teaching of the law books and of the classroom seemed to me to be against justice."[40] That is to say, lawyers had to serve their clients first rather than uphold the righteousness of justice. "The *caveat emptor* side of the law, like the *caveat emptor* side of business, seemed to me repellent", he claimed, "it did not make for social fair dealing."[41] It is hard to believe Roosevelt's own reason for quitting law. The law—public law, social law, Constitutional law—all could have certainly provided opportunities for socially fair dealings. Perhaps what Roosevelt meant was that he never wanted to walk the thin line between serving clients and pursuing justice. He knew he simply could never do it. Many years later, he would explain his doctrine on chasing righteousness: "What we need is . . . young men with ardent convictions on the side of the right; not young men who can make a good argument for either right or wrong as their interests bid them."[42]

The real reason that he gave up law so quickly was his distraction with politics. The Garfield assassination, the calamity of

American political affairs, and the fact that his father's rival was in the White House had ignited something in Theodore. He did not have to look far for motivation. Thee's last letter to Theodore, written from the hand of a dying man on December 16th, 1877, was cryptic inspiration, "The 'Machine politicians' have shown their colors." Thee wrote, ". . . I feel sorry for the country, however, as it shows the power of partisan politicians who think of nothing higher than their own interests, and I feel for your future. We cannot stand so corrupt a government for any great length of time."[43]

Just four days back from Europe, Theodore offered his services at Morton Hall in order to "kill our last year's legislator."[44] The legislator, William Trimble, a loyal servant to the machine and a Stalwart through and through, was up for annual re-election on the Republican ticket in the twenty-first district. A man like Trimble represented all that was wrong in government. The election date was November 8th, and the district Republican convention was set to meet on October 28th. If Roosevelt wanted him gone, he would have to act fast.

The Republican primary selection was controlled by Jake Hess and Joe Murray, the leadership at Morton Hall. Either one could make or unmake a candidate. Hess, a German Jew, was the leader of the district. Murray, an Irish Catholic, was Hess's lieutenant. Both men had earned their stripes through years of door-to-door networking and "late nights in smoke-filled strategy sessions."[45]

Joe Murray's story epitomizes the political worker of New York. Born in Ireland and "raised in barefoot poverty on First Avenue," it is claimed that he got his start in politics "on a free-lance basis, to influence the course of local elections with his fists."[46] Fifteen years later, having landed punches his entire career, he was in his mid-thirties and in a leadership role of the local party. It was Murray's job to ensure that the twenty-first district voted Republican.

Many historical accounts suggest that Joe Murray was impressed by a speech that Roosevelt gave in April before Theodore and Alice left for their honeymoon. The topic was the partisan method of street cleaning, and accordingly, Roosevelt stood up amidst the shouting at Morton Hall and spoke out against corrupt practices and inefficiencies. According to several biographical accounts, Joe Murray supposedly had "not forgotten the young man's courage and outspokenness."[47] This story does not seem to be true. Roosevelt did give an impromptu speech, but it was not very effective and Murray took no notice. Murray would later claim in a private unpublished interview that he did not even know Theodore Roosevelt until October of 1881.

"He had only been in the club six weeks," Murray flatly stated, referring to the time when Roosevelt got off the boat from his honeymoon through Election Day.[48] In fact, the only thing that Murray was initially impressed with was Theodore's last name.

About a week before the nomination, Roosevelt called on Murray to see how he could help ensure that Trimble be defeated. Murray recounted the meeting to a historian, highlighting that Theodore Roosevelt's entry into politics had all the awkward qualities of a first kiss:

> Roosevelt wanted to oppose Trimble's return to the Assembly, I said to Mr. Roosevelt that I objected to Trimble as much as he did.[49]

> Finally, I says, "Oh, I'm looking around for some good man as candidate.

> So he [Theodore] says, "Why there won't be any trouble about that."

> I says, "Why no, I haven't found any difficulty so far. By the way, Mr. Roosevelt, how would you like to run for the legislature?"

> He said, "Tut, tut. I won't take it."

> "Why?"

> "Well, won't it look as though I came around here with selfish motives?"

> "I don't look at it in that way. By the way, [could] you get the candidate?"

Roosevelt says. "You will not have any trouble about finding someone."

"Will you take it?" I says, "[or] will you get me a candidate?"

Roosevelt says, "Yes, I will do what I can."

So he came around the next night. I says, "By the way, have you got a candidate?"

Roosevelt says, "No. Have you got one?"

I says, "No. In case we cannot find any suitable candidate, will you take it?"

He says, "I will think the matter over and report tomorrow night."

The following day Theodore charged down to Morton Hall and told Joe Murray that he would take the nomination only if Murray promised him that if he found a more suitable candidate he would withdraw Theodore's name from the ballot. Murray agreed, "but I don't think I was honest in making the promise," he recalled.[50]

Examining the Roosevelt family correspondence of letters and diaries, there does not seem to be any premeditated strategy on Theodore's part. It does not seem that he had a grand scheme or even intended to personally take Trimble's place in the legislature.[51] It was pure fate. Curiosity led him to the political meetings at Morton Hall and great timing got him nominated. "It is not often that a man can make opportunities for himself," Roosevelt claimed, "But he can put himself in such a shape that when or if the opportunities come he is ready to take advantage of them. This was what happened to me in connection with my experience in Morton Hall."[52] The kid had put himself in the right place, at the right time. It did not hurt that he had the right last name.

Joe Murray knew what he was doing. The twenty-first district, known as the "silk-stocking district," was the wealthiest constituency in New York whose voting bloc was affluent and Republican. It was Murray's job to appoint a candidate that would appeal to voters who "rated integrity and personal worth above the requirements of the party."[53] The current assemblyman, William Trimble, did not have the panache demanded by the wealthy citizens of his district and was viewed as an oily Stalwart by everyone else. Roosevelt the Harvard Man could get votes from "the swells and the Columbia crowd."[54] Roosevelt, the son of the elite, could generate funds from family connections.[55] Roosevelt the young chap could be viewed as a new face in the old dirty game of politics. He was well educated, rich, and full of energy.

On October 28th, 1881, Joe Murray stood up at Morton Hall and cleared his throat. "Mr. Chairman, I nominate Theodore Roosevelt," he said, and then sat back down.[56] On the first ballot, the twenty-five delegates voted sixteen to nine in favor. Joe Murray had come through. Roosevelt was the nominee; a political dynasty had begun. Theodore had turned twenty-three years old the day before.

Theodore would state that it was "plain duty" that led him into government.[57] Certainly he inherited the ideals bred from his family lineage where men held a variety of public positions, ranging from legal to military to philanthropic. But his decision to become a New York assemblyman was different from his ancestors. He was starting at the bottom where filthy politics reigned supreme, heading right into the belly of the beast where men of society did not begin their careers. But it was just that, debunking the trend of the wealthy elite, where he admits to drawing his sense of responsibility. When told that society men do not become lowly state politicians, Roosevelt retorted, "that if this were so it merely meant that the people I knew did not belong to the governing class, and that the other people did—and that I intended to be one of the governing class."[58] He wanted to prove that the young rich kid could hang in the world of seedy politics.

His family was skeptical. "When he announced," Cousin Emlen stated, "we thought he was, to speak frankly, pretty fresh. We felt that his father wouldn't have liked it, and would have been fearful of the outcome."[59]

But becoming a politician gave Theodore Roosevelt a platform for his most visceral need of all: to live a life of purpose, a life free from obscurity.

Many years later he pondered on the twelve months that he lived Thee's life. "I tried faithfully to do what father had done, but I did it poorly," Theodore claimed, ". . . in the end I found out that we each have to work in his own way to do our best; and when I struck mine, though it differed from his, yet I was able to follow the same lines and do what he would have had me do."[60]

The son never harbored the intrinsic and compassionate love of charity that the father embodied. Theodore, unlike Thee, never viewed aid as a matter of the heart, where selfless acts manifested from pure altruism.[61] To the son, the best way to help those who could not help themselves was through efficient government, which required hard-fighting, bare-knuckled ethical politicians.[62]

Son, also unlike father, had a visceral need for people to know his name.

Roosevelt's competition for the state legislature was Democrat Dr. W. W. Strew, a man who had been in charge of the lunatic asylum on Blackwell's Island but was removed for ineptness. Evidently, Strew felt his incompetence was fit for government. Though Joe Murray knew Strew was a terrible candidate, he took no chances. Murray only had eight days to get his boy-wonder elected.

"It was customary, [in] those days for candidates to pay a visit to stores and business men of the district, particularly the saloons," Joe Murray stated.[63] Candidates canvassed for votes rather than give speeches and manage campaigns.

On the very first canvass, Murray, Roosevelt, and Hess hit the saloons on Sixth Avenue to appeal to the working man who had just gotten off and was looking to wet his whistle. Hess and Murray had built a reputation and trust with the laborers and saloon keepers, most of them Irish or German. When Hess and Murray accompanied a candidate into a saloon, their status alone could "sew up all the votes in the joint."[64] Their reputations were also at stake with each candidate they paraded into the bar.

There is one story that sums up Theodore Roosevelt's political career. Joe Murray narrated Roosevelt's first attempt to win votes:

> The first place we went into was a German lager-beer saloon on Sixth Avenue between 55th and 56th Street. Saloonkeeper was Carl Fischer. We had a small beer before Jake Hess introduces Roosevelt to Fischer.
>
> "By the way, Mr. Roosevelt," Mr. Fischer inquired, "I hope you will do something for us when you get up to Albany. We are taxed much out of proportion to grocers and we have got to pay $200 for the privilege."
>
> "How much do you say you pay for the license fee?" The young candidate questioned.
>
> "200," was the reply.
>
> Theodore quickly did the math. "200? Why that's not even half enough. It ought to be $1,000!" he shouted.[65]

The saloonkeeper was stunned. He scoffed and then shrugged. Was this a joke, he thought?

Joe Murray, in a rage, grabbed his candidate by the shirt collar and yanked him to the street.

"The conversation threatened to become stormy," Roosevelt recollected.[66] Murray was fuming and scolded Theodore like a child. The canvass on Sixth Street was over, Murray shouted, before demanding that Theodore "see to the college boys and his friend on Fifth Avenue," while he and Hess "did the other end."[67]

Theodore's first political campaign lasted all of one stop on one night.

Though not regretting his actions, Roosevelt heeded Murray's advice and stayed on Fifth Avenue to secure the financial backing of his father's friends: Morris K. Jesup, Joseph H. Choate, William Evarts, and J. Pierpont Morgan.[68] A *Tribune* editorial two days before the election highlights Thee's influence on Theodore's candidacy:

> The name of Theodore Roosevelt is one of those most loved and respected in our annals. The son of the lamented citizen who bore it with such honor is now a candidate for Assembly in the XXI'st. The voters of the district will have an opportunity on Tuesday, in voting for Mr. Theodore Roosevelt, to show their regard for an honored name, and to bring into the service of the State a gentleman every way worthy of his parentage.[69]

On Election Day, the good Roosevelt name and Joe Murray's politicking proved victorious: 3,490 votes to 1,989.[70] Roosevelt, having made his good fortune by having the fortitude to join the political ranks at Morton Hall, learned of his victory while putting the final touches on his book. Immediately appreciating the sanctity of public service, Theodore declared that week that he was "untrammeled and unpledged" and "would obey no boss and serve no clique."[71]

He kept this promise his entire life.

7. ENTERING THE STAGE

◇

THEODORE ROOSEVELT ARRIVED IN ALBANY, NEW YORK ON the afternoon of January 2nd, 1882.[1] The weather was cloudless and frigid, only seventeen degrees.

Congressmen and the newspapermen had already convened at the Delavan House, the old and prominent hotel directly across from the railroad station that served as the private head-quarters of both parties. The Delavan was, in many respects, more powerful than the statehouse itself. In its private rooms, powerful men bought and sold legislation while smoking cigars and drinking whiskey. Politicians and laws were made and unmade in its backrooms.

Assemblymen and journalists were congregated in the lobby of the Delavan, eager to size up the legislative class of 1882, when Theodore burst into the room. In a rush to get to the hotel, Roosevelt had forgotten his overcoat and gloves. But he did not care; the show had already started and he could not be late. In what has been described by one historian as "an actor's trick that quickly became habitual," Theodore burst on to the scene, as if the entire world was a stage.[2]

"His step across the hotel corridor was quick and vigorous," a witness recalled, "his whole manner alert, his salutation as he shook hands with the newspaper men . . . I am 'deelighted' to meet you. There was the same broad smile, the same dental dis-play, the same frank and courteous greeting so well known in the coming years."[3]

Roosevelt's "good, honest laugh" boomed; "you could hear him for miles."[4]

After sizing up Roosevelt's dress, antics, smile, and cackle, legislator John Walsh perplexingly blurted, "Who's the dude?"[5]

"That's Theodore Roosevelt of New York," came a chorus of answers.[6]

For all of his theatrical efforts, Theodore left a poor impression on his new colleagues.

"We almost shouted with laughter to think that the most veritable representative of the New York dude had come to the chamber," an assemblyman noted.[7]

"They looked upon him as a joke, a dude, his dress, the way he combed his hair, the way he talked, the whole thing," another stated frankly. "He was a regular dude."[8]

"What on earth will New York send us next?" Edgar Murlin of the *Tribune* thought to himself.[9]

George Spinney, the legislative correspondent of the *New York Times*, was unimpressed. "He was the homeliest pup you ever saw, with little Dundreary whiskers, a string on his glasses, and a face full of teeth. He still had his side-whiskers—his eyeglasses he wore at the end of a long, black cord passing around the neck and over the right ear."[10]

No one took Theodore seriously. He was simply too different, too young, too rich, too oddly dressed, too loud.[11] The monikers used of Theodore were persistent, and unflattering: "Jane-Dandy," "Young Squirt," "Weakling," "Green as Grass," "Punkin-Lily."[12]

"He is just a damn fool," snarled Tom Alvord, a man who had been a state legislator since before Theodore was born. Alvord, nicknamed "Old Salt," told anyone that would listen that the Republicans only had "sixty and one-half members" in the assembly.[13] The one-half was "that damn dude" Roosevelt.[14]

As Theodore became more acquainted with his fellow legislators, he too was appalled. Not by their looks or antics, but by their greed. Graft was not just a part of the game in Albany; it was the game. It was no secret that as many as sixty to seventy members of the legislative body made it known that their vote was for sale to the highest bidder, whether it be a political machine, corporation, or state entity.[15] The Black Horse Cavalry, as they were known, were a group of corrupt legislators that would require payment for votes regardless if the bill was proper or not.[16] It is rather telling of the political environment of the day that the Black Horse Cavalry were not seen as blatantly corrupt, just powerful legislatures playing by the unwritten rules.

In all, the 128 total members of the assembly were indeed a mixed lot: "three were newspapermen, six were liquor sellers, two were bricklayers, half a dozen were carpenters and machinists, one was a cooper, one a butcher, one a tobacconist, one a pawnbroker, one a compositor, and one a typesetter. There were thirty-five lawyers and an almost equal number of farmers."[17] But together, as a single body, according to *The New York Times*, the Assembly of 1882 was "the most corrupt Assembly since the days of Boss Tweed."[18]

As soon as he got to Albany, Theodore began sizing up the men he was working with and reverted back to his instincts as a natural historian. His meticulous study of birds and natural wildlife transferred to a careful study of human beings as he began to take copious notes on his peers. Observing legislators as if they were birds in nature, he put to a notebook his observations, his impressions, and interpretations of their actions. Where was their home? How did they act? Who were their associates? Like a good scientist, he classified them along taxonomic rank, based on their party affiliation and whether they were "a bad old fellow . . . corrupt," like Alvord or, "a country lawyer from Jefferson, thoroughly upright and honest," like Isaac Hunt.[19] He segregated the eight Tammany Hall Democrats who were henchmen for the machine from "the some twenty-five Irish Democrats," who, though "a stupid, sodden, vicious lot," might be swayed in a close vote.[20]

Every man was classified, according to Theodore, "to find out whether they were their own masters or were working under the directions of someone else."[21]

Isaac Hunt, "the country lawyer from Jefferson," recalled the day he found Theodore's little notebook of human observations.

"Leave that down," Roosevelt barked to Hunt. "Can't anybody look at it! There's enough in there for fifty slander suits."

"What in the world is it?" Hunt replied.

"Well," Theodore said, "I have written up my estimate of all the members in the legislature and assembly."

"After a good deal of persuasion I got him to let me see what he had written about me, and I turned and found it." Hunt said. "I was surprised at the diagnosis he had made of my character."

Isaac Hunt, who recounted the incident to a reporter, then paused to reflect. "They said he got to be a pretty good judge of human beings. Suppose when you were twenty-three years old, you sat down and wrote your analysis of one hundred and fifty or so men and put it in a book and then checked up on your estimate with your experience; of course you would get to be a good judge of human beings. He certainly did that."[22]

Roosevelt's second day in Albany was January 4th; it was an uneventful day save for a single action. At four o'clock in the afternoon there was a drawing for seat selection in the Capitol room. Ballots bearing the names of the 128 Assemblymen were placed in "the well," a small half-circle enclosure beneath and in front of the clerk's desk.[23]

Where a legislator sat in the rotunda was a symbol of prestige as well as political conviction. The two ex-speakers, given the courtesy of choosing their seats before the drawing, were, according to George Spinney, the "shepherds to lead the flock"—the party leaders that instructed legislators where to sit and subsequently how to vote.

To a chorus of cheers, Old Salt Thomas G. Alvord, Democrat from Syracuse, chose the seat he had occupied for twenty years: half way down the center aisle, on the left. Alvord got to his seat, opened the lid to his desk and threw in a soiled package of fine cut chewing tobacco and then sat down. Next, ex-speaker George H. Sharpe, Republican from Kingston, selected a seat on the opposite side of the aisle, on the right.[24]

Democrats sat on the left, Republicans on the right.

As name after name was called, legislators picked their seats, following their leaders like lemmings. Erastus Brooks, a sixty-seven-year-old politician from Staten Island—known as the "Democratic Warhorse"—picked an aisle seat in the middle tier. "A staunch Democrat," Spinney recounts, "Mr. Brooks was "the gentleman of the old school," both hardened and disciplined by a lifetime in politics.[25] Brooks had the longest and most respected record of any of the legislators.

When the youngest assemblymen's name was called, Theodore jumped up, passed by the Republican clique and a rotunda of open seats and plopped down in seat no. 40, right next to Erastus Brooks. The Republican brethren were stunned. To the ever curious and inquisitive young Roosevelt, Brook's wealth of experience and political acumen was a learning opportunity not to be missed.

The symbolic event in many ways foreshadows Roosevelt's political career. From seat no. 40 in the New York Assembly to his desk in the White House, he would choose to associate with individual thought leaders, not pledge blind allegiance to the party.

"I do not number party loyalty among my commandments," Theodore claimed as a maxim.[26] It was Roosevelt's lifelong belief that the party alone could not lead the public to a new frontier. The new frontier could only be attained through strong leadership from strong individuals.

"His one great study was men," Spinney recounted, "how they achieve[d] prominence, what they had done, how they maintained relations with the party and public and managed to prolong their careers, their peculiarities of mind or body, their use of power."[27]

Leaders led the party; the party did not lead the individual.

As Roosevelt took his seat next to Brooks, he immediately wanted to change the world. To his greatest horror, he could not. For the next thirty days nothing happened; the legislature was completely shut down due to the actions of a small influential cohort. Of the 128 Assemblymen, 61 were Republicans, 59 were Democrats and 8 were Tammany Hall Democrats.[28] The 8 Tammany men, hoping to secure a speaker position for the corrupt Tammany cause, refused to give their votes to either party for confirmation of a new speaker and held the entire legislative body hostage. No work could be completed until a speaker was chosen; no speeches given, no debate on laws, no legislation voted for or against. The Tammany clique—"not even one of them can string three intelligible sentences together to save his neck," according to Roosevelt—shut down the entire legislative branch for more than a month.[29]

It was the best thing that could have happened to Theodore.

"He grew like a beanstalk," a friend recalled. "All he could do was answer roll call, after roll call, after roll call. He was forced to sit and listen. He was like Moses in the wilderness. I don't think Roosevelt ever sat forty days anywhere else without saying something."[30]

"He was so altruistic, he wanted to accomplish all the good that could be accomplished right away, he wanted to do it in a minute," Isaac Hunt explained. [31]

On account of the gridlock, Roosevelt was relegated to seat no. 40, unable to speak, unable to act, and forced to appreciate the politics at play around him. "He learned more out of that than almost anything in his early experience," Hunt clarified. "He . . . in that contest to organize his forces, and he also learned another thing, that if he could not get all he wanted, he would take all he could."[32] That is to say, he was forced to learn how to work with the tools at hand.

During the legislative lockdown, monotony seized Albany. "Men just toiled up State Street to their seats in the capitol, indulged in the formality of taking a vote," a legislator recounted, "and the rest of the day—about twenty-three hours and thirty minutes—their time was their own, to be spent as they inclined, some at cards, some at the bottle, some at cock fights, and some at practical jokes."[33]

The most prominent jokester was John McManus, a man of "powerful build and as strong as a giant."[34] An Irishman, ex-prize fighter, and longtime Tammany Hall Stalwart representing the Bronx district, McManus listed his government credentials as "a liquor merchant" and "formerly a bricklayer."[35] McManus was tough and he knew it. One day, for fun, Big John decided to team up with a few others to "throw that damned dude [Roosevelt]" into a blanket, presumably to roll the new guy down a flight of stairs.[36] Theodore, the 5'8" 130-pound runt of a congressman with his Harvard pretension, bulging bank account, flawless family name, side whiskers, glasses, cane, and a morally righteous attitude, was a predestined and helpless victim. Or so McManus figured.

When word reached Roosevelt of McManus's plan, the little legislator lost it. Perhaps remembering the Moosehead Lake manhandling incident several years prior, Theodore burst down the corridor of the statehouse shouting "McManus, McManus, McManus!" Salivating from the mouth and heaving heavily, Theodore ran up to the Irishman, and though a hundred pounds lighter and a head shorter than the prizefighter, laid into him. "See here McManus!" his falsetto voice shrieked, "I understand some of you fellows are planning to toss me in a blanket. I want to serve notice on you now that I'll fight you, I'll bite you, I'll kick you, I'll do anything to you that my fists and feet can do!"[37]

With his fists tightened, neck veins popping, and teeth clenched, Roosevelt stood there, his head at McManus's chest. McManus chuckled; *is this really happening*, he must have thought. A long moment passed before McManus smiled and turned away. The blanket tossing plan was called off later that day. The wiry runt had stood up to the bully of Albany.

Roosevelt was not done fighting.

Just a few days later the dandily dressed Roosevelt—cane, doeskin gloves, pea jacket, hair parted in the middle—strolled into Hurst's Roadhouse with three other young legislators for a beer.[38] J. J. Costello, another Tammany man and "a thorough face scoundrel" according to Roosevelt, hurled an insult toward the dude: "Won't mamma's boy catch cold?"[39]

According to an eyewitness, Roosevelt put his glasses in his pocket, took a long breath and then snapped. "Teddy knocked him down, and he got up and he hit him again, and when he got up he hit him again, and he said, 'Now you go over there and wash yourself. When you are in the presence of gentlemen, conduct yourself like a gentleman.'"[40] Roosevelt then bought Costello a glass of beer and told him to drink it.

"I'm not going to have an Irishman or anybody else insult me," Roosevelt snarled for everyone in the bar to hear.[41]

Roosevelt was still not done fighting.

Legislator Dominick F. Mullaney, recalled yet another "incident that showed what a lion-hearted red blooded man [Roosevelt] was":

Patrick Burns was a labor agitator who represented a district from Brooklyn. His principal delight was in baiting young Roosevelt, whom he termed "that dude aristocrat from the diamond-back Fifth Avenue district." Burns was a giant. One day in the House he made a nasty, vulgar, brutal, and cowardly attack on Roosevelt.

It was such a mean tirade that we of the minority were absolutely disgusted with him. Roosevelt looked him square in the face while he was talking. No sooner had Burns sat down than young Roosevelt leaped to his feet. "Mister Speaker," snapped the young man, as we looked in amazement at him. His glasses were off and those prominent teeth were shoved further out than ever. But none of us were prepared for what happened. The House was still, Titus Sheard, the Speaker, looked in wonderment at this slender young man, who did not weigh 130 pounds, and whose body quivered with intense excitement, but who otherwise appeared to be the calmest of the 128 members.

"I appreciate that this place and this time is not the proper one to make a proper reply to the remarks of the gentleman from Brooklyn," he continued, "but if the gentleman from Brooklyn will step outside of the Capitol I will give him the only kind of reply his remarks deserve."

The audacity of this challenge took the breath of every one. We glanced at the courageous young man. We saw Burns look at him and then we saw Burns's eyes drop. Roosevelt made no move to sit down. Burns made no move to stand up. He did not leave the Capitol until Roosevelt had been gone a long time.[42]

In his memoir, when describing his time in Albany, Roosevelt does not discuss his aggressive incidents or fisticuffs in any detail. He does, however, give advice on fighting: "Do not hit at all if it can be avoided," before clarifying, "but *never* hit softly."[43]

When the Tammany clique finally caved in and the legislative gridlock ended, Roosevelt introduced four bills that were certainly not a part of a larger, well-thought-out reform agenda.[44] It is clear that Roosevelt went to Albany with no focused legislative strategy, bringing with him just his attitude and ambition, as well as a great desire to change the political system.

"He was just like a Jack coming out of the box," Isaac Hunt recalled of Roosevelt's first few days on the job. ". . . [T]here wasn't anything cool about him. He yelled and pounded his desk, and when they attacked him, he would fire back with all the venom imaginary. In those days he had no discretion at all. He was the most indiscreet guy I ever met. . . ."[45]

In his high-falsetto voice, from seat no. 40, Theodore would leap to his feet, lean across his desk at a forty-five-degree angle and with his right arm stretched high and his fist shaking to the heavens, shout across the chamber: "Mis-tah-Spee-kar! Mis-tah-Spee-kar! Mis-tah-Spee-kar!"

Spinney recollected, "And if this did not answer, Roosevelt was known to push his way into the main aisle and step-by-step move determinedly down to the well with his insistent 'Mr. Spee-kar' and his menacing forefinger."[46] Roosevelt thought nothing of shouting at the speaker for forty minutes straight.[47]

When the speaker finally capitulated and gave Roosevelt the floor, Theodore's voice sounded like "a man biting ten penny nails."[48]

"He spoke as if he had an impediment in his speech, sort of as if he was tongue tied," a legislator remembered.[49] Of his maiden speech, when Theodore used the expression "rather relieved," the *New York Sun,* mockingly printed it as "r-a-w-t-h-e-r r-e-l-i-e-v-e-d."[50] When speaking, Lucious Littauer found it funny that Theodore "didn't know what to do with his hands."[51]

"I had considerable difficulty teaching myself to speak," Roosevelt admitted.[52] In fact, his speaking ability was a work in progress during his time in the assembly as well as his entire adult life.

The only thing that seemed to save him in the early days was the genuineness in his approach. "It was hard for him to speak, but what he said was all right," Hunt explains. "[T]here was always meat in what he said. He improved on it, but he was always a speaker whose individuality dominated his speech. He was not like anybody else. He was like himself. There was but one Teddy."[53]

As Theodore shouted and fought his way to be heard, the distinguished old timers of the legislature were perplexed. "The men who were trying to handle that house and direct affairs," a member stated, "looked on him as a man would a ball of dynamite with a fuse in the process of burning."[54] All would agree that Roosevelt was both a perfect menace and entirely inexperienced.

Roosevelt's first political lesson took place when he became involved in the Cigar Bill, a piece of legislation from the Cigar Makers Union, led by Samuel Gompers, which moved to prohibit the manufacture of cigars in the immigrant tenements. "I was appointed one of a committee of three to investigate conditions in the tenement-houses and see if legislation should be had," Theodore explained.[55]

Of his two colleagues, Roosevelt writes, "one had to vote for it because the labor unions were strong in his district" and the other "had dealings [that] required him to be against it."[56] Theodore was the wild card on the committee.

An ardent believer of leaving a man to fend for his own, Theodore was against the legislation. "It was contrary to the principles of political economy of the laissez-faire kind," Roosevelt wrote, "and the business men who spoke to me about it shook their heads and said that it was designed to prevent a man doing as he wished and as he had a right to do with what was his own."[57]

Roosevelt's central tenets in life had long since held that individual freedom was paramount; self-reliance, hard work, and responsibility were supreme. But rather than vote on his instinct, Roosevelt as the free agent on the committee, decided to visit the tenement homes in question. He was unprepared for the stench and wretchedness that would forever alter his view on leadership and government.

I have always remembered one room in which two families were living [Roosevelt recalled thirty years later]. . .There were several children, three men, and two women in the room. The tobacco was stowed about everywhere, along-side the foul bedding, and in a corner where there were scraps of food. The men, women, and children in this room worked by day and far on into the evening, and they slept and ate there. They were Bohemians, unable to speak English, except that one of the children knew enough to act as interpreter.[58]

"These conditions" Roosevelt discovered, "rendered it impossible for the families of the tenement-house workers to live so that the children might grow up fitted for the exacting duties of American citizenship."[59] His firsthand experience bore sympathy, a realistic understanding of the true nature of the condition in the tenement homes. Back in Albany Theodore ardently championed the bill, got it passed through the State House, and Governor Grover Cleveland signed it into law.

A short time later, the Court of Appeals, no doubt influenced by the cigar manufacturers, declared Roosevelt's bill unconstitutional. Government, the court decided, had no right to infringe on business and the "'hallowed' influences of 'home.'"[60]

"The judges who rendered this decision were well meaning men," Roosevelt explained. "They knew nothing whatever of tenement-house conditions; they knew nothing whatever of the needs, or of the life and labor, of three-fourths of their fellow-citizens in great cities. They knew legalism, but not life."[61]

Theodore knew that judges had no idea what they were deciding upon. They had not actually spent any time in the tenement housing looking the poor in the eye, smelling the stench of rotting tobacco and foul bedding. Almost a century later, in the 1970s, the business leadership saying "management by wandering around" became popular, a style of managing whereby executives walked through the workforce in an unstructured manner, just listening and interpreting. Several historians believe that it was Abraham Lincoln who first implemented the informal management style when he visited Union Army camps to inspect the troops in the early part of the Civil War. For Roosevelt, the Cigar Bill incident was a learning experience: leaders learn best by interpreting a situation firsthand.

In the following month the Cigar Bill made Theodore instantly popular and provided a crucible event in his journey to lead. On March 29th, he stood up from his seat, no. 40, and tersely called for the immediate investigation and impeachment of State Supreme Court Judge T. R. Westbrook. As soon as Roosevelt sat down, pandemonium erupted in Albany.

It was the first time Roosevelt enacted his maxim, "[I] believe in waging relentless war on rank-growing evils of all kinds."[62] For his first victim, he had set his sights on the *most* powerful justice in the state.

"We used to spend a good deal of time in industrious research into the various bills introduced," Roosevelt explained, "so as to find out what their author really had in mind."[63] That is to say, in an effort to discern good legislation from corrupt legislation, Roosevelt took on the role of detective. When Isaac Hunt, who had been investigating judicial corruption, discovered irregularities of "suspicious insolvency of a number of New York insurance companies," he confronted detective Roosevelt.[64] The tip-off for Hunt was that all the suspicious irregularities and the judicial graft involved the same person: State Supreme Court Judge T. R. Westbrook.[65]

As Hunt explained his findings, Roosevelt recalled a recent *New York Times* article that had charged Judge Westbrook with complicity for his involvement of the Manhattan Elevated Railway Company and, more specifically, his close ties with Jay Gould, a railroad tycoon and speculator, one of America's original Robber Barons. Back in Manhattan the following week, Roosevelt met with the editor of the *Times*, Henry Loewenthal, and poured through the evidence that the newspaper uncovered. Probing the events and shady characters involved, not to mention the large amount of money that changed hands, the evidence certainly reeked of corruption.[66]

"Recognizing the tremendous future in store for any rapid-transit system in New York," a historian writes, "Gould had decided he needed the Manhattan Elevated. His scheme, as usual, was to harass and intimidate the existing owners at every opportunity, drive the stock down below its true value, then begin buying."[67]

Gould elicited Russell Sage, a cavalier Wall Street financier who, with the help of the editors at the *World*, relentlessly attacked Manhattan Elevated, implying the company was fraudulent and on the verge of bankruptcy.[68] Judge Westbrook, a man supposedly representing the best interest of the public, declared Manhattan Elevated Railway insolvent, and appointed Gould's business associates as the receivers. As planned, Westbrook's declaration of insolvency sent the stock plummeting and Gould, orchestrating the entire scheme, bought majority ownership during the ensuing fire-sale. Shortly thereafter the stock price rebounded and Judge Westbrook reversed himself. Voilà, the Manhattan Elevated was now solvent again with Gould as new majority owner and in charge of operations.[69] Manhattan Elevated was stolen outright and in broad daylight. A white collar crime executed to perfection.

It turns out that robber baron and the judge had been at it for a while. When Gould was starting out as a young financier, T. R. Westbrook was his first lawyer.[70]

The shady facts of the Manhattan Elevated acquisition were in the open for all to see. It had been written about in the papers and discussed in the local bars. It had only taken Roosevelt two days of research to uncover the entire web of corruption. It was, safe to say, not a secret.

But nobody in Albany wanted to take it on—it was one thing to go after a state supreme court judge, it was another thing to go after Jay Gould, the most powerful man in the country. Gould, the ninth richest-man in U.S. history, had a net worth of seventy-seven million dollars, or roughly, a half of one percent of the *entire* GDP of America.[71] He owned the *New York World* newspaper, a substantial portion of the railroads in America, as well as the Western Union Telegraph which gave him immense personal decision rights to decide what news to report, or not report, via the Associated Press.[72] No person had as much influence on the state house in Albany as Jay Gould. He was *the* untouchable.[73]

On the late afternoon of March 29th, with fifteen minutes to adjournment, Theodore Roosevelt rose shouting his trademark "Mis-tah-Spee-kar! Mis-tah-Spee-kar!"

When Speaker Patterson gave Theodore the floor, he no doubt expected a self-fulfilling declaration on a meaningless bill from the House's most inexperienced member. When Theodore spoke, he tersely called down the thunder:

> *Whereas,* charges have been made from time to time by the public press against [the resolution read] . . . T. R. Westbrook, a Justice of the Supreme Court of this State, on account of . . . official conduct in relation to suits brought against the Manhattan Railway, and *Whereas,* these charges have, in the opinion of many persons, never been explained nor fairly refuted . . . therefore *Resolved,* That the Judiciary Committee be . . . empowered and directed to investigate their conduct . . . and report at the earliest day practicable to this Legislature.[74]

The indictment was "like the bursting of a bombshell," Isaac Hunt recounted.[75] Roosevelt sat down to no applause, there was no noise. Hushed excitement seized the chamber. *What the hell had just happened,* no doubt many members thought, jaws dropped. The twenty-three-year-old, with sixty days of legislative experience—really only sixty days of experience in *any* career— had just asked for an impeachment investigation for a supreme court judge and his dealings with the most powerful business man on planet earth.

Sitting down after the indictment was an inexperienced move, leaving ten minutes in the session. The cunning veteran "Old Salt" Alvord immediately stood up, leaned on his cane, and began to stall.[76] The most capable of the "Black Horse Cavalry," Alvord eyed the clock and asked Roosevelt for real proof. The legislature was no "prying committee," he warned.[77] It was a terrible wrong— *tick, tock*—to ruin the career—*tick, tock*—of a virtuous man—*tick, tock*—on a hunch from a child legislator. Alvord rambled on, the big hand on the clock hit the top of the hour and the gavel fell. The house adjourned without a vote.

At the Delavan lair that night the assemblymen were scrambling. Should they support Roosevelt's reform effort or continue to play the game? Alvord's stall tactic proved valuable; the machine leaders had time to meet with their flock and make certain that Roosevelt did not have enough votes in the morning. And the next day, when the motion finally went to a roll call, fifty-nine members voted with Roosevelt and forty-five against, failing the two-thirds requirement. No investigation was warranted, the legislature believed.[78]

But word of Roosevelt's desire to investigate Judge Westbrook travelled swiftly and public sentiment rallied around the young crusader. *The Times, Evening Post,* and *Herald* all gave Theodore glowing reviews. "In these days of judicial, ecclesiastical and journalistic subserviency to the robber barons of the Street," the *Times* reported, "it needs some little courage in any public man to characterize them and their acts in fitting terms."[79] Only the *World,* owned by Gould, would vilify Roosevelt, claiming that he was making a "spectacle of himself."[80]

On April 12th, driven by a substantial ground swell of public support, the motion was passed, 104 to 6.[81] The assemblymen had changed their minds; they would look into the seedy business dealings and arrive at a verdict.

The lesson proved valuable for Theodore: the press could impel the politician to change his mind.

As the case went to the Judiciary Committee to issue a report to be voted on, it was clear that Roosevelt had disrupted the equilibrium of Albany. In a matter of hours, the state capitol was "teeming with prominent men from all over the state."[82] The invisible hand of the political machine went into silent action in defense of the judge and the robber baron. Tammany Hall thugs descended upon the Delavan like moths to the flame. Gould's henchmen met behind closed doors with legislators, to make it clear that at a time like this a politician's career could be destroyed with a single vote.

One such prominent man came down from Watertown to meet with Isaac Hunt to cryptically warn him, "you don't want to go to work and destroy a good judge like judge Westbrook!"[83]

Gould's operatives then set their sights on Roosevelt. Knowing that Theodore had inherited Thee's character and wealth, they quickly recognized that he was immune to bribery. So they turned to sex to entrap him. Walking home one evening, a sultry woman slipped and fell on the sidewalk in front of Theodore. He picked her up, helped her to her feet, and called a carriage to take her home. The woman—a siren leading a sailor to shipwreck—pleaded with Roosevelt for several minutes to accompany her home. He said no, she began to cry. As he paid the driver, he memorized the address the woman provided and passed it along to a police detective. The officer quickly dispatched to the address and found "a whole lot of men waiting to spring on him."[84]

"But no man can lead a public career really worth leading, no man can act with rugged independence in serious crises, nor strike at great abuses, nor afford to make powerful and unscrupulous foes, if he is himself vulnerable in his private character," Roosevelt claimed as belief. "He must be clean of life, so that he can laugh when his public or his private record is searched."[85]

The Westbrook case was a seminal moment for Roosevelt, not for his actions and the publicity it generated, but for what he chose not to do. Up until this point, he had really done very little on his own; all his life he had been a joiner and dependent. His father carried him through his childhood. At Harvard he joined the ready-made, safe, and luxurious clique. Joe Murray got him elected on Thee's good name. But as the Westbrook investigation took Albany by storm, an old family friend from a prominent law firm paid Theodore a visit to give the boy counsel. Roosevelt's wealth, his stellar last name, his new book, and his actions as a reformer, had all set him up to play the political game inside the inner circle with the power brokers. The family friend told Theodore, in no uncertain terms, that the men in the "inner circle" could make him a governor, a captain of industry, a senator, or perhaps one day, even a president. Nobody, the powerful ally told him, made it on his own. "The inner circle—included certain big business men, and the politicians, lawyers, and judges who were in alliance with and to a certain extent dependent upon them," the family friend explained, "and . . . the successful man had to win his success by the backing of the same forces, whether in law, business or politics."[86]

Theodore's bombastic actions as a reformer meant that he was on the verge of ending his career, even before it began. Acting like a reformer was one thing, but actually fighting hard as a reformer meant for a short career.[87] The family friend was experienced in the workings of the inner circle, and thought it appropriate to counsel the young man on how to "play the game," to follow the rich person's path to national leadership.

A strong case could be made that Roosevelt could have joined the inner political ring and still had a meaningful political and private career. He could have made small incremental changes from within the political game, until he got the time to lead, and then, armed with power, instigated sweeping reform. But he did not see it that way; he felt he would have lost a part of himself, the part of his conviction that held that government reform required an element of moral crusading at every rung of the ladder.

After the meeting Roosevelt decided not to join the game, to press on. He was going to continue after Westbrook like a dog on a bone. Evidently his ambition was held in check by his principle.

Roosevelt would later claim that he never knew if Judge Westbrook was corrupt, stating simply that "he may have been."[88] This is a profound admission. Theodore confesses that he put his political future on the line for something that just *may* have been.

"And for sheer moral courage, that act is probably supreme in Roosevelt's life thus far," the *Saturday Evening Post* reported shortly after the Westbrook affair. "He must have expected failure. Even his youthful idealism and ignorance of public affairs could not blind him to the apparently inevitable consequences. Yet he drew his sword and rushed apparently to destruction—alone, and at the very outset of his career, and in disregard of the pleadings of his closest friends and the plain dictates of political wisdom."[89]

What the *Post* writer had no way of knowing at the time was that this account would summarize the entirety of Theodore Roosevelt's career.

In May, the Judiciary Committee came back with its findings that Judge Westbrook had been "indiscreet and unwise" but recommended "against impeachment."[90] Three committee members, to no one's surprise, took bribes of $2,500 each.[91] The money undoubtedly came from men in the inner circle.

The assembly adjourned for good just two days later, and though Roosevelt had failed in the Westbrook case, and his Cigar Bill was later ruled unconstitutional, he had, according to Isaac Hunt, "won his spurs."[92]

Sometime later, Judge Westbrook was found dead in a hotel room in Troy, New York. Suicide the likely cause of death.[93]

At the end of his first term Theodore was a star. The New York newspapers, save Gould's *World,* were in lockstep agreement that Roosevelt was for real. *Harper's Weekly* ran a national piece on the kid legislator.

> It is with the greatest satisfaction that those who are interested in good government see a young man in the Legislature who . . . does not know the meaning of fear, and to whom the bluster and bravado of party and political bullies are as absolutely indifferent as the blowing of the wind.[94]

"I rose like a rocket," Theodore understated.[95] Re-elected by a two-to-one margin the following year, Roosevelt was selected, among his legislative peers, to be the Republican Speaker. Though a subdued honor, as the Democrats had the majority, it was nonetheless an incredible achievement considering that he was now the head of his party at just twenty-four years old with a mere five months of legislative experience. It was an even more amazing accomplishment considering that his polarizing reform activities offended both Democrats as well as the machine element within his own party.[96]

The assembly was elected annually. Theodore's first term in 1882, ran from January 1st to June 2nd. His second term, just four months, ran from January 1st to May 4th. Over the course of the two years, he was only in Albany for a total of nine months. His inexperience soon caught up with him. If his first five months were a tremendous success, his next four months can only be viewed as a considerable disappointment, and also a learning experience.

Roosevelt's second term got off to a running start. Once elected as the speaker, he was summoned to Governor Grover Cleveland's office to discuss civil service reform. The Reform Bill represented a countrywide effort to ensure that government jobs were awarded on the basis of merit and not simply distributed to cronies by those in power. President Garfield's assassination had thrust the idea of merit-based appointments to the forefront of America's consciousness.

When Cleveland and Roosevelt discussed civil service reform in the state of New York, neither of them realized that six years later Cleveland would be the president, and he and Roosevelt would team up again on the national stage to enforce a Civil Service Reform Act that would forever change America. But in 1883, the two met for three hours to discuss how to get the state bill passed through the state legislature and the governor was only mildly impressed with the twenty-four-year-old. "There is a great sense in a lot of what he says," Cleveland stated, "but there is such a cocksuredness about him that he stirs up doubt in me all the time . . . he seems to be so very young."[97]

As his second term began, Roosevelt wore his youth and cocksuredness on his sleeve. He began to refer to his elder party members as "my men" and, in the words of another legislature, "his political judgment was a decimal. It was not that he did not love politics, and know the game well enough from the start—*but he loved himself more.*"[98]

His tough crusader leadership style left everyone confused. He had put himself at the center of attention and soon became a man leading no one. "What's got into Roosevelt?" was the standing question. "He won't listen to anybody. He thinks he knows it all."[99]

When Theodore, as the minority leader, failed to produce legislative victories and rally the Republican caucus around his vision, he grew frustrated and more certain that *everyone* was corrupt. If you did not agree with him, you must be crooked. Worse, he never doubted the principles of his own position. If he made up his mind about something, then it *had* to be right. On every issue, it was a matter of good vs. evil, right vs. wrong, reformer vs. corruption, Roosevelt vs. the bad guys.[100] Theodore also felt that his title—Minority Speaker—gave him the right to exercise his authority, still too young to realize that a fancy title does not automatically equate to leadership. And the more he tried to exercise his authority, the more he came across as a righteous dictator. One Albany newspaperman quipped, "There is increasing suspicion that Mr. Roosevelt keeps a pulpit concealed on his person."[101] The papers gave him a new nickname: His Lordship.[102]

The *Albany Argus* began to reprimand Roosevelt, reminding him that the tough issues of the day had two sides, "with sincere men on both," and Roosevelt's habit of "claiming all of the public virtues for one party" was a terrible example of "flippancy, prejudice, and want of patriotism, as well as execrable ignorance."[103] The *Argus* concluded that Theodore's "limitations make him look ridiculous."[104]

"I suppose that my head was swelled," Theodore told his friend Jacob Riis. "It would not be strange if it was. I stood out for my own opinion, alone. I took the . . . stand; my own conscience, my own judgment, were to decide in all things. I would listen to no argument, no advice. I took the isolated peak on every issue, and my people left me."[105]

In fact, they did not leave him. He never had them.

"He was the leader, and he started over the hill and here his army was following him, trying to keep sight of him," George Spinney stated in an interview several years later. Isaac Hunt, upon hearing Spinney's assessment, would clarify that the "army only followed" Theodore to try and "keep him from rushing into destruction."[106]

Roosevelt's incomplete view on leadership held that if a leader stood strong by his convictions, then those that shared those convictions would follow, no matter what—just like the independent heroes of his mother's stories and the characters in his Mayne

Reid novels. What he failed to realize was that a leader has to start where his followers are and mobilize them around a shared, common goal. Only a small handful of Roosevelt's colleagues fervently shared his vision of moral crusading and reform; others simply desired it, and the majority, while conceding it would be great for the country, still speculated as to whether it was a fad. The issue of reform was not ripe enough to unite the majority around the cause. Theodore needed to focus on incremental victories; instead, he tried to change the entire culture overnight. Worse, the more pushback he received, the more independently radical he acted. The more radically he acted, the less people wanted to follow him.

Theodore's impulsiveness derailed any chance he had to lead. "Billy O'Neil and I used to sit on his coattails," recalled Isaac Hunt. "Billy O'Neil would say to him: 'What do you want to do that for, you damn fool; you will ruin yourself and everybody else!'"[107]

Years later Theodore would admit to his failure. He learned, rather spectacularly, that an adaptive leader can only lead others by listening, truly listening, to understand what the followers believed at that moment in time. It cannot be done by charging ahead alone, simply espousing virtues. Once a leader knew what his followers believed—as well as their prejudices—he could empathize with them. Only then could he lead them.

> Like most young men in politics, I went through various oscillations of feeling before I "found myself." [Roosevelt later wrote] At one period I became so impressed with the virtue of complete independence that I proceeded to act on each case purely as I personally viewed it, without paying any heed to the principles and prejudices of others. The result was that I speedily and deservedly lost all power of accomplishing anything at all; and I thereby learned the invaluable lesson that in the practical activities of life no man can render the highest service unless he can act in combination with his fellows, which means a certain amount of give-and-take between him and them.[108]

But in 1883 he had not learned this lesson yet. And things just got worse.

The Five-Cent Bill, as it was aptly called, was a piece of legislation to halve the ten-cent fare for the Manhattan Elevated Railway. It was introduced to cut into Jay Gould's excessive profits and please the thousands of patrons who rode the railway. A safe bill, aided by public support, it passed 109 to 6.[109] But upon delivery, Governor Cleveland vetoed it swiftly on the grounds that it was unconstitutional. Cleveland rightfully argued that though he loathed Gould's scheme, the state of New York did in fact have a contract with Gould, and, as a nation of laws, the state must uphold that contract. Theodore, originally in favor of the bill, quickly realized that Cleveland was right.

Roosevelt did not have to do anything; the house did not have enough votes to reverse the veto so the Five-Cent Bill was inconsequential. All Theodore had to do was keep his mouth shut and move onto the next piece of legislation. Instead, he took to the floor and in a single speech almost ruined his young career.

I have to say with shame [Roosevelt shouted] that when I voted for this bill . . . I weakly yielded, partly in a vindictive spirit toward the infernal thieves and conscienceless swindlers who have had the elevated railroad in charge and partly to the popular voice of New York.

For the managers of the elevated railroad I have as little feeling as any man here. If it were possible, I would willingly pass a bill of attainder on Jay Gould and all of Jay Gould's associates. . . . I regard these men as furnishing part of the most dangerous of all dangerous classes, *the wealthy criminal class*. . . .[110]

The speech was all at once an admirable *mea culpa*, a contradiction of political philosophy, and just plain odd. He took both sides of the issue, defending Cleveland yet berating the "wealthy criminal class." He had no idea how self-righteous and inconsistent he sounded. Was he himself not of the wealthy class? Was he himself not a reformer? Whose side was this kid on?

"What a storm that stirred up among the newspapers of New York," Hunt recalled. "How they lambasted him, *the Herald* and the *World*, as a fellow who did not know his own mind, and that this was the end of this young silk-stocking's career."[111] Roosevelt's

sermon appealed to no one. The reformers thought he was a traitor, the journalists thought he had a credibility gap, and everyone
else was just plain confused.

The backlash was harsh. The newspapers lined up against him:
"bogus reformer" declared the *Star*, he only wanted his opinion
known and did not care about the people, claimed the *Post*; "weakling" shouted the *Sun*[112]; a newspaper in Boston even chimed in
stating that it was certain that Theodore had dug his own grave.[113]

The *World* ran the nastiest piece: "The friends who have so long
deplored the untimely death of Theodore Roosevelt [Senior]
cannot but be thankful that he has been spared the pain of a
spectacle which would have wounded to the quick his gracious
and honorable nature."[114]

Amidst the journalistic uproar, Roosevelt doubled down.

A day or so after the Five-Cent debacle, Theodore again let his
emotions get the best of him.[115] Frustrated and angry that nobody
was following him, he offered his resignation from a committee
before giving an unprompted speech insinuating that God was
a Republican and the Devil was a Democrat.[116] The kid-speaker's
lashing out was described as "a wild, childish diatribe against the
whole Democratic Party. It was as if, like the tiny shrew in the cage,
he would fling himself at the great Democratic snake and tear it to
pieces before anyone knew what happened."[117] The speech was a
disaster. It was rash, irresponsible, silly, and incoherent. He was proving himself a pompous know-it-all that nobody wanted to follow.

"When Mr. Roosevelt had finished his affecting oration," the
New York Observer recounted, "the House was in tears—of uncon-
trollable laughter."[118]

When Roosevelt finally sat down, Erastus Brooks, the man
Theodore had chosen to sit next to on account of his wealth of
experience, stood up and reprimanded the young novice. In his
late sixties and polished, Brooks scolded Theodore: "The idea of
a man reared in the home of culture, a graduate from college,
appearing in the legislature and expressing himself in such language as 'rotten democracy,' was an embarrassment."[119]

Later, Brooks and Roosevelt would exchange words again, and
the old timer, in a fit of fury, lunged at Roosevelt, with what was
described as "fire flashing from his eyes."[120] The two had to be separated before Brooks, the experienced professional, took the fight
to the floor and gave an effective speech rebutting Roosevelt.[121]

When the speech finished, Theodore rushed over to Erastus with all of Brooks's men expecting fisticuffs. Instead, Roosevelt with tears in his eyes extended his hand, "Mr. Brooks I surrender. I beg your pardon."[122] The young gun had messed up, and he knew it. Of the surrender, an eyewitness would conclude it to be "one of the finest exhibitions of manly confession and honest emotion they ever witnessed."[123]

Though Roosevelt did apologize for his actions and words, the damage had been done. The *Observer* on March 10th reported what everyone already knew:

But the end came at last and now the careless Republicans who let the poor fellow run on and destroy himself are overcome with remorse. Yesterday in a speech Mr. Roosevelt got up and said in effect that he couldn't have his own way in that House and he wouldn't stand it, so there! And he couldn't even bring his 'own men' to time. And they were miserable, ungrateful creatures, so there! And he was a statesman who knew what he was talking about and not a child at all . . . *it was painfully evident that at last the young man's friends had tired of his 'leadership. . .'*[124]

Journalist Mark Sullivan would rightfully state that "Roosevelt did not regard politics as a gentleman's sport, to be played in the spirit of a private duello, with a meticulous code about choice of time and place. Roosevelt had a trait of ruthless righteousness."[125] For Roosevelt, politics was indeed a barroom fight. The righteous reformers, whom he trusted, got in the middle of the room, stood back to back, and started swinging at whoever came at them. He won in the moment, and failed in the moment. At this moment, nobody was fighting with him.

It is clear that success had come too quickly. Years later, in a letter to his son, he would admit that he lost perspective: "I came an awful cropper, and had to pick myself up after learning by bitter experience the lesson that I was not all-important and that I had to take account of many different elements in life."[126]

For all of his failures in his second term, the Civil Service Reform Bill that he championed with Governor Cleveland became law, and Theodore was later re-elected to a third term, his final one.

8. "THE LIGHT HAS GONE OUT OF MY LIFE"

The New York Times, February 13th, 1884

It is suicidal weather. Life does not seem worth living to a sensitive person easily influenced by atmospheric conditions. There is something comfortless and unhappy in the raw and chilly air, something suggestive of death and decay in the dampness that fills the world.[1]

Theodore Roosevelt committed to his diary that an evening alone with Alice, his "heart's dearest," was his ideal. "Back again in my own lovely little home, with the sweetest and prettiest of all little wives—my own sunny darling. I can image nothing more happy in life than an evening spent in my cosy little sitting room, before a bright fire of soft coal, my books all around me, and playing backgammon with my own dainty mistress."[2]

In the winter of 1884, much to the couple's delight, Alice was very pregnant. The couple had been planning for their future for some time and construction had recently begun on the ninety-five acre parcel of land Theodore had bought at Oyster Bay, New York. The house was to be enormous: twenty-two rooms, ten bedrooms, eight fireplaces, a grand dining room, and four living rooms.

From the rambling front piazza, the Roosevelts and their many children could lookout on the steamers heading up Long Island

Sound, or read a book, or memorize prose, or organize a game of kick-the-can. During the summers, on the shores below, the children would romp and climb and row; free to be free. In the winter, the family would nestle by the fire and read, or recite the poetry of Sir Walter Scott, or give spur-of-the-moment speeches on the topic of the day. The entire family—children, husband, wife—would no doubt succumb to bursts of spontaneous laughter. Here Theodore could be Thee, and Alice could be Mittie; the idyllic Victorian Roosevelt family raising their children in the blithe manor high upon the hill.

Theodore christened the home Leeholm, after his dearly beloved. His home life was perfect; he could not have known more merriment.

◌◌◌

During the second week of February 1884, Theodore returned from his legislative duties in Albany to his home on Fifty-Seventh Street. The weather was dark and brutal. The entire eastern seaboard was under siege from an unrelenting squall. Torrential rainfall pounded the Ohio Valley. Coal mines in Pennsylvania, fearing flash flood, shut down operations. Reports from Cincinnati told that the river was at a one-hundred-year high mark. Flood warnings were issued as far south as Louisville.[3]

A heavy fog imprisoned New York City. Shipping was shut down on the Hudson. Elevated trains inched forward unable to see the signals, traffic across Brooklyn Bridge was halted.[4]

Inside the Roosevelt home, to Theodore's joy, his pregnant wife was feeling well. She was due any day now. There was one cause for concern. Mittie had come down with a bad cold, but she seemed to be doing just fine.

Theodore left for Albany first thing Tuesday morning.

Late in the afternoon of February 12th, Alice went into labor, and a baby girl was born. There seemed to be no complications, mom was tired and the baby was healthy. A telegram went off to Theodore the following morning.

"I shall never forget when the news came," a friend remembered. "We congratulated him on the birth of his daughter. He was full of life and happiness."[5]

A few hours later a second telegram arrived that sent Roosevelt racing for the train depot. The words on that summons have been lost to history. A friend just remembered "how worn" Theodore instantly looked.[6]

On the train home Theodore was left alone with his thoughts. Six years and four days before, he had received a telegram, charged home on a train, and found his father dead. Just less than four years ago, almost to the day, he and Alice had announced their engagement.

Summoning up strength to temper his emotions, Theodore stared out the train window into a world of darkness. In the deep fog, the locomotives only inched down the line. At station depots train cars were backed up, hours behind schedule.

The man of action could only sit and think. Off in the distance, the lonesome and melancholic sound of the train whistle was barely audible.

He arrived at Grand Central Station at 10:30 p.m. The streets of New York were wet and quiet. The light from the lampposts were cloaked in darkness, as if a wool blanket had been draped over them.[7] It was another hour before he got to the home.

In the distance the church bells would soon toll midnight, Saint Valentine's Day, 1884.[8]

Hearing footsteps outside, Elliot flung open the front door, his silhouette the only thing visible from the walkway.

"There is a curse on this house," Elliot shouted hysterically to his brother. "Mother is dying and Alice is dying too!"[9]

At Alice's bedside, Theodore clutched his wife. She was comatose, slipping in and out of consciousness. She did not recognize him. He seized her and held her close, trying to infuse her body with his strength, his vitality, his vigor. As if his love, his grip, could remake her body.

In his arms Alice lay, until a horrible message came up the stairs. It was just before three in the morning. It was time to say goodbye to mother. In the same room where Thee died, Mittie breathed her last. A soft gaslight shone upon her moonlight complexion. The Southern belle looked as lovely as ever.[10]

Mittie had had typhoid fever, not a cold.

Grief settled on Roosevelt. Staring at his dead mother and thinking about his dying wife, he whispered his brother's words, "There *is* a curse on this house."[11]

Theodore turned, walked up the stairs to his wife, and again took her in his arms. At two o'clock in the afternoon Alice Lee Roosevelt died in her husband's embrace. She succumbed to Bright's disease; her kidneys had failed. She was twenty-two years old. She had been a mother for just over forty hours.[12]

In his diary, under the date February 14th, 1884, Theodore drew a large cross:

"The light has gone
out of my life."

His pen stopped; he wrote no more.[13]

In the sad interlude between the deaths Bamie sent a wire to Liverpool. "The cable has never carried through the depths of the sea a sadder message than it has brought us today," Uncle Jimmie Bulloch replied.[14]

By Saturday morning the storm had passed, the skies cleared.[15] A bitter cold settled in; it was twenty-four degrees.[16]

Two horse-drawn hearses, each containing a single rosewood coffin, lumbered side-by-side down Fifth Avenue to the

Presbyterian Church on 55th Street. The massive congregation was full, every pew accounted for.[17] The immediate family sat in the front. "Rock of Ages" was sung.[18]

The minister and family friend, Dr. Hall, started the terrible ceremony with a prayer for the surviving four-day-old baby. Stifled sobs reverberated throughout the church. He had never experienced anything quite like this, Dr. Hall revealed, weeping openly as he pressed on.

There was a disparity between the two tragic deaths. One, though she was only forty-eight years old "her work could be regarded as done."[19] But Alice, a young mother in the morning of her life, her death was different; her fate was "strange and terrible."[20] Nothing could be said to help anyone understand, except perhaps, "The Will of God."[21] With tears flowing down his cheeks, Dr. Hall ended the service by praying for the man who lost his mother and wife. The new father sat stone faced, expressionless.

That afternoon, the coffins were put to the earth at Greenwood cemetery, next to Thee and Grandma Bulloch.[22]

"Theodore is in a dazed, stunned state," Arthur Cutler wrote to Bill Sewall. "He does not know what he does or says."[23] But in contrast to his stunning reaction and multi-year healing process after Thee passed away, Theodore immediately looked inward, stoically, to find strength. He wrote no impassioned letters that he was helpless and lost, no diary entries of depression. He reached out to no one. On nobody's shoulder, at least in the immediate aftermath, did he break down and cry.

Of the entire experience, we have one lone insight into his grief during that terrible week, a diary entry on the day of the funeral:

Alice Hathaway Lee. Born at Chestnut Hill, July 29th 1861. I saw her first on October 18th 1878; I wooed her for over a year before I won her; we were betrothed on January 25th 1880, and it was announced on Feb 16th; on October 27th of that same year we were married; we spent three years of happiness greater and more unalloyed that I have ever known fall to the lot of others; on Feb 12th, 1884, her baby was born, and on Feb 14th, she died in my arms; my mother had died in the same house, on the same day, but a few hours previously . . . For joy or sorrow, my life has now been lived out.[24]

With that entry Alice ceases to exist. Save for one farewell letter for close family and friends, Theodore would never speak openly of Alice again. In his memoirs, not a single word was dedicated to her, not one mention of her life. The surviving daughter would grow up and never once hear her father speak of her mother. He never told the child anything. What her mother looked like, how her voice sounded, what made her laugh, what dresses she wore, how she danced, or if she wore bows in her hair. Nothing.

Later in life, Theodore would give advice to a friend who had lost a loved one: "Yet there is nothing more foolish and cowardly than to be beaten down by a sorrow which nothing we can do will change."[25] In a letter to Corinne, in 1908, and near the end of his presidency, Theodore gives his insight regarding the unexpected death of his niece's fiancé:

The only thing for her to do now is to treat the past as past, the event as finished and out of her life; to dwell on it, and above all, to keep talking of it, with you or anyone else, would be both weak and morbid. Let her try not to think of it; this she can not wholly avoid; but she can avoid speaking of it. Let her show a brave and cheerful front to the world, whatever she feels; and let her never speak one word of the matter, henceforth, to you or to anyone else. In the long future, when the memory is too dead to throb, she may if she wishes again speak of it.[26]

The baby was christened the day after the funeral and given the name Alice Lee, after her mother. Bamie, it was decided in accordance with the custom of the day for male widows, would take care of the child.

Just three days after the funeral, Roosevelt returned to Albany.

"I shall come back to my work at once; there is nothing left for me except to try to so live as not to dishonor the memory of those I loved who have gone before me," Theodore wrote.[27]

To Bill Sewall, he confided, "It was a grim and evil fate, but I have never believed it did any good to flinch or yield for any blow, nor does it lighten the blow to cease from working."[28]

"And I never shall forget how he looked when he came back," Isaac Hunt explained. "You could not talk with him about it. You could not mention the fact that his wife and mother had been taken away. You could see at once it was a grief too deep. He came back and so far as his acts were concerned and his conduct you would never have known anything had happened to him at all. He simply would not yield to those things . . . He was a changed man. From that time on there was a sadness about his face that he never had before."[29]

In the weeks after the double tragedy, Theodore's schedule became increasingly punishing. He was an assemblyman on Tuesday, Wednesday, and Thursday, and chairman of the City Investigating Committee on Friday, Saturday, and Monday.[30] He did not sleep, always in permanent motion, always working.

His decision to labor through the tragedy left everyone to believe that if he stopped to think about his calamity, he would go mad.

"He feels the awful loneliness more and more," Corinne wrote, "and I fear he sleeps little, for he walks a great deal in the night and his eyes have that strained red look."[31]

To a friend, Roosevelt wrote, "Although not a very old man, I have yet lived a great deal in my life, and I have known sorrow too bitter and joy too keen to allow me to become either cast down or elated for more than a very brief period over success or defeat."[32]

"He was carrying a grief that he had in his own soul," a confidant recalled, ". . . he felt those things more than people thought—[the tragedy] *hounded him to death*."[33]

The devastating double event galvanized for Theodore that life could end in a moment. The prevailing feeling that the end was always near was not an abstract feeling, but an integral part of his character. Death had tried to steal him as a child. His heart, he was told at Harvard, could give out at any minute. His father had died at forty-six; mother had died at forty-eight; his wife died at twenty-two. Life on earth—just like a candle—could be snuffed in an instant.

"Get action!" and "Seize the moment!" were not hollow instructions from Thee. They were doctrines for survival.

Though the world would come to know Teddy Roosevelt for his bombastic and cheerful personality, the private man was much more forlorn and pensive than the public ever realized. The quick-stepping and verbose Teddy would surrender to what his daughter called "a melancholic streak"—a quiet and abrupt retreat to his inner thoughts, his mind a thousand miles away, his body despondent. His young children and aides would often find Theodore in his study staring out the window, a sad look in his eyes, almost as if under a spell. One of his favorite poets was Edwin Robinson, a man who wrote on the "loneliness and the burden of personal memory."[34]

Then, as it is now, the American public never embraced Theodore's melancholy, perhaps due to the misperception that those who are melancholic to their core cannot be inspirational leaders. But it was Roosevelt's forlorn streak that made him reflective and thoughtful. It made him the leader he would become.

II

---✧---

RULING

9.   1884 REPUBLICAN NATIONAL CONVENTION

———————————————◇

As THE 1884 REPUBLICAN NATIONAL CONVENTION neared, the GOP was worried as to who would come out victorious in Chicago, IL. Since Garfield's assassination in 1881, President Chester Arthur had, to the surprise of the country, led quite admirably. The economy was growing, he supported the popular Civil Service Reform Act, and he stood strong on international trade. But Arthur's prior graft had already solidified his crony image and the Republican masses wanted their own man out of the White House. They decided that another Republican, James G. Blaine, ex-senator from Maine and Garfield's secretary of state, should be the party's next nominee.[1] Known as the "Plumed Knight," James Blaine was the resolute leader of the Republican Party, a man who had both the magnetic personality to inspire rank-and-file Republicans and the qualification of long-term obedience to the party. Blaine believed that loyalty to the party was a prerequisite to national leadership.[2]

This was the opposite of Theodore Roosevelt's belief. And worse, Blaine was severely corrupt.

James Blaine was the frontrunner for the 1876 presidential campaign before rumors circulated that the Union Pacific Railroad had paid him $64,000 for bonds he held in the Little Rock and Fort Smith Railroad. The problem was that the bonds were worthless and the transaction was nothing more than a disguised bribe. Though Blaine and the Union Pacific Board of Directors vehemently denied the charges, Democrats in the House of Representatives demanded a Congressional investigation. Just one month prior to the Republican Convention of 1876, James

Mulligan, an assistant formerly employed by Blaine's brother-in-law, testified that he had arranged the bribe and had the letters between Blaine and Union Pacific to prove $64,000 worth of wrongdoing.

The investigative hearing brokeout in an uproar and a recess was called. During the break, Blaine ran up to Mulligan's hotel room. What transpired there is unknown. What *is* known is that Blaine left with the critical letters under his arm and refused to turn them over to the committee, instead providing highly censored accounts.[3] James Mulligan refused to give further details on what he knew, and Blaine was shortly thereafter acquitted for a lack of evidence. Now, eight years later, Blaine was running for president of the United States, hoping the Mulligan Letter Affair had been erased from the public's awareness.

To Theodore, the choice between the two frontrunners was appalling. Both Arthur and Blaine were corrupt party loyalists, both dishonest men. Theodore's man was reform candidate Senator George Franklin Edmunds of Vermont, who in the words of *Harper's Weekly*, was "in full sympathy with the intelligent progressive spirit" as well as a man "of spotless personal character."[4] Theodore had never met Edmunds, but the accounts of his progressive spirit and spotless personal character were enough to garner his support.

Though Edmunds did not stand a chance of winning the nomination, fortune was smiling on Roosevelt. When the New York Republican Party convened at Utica's Grand Opera House to select its delegates for the national convention, they found themselves in a sticky situation. Of the 496 delegates, seventy were reform republicans—Independents—and the rest were divided evenly for Blaine and Arthur.[5] The Arthur supporters knew that if Blaine carried New York—President Arthur's home state—then it would seal both Arthur's chances and Blaine's nomination. The Arthur men were in a conundrum: if they could not persuade the seventy Independents they would be forced to give the Edmunds men all of their votes. At the center of this quandary was Theodore Roosevelt. He had all the power as the leader of the "spoiler's faction."[6] He was the youngest delegate present.

In his first year in the assembly, Theodore had witnessed how a spoiler's faction could influence the majority when eight

Tammany men held up the entire legislative body for several weeks.[7] Now the tables had turned, and he was the one who had the small influential cohort.

And so it was that when the powerful minority of seventy delegates stood firm behind Roosevelt, unwilling to split their votes, the Arthur men were forced to choose the lesser of two evils and all of Arthur's support was placed with Edmunds and the reformers. A delegation of four Edmunds men—more aptly put, four non-Blaine men—were off to Chicago to cast New York's votes for the president of the United States. The man in charge of the delegation was Theodore Roosevelt. He had been in the right state—Arthur's home state of New York, at the right time—the year of a national convention, with just enough votes from a new wing of his party—the reformers.

Henry Cabot Lodge, delegate-at-large from Massachusetts, was Roosevelt's equal in the reform movement and a supporter of Edmunds. Eight years older, Lodge had much more national experience and a better national brand. But Lodge was impressed with Roosevelt's earnest determination towards the cause of better government and knew he could leverage Theodore's bulldog tenacity on the floor of the national convention. Though Roosevelt had dodged Lodge's class when he was a professor at Harvard—simply because Lodge was a tough grader—he was now eager to join forces and welcomed him to his home in New York to discuss strategy.

"We are breaking up house," Theodore coldly warned Lodge regarding the visit, "so you will have to excuse very barren accommodations."[8] Mittie's and Alice's belongings had been placed in boxes, somber reminders scattered throughout the home.

Upon meeting in person, Roosevelt and Lodge quickly realized that their personal and political principles were tightly aligned.[9] Both men were born into wealth; both graduated from Harvard; both were in the prestigious Porcellian Club. Now later in life, both desired distinguished political and literary careers, and both thought of themselves as great men. Perhaps most importantly, both harbored the deep conviction that political reform was absolutely mandatory for the success of America's posterity. In time, the Lodge-Roosevelt relationship would prove to be among the greatest alliances in American political history, and time and again Lodge would prove to be the single most important ally in aiding Roosevelt's leadership journey.[10] It is almost impossible to imagine Theodore's rise to the presidency without the influence of Henry Cabot Lodge.

But in 1884, the cards were stacked against the young reformers. The "Old Guard," as they were called, consisted of veteran party members who had prospered mightily in the twenty-five year Republican dominance after the Civil War. When the South was defeated in the Civil War, so too were the Democrats, and the elder Republican leaders wielded expansive control on the party, and therefore, the country. The Old Guard detested young reformers like Roosevelt and Lodge who were disrupting the natural order of things.

"[The Republican machine] was probably the most efficient piece of political machinery for perpetuating a party in power that ever existed," George Spinney explained. "It rewarded its friends royally in the states, the counties and districts, disciplined its members vigorously who failed to produce majorities, and punished its enemies within by speedy banishment to private life or hamstringing them in their every endeavor to participate in public affairs and governmental activity."[11] The Old Guard thought nothing of the impropriety of the corruption charges against Blaine—they had won every election since the Civil War and fully intended to win again.

Both Lodge and Roosevelt realized that the nomination of Edmunds was not grounded in reality. However, they did appreciate that they might be laying the groundwork for future elections, perhaps at a time in the not too distant future when the reform movement was more nationally accepted. That is to say, when the next generation of national leaders outnumbered the Old Guard and would begin to take power.

On May 31st, the day Theodore arrived at the national convention, Chicago was abuzz with excitement. "Fast and thick the delegates to the convention are flocking into this city," a newspaper proclaimed before stating the obvious, ". . . a canvass of the members of the convention here shows Blaine to be in the lead. . . ."[12]

The entire scene made Theodore cringe. Undeterred that public sentiment, as well as the powerful political bosses, were both squarely behind Blaine, Roosevelt and Lodge immediately began working the backrooms of the Grand Pacific. "[We] pulled together and went in for all we were worth," Theodore admitted.[13]

The Republican National Committee, ripe with pro-Blaine delegates, had nominated Powell Clayton to serve as the chair of the convention. The powerful post meant that Clayton could dictate the proceedings and the ever important timing of votes. Blaine's huge lead, coupled with Clayton's support, meant that the convention could nominate Blaine immediately after the proceedings began and end the process instantly.

But Clayton was a poor choice. As the first Reconstruction governor of Arkansas, Clayton's personal reputation was rotten— the crudest of the cronies, he was a man for sale.[14] In every way, Clayton exemplified the dark cloud of seedy dealings that had hung around Blaine, and almost immediately upon arriving in Chicago, he had offered up the fourteen Arkansas delegates to the candidate that would appoint him to a cabinet post.[15]

The committee's poor decision to appoint Clayton gave Lodge and Roosevelt an opening to challenge Blaine early. However, to defy the National Committee's choice for the chairmanship, before the proceedings even started, was uncharted territory. No one had done it before. But Roosevelt could not have cared less for tradition and in an unprecedented move he convinced Congressmen John R. Lynch, an African American from Mississippi, to run for the chairmanship. That night, Roosevelt and Lodge canvassed the hotel corridor securing support for Lynch, aligning Arthur and reform candidates in an effort to slow down Blaine. All night Roosevelt romped from room to room urging support for Lynch. If they could win the chair of the convention for Lynch, Roosevelt figured, they would be assured a neutral representation when the convention began.

Theodore had gotten no more than three hours sleep when he awoke the next morning to make his national debut.[16]

At the Exposition Hall on June 3rd, 1884, the scene was chaotic. Below a massive banner that read NATIONAL REPUBLICAN CONVENTION, a crowd of ten thousand people were "converging from all directions, stopping traffic, backing up at six or seven different entrances."[17] Inside the hall, the scene was monstrously patriotic: state flags, American flags, red and white buttons, pennants, pins, straw hats, banners.

Twenty-eight minutes past noon, Johnny's Band started into "My Country 'Tis of Thee" and the convention was gaveled into order. Lodge, wasting no time, jumped to his feet, "I move you, Mr. Chairman, to substitute the name of the Hon. John R. Lynch, of Mississippi!"[18] The convention clamored, delegates began to shout. This was an act of disloyalty and betrayal. Members of the Old Guard demanded a prompt denial of the motion. One delegate, visibly shaking, reminded the crowd that nobody had ever challenged the National Committee's choice for the chairmanship at the beginning of the proceedings. Nobody, ever.

On cue, Roosevelt removed his delegate-issued straw hat, pushed in his spectacles, and climbed onto his chair. He had a "boyish figure," the *Times* reported. "He look liked a college boy," said another commentary.[19] His voice boomed over more than ten thousand people.

First he spoke of corruption:

> Mr. Chairman . . . I hold it to be derogatory to our honor, to our capacity for self-government, to say that we must accept the nomination of a presiding officer by another body; and that our hands are tied, and we dare not reverse its action.[20]

Then he spoke of Lincoln and the rights of all men:

> It is now, Mr. Chairman, less than a quarter of a century since, in this city, the great Republican party for the first time

organized for victory, and nominated Abraham Lincoln, of Illinois, who broke the fetters of the slave and rent them asunder forever. It is a fitting thing for us to choose to preside over this Convention one of that race whose right to sit within these walls is due to the blood and the treasure so lavishly spent by the founders of the Republican party. And it is but a further vindication of the principles for which the Republican Party so long struggled. I trust that the Hon. Mr. Lynch will be elected Temporary Chairman of this Convention.[21]

The speech lasted no longer than four minutes, and was interrupted several times by applause. Though it was praised in the papers as "neat and effective,"[22] it would be several years before the speech could be fully appreciated. In his introduction to national politics—his very first time in the national spotlight—Roosevelt called out corruption in his own party and then elevated a black man to the most important position of the entire proceeding.

A few minutes after Theodore sat down, roll was called, and John R. Lynch was elected by a margin of forty votes.[23] Lodge and Roosevelt, the young reform duo, had put a wrinkle in Blaine's easy path to the White House.

But the victory would not last. Over the next three days the inevitable gradually took hold. Roosevelt's nights of furious activity could not compete with the cash and promises dispersed from the bottom of the deck by Blaine's men. Nervous that the ship was sinking, reform delegates began ditching Edmunds, supporting John Sherman and then Robert Lincoln, son of Abraham Lincoln.[24] Frustrations mounted. A "cane-whacking" and "sporadic fistfights" broke out during the proceedings.[25] As tensions raged, it became clear that the 1884 nomination for president had become a watershed moment for the Republican Party. Would the Party of Lincoln finally stand up to its own corruption and embrace reform?

"It is a life or death struggle for the Republican Party in Chicago," wrote the editor of the *Times*. The nomination of Blaine, the *Times* continued, meant "a disastrous defeat for the Republican Party, and from that defeat the party would never recover except under other leaders and perhaps another name. The party has assuredly fallen upon evil days."[26]

And then came Black Friday.

At 11:30 a.m. Chairman Lynch called a vote to order. Amid a chorus of emotions from the ten thousand in attendance, the tally stood at 334 ½ for Blaine, 278 for Arthur, and 93 for Edmunds. The magic number for Blaine was 411.[27]

A short while later, a second, and then third ballot was issued. Edmunds' support began to erode as reform delegates defected to Blaine, who was now at 374 votes. Roosevelt ran frantically from delegation to delegation, his arms thrashed the air, his voice broke, he shouted and screamed, his entire body seemed to convulse.[28] Delegates stood on their chairs, shouting. Blaine's men rushed the stage, surrounding the chairman, and demanded a final vote. Nobody could hear a thing; chaos was king.[29]

A New Jersey delegate shouted at Theodore to shut up and sit down, which prompted Theodore to retort, "Shut up your own head, you damned scoundrel you!"[30]

Amid the disorder, Judge Foraker made a motion to recess the vote to halt the raging tide of support for Blaine. The motion was denied. At the doorstep was the inevitable, when William McKinley, congressman from Ohio, seeking to unify the party, stood up and asked for a vote to end the madness. Theodore sank in his chair as a fourth ballot commenced.[31] When Ohio cast its votes, it was all over. Blaine was the nominee.

The crowd erupted in what would come to be known as the "loudest roar in the history of American politics."[32] Triumphant hordes of people poured into the streets of Chicago, shouting, "Blaine, Blaine, hurrah for Blaine!"[33] Cannons and fireworks began to explode.

As the crowds erupted, William McKinley sprinted up to Roosevelt and urged him to make the vote unanimous, to concede defeat, and unite the reform faction of the party behind Blaine. McKinley wanted a unified Republican Party and asked Roosevelt to make it happen.

Here was the opportunity for Theodore, in his first national convention, to be *the* individual to unite the party. He could have taken the screaming masses to a new hysteria. But rather than be the hero of the moment in front of ten thousand, he shook his head and did not move. To him, this was not about accolades. He was fighting for the future of the country, not party unity. After all, how could he concede when the party seemed destined for more corruption?

So he remained in his seat, beaten.

A few moments later, in the middle of the pandemonium, he finally made his way for the exit, head down. A reporter rushed to Theodore's side to find that his face was red and his "eyes flashed with indignation behind his gold-rimmed spectacles as he contemplated his first real defeat."[34]

"You will support Blaine, will you not?" the reporter inquired.

"That question I decline to answer. It is a subject that I do not care to talk about."

"Will you not enter the campaign in the interests of the Republican Party?" was the follow-up.

"I am going cattle ranching in Dakota for the remainder of the summer and part of the fall. What I shall do after that I cannot tell you."

Then he pushed past several more reporters, all shouting questions.

Physically, emotionally, and politically, he was hanging on by a thread.

The following morning, the Exposition Hall was noiseless. A cluttered mess of banners, hats, and button pins were the only indication that something had just taken place. For all the commotion of the day prior, the Hall was now soundless, empty. Theodore Roosevelt was already on a train charging west, to the Badlands of North Dakota. He had brought with him to Chicago all of his baggage, literally and figuratively. As he looked out the window at the passing landscape, one could not help but realize that for all his activity, he too was vacant inside.

Within two days Roosevelt would be alone on the grim prairie of the frontier. He would finally have the solitude to reflect on his tragedy.

Alice Lee had been dead for just over one hundred days.

10. BADLANDS

———————————————————◇

THE SUMMER BEFORE ALICE DIED, THEODORE HAD TAKEN A buffalo hunting trip to Medora, North Dakota, and had spontaneously purchased an entire cattle ranch, tying up about ten percent of his inheritance. Medora, a hamlet on the Little Missouri River near the Montana border, had roughly a hundred citizens—ninety or so males and six females—and was earnestly striving to become a cattle town. The fertile rolling valleys and gentle hills provided seemingly endless grassy feed for as far as the eye could see. The railroad, running right through the town, provided west-to-east transportation for the beef. Numerous small homes were half-constructed, indicating that business was booming and more people were on the way. A newly erected slaughter house, with an immense brick chimney, beckoned to all that there was money to be made in the business.[1]

Theodore's desire to invest in a cattle ranch was a hedge against his non-money-making career as a politician. He claimed that he wanted a career outside of politics, should he get booted from office. One of his earliest convictions held that good government required leaders willing to risk their careers fighting for the cause of good government.

But now that his wife was dead, the ranch would serve an entirely different purpose. Less than three weeks after the double tragedy, Roosevelt knew he needed to go west to heal and wrote a letter to Bill Sewall to persuade the Maine hunting guide, and Sewall's nephew, Wilmot Dow, to move to the Badlands and help him raise cattle in North Dakota. He even made them an offer they could not refuse. "He said he would guarantee us a share of anything made in the cattle business,"

Sewall explained, "And if anything was lost, he would lose it and pay our wages."[2]

Hermann Hagedorn, a contemporary historian and friend of Theodore Roosevelt, wrote *Roosevelt in the Bad Lands* in 1921, just two years after the President had died. The book heightens Roosevelt's conquest of the frontier; a gladiator's triumphant story of renewing himself by dominating the western Badlands. But Hagedorn lived in an era of manly vigor, where toughness was promoted and weakness spurned. His account, influenced by the era in which he lived, would prove a substantial catalyst in promoting the spirited image of Theodore Roosevelt, the "Western Warrior." But after a lifetime of introspection, the historian that intimately knew Roosevelt would privately confide that the "real story of Theodore Roosevelt's ranching days has never been told."[3] Hagedorn's cryptic letter is a much more accurate account of Roosevelt's true state of mind.

> . . . when I wrote "Roosevelt in the Badlands," almost forty years ago, I was not in a position to tell all I knew, and in fact, I knew only part of the story. In the perspective of almost seventy-five years, the whole picture is now unfolding, and can be told.
>
> It is a story of a brilliant and successful young man who came out to the Badlands in the summer of 1884, outwardly alive and alert but inwardly shattered by the death in childbirth of the young wife he had devotedly loved. He had grown up in a society in which the romantic conceptions of Victorian literature were indisputable realities, and was convinced that, when his wife, Alice, died, happiness for him had forever died with her. Like the familiar heroes of fiction who had loved and lost, he fled to the wilderness, not so much to forget what he had lost but to live his life in its afterglow. His attitude of mind was sentimental, morbid, and unreal.[4]

The Theodore Roosevelt in the history books is the man that emerges from the Badlands in 1886. The Theodore Roosevelt in 1884 was severely morbid and melancholic. He looked gaunt, sickly and pale. "When he first came out," a ranch woman recalled, "he was sad and quiet."[5]

"You could have spanned his waist with your two thumbs and fingers," a cowboy remembered.[6]

On the 10th of June, Theodore arrived at the Medora train depot and, alone on his horse, Manitou, loped through the open sage en route to his new ranch, the Maltese Cross, some thirty miles from town. What was on his mind he did not document. He had with him a rifle, dry biscuits, a book, a metal cup, and salt.[7] Ahead of him lay the naked prairie, surrounded by jagged buttes of clay, coal and limestone deposits that had been cut by the waters of the great flood. The prairie breeze silently stirred the grass afoot, while rays of the morning sun danced off the red scoria buttes above. There was not a human for miles. The only sign of inhabitants was the faint imprint of a wagon trail that meandered alongside the bends of the river.

The land was desolate, and looked, Roosevelt wrote, just as Edgar Allen Poe sounded.[8]

After an hour of travel, Theodore was near the mouth of Davis Creek, when he spotted an abandoned log home. Colonel George Armstrong Custer had set up camp in that cabin just eight years prior. The year the wild colonel left the cantonment to continue his chase of the Lakota Tribe he was gunned down at Little Big Horn in Montana, just a few miles west. It had been Custer's Last Stand.[9]

In the wilderness that the Sioux Native Americans called "Land Bad," Roosevelt found his solitude.[10] When he discovered two magpies perched on an old buffalo skull that had been bleached white by the sun and snow, he was struck by both the permanence and impermanence of the object. Life and death.

At nights he would turn Manitou loose, build a fire to cook his kill, and lay down alone in the fathomless grassland. Awakened in the pre-dawn hour to the melodious chirp of the prairie dogs, he would cook his breakfast in the dark and then ride on deeper into the wild.

He had a despondent worldview. A meadowlark called out in "a cadence of wild sadness, inexpressibly touching," he recounted.[11] In the sounds of the birds he heard despair: "sad songs" of the hermit thrush, "boding call" of the whippoorwill, "the soft melancholy cooing of the mourning dove, whose voice always seems far away and expresses more than any other sound in nature the sadness of gentle, hopeless, never-ending grief."[12]

The vast and empty landscape moved him. "Nowhere, not even at sea, does a man feel more lonely than when riding over the far-reaching, seemingly never-ending plains; and after a man has lived a little while on or near them, their very vastness and loneliness and their melancholy monotony have a strong fascination for him," Theodore would write. "Nowhere else does one seem so far off from all mankind; the plains stretch out in death-like and measure-less expanse, and as he journeys over them they will for many miles be lacking in all signs of life."[13]

Everywhere he looked, internally and externally, Theodore found sadness.

On the prairie, thirty miles from any civilization, Theodore was unaware, and simply did not care, that the Republican Party was in a revolt. Independent Republicans, fed up with corrupt politics-as-usual, were leaving the party of Lincoln en masse. The faction, later known as the Mugwumps, were rich men from the Northeast whose desire for reform trumped party affiliation. The Mugwumps, men of wealth and consequence, rushed to support the Democrat nominee, Grover Cleveland. The list was impressive: Charles Francis Adams Jr., president of the Union Pacific Railroad; Henry Ward Beecher, iconic abolitionist; E. L. Godkin, editor of *The Nation*; Carl Schurz, senator from Missouri and editor of the *Evening Post* as well as a former general in the Union Army; Horace White, editor of the *Chicago Tribune*; and Mark Twain, author.[14]

As the Republican exodus captured headlines, Roosevelt became very important. He represented the opposite of the Old Guard and, to thicken the plot, one newspaper account had claimed that Theodore was leaving the party for good. This story, aided by the fact that Roosevelt was in the middle of nowhere and nobody could get a hold of him, provided for grand intrigue. The *Tribune* put the story on page one. Was the young reformer still a Republican? [15]

One wonders what Roosevelt would have decided to do at this critical moment in the history of the Republican Party had he not lost his wife and mother just a few months earlier. If he was not living his life, as Hagedorn put it, in "its afterglow," would he, chock-full of ambition, have become a Mugwump? Rather than living alone on the prairie for the better part of the next three years, would he have been hard at work in the New York state Assembly, plotting his next political move as the leader of a new third party?

Based on his track record in the Assembly and his efforts to elect Edmunds, Theodore could have very likely gone rogue and become a political warrior in a new party. Instead he chose to remain a Republican.

On July 19th, he gave a brief interview stating he had "time to think the whole matter over" and though he did his best in Chicago, he had "got beaten," and would "stand by the result."[16] Concluding that he was still a Republican, Roosevelt made it clear that he acted with the party in the past and would act with it in the future.[17]

His fellow reformers were beside themselves. Roosevelt was a traitor, they claimed. This was the reform movement's chance, this was their opportunity to change the Republican Party once and for all and now, not only was Theodore fleeing to the Badlands, he was still supporting the Old Guard.

What Roosevelt could see amidst the hysteria was that the party was still exceptionally valuable. The masses had chosen Blaine— the masses coveted Blaine. True leadership for the future required changing minds within the party, not the fiery actions of a right-eous reformer on the outside. The Republican Party was in flux, but it was, after all, still organized.

Roosevelt's favorite leader was Abraham Lincoln, and for the first time in his life, he set out to follow Lincoln's lead. Though the sixteenth president was adamant against slavery, he never aligned himself with abolitionists, the fringe of his movement. Lincoln instead focused on winning over the everyday person, the border-states, so to speak. Leadership, Lincoln knew, required changing the minds and motivations of the common American, not an empowerment of the fringe element. To Roosevelt the situation was similar: the common people were behind Blaine and had overwhelmingly endorsed him. Theodore believed that he needed to change their minds over time, not challenge their resolve today. He needed to win over the common American.

The new and exciting Mugwump faction of the party quickly morphed into a bunch of elite "holier-than-thou" Northeastern-ers who were out of touch with the working class. If Roosevelt aligned with them his political career would have probably been finished.

The "most impulsive man" that Isaac Hunt had known as an assemblymen had morphed into a man of longer term perspec-tive. The death of his wife and mother marked a distinct change in Theodore.

The Chicago convention and subsequent Mugwump uprising was Theodore's first contact with the power of the masses. Why had so many people, from every city in the country, fervently supported Blaine? Why had they not been influenced by the Mulligan Letters, the obvious corruption? This he could not answer. But he did pon-der the idea of majority rule.[18]

"It may be," he wrote to Bamie, "that 'the voice of the people is the voice of God' in fifty-one cases out of a hundred; but in the remaining forty-nine it is quite as likely to be the voice of the devil, or, what is still worse, the voice of a fool."[19] In Chicago, it was evident to Theodore that the voice of the people could be easily led astray. The true failure of the convention was that President Arthur had "absolutely no strength with the people."[20] Arthur did not know the people on the ground, nor did they know him. And it was Arthur's disconnect with the common man that allowed Blaine's magnetism to carry the convention. It was the leader's responsibility to know the people, to gain their trust, and then help them pursue moral ends.

The elemental lesson of it all was that strength with the people mattered most in leadership. The key was to know, and be known by, the common man.

For all of the corruption and self-inflicted political wounds, it would be alcohol that brought down James Blaine.

In the final week of the campaign, at a rally in a Fifth Avenue hotel, Blaine was introduced by Reverend Dr. Burchard of the Murray Hill Presbyterian Church in New York. As Burchard ended his introduction he vehemently roared: "We are Republicans, and don't propose to leave our party and identify ourselves with the party whose antecedents have been rum, Romanism, and rebellion! We are loyal to our flag!"[21] Blaine, preparing for his speech did not pay attention to Reverend Burchard's remarks and simply walked up to the lectern and gave a speech that nobody would remember.

Reverend Burchard's "rum, Romanism, and rebellion" introduction offered up political propaganda that remains unmatched in American political history. It was the exact wrong thing to say, at the exact wrong time, at the exact wrong place. Newspaper accounts made it seem that Blaine sat quietly as the minister attacked Catholics and Irish voters. The damage was swift and irreparable. Overnight, the Irish, the working man, and the beer drinkers, switched their votes to Grover Cleveland. On Election Day, New York decided the presidency by awarding Cleveland the state's thirty-six electoral votes from a razor thin margin: 1,149 out of 1,167,169 votes decided the election. If just

575 New Yorkers had switch their vote to Blaine, then he would have become president.[22] Nationwide, Cleveland won the popular voted by just .3 percent.[23]

The Republican Party had found a way to lose the White House for the first time since Abraham Lincoln saved the Union.

The scene around Theodore's ranch was striking, a picturesque backdrop that would allow a soul to brood. The ranch sat on a bluff overlooking the valley, some three hundred yards east of the Little Missouri River. Below the bluff, the river—its bank lined with lanes of cottonwoods—made a sweeping loop around Chimney Bluff. To the west was a series of jagged buttes, sheared at the top. Farther east and across the lane was a broad semicircular clearing covered with sage brush. In the distance, southwestward, a long flat line of foothills closed in the valley. The bottom lands, where the river ran through the scene, was a succession of green glades and grassy floors; the sunlight always seeming to dance through the canopy of cottonwoods. On the river bottom the tree leaves were never still, the green land bespoke fertile and lush, giving the impression of peace. In contrast, the bluffs on the horizon were stark and challenging, as if an impending doom waited.[24]

Bill Sewall recalled that his melancholic friend had many square breakdowns, and that on more than one occasion Theodore proclaimed that he absolutely "had nothing to live for."[25]

Sewall knew Roosevelt needed a challenge, if not a distraction from the tragedy. Theodore must do something; anything but wander the prairie alone wallowing in the sadness of the world. In short order, it was decided that Theodore, a ranch hand named Bill Merrifield, and a teamster named Norman Lebo would leave for the Big Horn Mountains, a massive range rising from the plains of North-Central Wyoming. The Big Horn Mountains were 235 miles away. The trio would be in the wild for two straight months. The quest was to kill a grizzly bear.

On August 18th, 1884, the party left the Maltese Cross ranch following the Keogh Trail. "We had no directions as to where the Big Horn Mountains were," the most experienced member of the group Bill Merrifield stated, "except that they lay to the southwest."[26]

Norman Lebo—short and stocky with a thick beard—drove the prairie schooner of supplies and did the cooking. Merrifield, the rancher, navigated. Roosevelt, the easterner, shot at everything that moved. And he was a terrible shot.

"The trouble with his eyesight was peculiar . . . he was unlike other men," a hunting guide remembered, "He could not recognize his best friend at a distance of ten feet without them [his glasses]."[27]

Once asked if he was a good shot, Roosevelt snapped, "No, but I shoot often."[28] He had the data to prove his inability. In his field notebook, Theodore kept scrupulous accounts of the number of cartridges used per kill. The results were underwhelming: three bullets for every bison, moose, elk, and mountain goat; a whopping fifty cartridges for every wolf and coyote; four cartridges for every deer and nine shots per pronghorn.[29]

The idea of one shot, one kill did not apply to Roosevelt. Undeterred by his inability, he set out to kill the most dangerous beast on the continent, the kingly grizzly bear. He had nearly 1,500 rounds of ammo in his pack.[30]

On September 1st, after several weather changes of rain, sleet, and a blistering heat wave, the men neared the foothills of the Big Horns. Near Crazy Woman Creek in Buffalo, Wyoming, Merrifield saw a camp a mile or so ahead in a far off thicket. He hitched up his horse to check them out.

"Where are you going?" Roosevelt asked

"Going to see who these people are," came Merrifield's response.

"Does it make any difference to us?"[31] Theodore asked.

It certainly does, Merrifield explained to the Easterner. In the city, you could pass by anyone and not look them in the eye. In the West it was different. You rode a mile out of the way just to look a passerby in the eye. An individual who did not adhere to this Western custom was suspect, a shady character, perhaps a horse thief. Only rogue thieves and lawless men went into hiding.[32]

Of the danger, Roosevelt shrugged. "Well, then can I go?"

The camp proved to be that of a ranchman named Frewen who had told Merrifield and Roosevelt that the area was teeming with large bears and that "several hunters had been badly injured and some of them killed by the grizzlies."[33]

The ranchman directed Roosevelt and Merrifield to a nearby Army Post that was manned by a giant Swede who, as an agent for the government, had lived the past seventeen years alone in the wilderness. Upon discovering Roosevelt's desire to shoot a grizzly, the grizzled old Swede shot his head back and pointed a crooked finger to the mountain, terrified. "I'm telling you that those bears are fierce," the Swede said tersely, "and you have to watch out for them and be a good shot or else you'd get into trouble for sure."[34]

The warning to be a "good shot or else" was lost on Roosevelt. The forlorn man tramped up the mountain at the fork of Crazy Woman Creek, right into bear country. The Swede must have wondered if the man with the funny eastern accent and thick eye glasses was suicidal.

By day, the men hunted for grizzly, and by night Theodore divulged his inner thoughts to Bill Merrifield.

"He said the doctors told him that he could not possibly live more than four years," Merrifield recounted in an interview several years later, "when we were together he said he talked things with me that he never talked with anyone else."[35] The four years remark is the only timetable ever spoken by Theodore—was this from Dr. Sargent at Harvard? If it was from Dr. Sargent, then Theodore was already living on borrowed time.

Over the crackling of the fire, alone in the vast wild, Theodore then admitted to his traveling companions that if he could just survive to adulthood, he thought he would make a great president someday.

Once atop the Big Horn Mountains, Merrifield and Roosevelt were at an altitude of nine thousand feet. The valley below them was expansive; the skyline seemed to slip the surly bonds of the horizon. Near Ten Sleep Creek, they had killed an elk, and returned to the carcass to find the fresh tracks of a massive bear. Though the sun had set, Roosevelt, the blind man and bad shot, talked Merrifield into stalking the animal into the thick timber. When darkness finally enveloped them, they set up camp, convinced that the grizzly was still in the area.

"[That night] we heard the bears growl," Merrifield explained. He said ". . . I'm telling you it made weird noises . . ." before adding that his hunting partner "enjoyed it."[36]

Theodore had, no doubt, read the stories of one bear killing two men. It was nothing, he knew, for the monster to run several hundred yards, with several bullets in him, and kill the man holding a rifle.

Shortly before dawn the men started on the grizzly trail again.

"Where the timber is ridgepole pine," reads an account of Ten Sleep Creek, "whose branches do not begin for thirty or forty feet above the ground, it is possible to see for considerable distances in the dim, cathedral light, and the imagination invests a charred stump or fallen log with weird possibilities. Walking alone over the silent carpet of pine needles, the effect is spectral enough in the day time."[37] At dawn, the cathedral lighting of the canopy created disquieting images; the shadows played tricks on the eye. Undeterred, Merrifield and Roosevelt stealthily followed the massive bear tracks into the lodge pole pine.

"When in the middle of the thicket," Roosevelt recounted, "we crossed what was almost a breastwork of fallen logs, and Merrifield, who was leading [on account of his eyesight], passed by the upright stem of a great pine. As soon as he was by it, he sank suddenly on one knee, turning half around, his face fairly aflame with excitement."[38]

Roosevelt charged past Merrifield, rifle at the ready. "Not ten steps off, was the great bear, slowly rising from his bed among the young spruces."[39]

The twelve hundred pound, nine foot tall beast reared on his haunches, and then fell on all fours—the action to charge. The ten steps would have been covered in less than one and a half seconds.

"The shaggy hair on his neck and shoulders seeming to bristle as he turned towards us," Roosevelt wrote later. "As he sank down to his forefeet, I had raised the rifle; his head was slightly down, and when I saw the top of the white bead fairly between his small, glittering, evil eyes, I pulled the trigger."[40]

The bear fell dead.

The visionless man, the horrible shot, had charged a grizzly and conquered it.

"There were all kinds of things of which I was afraid at first," Theodore wrote about his time in the Badlands, "ranging from grizzly bears to 'mean' horses and gun-fighters; but by acting as if I was not afraid I gradually ceased to be afraid. Most men can have the same experience if they choose . . . after a while the habit will grow on them."[41]

For all of his impressive accomplishments and interpersonal growth, Theodore had still not shown the ability to lead. Certainly he was no leader as a child or at Harvard. He had been elected to the speaker position but abruptly lost his leadership post the following year. He had been selected a New York delegate but his man Edmunds had finished third at the Republican convention in Chicago. He had shown tremendous promise as an individual, but not as a leader. He had yet to show whether he could capture the strength of the people, even those closest to him.

By the spring of 1885, this started to change for Roosevelt. Theodore had spent the majority of his time in the Badlands on his own ranch—with Merrifield, Dow, and Sewall—or alone on the prairie. He hardly went into the town of Medora, save to send mail or get the news at the *Badlands Cowboy*. He did not drink or smoke and had not mingled with the townsfolk. The time he had spent in the Badlands was personal and lonely.

And because they did not know him, the residents of Medora felt that Theodore did not belong in their world. "My first impression was not exactly favorable," a cowpoke stated several years later. "He was dressed in a fringed buckskin suit and wore glasses. A fringed buckskin suit, in that country at that time, was undisputable evidence of the rank of a tenderfoot and backed up by the glasses made it a dead certainty; he was slim, [a] rather anemic looking young fellow then."[42]

Out of ear shot, he was universally known as "Four Eyes" or "Teddy Roosenfelder". He looked funny, more like a Fifth Avenue cowboy poser than the real thing: he wore a hand-crafted and fringed buckskin shirt, expensive alligator boots, bowie knife from Tiffany's, and a custom Colt revolver plated with silver and gold.[43]

He also sounded funny. When a few head of cattle had broken out of alignment, Roosevelt shouted to a couple of cowboys, "Hasten forward quickly there!" in an effort to get them to cut off the lead cow. The cowboys almost fell off their horses in fits of laughter. The easterner's phrase became legendary overnight, and cowpokes began ordering their glass of beer and sidecar of whiskey while barking at the barkeep to "hasten forward quickly there!"[44]

Theodore was an outsider and was branded as such. But in the spring of 1885, he emerged from his cocoon of sadness and inquisitively took steps to fit in to his surroundings. On the frontier, the annual spring round-up was where you could prove your worth in salt. Lasting for roughly forty-five days straight, cowboys and ranchmen from a two-hundred-mile radius would converge on the valley of Little Missouri to collect and brand the free-range cattle. Each rancher sent five or six men, who were put under the supervision of "The Boss"—the foreman's foreman. The length of the drive was over a thousand miles long and chuck wagons— drawn by four horses and driven by a teamster, who was also the cook—were stationed along the countryside dispersing basic supplies, clothing and bedding, as well as cornmeal, bacon, tack, lard, sugar, coffee, and biscuits.[45] All of the cowboys in the county would work together, regardless of which ranch they belonged. The roundup was crude and violent. No poser could survive it.

"We were given a certain ravine or a certain territory and sometimes it would take two or three days to get all the cattle rounded up in this territory," Merrifield recounts. "Certain riders would be sent up certain ravines, others up on the plateaus and so on. Not all the men in our outfit necessarily were *of* our outfit. All the different ranchers met at a certain place, and so many wranglers, riders, cooks, mess wagons, etc. were sent out in separate groups, each having a certain, specific territory to cover."[46]

The day would start at three in the morning, and the aggressive cowboys—almost all of whom had never met Theodore— wanted nothing to do with the inexperienced Easterner. He was too much of a liability. Theodore knew this and realizing that he could not rope well on account of his eyes, and that he was only an average rider, he decided that what he lacked in talent, he could trump with determination.

He never shirked his duty, cowboy Frank Roberts recalled— "He was always there ready to do everything he possibly could. He wanted to do it. Tried to do it."[47]

"Roosevelt used to take his trick at anything he could do," another Westerner stated, "He would grab a calf or cow and help drag them right into the fire to be branded. He could wrassel [sic] a calf as good as anybody. He used to be all over dirt from head to foot. I'm telling you wrasseling calves is no easy job. He took his trick at everything. . . ."[48] Cowboy Jack Reuter was impressed. "He struck me like a sort of rough and ready, all-around frontiersman. Wasn't a bit stuck up—just same as one of the rest of us."[49] Cowboy W. T. Dantz, quickly recognized Theodore's "grit" and "bull-dogged energy."[50]

Theodore owned the ranch. He did not even have to go on the round-up or, at a minimum, he could have picked the easy jobs. If he just wanted to act like a Westerner, he had already done that by simply moving to the Badlands. But Theodore wanted to genuinely become a frontiersman.

"Everybody worked," Theodore wrote, "everybody was willing to help everybody else, and yet nobody asked for any favors."[51]

"Riding circle twice a day," cowboy Lincoln Lang wrote, ". . . he [Theodore] was in the saddle all of eighteen hours per day, throughout the trip, like the rest of us, frequently riding well over a hundred miles within the twenty four hours."[52]

"We are working pretty hard," Theodore wrote in a letter to Lodge. "Yesterday I was in the saddle at 2 a.m., and except for two very hearty meals, after each of which I took a fresh horse, did not stop working till 8.15 p.m.; and was up at half-past three this morning."[53] Adding that the "eight hour law does not apply to cowboys."[54]

On June 2nd, the roundup was camped near Garner Creek when a terrific storm rumbled in. Roosevelt was on night duty when a strike of lightning broke near the heard. Before the world became dark again, the cattle thundered into a stampede.[55]

"We called to Roosevelt to come back toward the wagon. We yelled for him to come back," a cowpuncher remembered. "He yelled back that he was not afraid of a little rain; that it wasn't going to hurt him."[56]

Riding hard into the night Theodore tried in vain to cut off the lead steer. "I could make out nothing except the dark forms of the beasts running on every side of me," he later wrote.[57]

Several hours later, on his way back to camp in the grey of dawn, he passed a cowboy on foot. In the stampede the cowboy's horse, blinded by the darkness of the night, had run full speed into a tree and killed itself. The rider, rather miraculously, was unhurt.[58]

Back at camp just to change horses, Theodore and a team of ranchmen again went out in search of the night herd that had vanished. It was a full ten hours later—as night settled once again—before Theodore finally had his chance at a bed. By this time, he had been in the saddle forty hours. The rest was short-lived; he was back up at four in the morning to man the herd.[59] He had been in the same clothes for over a week.

On all occasions Roosevelt fraternized with the cowboys; he rode, ate, laughed, and slept next to them. At night he listened as they told stories next to the campfire, he joined in on the chorus of the quaint cowboy songs, sung soft and low: "Roll on, roll on; roll on little dogies, roll on, roll on. . ."

And again, by the campfire, he was tested.

"Everything was all right for spending the night around the campfire, smoking and talking, and one young fellow he thought he'd pick on Mr. Roosevelt," Frank Roberts, a witness to the event, recalled.[60]

The young fellow was a Texan named Jack Tisdale and the comment had something to do with Theodore's "four eyes" or "storm windows."

When Theodore had enough he barked, "You're talkin' like a fool. Shut up. Put up. Be friends, or fight."

Tisdale stammered, not expecting the Easterner to confront him, ". . . make it friends."

Roosevelt extended his hand, "Shake and forget it."

"Nobody said anything," Roberts remembered, "but we was all thinking the same thing, I guess. We wanted to get up and shake his hand, too. We were proud of him."[61]

Roosevelt did make friends and hired Jack Tisdale the following year to help him at the Maltese Ranch. The employment was short lived. One afternoon Roosevelt witnessed Tisdale putting a brand on a cow which obviously did not belong to the Maltese.

"What are you doing there?" Theodore questioned.

Tisdale said with a grin, "Never you mind what I'm doing. I know my business. I always put on the boss's brand."

Roosevelt snapped, ordering Tisdale to see the foreman, get paid for his time and leave the ranch immediately.

Tisdale was beside himself. You're firing me for making you money, he no doubt asked.

"If you will steal for me," came the reply, "you will steal from me."[62]

Roosevelt won respect through his enthusiasm and authenticity. But he was also deliberate in his actions. For the first time in his life, he began to sense what others wished to see from a leader, and then acted on it.

When a cowboy from another outfit was struck by lightning and killed, Roosevelt listened as other cowboys worried that the dead man, a drifter, would not have a proper burial.

"We were camped about three miles from Sentinel Butte when one of the boys brought word of the accident and told of the removal of the body to Medora," George Myers recounted. "Roosevelt knew that the unfortunate man had no relatives in the state to arrange for his burial, and he immediately expressed his determination . . . that a fitting disposition of the body was made."

"We will flag the next train and go to Medora," Roosevelt said, referring to the Northern Pacific train number two, due to pass by in a few minutes.

"They won't stop here for nothing," said one of the boys.

"By Godrey, they'll have to stop," retorted Roosevelt, and he immediately ordered the men to go down the track to flag the train.

Meyers continues, "When the engineer saw the warning signal he slowed up the train, but did not stop. Some of the boys on horses then rode alongside the train, firing shots into the air until the train came to a standstill. Train crew and passengers alike thought they were in for a hold-up, and a wild scramble followed. . . . Roosevelt, Sylvane Ferris, Bill Merrifield, John Goodall, Ed Turner, and I boarded the train. When the conductor saw that we were on a peaceful mission, he flew into a rage and threatened to put us all off."

"By Godfrey, you be good or you'll be the one to get off," snapped Roosevelt.

Roosevelt and crew got off at the Medora depot, escorted by "some very bad language from the train crew." The train engineer threatened that Roosevelt and company would get arrested. But when asked if they heard from the engineer again, Meyers confirmed that "we never did."[63]

The charred cowboy, George Frazier, was buried the next day, with Theodore and his men seeing to it that all accommodations were accounted. By the time that he returned to the round-up, word had already passed through the area of Theodore's bold actions to stop a train and take care of the funeral of a cowboy that was not even in his outfit.

Certainly Mittie Roosevelt's son loved the flair for theatrics. But upon closer examination of Theodore's theatrics, it is clear that he carefully chose his dramatic acts to maximize his influence on others. That is to say, his dramatic acts were not impulsive, but rather calculated.

Another theatrical instance took place shortly after citizens and ranchmen began to express the need for a Stockmen's Association in Medora—a central group who could decide and enforce range rules for the cattle in the area, as lawlessness and theft were proving too rampant for sustainability. Leveraging his experience in Albany, Theodore helped draft and implement the organization's first charter, and, on account of his abilities in law and writing, he was selected chairman of the organization. The post came with no real formal authority so Theodore set out to increase his stature. To win the hearts and minds of his peers, he decided to take down a man who was wildly corrupt.

Fred Willard was the stock inspector at Medora, the last man to inspect brands and certify the shipments before they were sent off to the packing plants. He was thoroughly hated, a scoundrel who miscounted cattle to make money for himself. "Everybody knew he was crooked," a cowboy claimed, but nobody had done anything about it because Willard was tremendously powerful in his small neck of the woods.[64]

At a Stockmen's Meeting the cowboys had finally lined up to rebuke Willard and take him on publicly. Theodore knew this and seized the moment. He lept to his feet, skinned his teeth, and spoke first; thereby looking fearless as well as becoming the spokesman for the entire group. "He openly accused the sheriff of incompetence and dishonesty," a newspaper account relived the story, "and with the reflected light of the officer's pearl-handled revolver at his belt flashing across his glasses, the speaker scored him as a man unworthy and unfit for his trust."[65]

The printed account made it seem as if Theodore was a man of steel. "It is one thing to deliver a fiery accusation of general or personal charges before a crowded meeting of law-abiding citizens. It is another to stand coolly before a silent handful of frontiersmen and openly accuse one of dishonesty. Death stares a man closely in the face who attempts it, for these men, bred in isolation, are sensitive to the quick of their personal honor, and an accusation that would be laughed at in a convention hall would eat out [a] man's heart here."[66]

The local newspaper did not get the story right. The truth of the matter was that Theodore knew that the other cowboys in the room were not only thinking the same thing, but had his back. He had listened to their frustrations and knew what the men needed to hear. He simply led the charge. Years later, in private, Theodore was asked about his heroic deed. "I was right, and he knew it," he claimed. Everyone else knew Roosevelt was right, also. By speaking forcefully about what others were also thinking, his authority grew.[67]

But there is no better example that Theodore understood what the men needed to see than his actions with his string of horses.

On the frontier, everything of value was done on a horse: getting to town for whiskey, hunting for food, branding for money, fleeing trouble to save one's life. In a given day on the round-up, a single man could ride seven different horses and, in the ever competitive world of the cowboy, how one managed a horse was proof of his worth. Riding bad horses—those prone to bucking the rider—was both a dramatic hindrance and a rite of passage.

"I am not going to ride any one of those horses," Sewall told a cowboy one day, the Maine outdoorsmen unaware of the unwritten law in the West.

"You will have to," the cowboy responded.

"I don't know so much about that."

"If you don't," remarked the cowboy, "you will have the contempt of everybody."

"That won't affect me very much," Sewall answered as a fact.

"Oh well," said the cowboy, knowing the law of the land, "*you will have to ride them.*"[68]

In time the cowboy proved right. Sewall, in order to authenticate himself, indeed "agreed to ride them."[69]

Theodore listened to this exchange, and many more like it.

At the beginning of the round-up, ranch hands would draw straws to select horses, ensuring that all would share in the misery of a bad horse. As the owner of his own ranch, it was customary for Theodore to pick out his horses—the tame ones—before the draw. He chose not to and it made a world of difference.

A cowhand was asked to define the character of Theodore Roosevelt. He told this story: ". . . Roosevelt gave us all an exhibition of the stuff he was made of in riding a bad horse. He didn't have to have any of that kind in his string if he didn't want to, his position as the boss of his own outfit giving him the choice. But in his characteristically square-deal fashion he had pulled straws with his own men, as customary in the selection of strings, cheerfully accepting whatever the fates handed him in consequence drawing one or two ugly ones."[70]

A nasty draw for Roosevelt was a horse named Ben Butler, the name bestowed upon the animal because its large Roman nose bore an uncanny resemblance to General Benjamin Butler, a Democrat from Massachusetts.

"He [Ben Butler] viciously fought bit and saddle and was at times violent and dangerous," cowpoke W. T. Dantz remembered. "Both ranch managers, and even the cowboys, begged permission to take the horse out and shoot him as an outlaw."[71]

Roosevelt not only refused to have the horse killed, but drew the horse for his own string.

"That hoss will shore kill you, boss" came a plea. "Sooner or later they all kill."[72]

Theodore, inexperienced, probably did not appreciate that Big Ben could actually kill him. He just wanted to prove his grit with an egalitarian gesture.

While Theodore was riding Butler on the outside of the circle near a washout, the horse shot its head to the air and snorted. Roosevelt swerved heavily in the saddle before Ben Butler went wild. The horse was bucking fervently when, without warning, Butler "sunfished"—twisting its body in the shape of a crescent—before falling over backward on its rider.[73]

The fall was horrendous. The weight of the horse broke a bone in Theodore's shoulder, knocking the wind clean out of him. Pale, weak, and dazed, Theodore just got up, remounted a different horse, and carried on. He had no choice. The nearest doctor was well over fifty miles away.[74]

"The effort both to ride them [bad horses] and to look as if I enjoyed doing so," Theodore wrote, ". . . doubtless was of benefit to me, but lacked much of being enjoyable."[75] He drew straws and rode bad horses to win the favor of his men. He did this not because he enjoyed it, but because he knew what the men of the frontier wanted to see from a leader.

"By gollies, he rode some bad horses," Dutch Wannigan exclaimed in an interview twenty years after Theodore had left the Badlands. "Some of those Eastern punkin-lilies now, those goody-goody fellows, if they'd ever get throwed off you'd never hear the last of it. He didn't care a bit. By gollies, if he got throwed off, he'd get right on again. He was a dandy fellow."[76]

On the frontier, Theodore proved that he had an overabundance of toughness, and there is a strong urge to depict him simply as a man of vigor, rebuilding his body, conquering himself and the frontier. But this line of thinking is flawed, and frankly, not holistic. Yes, he did shoot a grizzly at ten steps, he did threaten a known assassin, he did punch a guy out at a crude hotel, and he rode for several days on horseback with broken ribs. But lost in the bravado is the fact that Theodore was also tremendously introspective and reflective on the frontier, and it built his character. Silenced from history have been the stories of his tenderness.

In an old log house just outside of Medora, lived Mrs. Roberts, a leather-faced woman whose husband, Floyd, had flown the coop, later to be murdered outside of Cheyenne, Wyoming. Mrs. Roberts, one of six women in the entire county and described as tough as a "meat axe," was all alone with five children to feed. Whenever he could, Theodore checked in on Mrs. Roberts by riding to her house just to say hello, sending a ranch hand over with a quarter of beef, or helping her fix her leaky roof. She came to expect Theodore's visits and each time would whip up a batch of buttermilk, which Theodore hated.

"I don't like your buttermilk," Theodore got the courage to say one day, "But I like you, Mrs. Roberts. May we just talk?" Widower to widower, the dialogue was undoubtedly affectionate.

"[He] would stop in to chat," Mrs. Roberts would state several years later. "Mr. Roosevelt was a wonderful man, and a wonderful friend."[77]

"Many seem to have assumed that he admired men of iron; liked the cactus," wrote a close friend, Lincoln Lang. ". . . [A]s a matter of fact, nothing could be wider of the truth."[78]

On a ride one afternoon Lang and Theodore heard "a loud squeaking of an animal in distress" from a nearby sagebrush.[79]

The duo came upon a half-grown jack rabbit entrapped in the coils of a large snake. Theodore leapt from his horse and shot the snake with his six-shooter. He then picked up the rabbit, and "carefully he set it in the crook of his arm and felt it over gently for broken bones," Lang recalled. "Satisfied at length that it was all right and able to take care of itself, he released it beamingly while expressing joy over the happy outcome."[80]

"There goes a sore but wiser rabbit," Theodore said affectionately as the rabbit bound away.[81]

Later that spring, Roosevelt was riding day herd when he came across a cow with a new born calf which had been born very late in the season. The weak calf could not keep up with the herd.

"The boys wanted Roosevelt to leave the calf behind," a cowboy named Lehmicke recalled, "and to drive the mother on."

Roosevelt refused, saying that it was not the right thing to do.

Lehmicke picks up the story, "Usually in such cases, the mother cow is driven along with the day herd, and the abandoned calf soon dies of hunger and exposure . . . . He [Theodore] had been watching the feeble efforts of the calf to keep along with the mother, and he was touched by the little fellow's plucky struggle to follow. He rode over to Bentley [another cowboy] and in a good-natured way asked him to exchange positions. Bentley galloped off to another part of the field, glad to get rid of the troublesome calf."

"Teddy rode along slowly to accommodate the pace of the calf, but after half an hour's struggle the little fellow had to give up. With a bleat he fell from exhaustion. Teddy got off his horse, picked the calf up in his arms, put it on the saddle in front of him, and rode along for a couple of miles. The mother cow trotted along at the horse's side."[82] The parallel to Theodore's childhood goes without explaining.

Theodore's contemplative actions on the frontier built his character. Bill Sewall—who first met Roosevelt when he was an aristocratic Harvard chap and had paid close attention to Theodore's bombastic actions in Albany—was his closest friend in the Badlands. Years later, Sewall was asked to describe the lessons that Theodore had learned in the West. "I always think of that verse from the Bible," Sewall responded matter-of-factly, "He that ruleth his spirit is greater than he that taketh the city."[83]

Sewall, a man of God who studied the Word, was referring to Proverbs 16:32.

Every leader wants to be a mighty man of valor, the scripture indicates, but the greater measure of individual glory is the ability to rules one's spirit. The men that were easy to idolize included Gideon, who defeated a huge army of Midianites; Samson, who killed a thousand Philistines with the jawbone of a donkey; and David, who took down Goliath with a slingshot. But the true warrior, the Proverb urges, is the wise and calm soul. The ambitious man who wants to take the city is ruled by his spirit; the true warrior could temper his impulses, the true warrior had an introspective dialogue.

What Sewall witnessed firsthand was the beginning of Theodore's change from a brutishly driven man, to a driven man who took time to reflect on the tenderness in the world around him. A man more thoughtful, more pensive, more contemplative. A man who learned how to rule his spirit.

March 30th, 1886, marked a convergence of two of Theodore's most prominent strengths: his historical perspective and his sense of adventure. On this day he put down his pen, having finished the first chapter of his third book, a biography on Thomas Hart Benton, and went out into a furious blizzard in pursuit of thieves. He was both an author writing a literary history as well as a vigilante of justice. Mayne Reid could not have set the scene any better.

Three days earlier, Bill Sewall had gone down to the river to discover that their boat had been stolen. Immediately, Sewall suspected Mike Finnigan and two other seedy characters that lived in a cabin twenty miles upstream. Everyone knew that Finnigan needed to bolt from the area because some cattlemen wanted him dead. A boat would provide his means of escape.[84]

Sewall told Roosevelt of the theft and reminded him that the river was walled off on both sides with ice; a horse chase would be of little use. The only way to pursue the thieves was to build a new boat and float down the river after them.

But do we really want to chase the thieves in a harsh winter blizzard just to retrieve a boat valued at thirty dollars, Sewall no doubt asked.[85] The millionaire Roosevelt could afford to replace the water craft. Why would he risk his life, either due to the weather or at the wrong end of a thief's gun, over a thirty dollar boat?

It was not the value of the boat that impelled Theodore into action. He had recently been appointed to the role of deputy sheriff of Billings County, and the role of a lawman pursuing thieves was one Theodore was not passing up. Besides a great adventure, it would make one hell of a story. *Century Magazine* would love it, he knew.

While Sewall and Dow built the boat for three days, Theodore poured over his research of Thomas Hart Benton, a senator from Missouri who died in 1858 at the age of seventy-six. Benton, a champion of Manifest Destiny, was one of the country's first and staunchest advocates of westward expansion, exactly the type of man that Theodore desired to portray himself as: an adventurous Westerner who was also a public leader full of conviction.

While taking a break from his work on *Benton*, a friend overheard Theodore pacing the ranch home, practicing his lines for his upcoming adventure down river: "I've got the gun on you!" Theodore shouted, probably throwing his thumb up with his pointer finger straight out like a gun. "I know you stole my boat and I'm here to claim it!"[86]

On March 30th,the boat was finally ready and Dow, Roosevelt, and Sewall pushed out into the icy water—Dow in the front, Theodore in the middle, Sewall manning the rear. They had with them two weeks' worth of flour, coffee, biscuits, and bacon. Theodore also took with him Leo Tolstoy's *Anna Karenina,* and, of course, his camera.[87]

For two days the pursuers did not see one sign of human life. The world around them was frigid and deathlike. A bitter glacial wind drove up the valley at every turn, right into their faces. "The crookedest wind in Dakota,"[88] Sewall moaned under his breath. Ice began to form on the side of the boat, at night the temperature dropped well below zero.[89]

A shootout was a concern. "[The] extraordinary formation of the Bad Lands, with the ground cut up into cullies, serried walls, and battlemented hilltops," Roosevelt wrote, "makes it the country of all others for hiding-places and ambuscades."[90]

Early on the afternoon of April 1st, the amateur deputy sheriff and his moral vigilantes rounded a bend in the river to find their stolen boat moored on the bank. They frantically paddled to the edge of the river, afraid of imminent gunfire. From the safety of the bank, the men spotted the smoke of a camp fire and charged towards it through a grove of young cottonwoods.[91] At the campfire sat a solitary figure.

"Hands up!" Theodore said tersely, seeming to forget the lines he had practiced.

Caught unaware was a "half-witted German named Wharfenberger," who was quickly stripped of his rifle and knife.[92]

Wharfenberger, staring down the barrel, divulged that there were two other men with him who were out hunting for food. Theodore commanded him to continue to sit by the campfire, as if nothing had happened. As the pursuers took cover in the brush, Theodore made it clear that if Wharfenberger made any movement, he would be shot dead.[93]

About an hour before sunset, Mike Finnegan and his companion, both carrying rifles, romped straight through the open sagebrush towards the riverbank. Theodore and Sewall waited until the men were just twenty yards out before jumping up and covering the thieves with cocked rifles. Both men did as they were told, dropping their arms to the ground.[94]

Now what? Roosevelt, Sewall and Dow had captured the thieves, but the nearest town downriver was Mandan, 150 miles away.[95] The thieves' hands and feet could not be tied up because they would freeze off in the biting cold. There was not enough food for six people to survive for more than a few days. It was instantly clear that Roosevelt and company had not thought the entire operation all the way through. Adventure had trumped reason.

For the next six days, the men floated down the river, making little headway as floes of ice jammed the waterway. It was sheer drudgery, a test of endurance. At night, the prisoner's boots were removed, and Roosevelt was the watchdog. "I kept guard over the three prisoners, who were huddled into a sullen group some twenty yards off, just the right distance for the buckshot in the double-barrel," he stated.[96]

One afternoon while Theodore stood guard, a picture was taken for verification, later to be published in *Century Magazine* under the title "Sherriff's Work on a Ranch."[97]

After a miserable eight days the food rations ran dry, and the biting wind and ice had made traveling farther downriver with six men impossible.

Roosevelt went on a mission by land to find human life, and luckily for thieves and lawmen alike, stumbled upon a cow camp. Borrowing a bronco from the foreman, he rode another fifteen miles to the C Diamond Ranch at the foothills of the Killdeer Mountains, where he bartered the use of a wagon and a teamster.[98]

Back at the river it was then decided that Sewall and Dow would continue downstream with the two boats, and Theodore, using the borrowed wagon, would take charge of the prisoners and ride them forty-five miles due south to the county jail at Dickinson, North Dakota.

Alone with the three thieves and a teamster he had not met, Roosevelt walked behind the wagon, at a distance of twenty yards, in ankle deep mud. After thirty-six hours without sleep, the men drifted onto the main street in Dickinson, where Theodore turned the thieves over to the authorities.[99] The locals were baffled—why had he not just shot the thieves or hung them by the end of a rope? The thought, Theodore answered, had never crossed his mind.[100]

Theodore had done it for the thrills. He had been gone for two weeks, floated the icy river for over two hundred miles, rode on horseback for twenty miles, and walked forty-five miles on foot. He read *Anna Karenina*, caught three thieves and had his thirty dollar boat returned.

Dr. Victor Hugo Stickney of Dickinson remembered vividly Theodore limping into his practice covered in mud, blisters all over his feet. "I took him into my office and while I was bathing and bandaging his feet, which were in pretty bad shape, he told me the story of the capture of the three thieves. . . . He was frankly thrilled by the adventures he had been through. It did not seem to occur to him that he had done anything particularly commendable, but he was, in his own phrase, 'pleased as Punch' at the idea of having participated in a real adventure. He was just like a boy."[101]

For all of Theodore's personal authenticity there is also a show-manship quality that is unsettling. He wrote dozens of articles of his feats in the West to be published in Eastern magazines. The fact that he brought a camera to take a picture of himself captur-ing thieves seems a bit premeditated. Also, just nine weeks after he got to the Badlands he began to write a ninety-five-thousand-word account of the terrain, wildlife, and peoples of the great frontier, later to be titled *Hunting Trips of a Ranchman*. But by the time Theodore had finished the book, he had spent less than half a year in the Badlands. Many wondered, then and now, whether Theodore was using his experiences in the West to gain public-ity. As if his time in the Dakotas was one large effort to build the Roosevelt brand.

Especially unsettling is the image of Theodore taken in a New York studio for the frontispiece of *Hunting Trips*. Adorn-ing his Dakota buckskin costume complete with moccasins and silver dagger in his belt, he stands on artificial grass in front of a painted backdrop of ferns and flowers. His hands clutch his Winchester and his finger is near the trigger as he stares off into the distance, looking for a grizzly or a buffalo.[102] The picture is comical, a disingenuous image to the lessons he was learning on the frontier. Standing on the imitation grass, it seems that he was disrespecting all that he had done in the West to fit in, to be a regular.

Theodore knew that the mythic figure of a cowboy was the ideal in the East, an emerging marvel. Horace Greeley's call to "Go West, young man, and grow up with the country" embodied a sense of adventure and toughness that was universally revered. Western dime novels had recently begun entertaining children with lurid stories of savage natives and gunplay. However, the Western ideal of Owen Wister's writings, Buffalo Bill and Annie Oakley's Wild West shows, and Frederic Remington's paintings, were all still a thing of the future, as were John Wayne, the Lone Ranger, and Ronald Reagan, for that matter.[103] Theodore Roosevelt's generation was the first to romanticize the West. "To be off to one's ranch in the Wild West," a commentary writes of that era, "or the ranch one had taken a 'flier' in, or better still, to be just back from one's ranch, full of stories, looking brown and fit, was all the rage. . . It was adventurous. It was Romantic."[104]

No doubt Roosevelt cherished his public image as a character straight out of a Mayne Reid novel. He told and retold the account of the grizzly hunt to any journalist that would listen, he was repeatedly photographed in eccentric Western garb, his trophy animals were displayed prominently, he wrote publicly about his love for guns and he penned a commentary in the *New York Tribune* that he had "eaten, slept, hunted, and herded cattle" with the cowboy and "never had any difficulty."[105]

Was he trying to create his own brand? Certainly. Did he embellish his own feats? Undoubtedly. Was he genuine in everything he did? Absolutely. He was simultaneously building his public brand and rebuilding his body and mind.

By his late twenties, it was obvious that Theodore was collecting defining roles for himself. He coveted being a man of letters and books, a historical author, a political reformer, a fighter for the poor, a survivor of childhood sickness, a hunter of dangerous game, a cattleman, a man of means and wealth, and a Badlands cowboy. All his roles were customized to his philosophy of a strenuous life and a strict moral code of leadership. Tellingly, his roles purposefully encompassed the diverse spectrum of American life: rich and poor, city and country, East and West, common man and academic, government reformer and objective politician. At any moment, he could genuinely play the part—the role—required for leadership.

In a curious footnote to history, several American citizens were arrested in Mexico in the summer of 1886, apparently illegally. Almost overnight, relations between the countries strained and anti-Mexican sentiment erupted along the border. President Cleveland intervened, demanding the release of the prisoners and, for at least a brief period, it looked as if a war could break out. But as quickly as the matter flared up, it died down. In a matter of days, the relations between the two countries were restored, and normalcy returned. But a story in the *Bismarck Tribune* indicated that one man in the Badlands was ready to lead the fight.

Bismarck Tribune
August 21st, 1886

Hon. Theodore Roosevelt of New York, the famous statesman, ranchman and hunter, came to the city from Mandan yesterday morning, and proceeded immediately to the capitol. He has been making inquiries since the announcement of the Mexican difficulties as to the available volunteer troops in the Northwest, and in the event of action being required, it is confidently believed Mr. Roosevelt would tender to the government the services of an entire regiment of cowboys, under his command. At a recent visit here he was assured of two companies of Dakota cowboys to accompany him. Mr. Roosevelt . . . no better man could be found to lead the daring cowboys to a seat of war and no commander would have more effective troops.[106]

Theodore was obviously searching for the opportunity to play the role of a lifetime, that of a heroic frontiersman fighter. This article ran *twelve years* before he became the colonel of the Rough Riders.

By the fall of 1885, Theodore had been in the Badlands for two years. No longer succumbing to long bouts of melancholy, he began showing signs of the affectionate nature that would come to dominate his personality. And it is no coincidence that Theodore's good mood coincided with his reconnection with his childhood friend, Edith Carow.

Theodore had believed that a second marriage was a betrayal to the memory of his dead wife. But sister Corinne did not care for Theodore's belief and purposely invited Edith over to the house the day her brother made a brief return trip to New York. Edith was on the staircase when Theodore blasted through the door, and when they saw each other, it was over. Just a month later, they were secretly engaged.

Initially, Theodore struggled with the engagement. He had only been a widow for twenty-one months. Family and house guests could hear him pacing the room upstairs, muttering, "I have no constancy, I have no constancy."[107]

But love and reason trumped inner confliction, and though he left to go back to Medora shortly after the engagement, the two had agreed to marry before Christmas 1886.

Another factor was propelling Theodore towards domestication. Both Sewall and Dow's wives had given birth to babies while in the Badlands, and not coincidentally, Theodore's letters were soon filled with references to baby Alice: "I miss . . . darling Baby Lee dreadfully; kiss her many times; I am hungry to see her. She must be just too cunning for anything."[108]

Fittingly, the enormous home at Oyster Bay had just finished construction. Theodore changed the name from Leeholm to Sagamore Hill, the Algonquian Indian word for "Chief."

Theodore's desire to make his ranching business profitable was thwarted by his lack of business sense. His trouble making money was a basic problem of supply and demand. Books published in the East—such as *The Beef Bonanza, or How to Get Rich on the Plains*—led to an influx of Eastern money into the Montana and Dakota cattle industry as rich easterners wanted in on the action. Theodore was an Eastern anomaly only in the sense that he invested not just his money but also his time into the Badlands. Within a span of three years, the flood of Easterners to the Badlands had dramatically changed the landscape. No longer was the range grassy and underutilized; it was now buckling under the weight of too many cows.

As more money and cattle poured into the region, land misuse increased and market prices fell. And while Bill Sewall and nature itself were telling Roosevelt that business was unsustainable, his own enthusiasm for ranching was waning. The lure of starting a family and getting back into the battle of political reform was pulling Theodore back east.

At the end of September, 1886—just three months before the Christmas marriage deadline—Theodore and Sewall sat down to discuss the future of the ranch. Sewall flatly told Theodore that he was throwing away money and that the operation must thin out. It was decided that Sewall, Dow, and Roosevelt would leave the Maltese Ranch, and Bill Merrifield would remain to manage the operation. All the Easterners were heading home.

Just as Roosevelt had done when he returned from his honeymoon with Alice several years prior, he returned to New York and went straight to the Republican Party headquarters. Again, it was an election year, and again, the party leaders asked him to be the nominee. Again, Roosevelt had not orchestrated the nomination, and again, he rose to the opportunity.

On the night of Wednesday, October 27th [1886] Roosevelt's twenty-eighth birthday, bonfires belched in the street outside Cooper Union, reddening the huge building's facade until it glowed like a beacon. For almost an hour, rockets soared into the murky sky, casting showers of light over Lower Manhattan and attracting thousands of curious sightseers. By 7:30 p.m. every seat in the hall was filled, and standing room was at a premium as Republican citizens gathered to ratify the nomination of Theodore Roosevelt for Mayor.[109]

Inside the Cooper Union, surrounded by American flags and a golden eagle, sixty-three-year-old Thomas Acton, chairman of the meeting, took to the stage.

"You are called here tonight to ratify the nomination of the youngest man who ever ran as candidate for the Mayor of New York!" Acton cries out, "I knew his father, and wish to tell you that his father did a great deal for the Republican party, and the son will do more. . . . He is young, he is vigorous, he is a natural reformer. He is full, not of the law, but of the spirit of the law. . . . The Cowboy of Dakota! Make the Cowboy of Dakota the next Mayor!"[110]

A roar erupted as the band broke into a martial tune.

Theodore bounded sturdily to the stage, his teeth on display. His speech, like the man, was short and effective.

"The time for radical reform has arrived," he cried as he wrapped up, "and if I am elected you will have it!"[111] Wild applause consumed the hall.

Inside the auditorium were his dad's people, the Choates, Astors, Rockefellers.[112] After a warm reception, Theodore mingled for a few minutes. Outside a rain began to fall on a large crowd that had gathered to see what the commotion was about. When Theodore heard of the crowd, he took to the street, shook hands, and patted backs in the rain for over an hour.

In this election, Theodore knew his chances to win were slim. He was only twenty-eight years old and the nominee of an unexceptionable ticket. The Democrats had an enormously strong candidate, sixty-four-year-old Abram Hewitt, who had been the head of the National Democratic Party after rising to fame by planning and financing the construction of the New York City subway system. The United Labor Union had also put forth a candidate, named Henry George, who represented the disenfranchised working man.[113]

Hewitt was an immensely capable candidate, and George, as third party candidates often do, would no doubt siphon off the Independent vote. "All that I hope for, at the best, is to make a good run and get out the Republican vote," Theodore wrote Lodge in private.[114] The editor of *The Sun*—who had come out in favor of Abram Hewitt—understood why Theodore chose to run even when the cards were stacked against him:

> . . . To be in his youth the candidate for the first office in the first city of the U.S., and to pole a good vote for that office, is something more than empty honor . . . He cannot be Mayor this year, but who knows what may happen in some other year? Congressman, Governor, Senator, President?[115]

On Election Day, Hewitt tallied 90,552 votes, George 68,100, Roosevelt 60,435.[116] Estimates indicate that 15,000 Republicans had defected to Hewitt, perhaps due to Theodore's age or Hewitt's popularity.[117]

Though it was his third political defeat in a row, Theodore lost falling forward. But for reasons still not appreciated today, he hardly ever spoke of his mayoral campaign; his autobiography only lends one sentence to the entire affair. "I have been fairly defeated," he told the *Tribune* shortly after hearing the returns, "But to tell the truth I am not disappointed at the result."[118]

On Saturday, November 6th, just four days after the election, Edith and Theodore boarded the liner *Etruria* under the pseudonyms "Mr. and Mrs. Merrifield." On December 2nd, they were married at St. George's in Hanover Square in London. The church was empty. Outside the grand doors and stained glass windows, a heavy early morning fog had settled.[119]

At the close of the ceremony, Theodore signed the registry identifying himself as a "Rancher." For one of the few times in his life, he lied.

Theodore knew that his ranching days were over and mother nature soon made certain of that fact. While he and Edith were honeymooning in the Mayfair district—the richest part in all of London—the Badlands were ravished by one of the harshest winters on record. Several children froze to death; a few men in isolated areas got cabin fever and shot themselves; a hired girl near Wibaux, Montana "blew her brains out in the kitchen"; cattle were buried alive in snow banks.[120] Temperatures hovered at forty below, staying there for days.

"It seemed as if all the world's ice from time's beginnings had come on a wind which howled and screamed with the fury of demons," a frontiersman wrote.[121]

A "Dutchman," whom Roosevelt knew, had gotten lost in the prairie for a few hours and died of exposure. In the morning, cowboy Jack Snyder found the body but could not bury it—no pick ax could break through the frozen ground. Snyder laid the Dutch-man outside his cabin, where the body was soon covered with ten feet of snow. The cadaver remained there until late spring.[122]

The snow and ice that had amassed was of epic proportions. When the balmy Chinooks wind of spring finally blew through the region, the thaw was astonishing.[123]

Cowboy Lincoln Lang remembered looking out his cabin door to a sight as awful as any he had ever seen. It took a moment for his mind to register what his eyes saw.

> Countless carcasses of cattle [were] going down with the ice, rolling over and over as they went, so that at times all four of the stiffened legs of a carcass would point skyward, as it turned under the impulsion of the swiftly moving current and the grinding ice-cakes . . . their carcasses being spewed forth in untold thousands by the rushing waters to be carried away on the crest of the foaming, turgid flood rushing down the valley. With them went our hopes.[124]

The great cattle herds of the Badlands had been wiped out. The few scrawny cows that had survived were stripped from the range to satisfy the demand of creditors back east. Overnight, people and money fled the area. The once booming cattle town went back to the way it had been fifteen years prior and the way it would remain for the next twenty years. The fragments of a few hastily built homes, isolated barbed wire fences, and one large packinghouse were the only signs that humans ever inhabited the land.

In all, Theodore had invested $82,500 in the Badlands. After selling off his remaining livestock and, deducting his losses from investment, he was left with a total number of $20,292.63. The total loss, including a modest interest if the money had been invested elsewhere, summed well into millions of dollars in present day money.[125]

Perhaps worse than his financial misfortune was the realization that he and his ranch had contributed to the misusage of the grasslands, rivers, and prairies. The over feeding of the grassland, the excessive number of cattle near river banks, and the killing off of beavers who built natural dams, had all culminated to make the treacherous winter of 1886–1887 that much more disastrous. The beef bonanza had ravished the countryside. Nature, he now knew, must be conserved.

Several years later at the Grand Canyon, on May 6th, 1903, Theodore, no doubt influenced by his own contribution to the great cattle die-up, urged the citizens of Arizona to preserve the natural wonder. "I want to ask you to keep this great wonder of nature as it now is . . . [never] to mar the wonderful grandeur, the sublimity, the great loneliness and beauty of the canyon. Leave it as it is. You cannot improve on it. The ages have been at work on it, and man can only mar it."[126]

Though he lost a tremendous proportion of his inheritance in ranching, his time in the West would prove the most influential in his life. In contrast to his sickly and gaunt appearance when he first arrived after the Chicago convention in 1884, Theodore left the badlands a man of physical vitality. No longer could one span his waist with two thumbs and fingers; Theodore was now "rugged, bronzed, and in the prime of health," an astonished reporter wrote in the *Pioneer Press*.[127] At a station stop in Pittsburgh he was interviewed by a correspondent that had interviewed him before he went West. "But what a change! . . . he is now brown as a berry and has increased thirty pounds in weight."[128] The *New York Tribune* observed that for the first time in his life Theodore's walk was "sturdy" and "firm," a clear indication of the "vigor he has acquired while hunting in the West."[129]

In the Badlands, a boy's quest to build his body had been fulfilled.

Roosevelt's time in the Badlands was also, unquestionably, the most influential period in his leadership development. "I never would have been President if it had not been for my experiences in Dakota," he flatly claimed.[130] The experience took the elitist out of him. Forevermore, a person's worth was based on character and ability; not on economic worth, or last name, or social standing. Theodore encapsulated the value of his Badlands education:

I never can sufficiently express the obligations I am under to the Territory of Dakota [Sioux Falls on September 3rd, 1910]. . . . I regard my experience during those years, when I lived and worked with my own fellow ranchmen on what was then the frontier, *as the most important educational asset of all my life.* It is a mighty good thing to know men, not from looking at them, but from having been one of them. When you have worked with them, when you have lived it with them, you do not have to wonder how they feel, because you feel it yourself. . . . I know how the man that works with his hands and the man on the ranch are thinking, because I have been there and I am thinking that way myself. It is not that I divine the way they are thinking, but that I think the same way.[131]

"He started out to get the fundamental truths as they were in this country," a friend reminisced, "and he never lost sight of that all the time he was here." What he learned, according to a cowboy, was "humanity."

"He got away from the New York life. Got to mingling with the people; got to know the people."[132]

Though Theodore would only return to the Badlands for short stays and hunting trips, he never really left the West in spirit or mind. For the rest of his life, he would always marry his personal experiences in the Badlands with his political leadership in the East. He would forever be the cowboy from the range, the common American who could bond the frontiersman and the aristocrat, the East and the West. At his presidential inauguration ceremony, the Sewalls and other friends from the Badlands sat so close to the president they could have reached out and touched him. At the White House, his Dakota and Montana friends were always welcomed guests—much to the merriment of the press, who would consistently embellish the story of an oddly dressed cowboy or mountain man eating dinner on White House china with the most powerful man in the world.

But it was no show. These were the president's friends, his people.

One newspaper complained that the president was inviting "thugs and assassins of Idaho and Montana to be his guests at the White House" obviously baffled why anyone would ever defile the office of the president with frontiersmen. One night, a gate-keeper refused to let a cowboy named Sylvane into the White House. When Roosevelt heard about it he was furious. "The next time they don't let you in, Sylvane, you just shoot out the windows!" he barked.[133]

In the late spring of 1900, Theodore Roosevelt returned to the Badlands as the candidate for vice president of the United States of America. During the whistle-stop campaign, his train charged farther down the line, deeper into the western frontier. A curious thing happened on his way to Helena, Montana. Theodore and his staffers were talking politics in the main locomotive car when the vice presidential candidate—the most popular and likable man in the entire country—abruptly stood up and walked out. His face was instantly worn and sad. On the rear platform, Theodore closed the door and sat alone in the loud, rushing wind.

The vast and desolate landscape—the fathomless prairies that rolled gently out into the expanse—once again occupied his soul. It stirred something in him.

A member of his staff, trying to discover what happened, was turned away.

"The governor don't want to see anybody for a while," the porter said, blocking the door.[134]

And so Roosevelt sat, on the rear of the platform, alone with the solitude of his thoughts, alone with the Badlands, alone with his memories and the lessons that he had taken from the land and its people. It was in this land where he learned to live with his melancholy; he learned to rule his spirit.

In Helena, Montana, thousands were awaiting for his arrival at the station. Theodore saw the crowds and changed his demeanor. His smile beamed, his actions were bombastic and verbose. He was once again the Theodore Roosevelt that America loved.

On the steps of the capitol building, he spoke to a crowd one hundred yards deep. Midway through his speech he spotted his old friend, cowboy Jack Willis, and brought him to the stage, to interrupt "politics long enough," as Jack put it, "to tell the crowd a lot of things that had happened on our hunting trips."[135]

After the speech, an onlooker squealed in amazement to Willis, "You are a lucky man to know as big a man as Mr. Roosevelt well enough to have him single you out of ten thousand people and send a messenger for you!"

"I am not a damned bit luckier than Roosevelt is in knowing me!" Jack shot back, the only response that made sense to a cowboy.

Roosevelt, who overheard the exchange, slapped Jack Willis on the back, "By George, that's right," Roosevelt blasted, "That's just the way I look at it!"[136]

In the West, Roosevelt found strength with the people; he both knew and was known by the common American.

11. VOICE OF THE FRONTIERSMAN

——————————————◇

WHEN THEODORE RETURNED FROM HIS SECOND HONEYMOON, on March 28th, 1887, he was at a loss as to what to do next. Within two weeks he would travel back to Medora to find a barren waste-land, "... it is even worse than I feared," he wrote. "I wish I was sure I would lose no more than half the money [$80,000] I invested here."[1] The storm had been crippling, a full two-thirds of his herd was dead.

While Theodore was on the plains discovering that he lost his fortune, his new wife, Edith, had gone over her husband's unbalanced check books to discover that he was hemorrhaging money, and had been for a while. Uncle James Roosevelt—the guardian of the family finances—had long thought his nephew was careless financially. Prior to leaving for Medora for the first time, Theodore had written a check for twenty-thousand dollars—near a million dollars in today's terms—to become a special partner in G. P. Putnam's Sons, the publisher of Theodore's *Naval War of 1812*. The check bounced. Bamie, who maintained Theodore's day-to-day accounts, had no idea what he had done. While everyone was left scrambling—the bank, Bamie, Putnam's, Uncle James—Theodore headed west to hunt buffalo, completely unaware that he needed to do anything other than sign a check. It was Uncle James who came to the rescue, borrowing the difference from Theodore's annual stipend to put sufficient funds into the account until Theodore returned home from the buffalo hunt.[2]

When word of his staggering losses in the West reached Edith, she demanded that they "cut down tremendously along the whole line." The financial strain was so intense that she urged her husband to "think very seriously of closing Sagamore Hill."[3]

Theodore's total net worth at this time has not been fully appreciated. What is known is that as soon as Edith moved into Oyster Bay, the careless outlays ceased immediately. Theodore had lived outside of his means for so many years, and his inheritance had dwindled so precipitously, that to save money and cut the heating expenses of the large home at Sagamore Hill, the family moved into Bamie's house at 689 Madison Avenue for an entire winter. Theodore criticized his own financial ineptness as "unworthy of a middleclass chimpanzee," and Edith, as hard as she would try, would never be able to teach Theodore about money.[4] Instead, like a mother often does with a child, she would give him twenty dollars when he left in the morning, only to find that when "he returned at night with empty pockets, he had no idea how he had spent it."[5]

That winter Edith also discovered that she was pregnant with a boy, Theodore Jr., due in September. Baby Alice, now three, had been taken from Bamie's care and Edith became her mother. Theodore came to fully embrace fatherhood. At nights, he would gambol with his daughter in the living room, or build block houses, or read to her. He was finally the present and loving father that the world would come to know. But never, not once, did he speak of Alice's real mother.

With the family growing and the finances dwindling, Theodore, for the first time in his life, had to find a job to make ends meet. But everywhere he looked, he saw Democrats. The president of the United States, the governor of New York, and of course, the mayor of New York City, were all of the wrong party. To compound matters, the Democrats were capitalizing on their long awaited opportunity to govern and "two-thirds of the entire federal bureaucracy" had been replaced. Or put another way, two-thirds of the Republican civil servitude had been replaced.[6] Longtime Republican officials were being expunged right and left.

If there ever was a time to get into the private sector, be it law or business, this was the moment. His finances were shattered, his wife was pregnant, and it seemed that he stood no chance of obtaining a government post. Worse, the Republican prospects in 1888 looked bleak. The economy was moving along and President Cleveland was popular.[7]

Theodore decided to make the risky decision to earn a living as an author.

By his thirtieth birthday, Theodore Roosevelt thought of himself as a great man. His life experiences had vindicated to him that he was a survivor, physically and emotionally. His grit and courage had propelled him to become a well-known politician in New York, and his keen self-awareness and tenacity of character had proven that he could hang with the frontiersmen in the West. He knew that his values and principles had been tested under pressure, and he gained strength from meeting those challenges. All of his intense tribulations and experiences, packed into such a short time frame, had crystallized who he was.

If the first requisite of a great leader is to know himself, and what he stood for, then Theodore Roosevelt had obliterated the primary obstacle. He was so certain of himself, and of his unique world outlook, that he believed he was the right man to catalyze America's dream of becoming a supreme world power. America was still reeling from the Civil War and was still an isolationist country. But in the near future, it was speculated that the country, with its roaring economy, might become a world power. Theodore sensed the shift and decided to shape America's future by igniting the frontiersman spirit of its past.

At Oyster Bay, he set aside his gun room as a writing sanctuary. The desk, in an effort to prevent distraction, faced a blank wall rather than the large window overlooking the picturesque Long Island Sound. And so it was that on May 1st, 1888 Theodore Roosevelt sat down to write the history, as he put it, "from the days when Boone crossed the Alleghenies to the days of the Alamo and San Jacinto."[8] From Daniel Boone to Davy Crockett, the project encompassed nothing short of the entire history of the United States from 1774 to 1836. He would look to America's past frontiersmen to provide the lessons for the future. He titled the grand project *The Winning of the West*.

When finished, the multi-volume saga tells the romantic and epic tale of America's heroic pioneers from the "gifted and robust people who were kin to the fearless sea voyagers of hundreds of years before," to more modern leaders like George Rogers Clark, James Robertson and John Sevier—leaders who, according to Roosevelt, "were men of might in their day, born to sway the minds of others, helpful in shaping the destiny of the continent."[9] One is left to conclude that the frontiersman was, and still is, America's greatest asset. "Nowhere else on the continent," Theodore exclaims, "has so sharply defined and distinctly American a type been produced as on the frontier, and a single generation has always been more than enough for its production."[10]

Again, there is a visionary quality to Theodore's writing. There is a valiant theme throughout that holds that American greatness was not a foregone conclusion or something that was just handed down from one generation to the next. Rather, America's greatness was earned through the heroic acts of selfless pioneers, generation after generation. One generation of Americans "triumphantly determined to acquire the right to conquer the continent," and the next generation took it upon itself to pioneer to the West. America was propelled towards greatness because of the ingrained belief of Manifest Destiny, the belief that the country must always push the limits of its frontier.[11] Theodore's not-so-subtle theme held that it was imperative for the next generation to lead America to the next frontier, whatever that frontier may be. He concluded that all frontiersmen were "one in speech, thought and character," no matter in what era they were born, what part of the country they had come from, or their social standing.

His message was timely, and he knew it. The story of the frontiersman, the strong individual who toiled hard, looked after others and would die for country, stood in contrast with the nonchalant attitude born of excessive wealth in the Gilded Age of the 1880s. The book was released into a country debating whether it had lost its drive for patriotic excellence in the pursuit of the almighty dollar. The theme of *winning* that begs for the next generation of American pioneers was perfectly matched for the country's debate. America increasingly looked "like a society that had lost its moral compass in the pursuit of wealth"[12] and Roosevelt took that moral decay head-on.

The *Atlantic Monthly* praised Roosevelt with a beaming review: "His style is natural, simple, and picturesque. . . . few writers of American history have covered a wider or better field of research, or are more in sympathy with the best modern method of studying history from original sources."[13]

"What is essential," Theodore later stated about his writings, ". . . [was] the power to embody ghosts, to put flesh and blood on dry bones, to make dead men living before our eyes."[14] In an effort to tell his view of American history, he sounded more like Sir Walter Scott and Mayne Reid rather than an academic. "Impartiality does not mean neutrality," he would later claim, "the best historians must of necessity take sides."[15]

Besides, Theodore was not writing a history, he was shaping the future.

From today's vantage point, it is clear that Theodore Roosevelt was not born to lead. His leadership persona was cultivated and refined his entire life as he continued to interpret and make sense of his own beliefs and the world around him. At first pass, his books and professional career may seem disconnected and without aim. Yet from the Badlands, to Pennsylvania Avenue, it is important to note that he took the same modus operandi wherever he went, always promoting the ideals of vigor, courage, strength, and reform. To Theodore, the pioneers of America's past were shining examples for leaders interested in modern-day American supremacy. Theodore Roosevelt was still cultivating and pursuing this ideal with hard devotion until the day he died. The country would embrace President Roosevelt because he embodied America at the turn of the century—the self-assurance, the enthusiasm, and the assertiveness. It was all there in America, and it was all there in Theodore. It was in his mid-twenties when Theodore began to position himself as the man who could meet the country's challenges at the turn of the century. He has often been described as a man of destiny, but his path was not carved by accident. He envisioned the entire thing.

12. CIVIL SERVICE COMMISSION

─────────────────────────◇

SHORTLY BEFORE 1888, THE POPULAR PRESIDENT GROVER Cleveland took an unnecessary stance on a controversial issue of the day, a move that sitting presidents have tried not to duplicate. The topic was tariff rates which Cleveland thought were "vicious, inequitable, and illogical sources of unnecessary taxations, [that] ought to be at once revised and amended."[1] Cleveland's rhetoric, though sound free-trade economics, was construed as favoring international business at a time when the public wanted to protect the American worker. On Election Day, 1888, Cleveland won the popular vote by .8 percent, but lost the Electoral College vote and his job.

"When I came into power," the new President Benjamin Harrison stated frankly, "I found that the party managers had taken it all to themselves. I could not name my own cabinet. They had sold out every place to pay the election expenses."[2] This is an exceptionally sad statement from a man whose campaign promise was focused on reform, the promise that only the most qualified would be given government jobs.

It is difficult for the contemporary American to fully appreciate the visceral emotions surrounding spoils system appointments and the subsequent civil service reform quest of the late nineteenth century. Today, it is common sense that government careers are bestowed upon those with merit. But as the turn of the century neared, many Americans disapproved of the merit system and its arrangement of competitive examinations for government positions. It was a new idea, labeled as "too Chinese," referring to China's rigid examinations to weed out incompetency.[3] Besides, the prevailing thought of the day was that politicians who had won an election in a free democracy should be able to reward hard working individuals who helped them along the way. But this arrangement—rampant after the Civil War—had created a currency in the form of lucrative government jobs, which were used as incentives for subordinates to loyally work for the political party, not the government.

To Roosevelt, the merit system was the only system that could both diminish incompetency and increase efficiency. Most importantly, the merit system could end corruption and was, according to him, "essentially democratic and essentially American, and in line with the utterances and deeds of our forefathers of the days of Washington and Madison."[4] The biggest enemies for posterity in domestic policy, he complained, were the party machinists, "whether Democratic, Republican, or Independent,"[5] who doled out jobs from the treasure chest of political capital.

After President Benjamin Harrison's victory Theodore saw an opportunity to get back into public life. He enjoyed writing his books, but confessed that "I would like above all things to go into politics."[6] In a contradiction that was lost on Roosevelt, he asked Henry Cabot Lodge to lobby on his behalf to find him a government post in the new Harrison administration so that he could fight against the spoils system. Lodge, the most loyal friend, immediately began politicking for Theodore. First, Lodge tried to persuade James G. Blaine, who had been appointed secretary of state. Lodge believed that Roosevelt would make a wonderful assistant secretary under Blaine, despite the fact that Theodore had campaigned against the former presidential candidate. In a letter that proved incredibly predictive, Blaine was not angry about Theodore's action in Chicago in 1884, but was more worried about Theodore's need for action:

My real trouble in regard to Mr. Roosevelt is that I fear he lacks the repose and patient endurance required in an Assistant Secretary. Mr. Roosevelt is amazingly quick in apprehension. Is there not danger that he might be too quick in execution? . . . Matters are constantly occurring which require the most thoughtful concentration and the most stubborn inaction. Do *you* think that Mr. T.R.'s temperament would give guaranty of that course?[7]

With the assistant secretary of state position out of the picture, Lodge went straight to the president to find that Harrison was also not at all enthusiastic to employ Theodore.[8] But Lodge—"certainly the most loyal friend that ever breathed"—continued to press Harrison and, after much discussion, the new president admitted that there was one position he was willing to give to Theodore Roosevelt: a post on the three-member Civil Service Commission.[9]

The job was minor. It paid only $3,500 a year and it did not come with any political power. It harbored the opposite of prestige, described as a position that was "as thankless as any in the government."[10] According to the job description, commissioners were tasked with firing the incompetent, which inevitably meant angering those let go as well as their wives, children, beer-drinking buddies, and fellow church members.[11] It also meant alienating the machine operatives and local politicians who had placed the incompetent into their current jobs and who feared the undoing of the spoils system that made the machine so powerful.

The Civil Service Commission was a job of legal obstacles that generated bad will, bureaucracy, and paperwork. It was the type of position an ambitious young man ought to turn down.[12] Roosevelt took it.

Prior to Theodore's arrival in May of 1889, the office at the Concordia Building at Eighth and E Streets was the scene of a quietly run government agency.[13] The president of the Civil Service Commission was Charles Lyman, a Presbyterian elder and a subtle gentleman, who oversaw the bureau with a nonchalant eye. Lyman's eight previous predecessors had all adhered to a laissez-faire policy approach towards government reform, and the pervasive culture of indifference meant that the commission suggested reform tactics rather than demand them.[14] To a young, virtuous Roosevelt this was dishonorable.

Roosevelt hit the ground running. In the first week, he went looking for corruption at the Customhouse in New York, both a personal charge to avenge Thee's loss to Chester A. Arthur, as well as a pragmatic move considering his experience on the Albany investigation committee. He knew that it would be easy to find corruption, and he chose the customhouse because it would provide the publicity to promote his cause.

What Theodore found, without effort, was that questions for the merit-based examination had been forwarded to "favored candidates" for a mere fifty dollars.[15] Customhouse officials were gaming the merit system and Theodore, in grand Roosevelt fashion, immediately exposed the fraud and mismanagement in a fiery report calling for the dismissal of three officials and possible criminal prosecutions. Stunned, one prominent reformer stated that Roosevelt's call to action was "the first emphatic notice that the Civil Service Act was a real law and was to be enforced."[16] The Civil Service Act, the landmark legislation that created the Civil Service Commission, had been passed in 1883, a full six years prior to Roosevelt's report. In effect, it had taken Roosevelt a week to make the six-year-old law a reality.[17]

The following month, June 1889, Roosevelt and his fellow commissioners left Washington for an inspection tour across the Midwest to examine whether local postmasters in the interior were adhering to the Civil Service laws.[18] In an effort to scare government officials straight—to "make the Commission a living force," as he put it—he brought the press along and, for the first time, illustrated an extraordinary gift as a propagandist. The press presence would put the country on notice: the Civil Service Act was going to be enforced, from sea to shining sea.

Roosevelt was horrified by what he found in the Midwest. The spoils system had created an environment infested with nepotism and incompetency. In Indianapolis, a postmaster who had been fired for operating an illegal gambling operation had been reinstated to his post because he promised to further the Republican cause.[19] In Milwaukee, Roosevelt found a postmaster "about as thorough paced a scoundrel as I ever saw" who had taken the liberty to appoint whomever he chose and helped friends cheat on the exams.[20]

Again, Roosevelt publicly demanded the removal of the inept postmasters, decrying that "the spoils system means the establishing and perpetuation of a grasping and ignorant oligarchy."[21]

But Roosevelt's call for the swift removal of the useless was futile. He had no power beyond that of revealing wrongdoing. It was up to President Harrison to act, and when the amicable president waffled, Roosevelt set out to force Harrison's hand by shooting off another fiery public report and feeding the press evidence of the graft he witnessed on the Midwestern tour.

This made for great publicity, but again nothing happened.

President Harrison had no desire to irritate his political base by dismissing several government officials. Besides, the status quo of the spoils system was the norm and the Civil Service Commission was supposed to *act* like they were reforming America, but actually not *do* too much. Had Theodore not noticed the culture of tranquility and comfort at the bureau when he arrived, Harrison wondered?

President Harrison also placed complete trust in John Wanamaker, the postmaster general and Republican heavy hitter whose deep pockets had bought him a spot in the president's inner circle as well as a cabinet seat. Wanamaker exemplified the spoils system and handed out jobs to political allies regardless of merit. Shortly after his appointment, he demanded the removal of 985 postmasters and 30,000 postal workers, all to be "replaced by deserving Republicans."[22] Wanamaker believed that the spoils should go to the victor and quickly grew annoyed with Roosevelt's righteously charged reports damning his agency.[23] It was the postmaster general's job, Wanamaker knew, to reward the president's allies with employment.

Roosevelt decided to pick a fight with the kingpin, Wanamaker.

Through shrewd detective work, Roosevelt uncovered rampant corruption among post office officials and U.S. marshals in the city of Baltimore. Several witnesses were prepared to testify that "friends of Benjamin Harrison" were using government offices to extort "contributions" of ten dollars from government officials to build a war chest for the upcoming election.[24] The money was "certainly to be used to bribe election judges."[25] Roosevelt sent a letter to John Wanamaker suggesting that he investigate the claims; after all, this was in Wanamaker's jurisdiction as the postmaster general. Wanamaker declined outright, and told Theodore to drop the investigation.[26]

Theodore, insubordinate and morally charged, left at once for Baltimore to collect firsthand evidence and to interview employees. On Election Day, March 30th, he arrived in Baltimore to a sea of sleaze:

> On every sidewalk fists flew and money—taxpayers' money—changed hands, while in house-windows overlooking the street, election judges sat in impassive groups of three, like monkeys who saw, heard, and spoke no evil. Relays of furniture carts rumbled in from all points of the compass, bringing hundreds of rural voters with no apparent connections to the local Republican party. Ward-workers entertained these transients in saloons where the beer flowed freely, compliments of Postmaster Johnson and Marshal Airey. . . . Elsewhere an anti-administration worker eliminated three pro-administration judges by the simple expedient of pulling a blind down over the window.[27]

The graft was incredible. The spoils system had infiltrated the Baltimore postmasters so thoroughly that a carrier on government payroll admitted on the record that he indeed "was a political worker and that cheating was one of the features of Republican methods in Baltimore," before clarifying innocently, "we always cheat fair."[28]

Roosevelt did not appreciate the distinction between cheating fairly and cheating unfairly, and decided to go over the head of Wanamaker and publish a damning indictment of Republican wrongdoing. The 146-page *Report of Commissioner Roosevelt Concerning Political Assessment and the Use of Official Influence to Control Elections in the Federal Offices at Baltimore* demanded that twenty-five of Harrison's own appointees be dismissed immediately, and some of them be sent to prison.[29]

Theodore had kicked over the hornet's nest.

Wanamaker was irate and spoils men from all over the country rushed to the White House calling for Roosevelt's immediate dismissal. The Republican Party bosses demanded that Theodore be fired to prevent him from dividing the administration and destroying Harrison's upcoming reelection bid. After all, the day after Theodore filed the Baltimore report, Grover Cleveland was re-nominated by the Democratic Party to contend for his old job. The *Boston Post* speculated that "the removal of Theodore Roosevelt from the Civil Service Commission is among the possibilities in the near future."[30]

But as the cry went out that he was destroying the party, Theodore took comfort. His hard devotion to uphold the law led him to believe that he was doing his job successfully. Never mind that he might be splitting the party and destroying Harrison's presidency; he had been hired to implement reform and that was exactly what he was doing. "We have administered a galvanic shock that will reinforce his [President Harrison's] virtue for the future," Theodore explained.[31]

In a very public way, Theodore had forced the president to take action. He had put his career on the line to find out whether Harrison was for the merit system or against it. If Harrison fired Theodore he would appease the spoilsmen, and send a strong signal that reform was not all that important to him. If he fired Wanamaker, he would rally the reformers, but alienate his Republican base.

Harrison decided to do nothing, and ended up looking weak.

"The little gray man in the White House looking on with cold and hesitating disapproval," Roosevelt snarled, "but [does] not see how he can interfere."[32] A good leader would have acted, Theodore knew. "I much prefer to really accomplish something good in public life," he explained, "no matter what cost of enmity from even my political friends than to enjoy a longer term of service, fettered by endless fear, always trying to compromise, in doing nothing in the end."[33] Not concerned at all that he placed the president in a precarious position, Roosevelt slept well at night, admitting "I think I have done good work."[34]

Interestingly, Harrison neither denounced nor supported Roosevelt. "The only trouble I ever had with managing him,"

Harrison stated years later, "was that he wanted to put an end to all the evil in the world between sunrise and sunset."[35]

As the election of 1892 approached, Theodore's hard obedience to his cause in Baltimore proved a hazard to Harrison's reelection bid. "Teddy at the Polls—Helping to Hurt Mr. Harrison," a newspaper headline touted, before adding that if Harrison were to lose, "the President will have nobody to blame more than his civil service commissioner."[36]

Backlash from his party was ferocious. A postmaster in Baltimore told the newspapers that he was hoping "that lightning may strike Theodore Roosevelt."[37] In no uncertain terms, the party faithful demanded that Theodore recant or suppress the damning findings. Members of the cabinet met with him one-on-one, seeking solidarity between Roosevelt and Harrison. Theodore did not budge. It did not matter whether it was an election year or not, for the sake of America's posterity the president must fire the twenty-five corrupt officials, regardless if they were his own appointees.[38]

On Election Day 1892, aided by the fracturing of the Republican Party and an uptick in the reform vote, Grover Cleveland carried the election by three percentage points. How much Theodore was responsible is up for debate. However, it is undeniable that he certainly did not help Harrison's cause.

But Theodore Roosevelt never intended for Harrison to lose the election. He campaigned for the president and even wrote an approving article on Harrison's behalf in the *Independent*, titled "The Foreign Policy of President Harrison." Theodore did indeed want his party to win, but he simply could not turn a blind eye to the corruption that he had discovered.[39]

"[I] have the profound gratification," Theodore told a friend, "of knowing that there is no man more bitterly disliked by many of the men in my own party. When I leave on March 5th [beginning of Cleveland administration], I shall at least have the knowledge that I have certainly not flinched from trying to enforce the law during these four years, even if my progress has been, at times, a little disheartening."[40]

But Roosevelt was not going anywhere. Shortly after President Cleveland re-took the helm of the country, he asked Theodore to stay and serve in his administration. It was a safe choice.

Roosevelt's public battles with his own Republican leaders had proven that the young leader was more interested in destroying the spoils system than promoting politics.[41] One friend quipped that if someone turned out the lights, then nobody would be able to tell if Theodore Roosevelt was a Democrat or a Republican.

Honored by President Cleveland's offer, Theodore decided to work for the Democratic administration. But the thankless job of civil service was wearing thin and he began to feel that his career was stalling. He was just barely content; for all the work he had done, President Harrison had not supported nor endorsed his actions. He knew at any moment Cleveland could fire him, and worse, he had little idea of what to do next for his career.

His family was also expanding. Edith gave birth two more times, to Kermit in 1889 and Ethel in 1891. The two new additions, plus Alice and Ted Junior, made for a "household swarming with bunnies."[42] The expenses of maintaining four children, two adults, a house in New York and a house in DC, had taken its toll. On the government payroll Theodore was earning just $3,500, and the family operating budget was at least $5,000. There was another heated discussion about selling off Sagamore Hill.[43] The disastrous financial outcome in the cattle business, coupled with a meager government salary and an expanding family, had precipitously decreased his inheritance. The entire period that Theodore served on the Civil Service Commission seemed to the family as if they were living in a "season of grinding poverty."[44] At one point, paper money became so tight that Edith paid household workers in gold.

Though Roosevelt was not making money, his tenure as civil service commissioner would prove successful in other ways. He travelled across the country broadening his network while further entrenching his name in the public consciousness as a young leader dedicated to the progressive government movement. But he also exhibited a great talent in cultivating personal relationships with like-minded power brokers in the most powerful city in the world.[45] In the West, he had learned the ways of the frontiers-man. In his six years in Washington, he learned how to interact with those of the political class and expanded his network through an incessant social schedule that had him dining out four times a week and entertaining a constant stream of visitors at his home.[46] He became close friends with Speaker of the House Thomas Reed, and with Henry Adams, the great-grandson of John Adams, and a leading journalist of the day. He cultivated a relationship with the congressman from Ohio that he met at the 1884 Republican convention, William McKinley.[47] He also got reacquainted with one of his father's old friends, John Hay. But in his time in Washington, one man in particular had an influence on Roosevelt that would forever alter American foreign policy.

Alfred Thayer Mahan was born in 1840 in West Point, New York, to a family steeped in military tradition. Alfred's father, Dennis Hart Mahan, served as the dean of faculty for the U.S. Military Academy and was the legendary professor to most of the great Civil War generals: Sherman, Grant, Beauregard, Sheridan, Jackson.[48] So great was Dennis's influence on his pupils that when a young Alfred Mahan, just a lieutenant, met Civil War hero William Tecumseh Sherman, just after Sherman's March to the Sea, it was the general who was "delighted to shake the hand of the son of old Dennis."[49]

Now, several years later, and in the twilight of an undistinguished career, Alfred Mahan had been appointed lecturer of naval history at the Naval War College in Newport, Rhode Island. At the age of fifty, he published a collection of his lectures under the title *The Influence of Sea Power upon History*, a summary of his view of the "intricate relationships between political power and sea power, warfare and economics, geography, and technology."[50] Mahan's theme held that the decrepit naval fleet made America unsafe and only a rapid rebuilding effort would allow America "to assert itself in international markets and in power politics."[51]

In May of 1890, Roosevelt read *The Influence of Sea Power upon History*, in rapt awe. Mahan's assertion that larger ships should be built and deployed to other parts of the world—to promote defense—was aligned with Theodore's long-held conviction. Roosevelt particularly loved how Mahan defended his position that a quick strike by a concentration of ships at various "pressure points" of global commerce routes could paralyze an entire nation—the country that took such action could easily win a war of the oceans in a matter of days.[52] The idea that a great offense provided the best defense was the genesis of gunboat diplomacy.

Theodore knew that Mahan was a frontiersman like himself. Since his own work on *The Naval War of 1812*, he had passionately argued for a transformation of the navy and now, a professor at the heart of the war-planning institute was advocating the same strategy.

"My dear Captain Mahan," Roosevelt immediately wrote to Mahan, "I can say with perfect sincerity that I think it very much the clearest and most instructive general work of the kind with which I am acquainted. It is a very good book—admirable; and I am greatly in error if it does not become a naval classic."[53]

To entrench his friendship with Mahan, Roosevelt penned a book review for the *Atlantic Monthly*:

> Captain Mahan shows very clearly the practical importance of the study of naval history in the past to those who wish to estimate and use aright the navies of the present. . . . the tacticians of to-day can with advantage study the battles of the past.[54]

In other words, the leaders of today can learn from history.

What Roosevelt feared most was that Mahan's philosophy could become the operational doctrine of global powers Germany, Japan, and Britain. How could he get political leaders, and the American public, to subscribe to Mahan's theory before the German, Japanese, and British governments implemented it?

Roosevelt had visionary leadership. He was on the balcony, looking to America's future. What he saw was the most powerful economy in the world secured by the most powerful military force in existence.

Theodore Roosevelt's rapid ascension has been compared to that of a charging locomotive on the inevitable track to the presidency.[55] In the six short years from 1895 to when he took the oath of office as president of the United States in 1901, Roosevelt's career trajectory was indeed frantic: federal civil service commissioner, president of New York City police board, assistant secretary of the navy, colonel of the Rough Riders, governor of New York, and vice president of the United States. The entire ride would prove frighteningly rapid, and at times as if guided by a divine power.

But it is important to distinguish that Theodore's good run of fortune did not occur until after the spring of 1895. In taking inventory of his life before his dramatic ascension, there is a prevailing sense that he was underwhelmed with his accomplishments. Where was the heroic leadership, he wondered at the age of thirty-five? In the past decade he had proven to be a failure at business, squandering the majority of his inheritance. His once-promising political career—he was elected to assemblyman at twenty-three—had since stalled. He had lost his bid for the mayor of New York. His current job on the Civil Service Commission had since proven to be thankless.[56] His books, though popular, were written about other great men—but he wanted to be a great man.

There was no mistake that Theodore had the fortitude to be great, but the accomplishments to date were not all that significant—at least by his standards.

During the first week in August 1894, it looked as if it was all about to change. Congressman Lemuel Ely Quigg of New York called on Roosevelt to see if he would accept the Republican nomination for New York mayor. The election was only three months away, and the chances of a Republican victory were all but guaranteed. The city was itching for a reform candidate and if Roosevelt's name was on the ballot, it would be no contest. This was Theodore's big chance, Quigg told him; the office was his to lose.[57]

Theodore thought the matter over for two weeks before declining the nomination. Quigg was stunned. So certain was he that Theodore would accept the nomination, Roosevelt had to turn him down on three more occasions.[58]

It is no secret that Theodore coveted the mayor's office and wanted nothing more than to occupy it. But Edith was against it. To run for mayor meant Theodore would have to spend money on his campaign, as was the custom of the day. Also, Edith did not want her husband to be unemployed if he did not win. Edith's disapproval, coupled with their financial state, impelled Roosevelt to withdraw his name from the nomination. "I simply had not the funds to run," he admitted privately.[59]

Immediately upon making the decision, Theodore slipped into a deep depression. The sicknesses, the bronchitis, the obstructed breathings of his youth all returned with a fury. It was as if, for a brief moment, he had no future before him and his body just simply gave out on him. He was confined to his bed for over a week; plagued by vomiting, asthma, and headaches. At thirty-five years old, he felt that he missed his "one golden chance, which never returns."[60]

Theodore's depression moved Edith tremendously. She had persuaded him not to run and then had to stand by hopelessly, witness to his physical and emotional devastation. ". . . I cannot begin to describe how terribly I feel at having failed him at such an important time," Edith confided to Bamie, ". . . only if I knew what I do now I should have thrown all my influence in the scale . . . and helped instead of hindering him. . . . This is a lesson that will last my life."[61] It seems that Edith had yet to embrace just how much Theodore needed to be in politics, how much he needed to be somebody, and how much he needed the opportunity to run down the dream.

Miserable and depressed, Theodore divulged to a friend that he "would literally have given my right arm to have made the race."[62]

The Republican nomination was handed to William L. Strong, a businessman in his late sixties with little political experience. As expected, Strong positioned himself as the reform candidate and was elected comfortably.[63]

Roosevelt returned to the Civil Service Commission and likened it to "starting to go through Harvard again after graduating."[64] Shortly before Christmas 1894, he received a message from mayor-elect Strong, offering him the position of street cleaning commissioner in New York.[65] The offer, made in good faith, was devastating to Roosevelt. Had he just decided to run then he would undoubtedly have been the mayor. Could it be that his next best career opportunity was in garbage? Oh, the insult.

Theodore remained in a depression for several months; the man needed a challenge to help rid him of his melancholy. He needed something that he could conquer, much like when we went to the Big Horn Mountains in Wyoming to kill the grizzly bear.

The Lexow Committee Report provided just the challenge.

Clarence Lexow, a New York State senator, had recently introduced a bill to investigate the affairs and corruption in the New York City police force. The one year investigation was exhaustive, and the discovery was scandalous. The report consisted of 10,576 pages of testimony from 678 witnesses that uncovered a gamut of vice: extortion, bribery, counterfeiting, voter intimidation, election fraud, and racketeering.[66] The police, rather than upholding the law, were running a business of corruption.

> In addition to the government's official appropriations of $5,139,147.64, the department counted on brothel contributions of $8,120,000.00; [according to one account of the findings] saloon contributions of $1,820,000.00; gambling house receipts totaling $165,000.00; collections from merchants, peddlers, and others to the tune of $50,000.00; and $60,000.00 in fees squeezed from new members of the force. These sums brought the grand total to $15,354,147.64.[67]

Over two-thirds of the New York police force budget came from illegal activities.

The hubris of the graft was equally appalling. Police Inspector Alexander "Clubber" Williams, the "Czar of the Tenderloin," managed his district like a gangster. When queried by the Lexow Committee about why he chose to shut down only a few brothels in his district, Williams answered, under oath, that he in fact "made no attempt to close them all."

"Why?" an investigator asked.

"Well, they were fashionable," came Williams's response, implying that he was on the payroll and receiving kickbacks.

"Then you, the police officer charged with carrying out the laws, and paid by the people for doing so, say that you left the houses open because they were fashionable?" came the response from the investigation committee.

"Yes," Williams responded.

Senator Lexow was beside himself, "Don't you know that that is an extraordinary answer?"

"Well," Williams admitted, not at all concerned, "I haven't any other."

Then the conversation turned to Clubber's "bulging bank accounts, a home in the city, a mansion in Connecticut and ownership of a yacht."[68]

How had he afforded all of this on his policeman's salary?

"Lots of real estate in Japan," came the answer, an obvious and disrespectful lie.

Clubber Williams's remarks and the not-to-secret police budget were just symptoms of the corporate disease of corruption. The underworld, the Tammany politicians, and the police force were all working together to orchestrate the city-wide racket. The power players decided who got rich, which brothels got shut down, which brothels never got raided, and which saloons would suddenly have their rent quadrupled. They all served the racket, not the public.

"The time had come for a determined effort to bring about such a radical and lasting change in the administration of the City of New York as will ensure the permanent removal of the abuses from which we suffer," the Lexow Committee Report urged.[69]

But who could lead such an intimidating crusade? Who could carry out "business and not politics in city affairs?" the *New York Times* asked. "It has been the demoralizing influence of the politicians that has made corruption and favoritism possible, and honesty, discipline, responsibility, and efficiency difficult and largely impracticable."[70]

The *Times* had already had a frontrunner: "IF NOT MR. ROOSEVELT, WHO?"[71]

The ground swell of publicity flattered Roosevelt. He was wanted; he had his challenge. His blood began to boil.

At the end of March, Roosevelt sent word to Lemuel Quigg that he wanted the post of police commissioner and the opportunity to reform the entire force. To backup Quigg, Theodore asked Henry Cabot Lodge to discuss the matter directly with Mayor

Strong.[72] Again Lodge came through, and on April 17th, 1895, Theodore's appointment was confirmed.[73] He was heading back to New York.

In all, Roosevelt spent six years at the Civil Service Commission, the longest job he would ever hold, save for president of the United States. The quality of his work on the commission depended upon whom one spoke with. The spoilsmen hated him. The machinists hated him. Middle America liked the idea of Roosevelt, but was still unsure. The Mugwump faction of the Republican Party loved him. The Old Guard worried over him.

Tellingly, the *Civil Service Chronicle* of May 1895 correctly pointed out that Theodore's stint on the commission was "an educational process spread over the country."[74]

It would take several years for Theodore's actions on the commission to be fully appreciated. Not until the merit system was fully engrained into the American way of life did he receive the accolades he deserved. "Theodore Roosevelt probably contributed more to the development and extension of the civil service than any other person in the history of the United States," confirms a 1958 independent review of the civil service in America.[75]

But the lasting value was not what he did for the commission, but what the job did for him. Roosevelt was perhaps the greatest bureaucratic manager that ever held the presidential office, save perhaps Dwight D. Eisenhower. This would certainly not have been the case without his experience on the commission. During his tenure, the civil service bureau doubled in size, as six thousand new positions were put into classified service.[76] The logistical challenge of managing such great expansion introduced Theodore to administrative and managerial duties where he was forced to appreciate that practical technical actions are essential to bring reform. While visionary rhetoric was important, hard managerial processes were a vital requirement to create a lasting transformation. Some of President Roosevelt's mundane managerial actions included definitions for "just cause" to terminate an employee, requirements for stricter compliance between political entities and government officials, guidelines to appoint employees to jobs with specific classifications, and new measures that forbade the disbursement of money to persons appointed to civil service positions outside the set forth processes.[77] These actions became the foundation of the merit system.

As president, Theodore, unlike Benjamin Harrison, acted boldly to eliminate political appointments, marrying ambitious leadership with focused managerial activities. During Theodore's presidency, the number of merit-appointed government workers surpassed the number of patronage-appointed employees for the first time since before the Civil War.

This trend has now lasted for well over a century.

While in the trenches fighting for civil service reform in Washington DC, Theodore kept his eye on the prize. All of his efforts had one singular goal.

"I used to walk by the White House, and my heart would beat a little faster as the thought came to me," he admitted later in life, "that possibly—*possibly*—I would someday occupy it as president."[78]

13. POLICE COMMISSIONER

—————————————————◇

"I HAVE THE MOST IMPORTANT AND THE MOST CORRUPT department in New York on my hands," Theodore wrote the day before he was appointed to the Police Commission. "I shall speedily assail some of the ablest, shrewdest men in this city, who will be fighting for their lives, and I know well how hard the task ahead of me is."[1]

As a member of the state legislature, Theodore had presided over investigation after investigation that revealed just how deeply engrained the graft and corruption was in the police force. Everyone was involved. "From top to bottom, the New York police force was utterly demoralized by the gangrene," Theodore wrote. ". . . [V]enality and blackmail went hand-in-hand with the basest forms of low ward politics. . . . [T]he policeman, the ward politician, the liquor seller, and the criminal alternatively preyed on one another and helped one another prey on the general public."[2]

But unlike his time in the assembly eleven years prior, Theodore now had the ability to act, not legislate.

At ten o'clock on the morning of May 6th, 1895, Theodore walked into Mayor Strong's office and took the oath of office.[3] When the simple formalities were finished, he turned on his heel and bolted for the door and into the street. He ran through sixteen intersections along Pearl, Worth, Canal, Grand, Broome, and Houston, before turning onto Mulberry Street eighteen blocks later.[4] When Roosevelt came in sight of the police headquarters on 300 Mulberry, he literally was sprinting to his new job.

Lincoln Steffens, reporter for the *Evening Post*, was sitting on the stoop outside of police headquarters and had just received the message that Roosevelt, only moments before, had been sworn in as police commissioner at City Hall, a full mile away. Steffens was shocked to see Roosevelt so soon and in a sprint. Steffens narrated the scene for his readers:[5]

He came on ahead down the street; he yelled "Hello, Jake," to [Jacob] Riis, and running up the stairs to the front door of Police Headquarters, he waved us reporters to follow. We did. With the police officials standing around watching, the new Board went up to the second story . . . still running, he asked questions:

"Where are our offices?"
"Where is the Board Room?"
"What do we do first?"

Out of the half-heard answers he gathered the way to the board room, where the three old commissioners waited, like three of the new commissioners, stiff, formal and dignified. Not TR. He introduced himself, his colleagues, with handshakes, and called a meeting of the new board . . . had himself elected president—this had been prearranged— and then adjourned to pull Riis and me with him into his office.

"Now, then, what'll we do?"[6]

Theodore had not been in the building more than an hour "before he had made the personal acquaintance of every man in it," a newspaper said, "from the nursery up under the roof to Tim, the janitor, in the cellar."[7] Theodore's theatrical charge into headquarters was a clear message to all that he would act swiftly and boldly. His first press release was unambiguous: "Every man in the force will have to stand on his merits and all appointments will be made for merit only. . . ."[8]

The headquarters at 300 Mulberry was "an arena always live with drama, or at least the promise of drama," a commentary reads. "A sudden singing of the telegraph wires, which untidily connected police headquarters with every precinct in the city, might signify riots in Hell's Kitchen, or a brothel-bust in the Tenderloin; sooner or later, the latest victims of the law would be delivered in shiny patrol-wagons, and the press would dash across to meet them, pencils and pads at the ready."[9]

The actual office, much like its operatives, was dark and shady, looking more like a rat-infested dungeon than a place of justice.

Over the course of his first month, Theodore would boast that he had "never worked harder" and that the job had "not a touch of the academic."[10] It was pure practical action and he loved it.

The job to bring about reform was not Theodore's alone. He had been selected as the president of a board of four members and, in compromising fashion, the commission consisted of two Republicans—Roosevelt and Frederick D. Grant, the son of President Ulysses S. Grant, and two Democrats—Avery D. Andrews and Andrew D. Parker.[11]

From the start, there was tension. Theodore believed that only one person should call the shots and acted as such. He took command authoritatively, and his correspondence to the press referred to "my policy" rather than "our policy" to represent the board's views.[12] Theodore believed that dramatic change and reform was best concentrated in the hands of one man, an executive with ample power to enforce change to do the work necessary.[13]

Commissioners Grant and Andrews squarely supported Theodore from day one, but Democrat Andrew Parker detested Theodore's authoritative style, and soon protested to others that Theodore "thinks he's the whole board."[14]

On May 13th, just one week into his new role, the board, at Theodore's urging, sought the approval of the Albany legislature to reorganize the force. Reform could only happen if they could fire the corrupt, they explained.

Chief of Police Tom Byrnes was irate at the board's power play. He rightfully saw the legislative proposal as an infringement on his power, and indignantly he started an "anti-reform fund" to defeat the proposal. Byrnes made it known that each member of the force was expected to give fifty dollars "to help finance the efforts" to kill Theodore's appalling reorganization idea.[15] Byrnes then made a personal appeal to his legislative allies in Albany, and the Tammany men, never to miss the call of corruption, voted down the board's proposal. With Theodore's power play killed, Byrnes was confident in his entrenched authority, and faced off with Roosevelt. "It will break you," Byrnes shouted, "You will yield. You are but human!"[16]

Police Chief Byrnes was a grizzled veteran whose thirty-two years in the force had garnered him immense respect. He had captured notorious Manhattan bank robbers, which made him a hero, and benefactor, of Wall Street financiers.[17] He was loved by Tammany Hall, bankers, politicians, and the overwhelming majority of his own force. Described as "the personification of the police department," Byrnes was the leader, the head honcho, the untouchable.[18] Theodore did not care. "I shall move against Byrnes at once," he confidently wrote Lodge on May 18th, "I thoroughly distrust him . . ."[19]

Roosevelt did not have authority to reorganize the force or to fire Byrnes, so he decided to use politics to force him out. On May 24th, Theodore allowed the reading of a letter from a private citizen named "Thomas MacGregor" to be entered into the record of the police board's public meeting minutes. The letter stated that "Byrnes confessed [to the Lexow Committee] that he was worth $200,000 or $300,000 . . . [but he was actually worth] $1,500,000, and every dollar of it was wages of blackmail and corruption."[20] Byrnes's fortune, the letter acknowledged, came from "protection fees" he charged to brothels and saloons.

The indictment in the letter was not new news, but the press, probably at Theodore's back channel urging, ran with the story.

Immediately, there was backlash against the board. The citizen, Thomas MacGregor, did not exist. The story, though true, had obviously been written by someone who wanted Byrnes out. Theodore vehemently denied writing the story and immediately sent out a press release stating that "each of the Commissioners deeply regrets the unauthorized publication."[21]

But Theodore was a politician and quickly realized that the door had swung wide open on the question of Byrnes's finances. The public was demanding to know how a police chief had acquired so much wealth, regardless if Thomas MacGregor existed or not. And though Roosevelt apologized for the errant publication, he immediately set out to capitalize on the ground swell of public opinion and demanded that Byrnes go on the public record to explain his financial situation. Just to settle the matter once and for all, Theodore urged with a wink and a smile.

The mere threat of going under oath to answer his financial dealings was all it took for the heavyweight Byrnes to topple. The untouchable—the most important and prominent man in the entire police force—decided on the spot to stand down.

Byrnes retired on May 28th, nine days after Theodore had made the declaration to Lodge that the corrupt police chief had to go. All it had taken was for someone to stand up to the kingpin of police corruption and ask him to make a public statement on his finances.

The announcement was a major blow to the force. To the rank-and-file, it was a devastating act of epic proportions. Grown men were seen with tears rolling down their faces, hugging and consoling one another. Their leader, their stalwart, their captain, was now gone. On the day Byrnes left the precinct for good, almost the entire force lined the hallway to bid him a farewell, all angry that such a good man had been forced out so disrespectfully. One man, shocked that the captain was no longer the leader, remarked that the world had to be coming to an end.[22]

But the world did not end. "Men stopped and stood to watch him go, silent, respectful, and sad," Lincoln Steffens wrote, "and the next day the world went on as usual."[23]

Theodore was not done and the same week he forced another emblematic retirement. This time it was inspector "Clubber" Williams, the callous man who claimed he had made his millions in Japanese real estate. Lincoln Steffens recalled the event.

A few days later, TR threw up the second-story window, leaned out, and yelled his famous cowboy call, "Hi yi yi." . . .

I hurried over to his office, and there in the hall stood Williams, who glared as usual at me with eyes that looked like clubs. I passed on in to TR, who bade me sit down on a certain chair in the back of the room. Then he summoned Williams and fired him; that is to say, he forced him to retire. It was done almost without words. Williams had been warned; the papers were all ready. He "signed there," rose, turned and looked at me, and disappeared.[24]

The coerced retirements of Byrnes and Williams jolted the entire city of New York.[25] "The work of reforming the force was half done," Theodore exalted, "because it was well begun."[26] Roosevelt appointed Peter Conlin, an unobtrusive man of virtue, as the new police chief. Though Conlin was well liked and trusted by the men in the force, nobody doubted that Theodore was now the true authority.[27]

Roosevelt scored a great achievement with the removal of Williams and Byrnes. But he now knew he had to find a way to lead the rank-and-file, the same men that had recently paid fifty dollars each to ensure that Theodore did not have the legal authority to reorganize their force. Theodore appreciated that his actions had shaken the force, signaling that change was imminent. Now it was time to capitalize.

"It was all breathless and sudden," Lincoln Steffens wrote of Theodore's first few days on the job. "It was just as if we three were the police board, T.R., Riis, and I. . . ."[28]

In many ways, the police board was indeed Theodore Roosevelt and the two reporters, Jacob Riis and Lincoln Steffens.[29] Theodore appreciated that he was combating a deeply engrained culture of corruption without any real administrative authority to enforce discipline. He also knew that his bombastic actions, coupled with the citizens of New York City's desire for reform, gave the press ample opportunity for sensational stories. His most effective weapon for reform was publicity and he decided to use it forcefully with a grand scare tactic, taking his message directly to the streets, where the spoils of corruption were most rampant.[30]

Shortly after two in the morning on June 7th, 1895 Roosevelt and Riis stepped onto the stoop outside of the Union League

Club. Roosevelt turned the collar of his coat up and pulled his hat low. Then he bolted down Fifth Avenue. The world around him was dark and sinister. This hour in the morning belonged to drunks, thieves and prostitutes.

Riis and Roosevelt would walk as far south as Twenty-Seventh Street—over a mile—before they would encounter their first policeman.[31] At one point, Roosevelt and Riis were standing outside a late-night diner when the owner came out and peered down the deserted street, ironically quipping, "where in thunder does that copper sleep?"[32]

Later that morning Riis and Roosevelt approached two patrolmen shooting the bull outside a liquor store. "Why don't you two men patrol your post?" Roosevelt asked, which was responded to by a threat of bodily harm. "I am Commissioner Roosevelt!" Theodore shouted in response. The loiterers looked puzzled before bolting away in a sprint, no doubt stunned that the head of the police commission was patrolling at such an hour.[33]

On Second Avenue, Roosevelt saw a patrolman sprawled out on a butter tub "snoring so loud that you could hear him across the street." Roosevelt ran up to the sleeping cop, and got right in his face, "Is that the way you patrol your post?" The cop, awakened from a deep sleep and drooling, was the most bit annoyed. "Come now, get a hustle on before I dump you!" Theodore introduced himself and ordered the freshly awakened officer to the headquarters building later in the morning.[34]

On another occasion, Theodore saw a patrolman chatting with a prostitute, and inquired "Officer, is this the way you attend to your duty?"[35]

"What are you looking for, trouble?" the policeman retorted, then pointed to his nightstick in hand, "You see that street? Now run along, or I'll fan you and I'll fan you hard." To prove his manhood, the cop then turned to the prostitute, "Shall I fan him, Mame?"

"Fan him hard," was the hustler's reply.

"Oh no, officer, you will neither fan me hard or easy," Theodore barked, skinning his teeth, leaning in with his chin out. "I am police commissioner Roosevelt and instead of fanning anybody, you report at headquarters at 9:30 o'clock."[36]

Arriving back at Mulberry Street with the rising sun, Roosevelt was exhausted. But he had one hell of a good story to tell and the newspapers, on cue, dramatized his midnight patrols:

New York World: TRIALS ARE TRIALS NOW: NAUGHTY POLICEMEN FIND A BIG DIFFERENCE IN THE NEW BOARD'S METHODS

Journal: SLY POLICEMEN CAUGHT BY SLYER ROOSEVELT

New York Advertiser: TURN THEM OUT: POLICE BOARD WILL GIVE NO QUARTER TO TAMMANY RASCALS: "OLD SYSTEM" DOOMED.[37]

The *Washington Star* warned the men on the force "to memorize Roosevelt's features so as to be prepared for trouble whenever teeth and spectacles came out of the darkness."[38]

On June 14th, Roosevelt again took to his small hours patrol, this time convoyed with Richard Harding Davis, a correspondent of *Harpers Monthly*. Making their way by pale gaslight, the three men happened upon William Rath, who had "forsook his beat for an oyster saloon."[39] The *Excise Herald* captured the two-in-the-morning dialogue:

Roosevelt: Why aren't you on your post, officer?
Rath: What the—is it to you?
Man at the Counter: You gotta good nerve, comin' in here and interferin' with an officer.
Roosevelt: I'm Commissioner Roosevelt.
Rath: Yes, you are. You're Grover Cleveland and Mayor Strong all in a bunch, you are. Move on now, or —
Man at the Counter: Shut up, Bill, it's His Nibs, sure, don't you spot his glasses?
Roosevelt: Go to your post at once.
[EXIT patrolman, running][40]

Without a doubt, the highlight of the midnight patrols took place when Theodore visited the station house bathroom and emerged snickering like a school boy. On the wall was a graffiti sketch of him prowling the streets, teeth and spectacles on full display. It was a clear sign that his scare tactic was working. He was as honored as he could be.[41]

Theodore was the talk of New York, the one-man show, the popular night crusader of justice. "We have had Napoleons of finance, Napoleons of the banana trade, and Napoleons of the pulpit," shouted the *New York Journal*. "Now we have a Napoleon of the police!"[42] The *World* wrote a glowing feature story: "We have a real Police Commissioner. His name is Theodore Roosevelt. His teeth are big and white, his eyes are small and piercing, his voice is rasping. He makes our policemen feel as the little froggies did when the stork came to rule them."[43] The friendly press dubbed him "Haroun el Roosevelt," after Haroun el Raschid, "the caliph of Baghdad who had walked incognito at night through the city of the Tigris a thousand years earlier."[44]

Roosevelt would state that he only conducted his nocturnal excursions simply "to see exactly what the men were doing," to manage by wandering around.[45] But he undoubtedly knew that citizens were yearning for a good story and he met their need with feats that made for wonderful headlines. Newspapers in Philadelphia and Baltimore told of Roosevelt's actions. The *Chicago Times-Herald* called Roosevelt the "most interesting man in public life."[46] Immediately, there was a nationwide discussion that he was on the path to the presidency and the Ithaca *Daily News* declared Roosevelt its candidate for the 1896 presidential campaign.[47]

The uptick in presidential chatter impelled Lincoln Steffens and Jacob Riis to ponder Theodore's aspirations. One afternoon, in the lull of the day, the three men were chatting nonchalantly when Riis innocently put forth the question of the presidency. Theodore reared his head back as if he were a cornered bull moose and charged. "It was frightening," Lincoln Steffens recalled of Theodore's instant reaction.

TR leaped to his feet, ran around his desk, and fists clenched, teeth bared, he seemed about to strike or throttle Riis, who cowered away, amazed.

"Don't you dare ask me that," TR yelled at Riis. "Don't you put such ideas into my head. No friend of mine would ever say a thing like that, you—you—"

Riis's shocked face or TR's recollection that he had few friends as devoted as Jake Riis halted him. He backed away, came up again to Riis, and put his arm over his shoulder. Then he beckoned me close and in an awed tone of voice explained.

"Never, never, you must never either of you ever remind a man at work on a political job that he may be president. It almost always kills him politically. He loses his nerve; he can't do his work; he gives up the very traits that are making him a possibility. I, for instance, I am going to do great things here, hard things that require all the courage, ability, work that I am capable of, and I can do them if I think of them alone. But if I get to thinking about what it might lead to—"

". . . I must be wanting to be president. Every young man does. But I won't let myself think of it; I must not, because if I do, I will begin to work for it, I'll be careful, calculating, cautious in word and act, and so—I'll beat myself. See?"

Again he looked at us as if we were his enemies; then he threw us away from him and went back to his desk.

"Go on away, now," he said, "and don't you ever mention the—don't you ever mention that to me again."[48]

According to Augustine Costello, an NYPD commentator in the 1880s, the public's perception of the New York policeman was, "[that of] a bloated, drunken, ugly fellow, who depends on graft and political influence to retain his sinecure situation and who perfunctorily does his sixty minutes to the hour from pay day to pay day and from one blackmailed rum hole to another."[49]

Roosevelt disagreed with this assessment. "It is useless to tell me that these men are bad," he wrote. "They are naturally first-rate men. There are no better men anywhere than the men of the New York police force; and when they go bad it is because the system is wrong, and because they are not given the chance to do the good work they can do and would rather do."[50]

To lead these good men, Roosevelt knew he had to change the system. It started and ended with merit. "The first fight I made was to keep politics absolutely out of the force," Roosevelt would write, "and not only politics, but every kind of improper favoritism."[51]

His night patrols had seized the attention of the police force, but real leadership would require the implementation of managerial standards to change the system—nearly the same vitally important administrative requirements of reform that he had learned while in the civil service bureau.

Immediately, he centralized control measures to reduce political influence on police matters. He promoted the creation and training of special squads. He set new mandatory literacy and physical fitness requirements. He created the school of pistol practice, which became the first police academy. He insisted on sealed bids for contracts. He put new emphasis on rigorous budgetary management, where all monies had to be accounted for and documented. He instituted a hiring process from a set of standardized job descriptions.[52] And he introduced technology innovations to the force in the form of the telephone and the Bertillon system of criminal identification.[53]

To inspire the rank-and-file, Roosevelt instituted procedures for awarding medals of gallantry. The awards had two benefits, recognizing officer achievement and providing weight for promotion. For the first time ever, policemen were now incentivized for their actions, for actually doing work that advanced the cause of the force. "During our two years' service," Roosevelt boasted, "we found it necessary over a hundred times to single out men for special mention because of some feat of heroism."[54]

He also made a symbolic change by hiring a woman. THE POLICE BOARD'S NEW PRESIDENT CREATES SENSATION IN MULBERRY STREET — WOMAN SUCCEEDS MEN, *the World* shrieked."[55] The young lady was Minnie Gertrude Kelly, whose abilities were indisputable. But not only had Roosevelt hired Kelly; he gave her the job descriptions that had belonged to *two* men. It signaled both a move towards efficiency, as well as a symbolic gesture regarding gender capabilities. The woman could do the job of two men. Kelly became a star, her image inspirationally sketched in the newspapers.[56]

Perhaps Roosevelt's greatest act took place when he acted to end religious preferential treatment and hired numerous Yiddish-speaking Jewish policemen who understood the culture on the Lower East Side.[57] When Rector Ahlwardt, an anti-Semitic preacher from Berlin, visited New York to spew a hate-filled crusade against Jews, the New York Jewish community pleaded with Roosevelt to prevent Ahlwardt from speaking and, at a minimum, refuse any police protection.[58] Instead, Roosevelt sent an entirely Jewish contingent of forty officers to the event and as Ahlwardt disgorged wickedness from the lectern, New York's finest Jewish men were protecting him. "The proper thing to do was make him look ridiculous," Roosevelt wrote with pride.[59]

Roosevelt's outlook on diversity permeated the force. It was merit that mattered; not race, not religion, not gender, not social status. A reporter recounted an incident at 300 Mulberry where a cop was frustrated with a child who was crying hysterically because the young boy was lost. Theodore ran to the commotion.

"What's the matter," Roosevelt barked animatedly.

"I don't know whether this boy is Italian, German, or Yiddish," said the frustrated officer, not too worried about the boy's plight but the headache of getting the street rat home.

"That makes no difference," Theodore blasted, "The hearts of Italian, German, and Yiddish mothers are all the same. If you don't want to break one of the three get this boy home as soon as possible!"[60] Roosevelt then turned and stormed off.

Many in the police force felt that Theodore's actions were done to promote his own political ambition, arguing that he was solely interested in publicity. His next act proves this to be untrue. Rather than bask in the great publicity that he had garnered, Theodore decided to enforce the unpopular Sunday Excise Law that outlawed the sale of alcohol on the Sabbath. To the common New Yorker, it seemed that Roosevelt had become drunk on power. This was not reform. This was an intrusion of personal freedom, and in a matter of days, Theodore went from loved to loathed.

The Excise Law had been on the books for quite some time, but it had never been enforced. It was this lackluster administration of the law, Theodore believed, that enabled the machine to raise enormous sums of money by selectively deciding which violations to enforce.[61] Roosevelt was not a prohibitionist. In his mind, the law was the law and so long as the law was on the books, it was his job to enforce it.

"My task, therefore," he later exclaimed, "was really simple."[62]

The issue was nowhere near as black and white as Theodore viewed it. When he ordered officers to shut down saloons on Sunday, the city erupted in rage.[63] Rather than take the politically astute stance and reverse his decision, Theodore doubled down and closed more saloons.

The hardworking German Americans, who loved their family gatherings at the Sunday beer gardens where they danced to live music, were the most angered by Theodore's actions and took to the streets in thousands, protesting raucously. So vitriolic did the issue become that a mail bomb was sent to Roosevelt's office. It detonated en route and nobody was hurt. Of the bomb, Theodore simply called it a "cheap thing."[64]

Dry Sundays sent citizens, money in hand, fleeing the city for Coney Island just to get a beer. It was claimed that half a million mugs of beer were sold on one Sunday afternoon alone. "East Side, West Side, all around the town, yesterday went King Roosevelt I, ruler of New York and patron saint of dry Sundays," blasted the *Evening Journal.*[65]

Roosevelt's popularity was gone, his goodwill obliterated. He was the most hated man in large pockets of the city. "The outcry against me at the moment is tremendous," he wrote Henry

Cabot Lodge. "The *World, Herald Sun, Journal* and *Advertiser* are shrieking with rage."[66]

Again, it was an election year, and again, Roosevelt's actions were splitting his own party. He was accused of waging war against beer drinkers—"[holding a] grudge against Irish-Americans and German-Americans," a newspaper claimed—a traditionally solid Republican voting bloc.[67] The chairman of the Republican County Committee issued a decree trying to divorce Roosevelt's actions from the GOP, stating that the Republican Party "was not in any way responsible for Rooseveltism."[68]

Mayor Strong told Theodore to "let up on the saloon" or step down.[69] Roosevelt did neither and put Strong in the same position as he had President Harrison: damned if he fired him and damned if he did not. Firing Theodore meant that Strong was weak on reform; keeping him meant that Strong was disenfranchising a large portion of his party's base.

"I would rather see this administration turned out for enforcing laws than see it succeed for violating them," Roosevelt proclaimed.[70] "I do not deal with public sentiment. I deal with the law. . . . Woe be to the policeman who exposes himself to the taint of corruption."[71]

When the city-wide elections were tallied, it was estimated that an astounding eighty percent of the Republican German American vote defected to the Democratic ticket. The Tammany candidates running on the anti-Roosevelt platform were elected in landslides. Two things were clear: beer mattered in elections and, at least in the short run, Theodore's actions had empowered the political enemy.[72]

The morning after the election, Roosevelt, still determined, called together his precinct captains and confirmed his stance: "The board will not tolerate the slightest relaxation of the enforcement of the laws, and notably the Excise Law."[73]

But why did Roosevelt take such an unpopular position on an issue that he himself did not fully embrace? After all, he was no teetotaler and, as an assemblyman a decade prior, he voted against prohibition, warning, "that no more terrible curse could be inflicted on this community than the passage of a prohibitory law. . . . It is idle to hope for the enforcement of a law where nineteen-twentieths of the people do not believe in the justice of its provisions."[74]

Against his initial stance, Roosevelt now defended his action by stating that the excise situation was "perennially serious and difficult . . . one of the chief reasons for police blackmail and corruption."[75] It was his obligation to enforce the law. The men with pull were the ones that were benefiting from blackmail and the only way to deal with it, according to Theodore, "was to enforce the law."[76]

Roosevelt's explanation makes it clear that he had not sensed his environment or the sentiment of the people he was trying to lead. He had yet to master the art of political leadership.

The Sunday saloons were a social network in the immigrant neighborhoods, a place not just for drinks, but a safe haven to vote, of fellowship, to get a loan, to use a telephone, to play cards, to gossip, to complain about politicians, to complain about a boss, to meet the new son-in-law, to find a wife, to leave a wife. The saloon was the working man's union, the working man's social club. The Sunday beer was opportunity to leave the hellacious work week behind, to forget about life for a while. Getting drunk with friends and family was a form of therapy, described as the "favorite recreation of poor immigrant men."[77]

While Roosevelt tried to crack down on corruption and racketeering, he was instead penalizing the laborer. He was completely blinded by his hard devotion to the law, unable to see how his actions could be perceived from a faction of people that he had never known, the German and Irish beer drinkers. Theodore only saw the issue from his vantage point as police commissioner and expected everyone to appreciate his moral stance.

"The howl that rose [against me] was deafening," Theodore confirmed.[78]

As 1895 came to an end, rumors circulated that Mayor Strong had formally asked Theodore to step down. Both men denied the allegations, but had Theodore offered, Strong would have certainly consented.[79]

But another problem was developing for Roosevelt. Just as it happened with Postmaster General John Wanamaker, Roosevelt had found an enemy in his own organization, in his own inner circle. From the start, Theodore's actions had dwarfed everyone on the board, and the more unpopular Theodore became the more power board member Andrew Parker amassed.

Andrew Parker grew his authority by backstabbing Roosevelt among the rank-and-file, the common patrolman who was wary of Theodore's midnight patrols. While Theodore was out front in the press spotlight, Parker was behind the scenes, quietly telling those in the detective bureau that Theodore was abusing his power and needed to be replaced. Emboldened by the support of the patrolmen, Parker began to publically challenge Theodore at board meetings, "just to see the big bomb splutter, the boss leader of men blow up."[80]

A newspaper editor had warned Theodore that Andrew Parker was "a snake in the grass, and sooner or later, he will smite you."[81] A ward worker had warned Theodore that Parker "could not be trusted . . . that he was not loyal to him as head of the Commission."[82] Theodore refused to believe the rumors and carried on with his business as usual.

"It is impossible that two men like Mr. Roosevelt and Mr. Parker should long travel the same road," Lincoln Steffens reported in the *Evening Post.* "They run on radically divergent tracks. Mr. Parker fights secretively, by choice, while Roosevelt seeks the open. . . . Parker rushes swiftly to the punishment of any man. Roosevelt seeks ever a chance to reward and praise. Both are able and obstinate men. . . . There is war and nothing but war in prospect."[83]

Parker made a public spectacle of the hostility, and the feud was aired out like dirty laundry. The press loved the drama. At one meeting, city comptroller, Ashbel P. Fitch, objected to a budgetary expenditure. Roosevelt defended the expenditure, but egged on by Parker, thought his manhood had been called into question.[84] The *New York Tribune* printed the event.

Fitch: I would never run away from you.
Roosevelt: You would not fight—

Fitch: What shall it be, pistols or—
Roosevelt: Pistols or anything you wish.
Mayor Strong: Come, come. If this does not stop, I will put
you both under arrest.[85]

Never one to walk away from a fight, Theodore pushed even
harder on the Excise Law, which in turn made him even more
unpopular with the public. Soon he demand that other "Blue
Laws" be enforced, and soda fountains, florists, and delicatessens
were also shut down on the Sabbath.

"The law will be enforced in every particular," Roosevelt
shouted as he shut down a soda parlor.[86] The *Times* ran an
article about a peddler who was arrested for selling flowers to
a detective.[87] The *Evening World* made up a silly story about a
mother, who sought ice for her sick child on a Sunday morning and was arrested along with the shop keeper. The mother
was unable to get ice for her little sick darling and went home
to find that her child had died. The inference was simple:
Roosevelt's needless enforcement of the law had killed a
child who needed ice.[88] The public grew angrier with Lord
Roosevelt's actions and another parcel bomb was sent to Theodore, and again it was intercepted, this time by detectives.
Had it been opened, the sheer amount of Chinese gunpowder
in the package would have killed him dead before his body hit
the floor.[89]

The entire situation had become profoundly dysfunctional:
two mail bombs, the insinuation that Theodore was responsible
for a shortage of ice that led to the death of a child, and a grown
member of the police board backstabbing Theodore just to see
him get angry. About the only thing that was clear was that the
police board was in turmoil.

Theodore played the integral role in creating the environment of dysfunction, and his righteous stand on the Excise Law,
coupled with the infighting on the board, made it look like he
was a lost leader. His reform agenda had been derailed; it had all
become a circus act, with the focus on Theodore the man and
not on the crusade for good government. Pondering his situation
in the spring of 1896, Theodore admitted to "hours of profound
depression."[90]

Confronting his perceived failure, Roosevelt reflected to Lodge, "It really seems that there *must* be some fearful shortcoming on my side to account for the fact that I have not one New York City newspaper, nor one New York City politician of note on my side." But in true Rooseveltian grit, he concluded, "Don't think that I even for a moment dream of abandoning my fight; I shall continue absolutely unmoved from my present course and shall accept philosophically whatever violent end may be put to my political career."[91]

The violent end to his political career never came about. But it was brutally clear that Theodore had yet to understand political leadership, the ability to lead those who disagreed with him, to make meaningful changes at the margin. He tried to rid the world of evil between sunrise and sunset and it almost cost him his career.

Thankfully, the presidential election of 1896 would save him from himself.

The national election of 1896 is considered one of the most transformative in American history. The Republican Party had settled on William McKinley, a Civil War veteran, former governor of Ohio, and acquaintance of Theodore Roosevelt. Theodore was worried about McKinley's Old Guard tendencies as well as his incessant need for compromise. "He is not a strong man," Theodore wrote his sister, ". . . I should feel rather uneasy about him in a serious crisis, whether it took the form of a soft-money craze, a gigantic labor riot, or danger of foreign conflict."[92] But McKinley's timidity was pale in comparison to the much larger hazard rising up from the nation's interior: the populist crusade of William Jennings Bryan.

William Jennings Bryan moved masses with words. Nicknamed the Boy Orator of the Platte, Bryan was a man of unending personal magnetism, the present day poster-child of populism. A fervent Presbyterian and Democrat, Bryan lambasted eastern money and preyed on the tenets of class warfare, consistently flirting with anarchistic rhetoric. Bryan was an effective enemy of the gold standard—"You shall not crucify mankind upon a cross of gold!" He viscerally moved the excitable throng of Americans sensitive to the injustices of the day.[93] In an era of labor and economic tumult—the Haymarket bombing of 1886, the Homestead rioting of 1892, the Pullman Strike of 1894—Bryan gave a radical voice to the laborer and the poor—anyone who felt that the government was not working for him.

During the 1896 campaign, the greatest orator of the nineteenth century travelled thousands of miles and addressed millions of Americans in person. McKinley's strategy, dubbed the "front-porch campaign," held that the candidate should stay in Canton, Ohio, while his manager, Mark Hanna, raised money and surrogates spoke on his behalf. McKinley's strategy left the countryside wide open for Bryan to barnstorm from town after town and whip up the frenzied masses. As the Populist movement continued to grow and anti-establishment fervor consumed the West, it was clear that the election was going to be a dog fight.

To Roosevelt, Bryan was a populist agitator, not a leader, and the election represented the "greatest crisis" since the Civil War.[94] In July of 1896 Roosevelt offered his services to campaign manager Mark Hanna. Hanna appreciated Roosevelt's appeal in the nation's interior and knew that Theodore could, in the words of one historian, "explain the complexities of the Gold Standard in terms a cowboy could understand."[95]

Taking a leave of absence from the dysfunctional environment on Mulberry Street, Roosevelt hit the campaign trail with vigor and enthusiasm. The nation's prominent outdoorsman was a big draw, at least in cities where he was not banning the sale of alcohol. The middle of the county embraced Roosevelt's zeal to fight corruption. When they read about the Sunday excise tax debacle in the papers they viewed it as a crusader's quest to end corruption. Thirteen thousand showed up to hear him speak in the Chicago Coliseum and it was Theodore—the beloved Teddy—who was responsible for, according to *The Chicago Tribune*, "the most remarkable political gathering of the campaign in this city."[96]

Though Roosevelt was afraid of a Bryan presidency, he, more importantly, wanted to get back to Washington as a political appointee in the McKinley administration. His daily activities prior to the

Republican convention—when he was also consumed in the affairs of police commission reform—highlight that Theodore's mind was wandering into naval affairs.

February: Dined with Captain Alfred Thayer Mahan to discuss naval matters

March: Wrote a critique of Secretary of the Navy Abner Herbert's annual message

April: Reached out to German Diplomat Speck von Sternburg to discuss German naval strategy

May: Read a book on Admiral James and spent a "rather naval week" aboard the *USS Indiana* and the *USS Montgomery*[97]

On Election Day, 1896, McKinley received only half a million more votes than Bryan and only carried twenty-three states to Bryan's twenty-two. But the electoral vote victory was solid: 271 to 176. For Roosevelt, the national Populist crises had been diverted and, more importantly, he could now call upon the president-elect for the opportunity he had coveted since he first heard the stories of the Bulloch uncles: to run the United States Navy.

No doubt the last few months of Roosevelt's time as police commissioner bordered on failure. He had proven that he had not learned how to discern which action would be politically hazardous; that is to say, which fights to pick, and which fights to let be. But if evaluated on the aggregate of his actions, it was Roosevelt who first began to eradicate corruption in the New York police force and set it on the path to becoming the modern force it is today. "It's tough on the force," a police officer told Lincoln Steffens of Theodore's departure, "for he was dead square . . . and we needed him in the business."[98]

Theodore also grew personally. His time as police commissioner was his first experience in executive leadership. He learned what it meant to have every word observed, every action dissected—to be applauded unjustly, questioned unfairly. His actions appeared in almost every newspaper; he was on stage every day.[99] An executive must have command of the theater, he learned, complete with a clear vision and the willingness to take the heat for decisive action. His critics tore him up, a lesson which strengthened his resolve. He learned the importance of mitigating a dissenter in his inner-circle—Andrew Parker—and the requirement to surround oneself with people that would challenge him privately, not publicly. Most importantly, he learned that leadership is lonely. The person in the arena, the one who strives to be a leader of consequence, must be willing to take criticism and continue to fight on.

"We need fearless criticism of our public men. . ." Theodore wrote, ". . . but it behooves every man to remember that the work of the critic is of altogether secondary importance, and that, in the end, progress is accomplished by the man who does things and not by the man who talks about how they ought or ought not to be done."[100]

During his turbulent days as police commissioner, Roosevelt met Bram Stoker, the author of *Dracula*. Stoker was impressed with Theodore's ironclad courage amidst the political firestorm. This was a man different from others, Stoker sensed. "Must be president someday," Stoker wrote in his diary, "A man you can't cajole, can't frighten, can't buy."[101]

14. ASSISTANT SECRETARY OF THE NAVY

"IF I CAN ONLY GO OUT OF OFFICE WITH THE KNOWLEDGE THAT I have done what lay in my power to avert this terrible calamity I shall be the happiest man in the world," President McKinley told outgoing President Cleveland, the night before McKinley entered the White House. The terrible calamity was the issue of war with Spain over the island of Cuba.[1]

When McKinley was inaugurated on March 4th, 1897, there were many reasons that the Cuban topic was on the national conscience. The chief driver was humanitarian. Since 1492, when Christopher Columbus claimed Cuba as property of the Kingdom of Spain, the Spanish had ruled the fertile island with a strict adherence to colonialism. The entire history of nineteenth-century Cuba is a continuous stream of sporadic revolutionary uprisings as Cuban nationals sought equality through independence. But it was not until February 24th, 1895, that the *Guerra de Independecia*—the War of Independence—was declared. Journalists, plantation workers, and rebels united to overthrow the Spanish stronghold on the small island.

The under-matched Spanish government moved swiftly and brutally to smash the revolution. While Theodore was making his midnight patrols on the police force, Spanish General Valeriano Weyler y Nicolau put the entire island under martial law and implemented a Reconcentrado Policy which forced civilians to move into concentration camps controlled by the Spanish army. The policy was a disaster. Perhaps as high as one-third of Cuba's citizens—somewhere between 200,000 and 400,000 civilians—died from lack of nutrition and dreadful sanitary conditions.[2] As the atrocities were reported in the American press, the public was left to question whether America should intervene. Would America "look idly on while hundreds of thousands of innocent human beings, women and children, and old men, die of hunger close to our doors?"[3] Senator George Hoar asked the country. Theodore, the moral advocate, shared the same sentiment, "Cuba was at our very doors. It was a dreadful thing for us to sit supinely and watch her death agony. It was our duty, even more from the standpoint of National honor than from the standpoint of National interest, to stop the devastation and destruction."[4]

The root of the humanity question in Cuba was in the complex question of America's role in international affairs at the dawn of the twentieth century. By 1897, a new generation of young Americans was just now coming into leadership positions in entertainment, law, business, and politics. This generation, born at the beginning of the Civil War, grew up in a nation divided. When they were children, their families had been decimated and slaughtered; they witnessed two presidents assassinated—Lincoln and Garfield—in a span of sixteen years on account of political tumult; they watched as Reconstruction policies morphed into a corrupt spoils system which created gangster-like animosity in politics; they witnessed government policies spur economic growth in the North while the South's economy was left to flounder—exacerbating the truth that unity across the Mason-Dixie line had been completed in law, but not in spirit.

This entire generation had simply never known American patriotism, or its awesome power. This generation craved for America to take the mantle of global leadership, to give the country something to cheer about.

Since the Monroe Doctrine of 1823, no European government was allowed to colonize land or interfere with states in the western hemisphere. Spanish colonization in Cuba had been exempt. For Roosevelt, and other likeminded leaders, world supremacy could not be achieved so long as there was a European influence in the western hemisphere. The time had come, as Henry Cabot Lodge put it, "[to] make up our minds whether we are to be dominant in the western hemisphere and keep it free from foreign invasion or whether we are to stand aside. . . ."[5]

A third propelling factor for war was the remarkable growth of the American economy. By the mid-1880s, just twenty years after the Civil War ended, America was the world leader in meat, timber, coal, gold, iron, and steel production.[6] By 1893, only Great Britain was trading more goods and services.[7] As the American population doubled in the last forty years of the nineteenth century, American exports tripled, and the idea of "disposable income" and "millionaires" became relevant in society. America's greatest asset, its entrepreneurs, were leading the world in technology, putting to market a slew of amazing inventions: "turbines, internal-combustion engines, railway air brakes, telephones, phonographs, alternating current, incandescent electric light bulbs, automobiles, cinematography, aeronautics, and radio telegraphy."[8] The economic boom was so spectacular that five of the top eleven richest Americans of all time were born in the five year span from 1834 to 1839: John D. Rockefeller, 1839; Andrew Carnegie, 1835; Frederick Weyerhaeuser, 1834; Marshall Field, 1834; and, of course, Jay Gould, 1836.[9]

America in 1897 was resource rich in commodity production, transportation, steel, oil, finance, and entrepreneurs.[10] But had the country lost its moral compass in the pursuit of wealth? The question was floating around every pool hall and classroom, every church and saloon.

For quite some time, Theodore had tried to influence the debate through his books and writings that promoted a frontiersman mentality. Theodore worried that American citizens, coveting wealth and not security, had become blinded by prosperity and were unwilling to accept the maxim that economic strength must be secured with military power. The desire to safeguard national interests with a strong foreign policy made Roosevelt a target to his critics, who labeled him a "jingo," a derogatory term for those who advocated nationalism through force alone.

Regardless of one's belief, whether it be humanitarian, patriotic, or economic, the thorny issue of naval preparedness was *essential* to potentially go to war with Spain over Cuba. The likes of Mahan and Roosevelt had long since warned of the dangers of a supreme world economy protected by a dilapidated navy. While the post-Civil War U.S. economy was booming, the navy ranked sixth in the world behind Great Britain, France, Italy, Russia, and

Germany. As the American people looked beyond their borders, the question was increasingly posed: Could the American economy, now dependent on foreign exports, be quickly crippled in a war of the oceans by a well prepared enemy navy?[11]

America's unique debate of humanitarian, economic, patriotic, and military preparation had given Theodore a purpose for his next career move. His convictions, his morality, his character, and his pursuit of notable leadership, all converged onto the issue of Cuba. It was morally right to help the women and children of the island; a war would rebuild the navy; a powerful navy could sustain American world dominance; and, rather conveniently, a battle could provide the backdrop for notable military heroism. Roosevelt coveted the idea of leading America to the next frontier—it was as if his entire life had been preparing him for this opportunity, for this time.

"I am quietly a rampant 'Cuba Libre' man," Theodore wrote in a private letter on January 2nd, 1897—two months and two days before President McKinley was inaugurated. The time was now, according to him, to "recognize Cuba's independence and interfere; sending our fleet promptly to Havana."[12]

Conflict was the last thing that McKinley wanted. "We want no wars of conquest," he spoke at his inauguration, ". . . War should never be entered upon until *every* agency of peace has failed; peace is preferable to war in almost every contingency."[13] A decorated Civil War veteran McKinley was even more adamant in private. "I have been through one war; I have seen the dead piled up; and I do not want to see another!"[14] he screamed one night. In a private meeting with Carl Schurz, he lost formality and shouted, "There will be no jingo nonsense under my administration!"[15]

On November 30th, just three weeks after the presidential election, Henry Cabot Lodge went to Canton, Ohio, to meet with the president-elect about Theodore Roosevelt. McKinley started the meeting off by expressing his detest for war before Lodge, in the utmost of irony, changed the subject to Roosevelt. "I have no right to ask a personal favor of you, but I do ask for Roosevelt as the one personal favor," Lodge pleaded to McKinley.[16] Lodge relayed McKinley's reaction back to Theodore:[17]

He spoke of you with great regard for your character and your services and he would like to have you in Washington. The only question he asked me was this, which I give you: "I hope he has no preconceived plans which he would wish to drive through the moment he got in.[18]

Lodge knew Roosevelt wanted war and wanted it yesterday. McKinley, perhaps sensing Lodge's insincerity on the matter, did not agree to make Theodore an offer on the spot. Worried about McKinley's hesitancy, Lodge organized a lobbying campaign on behalf of Roosevelt that included John Hay, Speaker of the House Thomas Reed, Judge William Howard Taft, and Vice-President-elect Garret Hobart.

"I want peace," McKinley told a Roosevelt supporter, "and I am told that your friend Theodore—whom I know only slightly—is always getting into rows with everybody. I am afraid he is too pugnacious."

"Give him a chance," the friend pleaded paradoxically, "to prove that he can be peaceful."[19]

As the days passed, the silence on Theodore's nomination became more perplexing. Why had the heavy weights—Lodge, Hay, Taft, Reed, and Hobart—all not been able to secure a place for Theodore? Lodge began to speculate, rightfully, that somebody was working against Theodore's appointment.

Senator Thomas Platt, the leader of the New York State Republican machine, did not want Roosevelt appointed to the assistant secretary of the navy and voiced his concerns directly to McKinley. Platt was not worried that Roosevelt would take the country into war but rather that Roosevelt would interfere with Platt's business arrangements at the Brooklyn Navy Yard—known as "Mr. Platt's Yard." Platt had seen firsthand how Roosevelt fought corruption in the New York Assembly and how he had chosen the law over profit when he banned the sale of alcohol as the President of the Police Board. For Platt, it was Theodore's crackdown on party patronage that was bothersome, not his jingo tendencies.

When Lodge discovered that Platt was working against him, he advised Roosevelt to meet with the machine boss immediately and work out a truce.[20]

Roosevelt and Platt met privately, coming to an undisclosed compromise. The implicit counter argument that Theodore no doubt presented was that if he stayed on as police commissioner, he would remain on Platt's turf and could still come down on the old man's activities throughout New York in an instant. If Theodore were in Washington, DC, he would be out of the machine's way. After the meeting, a treaty was called, and Platt sent his blessings to McKinley so long as it "was not charged to him or New York,"[21] that is to say, if Theodore promised not to investigate the Brooklyn Navy Yard.

Still McKinley waffled. He was just too uncertain about Theodore's bombastic energy, too uncertain about his stance on the Cuban conflict. Ever the compromiser, McKinley deferred the decision to the newly appointed secretary of the navy, John D. Long.

John Long was exactly the man President McKinley wanted to run the navy department. An aging ex-governor of Massachusetts, Long harbored the judicial disposition of a restrained gentleman, the temperament of an elder: soft spoken, white haired, pleasantly plump, a mild hypochondriac. He even moved at the pace of molasses on account of his corn infested feet.[22] Long was, in every way, the opposite of Theodore Roosevelt.[23]

Long admitted that he liked Roosevelt but was concerned that Theodore wanted to both "fight someone at once" and try to rule the Navy from the start. "If he becomes Assistant Secretary of the Navy he will dominate the Department within six months!"[24] Roosevelt in an effort to appease Long, fired off a letter promising to be a perfect subordinate, to work hard, and do whatever possible to make the Long administration a success. Cunningly, Theodore appealed to Long, writing "I shall stay in Washington, hot weather or any weather," knowing full and well the elder Long desired to leave Washington during the heat of the summer.[25]

Evidently, the letter worked.

On the sixth day of April, six months after his first meeting with Lodge, McKinley conceded and sent the name of Theodore

Roosevelt to the senate for confirmation. On the day of confirmation *The Washington Post* warned that Theodore's appointment was "a matter of regret."

"Of course he will bring with him to Washington all that machinery of disturbance and upheaval," the *Post* declared, "which is as much a part of his *entourage* as the very air he breathes." But then the tone of the editorial switches, as if mirroring the paradoxes of the man it depicted. "He is inspired by a passionate hatred of meanness, humbug, and cowardice. He cherishes an equally passionate love of candor, bravery, and devotion. He is a fighter, a man of indomitable pluck and energy, a potent and forceful factor in any equation into which we may be introduced. A field of immeasurable usefulness awaits him—will he find it?"[26]

From the start, Theodore impressed Secretary Long. "Best man for the job," Long wrote in his diary, and followed by "entirely loyal and subordinate."[27] It is clear that Theodore astutely adhered to his boss's expectations and appreciated that Long, a simple indolent man, wanted no cause for alarm. Long's sole desire was to have the navy operate at a rate of zero turmoil. Theodore was purposeful; he knew that if he could win Long's confidence, more and more responsibility would be bestowed upon him as time wore on. So, in contrast to his running start on the Civil Service Commission and as police commissioner, Theodore was tempered and modest at the navy department. At least at the start.

The first few weeks on the job included making a trip to examine a boat and working on important, but rather monotonous, memorandums on technologically administrative matters. "His typewriters had no rest," Long recounted.[28] Theodore took such great pride in administrative intricacies and learning naval details that Long fondly exclaimed: "What is the need of my making a dropsical tub of any lobe of my brain when I have right at hand a man possessed with more knowledge than I could acquire?"[29]

Certainly Theodore harbored a passion for war preparations but he was not pugnacious in his actions. His activities were reserved, his bombastic tendencies curbed. He shrouded his agenda for war in administrative and technical memos. One memo, written his first week on the job, was sent to President McKinley and exhaustively examines battle provisions and hypothetical war maneuvers for the majority of America's naval fleet, including the *Indiana, Massachusetts, Iowa, Brooklyn, Texas, Maine, New York, Columbia, Amphitrite, Terror, Puritan, Cincinnati,* and *Raleigh.* The memo, written technically and systematically, could not be construed as jingo nonsense—just thorough preparative planning, or as Theodore explained, a "readiness for action should any complications arise in Cuba."[30]

Just in case something would happen, Mr. President.

Though Theodore plowed away at administrative duties, he was gearing up for something big. Every day at lunch he took a short walk from the state, war, and navy building—down Pennsylvania Avenue and up to Seventeenth Street—to the Metropolitan Club, a private establishment, created during the Civil War by six Treasury Department officials that had moved from New York and started "a proper city club" to further "literary, mutual improvement, and social purposes."[31] The crowd in the club was, and still is today, the "who's who" of Washington: cabinet members, diplomats, significant professors, politicians, prominent businessmen, military brass, journalists. At the turn of the century, lunch conversation focused on American expansion and what to do about Cuba. As talk of war consumed the capital, the men of power, realizing that President McKinley was noncommittal, began to wonder who would lead the cause. It is unknown whether Roosevelt chose to lead them or they chose to follow Roosevelt. What is known is that Theodore would leverage the men of the club to get action within fourteen months. Theodore would be a national war hero and two Metropolitan Club confidants, Commodore George Dewey and Leonard Wood—both of whom Theodore had not met prior to 1897 and both living in obscurity—would become two of the most famous men in America.

"In terms of their impact upon the history of the states, few meetings rise to the significance of Roosevelt's introduction to these two men," historian H. Paul Jeffers writes about the friendship between Leonard Wood, Commodore Dewey, and Theodore Roosevelt. "These meetings [at the Metropolitan Club] rank in importance with the Prussian-born General von Steuben presenting himself to George Washington at Valley Forge and offering his expertise on training soldiers, and Abraham Lincoln's first encounter with General Ulysses S. Grant. From the moment the men shook hands, the course of history and their own destinies changed."[32]

Commodore George Dewey, sixty years old, was a small sinewy man with a large, luscious white mustache and an impeccably ironed white uniform. A decorated Civil War veteran, Dewey was now in the twilight of his thirty-plus-year career in the Navy, staring down mandatory retirement in just three years. Recently he had been appointed to the important, albeit un-heroic, post as president of the Board of Inspection and Survey.[33] Dewey shared Roosevelt's dream that world power could only be achieved through sea power. He yearned for one more opportunity to get back into the battle—both to make a lasting name for himself and to usher in a new world order where America reigned supreme. He only had three years left until retirement; his time to get action was now.

Captain Leonard Wood was a young Army hero now serving as President McKinley's personal doctor. Born in Winchester, New Hampshire in 1860, Wood was tall and athletic and possessed a prominent jaw and a grave demeanor. His perfectly manicured mustache and strong eyes gave him an aura of significance that most men his age did not possess. Wood was a Harvard man who graduated four years after Roosevelt. The two men never crossed paths on the bank of the Charles River but if they had, they probably would not have been friends. Back then, Wood was interested in the world of military leadership and Theodore, at least in his first three years at Harvard, was still an insulated aristocrat. After college, Wood served as a surgeon at Boston City Hospital before receiving an appointment in the army and getting shipped out to Arizona. Shortly thereafter, he was awarded the Congressional Medal of Honor for his role in the capture of the Apache leader

Geronimo. Smart and accomplished, he was tapped to become physician and aide for President Grover Cleveland and then was kept in his post by President McKinley.[34]

Roosevelt had found in Leonard Wood and Commodore Dewey men of strength, valor, and ambition; men who wanted to change America's future. He had found fellow frontiersmen.

Theodore knew that the Cuba situation was gaining momentum but that the movement was leaderless. Certainly the topic was on the American consciousness and debated in the papers, but no leader had stood up to take a hard stand on the matter. Theodore also knew that at the end of June the navy would be releasing its all-important war planning document. To influence both—the war planning document and the American public—Theodore called on his good friend, Alfred Thayer Mahan, to get access to the stage at the Naval War College in Newport, Rhode Island. It would be Theodore's first public announcement as assistant secretary of the navy and it would be the greatest speech of his life.

The Naval War College was established in 1884 by Admiral Stephen B. Luce on Coaster's Harbor Island at Newport, Rhode Island. Its building was unassuming, formerly the city's poorhouse, but its charter was grand: "teach officers the science of their own profession—the science of war."[35] By 1897, the Naval College had become the epicenter of the debate on naval preparedness, on its grounds tacticians and strategists debated whether or not America was ready for a war against Spain.

On June 2nd, 1897, Roosevelt posed for pictures with officers of the war college, standing on the steps of the building overlooking Narragansett Bay. As the Naval Officers looked into the camera, Theodore turned his head to the left, his strong face peered out into the same bay where 121 years earlier, John Paul Jones set sail to take the American Revolution to the British. A man of history, Theodore was perhaps mentally reciting Paul's famous quote, the one supposedly shouted when his ship was sinking underneath him: "Surrender, Hell, I have not yet begun to fight!"[36] Like Theodore, Jones was a fellow frontiersman.

After the snap of the camera, the men filed into a cramped auditorium. In an unwavering voice, Theodore began his speech. His face was tight and strong, his jaw locked between sentences; a dull boom resonated when his fists pounded the podium. His words forever altered American foreign policy:[37]

A CENTURY has passed since Washington wrote, "To be prepared for war is the most effectual means to promote peace." We pay to this maxim the lip loyalty we so often pay to Washington's words; but it has never sunk deep into our hearts . . .

PREPARATION for war is the surest guaranty for peace. Arbitration is an excellent thing, but ultimately those who wish to see this country at peace with foreign nations will be wise if they place reliance upon a first-class fleet of first-class battleships rather than on any arbitration treaty which the wit of man can devise. . . .

PEACE is a goddess only when she comes with sword girt on thigh. The ship of state can be steered safely only when it is possible to bring her against any foe with "her leashed thunders gathering for the leap." A really great people, proud and high-spirited, would face all the disasters of war rather than purchase that base prosperity which is bought at the price of national honor. All the great masterful races have been fighting races, and the minute that a race loses the hard fighting virtues, then, no matter what else it may retain, no matter how skilled in commerce and finance, in science or art, it has lost its proud right to stand as the equal of the best. . . .

COWARDICE in a race, as in an individual, is the unpardonable sin, and a willful failure to prepare for any danger may in its effects be as bad as cowardice. The timid man who cannot fight, and the selfish, short-sighted, or foolish man who will not take the steps that will enable him to fight, stand on almost the same plane. . . ."[38]

The speech was as powerful as a lightning strike. He stood before the hearth of war preparations, which made it seem to the public as if he was the spokesperson of the institute, that he had support of the entire War College. The carefully crafted words were a national call to awaken the ghost of George Washington, bringing back to life the first president's important maxim: "To be prepared for war, is one of the most effectual means of preserving peace."[39] The thesis of Theodore's speech held that the navy should be prepared in an increasingly uncertain and globalized world. War was debatable, but naval preparation was not.

Strategically and systematically, Theodore laid out a brand-new foreign policy: peace required strategic preparation; diplomacy required force; the duty of Congress was to allocate funds to protect American interests—at home and abroad; the best national security for a country was a military that could quickly go on the offense; the world was changing, becoming more connected, and America must take the mantle global leadership immediately to preserve national growth in generations to come.[40]

"It was the voice of Roosevelt, and of Roosevelt alone, and it stirred the country like the sound of a trumpet," wrote journalist Joseph Bucklin.[41] The *Sun* praised the speech as a "manly, patriotic, intelligent, and convincing appeal to American sentiment on behalf of the national honor, and for the preservation of the national strength. . . ."[42] The *Herald* predicted that it would "inspire the youth of America with the same lofty spirit of devotion to our country's honor, glory and prosperity that actuated its utterance by the speaker."[43] *The Washington Post* claimed that Theodore ". . . honored both himself and the country. . . . Well done, nobly spoken!" The speech was printed in full in all the major newspapers in the country—from New York to San Francisco, from Chicago to Texas, citizens all over America were now questioning one another: do you agree with Theodore Roosevelt?[44]

It was the speech Theodore was born to give and the one that he had been rehearsing since he wrote *The Naval War of 1812*. It was everything he stood for, the theme of all of his books. The only thing that had changed was the environment in the country; Americans were now actively engaged in the debate on their country's role in international affairs.

Of all the lofty press Theodore received, it was *The New Orleans Daily Picayune* that credited Roosevelt with greatest compliment of rhetorical leadership: "[Theodore] undoubtedly voices the sentiments of the great majority of thinking people."[45]

It was clear that expansionist movement had found its leader.

John D. Long was angry. His underling's War College message that there was not "the slightest danger of an over-development of warlike spirit, and there never has been any such danger," stood in direct opposition to McKinley's wishes for "no jingo nonsense."[46] Under another boss, Roosevelt may have lost his job immediately, but Long, ever the cautious gentleman, knew that firing Roosevelt would have been a public relations fiasco. Roosevelt had tapped into the very core of the American spirit and his words had ignited passion across the country. The speech, as it was presented to the public, was a call for preparation, a call for strong leadership, not a call for aggression. Besides, what sane American would argue against the words of George Washington?

In a testament to Theodore's craftily chosen words, McKinley, upon reading the transcript of the speech, remarked to an aide, "I suspect Roosevelt is right, and the only difference between him and me is that mine is the greater responsibility."[47]

Long met privately with Theodore and requested that his subordinate temper the war rhetoric. But interestingly, the request came with no ultimatum. Theodore acknowledged Long's feelings on the matter, but promptly dismissed them. Just two days after the speech, Theodore wrote to Captain Mahan, that "he [Long] didn't like the address I made" but that the true folly was not his speech but the fact that Long was still "only lukewarm about building up our navy. . . . This is, to me, a matter of the most profound concern."[48] Theodore, rather than acknowledge that his actions were in conflict with his boss's wishes, instead urged Mahan to reach out to Long personally to persuade the secretary of the navy to their way of thinking. "I feel that you ought to write him—not immediately, but sometime not far in the future—at some length," Theodore urged Mahan, "explaining to him the vital need of more battleships now, and the vital need of continuity in our naval policy."[49]

The War College speech instantly made Theodore a national figure on the debate of war preparation. But almost as important, the speech had tested Long's authority and Theodore learned that the gentle old man wanted to avoid personal conflict at all cost. Whatever worry Long had toward Roosevelt did not prevent Long from leaving Washington DC for an extended summer leave and, in his absence, Long placed Theodore in charge of the entire navy department.

Long's actions to leave the capitol must be placed into context. During this period of American history, it was not uncommon for high-ranking government officials to leave the sweltering humid heat of a Washington summer for a several month vacation. But it was nonetheless peculiar timing for Long. As war rhetoric ran rampant across the country, Long was pruning his garden at his rural home on the South Shore of Massachusetts.

Just two weeks after the War College speech, Roosevelt was promoted to acting secretary, the "hot weather Secretary,"[50] as he called it. In the absence of his boss, Theodore was in command and in heaven; every action exuded a childlike enthusiasm. "The secretary is away and I am having immense fun running the Navy," he boasted euphorically.[51]

In the first few days in charge, one finds Theodore pouring through old naval reports looking for historical insights to leverage in the present; opening an investigation into the corruptive operations at the Brooklyn Navy Yard, against his commitment to Thomas Platt; recommending the now-common precedent that warships be named after historic American citizens, not geographical locations as was the custom; advocating the "installation of rapid-fire weaponry throughout the fleet;" and, as he had done in the Civil Service Commission, initiating a cataloging classification mechanism to reduce the burden of paperwork on the department.[52]

"I perfectly revel in the work," Theodore admitted.[53]

Over the Fourth of July weekend Theodore returned to Sagamore Hill to a cackle of "sixteen small Roosevelts," his children as well as a throng of cousins. The summer would prove influential for fifteen-year-old Franklin Delano Roosevelt, who had taken a break from the Groton School to spend his summer at Oyster Bay. Young Franklin would grow up to consider his cousin the "greatest man he ever knew" and would intentionally follow his hero's career path: Harvard College, Columbia Law School, New York legislature, assistant secretary of the navy, governor of New York, and president of the United States.[54] Perhaps it was Franklin's love of Theodore that compelled him to marry Theodore's niece, Eleanor, a homely, unattractive girl with buck teeth, who Edith Roosevelt worried had "no future."[55]

The remainder of the summer of 1897 found Theodore doing what he did best, leading on foot. As he had done at the Civil Service Commission, he left on a Midwest inspection tour of the Great Lakes Naval Militia in Detroit, Chicago, and Mackinac.[56] He also invited himself to partake in the war gaming exercises on the USS *Iowa,* the navy's newest and most impressive battleship.[57] As bells sounded and officers scattered to battle stations for target practice, Roosevelt took his place on the bridge, in the middle of the fray. The mounted eight-inch guns on the *Iowa,* when fired, shattered a floating target approximately two thousand yards away. Then the twelve-inch guns were let loose in a torrent so powerful that it knocked a steel door off its hinges and several skylights shattered.[58]

Theodore was impressed by the power and precision of the ship and did not miss the opportunity to get details. Charles H. Cramp, the engineer of the marvel battleship, recalled that amidst all the excitement, Theodore "broke the record in asking questions."[59] He grilled everyone on everything. "I have never enjoyed three days more than my three days with the fleet, and I think I have profited from it. . . . I met every captain and went over with him, on the ground, what was needed."[60]

In an effort to influence public opinion, Roosevelt invited Frederic Remington to witness the naval war games. Remington, the premier artist of the day, was ivy-league educated before finding his calling in the West where he gained popularity by painting romantic images of the frontiersman on the western plains.[61] Remington's images of cowboys, natives, and the U.S. cavalry stirred idealistic visions of the wild and adventurous West. Now Roosevelt wanted Remington to provide idealistic publicity for the Navy. "I can't help looking upon you as an ally from henceforth on in trying to make the American people see the beauty and the majesty of our ships," Theodore told Remington, "and the heroic quality which lurks somewhere in all those who man and handle them."[62]

The war gaming exercise brought all of Theodore's multi-faceted personality to bear. He exhibited the signs of a shrewd data-driven analyzer, a gifted propagandist, an astute administrator, and the exuberated enthusiasm of a boy on a ship.

The result of Theodore's actions was captured by the *Sun* on August 23rd, 1897:

> The liveliest spot in Washington at present is the navy department. The decks are cleared for action. Acting Secretary Roosevelt, in the absence of Governor Long, has the whole Navy bordering on a war footing. It remains only to sand down the decks and pipe to quarters for action.[63]

By the end of September, Secretary Long was ready to return to Washington. Evidently, the weather had cooled. The *Boston Herald* had printed a sarcastic story depicting Roosevelt's plan to replace the vacationing Long for good. Roosevelt shot off a letter to Long ensuring his loyalty. Long, unconcerned and indifferent, decided to return to Washington on September 28th, citing that it was simply "a liberal education to work with him [Roosevelt]."[64]

Though Roosevelt wrote of loyalty, he quickly took insubordinate actions. On Monday the 27th, as his boss was en-route to the capitol, Theodore got hold of a letter that New Hampshire senator, William Chandler had written to Long. Chandler, who had previously been the secretary of navy under Chester A. Arthur, had recommended that Commodore John A. Howell receive appointment as head of the all-important Asiatic Naval Squadron, the position that Roosevelt wanted for his friend and Metropolitan Club comrade, Commodore Dewey.

Theodore had vetted Dewey and knew that he was a frontiersman. "I've looked into his eyes," Theodore claimed; "he's a fighter."[65] The nation was on the verge of war with Cuba and in a crisis, the navy needed a man who could be counted on to act with strength and decisiveness. Dewey, according to Theodore, "could be relied upon to prepare in advance, and to act promptly, fearlessly, and on his own responsibility when the emergency arose."[66]

Theodore's next move can be viewed as entirely unethical or a master stroke in the art of politics.

Long was not due back in the office until the following morning, Theodore bought time by sending an appeal to Senator Chandler. "Before you commit yourself definitely to Commodore Howell I wish very much you would let me have a chance to talk to you. . . . I shall of course give your letter at once to the Secretary upon his return."[67]

Roosevelt then immediately met with Dewey. "Do you know any Senators?" he asked the Commodore, explaining that Chandler had nominated Howell and that Dewey needed a nomination from another senator as soon as possible.[68]

Dewey acknowledged that he was close with Redfield Proctor from Vermont, a man with whom he had shared expansionist thoughts as well as pork chop lunches at the Metropolitan Club.

Dewey quickly met with Proctor, and the Vermont Senator, a friend of McKinley, paid an immediate visit to the White House. McKinley took Proctor's advice, and unaware of Theodore's behind-the-scenes politicking, issued a memorandum to Secretary Long requesting the appointment of Commodore Dewey.[69]

Returning to the navy department Long was chagrined to find that McKinley had requested Dewey to lead the Asiatic Squadron. As a traditionalist, Long felt that Howell, with his senior rank and more action-adverse demeanor, would have been a better choice than Dewey. But McKinley was the president and his wishes were to be respected. Long obliged and appointed Dewey.[70]

Senator Chandler's recommendation for Commodore Howell sat in Theodore's care until Dewey's appointment had been finalized. "In a fortunate hour for the Nation," Theodore boasted, "Dewey was given command of the Asiatic squadron."[71]

Long later acknowledged that a letter had in fact "arrived while he was absent from the office and while Mr. Roosevelt was Acting Secretary. . . ."[72] But Long did not question the matter further, never suspecting what Theodore had done.

In his *Autobiography*, Roosevelt commended Dewey's decision to seek help from Senator Proctor to get the appointment: "But a large leniency should be observed toward the man who uses influence only to get himself a place in the picture near the flashing of guns."[73] Absent in Roosevelt's analysis is his view on the ethics of intercepting a letter, using its contents to assist a friend, and then withholding the letter until the manipulation had been completed. No doubt Roosevelt felt that he was doing what he thought was best for the navy, for the people of Cuba, and for the posterity of America. But the morality of his actions was questionable and Roosevelt's stance on the matter is lost to history. But the end result was that Dewey, a man Theodore could rely on to act on his own initiative, was in command of the critical Asiatic Squadron. It was all Theodore's political maneuverings, ethical or otherwise. Perhaps all is fair in war?

In reflecting on the summer that Theodore was the acting secretary, an unsettling question arises: How did Roosevelt move the navy to the doorstep of war without getting fired, especially in a department that embodied bureaucracy and hierarchy?

"It was mainly because he was beguilingly honest and open about his views, cloaked his decisions in a broad concept of a stronger defense, and based that concept on a powerful nationalistic philosophy," a Roosevelt family historian writes.[74] That is to say, Theodore garnered personal trust from confidants like John D. Long while hiding his war-hawk tendencies under the broad idea that a stronger defense meant for a more secure nation. Theodore also knew that the country, still under the ominous cloud of the Civil War, was yearning to feel patriotic pride. The American public was listening to him in an effort to interpret its future.

Despite Roosevelt's best effort, the prospects for war over Cuba seemed to be waning by the late summer of 1897. On August 8th, Spanish Prime Minister Antonio Cánovas del Castillo was assassinated by an anarchist. The rhetoric from the new government promised appeasement to the Cuban rebels, insinuating that independence was forthcoming.[75] Though Theodore still yearned for battle, he began to acknowledge that war was going to be averted. Intellectually restless, and despite his torrential activities at the navy department, he began to contemplate writing a historical piece "on the Mongol terror, the domination of the Tartar tribes over half of Europe during the thirteenth and fourteenth centuries."[76] But the history of the Mongol terror was never written. William Randolph Hearst made certain that a war would occupy all of Theodore's time.

Theodore Roosevelt and William Randolph Hearst had much more in common than either of them ever cared to admit. Both came from wealthy families, both went to Harvard, both had a flair for clothing and the finer things in life, both had fathers who avoided service in the Civil War, both saw themselves as important men, and both had grandiose visions of American military glory.[77]

Born in San Francisco in 1863, Hearst was the son of multimillionaire George Hearst, who had made his fortune in mining, and later bought himself a U.S. Senate seat. The elder Hearst enjoyed gambling and girls and left parenting to his wife Phoebe, twenty years his junior.[78]

After a carefree aristocratic youth, William left for Harvard in 1882, but unlike Theodore, Hearst was a party animal and drank heavily, spending his nights at dance halls and keeping a bar-maid as a mistress.[79] More interested in pranks than scholastics, Hearst presented each faculty member with a silver piss pot that had the professor's name inscribed in the basin. This promptly got him expelled from Harvard. But it did not matter; his family was rich. By the time Hearst was in his mid-twenties he was spending more than $40,000 a year—over a $1 million in today's dollars—on "personal entertainments," which his mother sus-pected rightly to be "theaters, horse shows, late suppers, and women. . . ."[80]

Yet for his carefree ways, Hearst harbored an intense determina-tion to make a name for himself. In 1895, when the family's stake in the mining business was sold for an astonishing $7.5 million dollars, he used the money to buy a small fledgling newspaper in New York called the *Morning Journal* where he quickly realized that sensational news, true or not, was profitable.[81]

In 1897, Hearst—now thirty-four years old—wanted to usher in a new American foreign policy and sent a reporter to Cuba to provide firsthand accounts of the atrocities on the island. From Cuba the correspondent sent Hearst a tame telegram:

EVERYTHING IS QUIET. THERE IS NO TROUBLE HERE. THERE IS NO WAR. I WISH TO RETURN.

Hearst allegedly responded:
PLEASE REMAIN. YOU FINISH THE PICTURES AND I'LL FURNISH THE WAR[82]

By late autumn of 1897, Hearst had grown frustrated that the prospect for war, as well as the prospect of selling more papers, was declining. He needed a story to counter Prime Minister Anto-nio Cánovas del Castillo's assassination and the new government's promise of peace.

James Creelman, a sensationalist reporter hired away from Joseph Pulitzer, recalled Hearst sulking in his office, bored and dejected, when a copyboy handed Randolph an innocent cable from Cuba.

HAVANA.

EVANGELINA CISNEROS, PRETTY GIRL OF SEVENTEEN
YEARS, RELATED TO PRESIDENT OF CUBAN REPUB-
LIC, IS TO BE IMPRISIONED FOR TWENTY YEARS ON
THE AFRICAN COAST, FOR HAVING TAKEN PART IN
UPRISING OF CUBAN POLITICAL PRISIONERS ON
THE ISLE OF PINES.[83]

According to Creelman, Hearst read the cable, whistled, and
then slapped his knee, "We've got Spain, Now!" he snarled, ". . .We
can make a national issue of this case. . . . The Spanish minister
can attack our correspondents, but we'll see if he can face the
women of America when they take up the fight!"[84]

On August 17th, just nine days after the Spanish prime minister was assassinated, the *Journal* embellished the dramatic tale
of the "Cuban Joan of Arc," Evangelina Cisneros, a brave and
charming woman from the "gentlest of families, she had come
to the Isle of Pines"—a small island thirty miles across the Gulf of
Batabanó where Spanish officials imprisoned political agitators—
simply "to beg for her elderly father's release."[85] She was a gentle
and innocent woman, the article insinuated, but that did not matter to the brutal Spanish men. Evangelina, the dove, was forced to
resist the sexual advances of a ruthless prison guard before being
thrown into a reformatory for "prostitutes and madwomen." The
article wondered: would America help Evangelina rise up against
Spanish oppression?

The truth was that Evangelina had likely been scheming with
several rebels to trap the prison warden, perhaps by luring him in
for sex. She was also not suffering in a desolate prison cell. The
Spanish authorities, wary that her plight might cause an international sensation, fed and clothed her appropriately.[86]

Irrespective of the truth, Evangelina the heroine who
resisted sexual advances from the degenerate prison commander and had been jailed with the prostitutes and the
insane, was *the news* in America.[87] Her story generated an outpouring of humanitarian concern across the country; the vulnerable young woman was in need of a gallant rescue from
America-the-brave.

By August 23rd, "More Than Ten Thousand Women in All Parts of the United States Sign the Petition for the Release of Miss Cisneros," the *Journal* proclaimed on its front page. Hearst's sensationalism had worked brilliantly. His office was flooded with letters from the likes of Clara Barton and Jefferson Davis's wife. Hearst even swayed President McKinley's own mother to "lend her voice" to liberating Evangelina.[88] Overnight, the crisis became a humanitarian cause where America could play the role of savior and liberator of Cuba. It was Hearst's fabrication that rallied the American public around decisive action.

Theodore Roosevelt, a student of public relations, had long since understood that "it is very difficult to make this nation wake up."[89] The public, Theodore knew, was now awake and could force President McKinley into action.

Since at least 1886, when he offered to fight against Mexico with "an entire regiment of cowboys," Theodore had dreamed of military glory. He wanted to restore honor to the Roosevelt name, to erase the one blemish of Thee's life.[90] But as military glory became an ever increasing possibility, Theodore faced the very real prospect that he would lose another wife to a premature death. Edith had fallen ill, and for over ninety days her life hung in the balance.

In November, 1897, Edith went into premature labor and gave birth to the couple's fifth child, a healthy boy named Quentin. Complications from childbirth and a subsequent illness confined her to bed, leaving her unable to take care of herself or the children. At different times, from different doctors, the illness was diagnosed as grippe, sciatica, and neuralgia.[91]

As Edith deteriorated, so did the conditions in Havana. She had been bed-ridden for over a month when news from Cuba trickled in on January 1st, 1898, that its citizens were rioting in the streets. On January 12th, Spanish officers demolished the printing presses of local newspapers that had been critical of Spain's occupation. The ensuing violence lasted less than a day but it gave the *Journal* the opportunity to report, erroneously, that throngs of protestors were attacking American citizens in the streets. Hearst's paper demanded, "Next To War With Spain," complete with the untrue prediction that "armed intervention" was imminent, perhaps within two days.[92]

U.S. Consul-General Fitzhugh Lee, the nephew of Confederate General Robert E. Lee, decided that the minor skirmish had indeed put American lives at risk and dispatched a coded signal to Captain Charles D. Sigsbee of the battleship USS *Maine.* The secret cable—TWO DOLLARS—alerted Sigsbee to immediately coal up the *Maine* and set sail for Havana.[93]

Stirred by the riots in Cuba, Roosevelt stormed into John Long's office and shouted his intentions "to abandon everything and go to the front."[94] Long, the old mediator, tried to persuade his zealous assistant by deriding any conflict with Spain as a "bushwhacking fight" where military glory would not be won, but where Roosevelt would only "improve every opportunity of dying with malaria."[95]

"I tried to persuade him that if it was his country which was at stake, or his home should be defended, such a course would be worthwhile," Long wrote. "I called him a crank, and ridiculed him to the best of my ability, but all in vain. The funny part of it is that he actually takes the thing seriously."[96] Long was perplexed by his subordinate's singular focus on fighting in Cuba. In a moment of reflection he confided the confusion to his diary, ". . . [Theodore] evidently regards it as a sacred duty which *he owes to his own character.*"[97]

Long's inclination was dead-on. Military glory had indeed become a tenet of Theodore's character. He had to restore honor to his family's name, he had to live up to Mittie's stories of valor, he had to practice the doctrine of action that he had been preaching in his books. Fighting had become a sacred duty which he owed to his character.

As for his sick wife, Theodore had already made up his mind. "I would have turned from my wife's deathbed to have answered that call," he wrote callously, "It was my chance to cut my little notch on the stick that stands as a measuring rod in every family."[98]

The USS *Maine* was brand new; its keel laid just the prior October. Built at the New York Navy Yard in Brooklyn, it had a length of 324 feet, a beam of 57 feet, and a draft of 21½ feet. Officially an armored Cruiser ACR-1, the *Maine* displaced 6,650 tons, had an armor belt 7- to 10-inches thick and was equipped with an impressive arsenal: four 10-inch guns in two twin turrets, six 6-inch guns, seven rapid fire turret 6-pounders, eight 1-pounders, and four surface torpedoes.[99]

McKinley, ever the diplomat, announced that the arrival of the *Maine* was "an act of friendly courtesy" and the Spanish government, still reeling from the assassination of its Prime Minister, accepted.[100]

The USS *Maine* dropped anchor in the clear, still water of Havana Harbor shortly after dawn on January 25th, 1889. Spanish officials went aboard for what was described as a "polite but chilly welcome."[101] After diplomatic pleasantries aboard the *Maine* had concluded, Consul-General Lee cabled to Washington: "peace and quiet reign."[102]

While the nation stirred for war, Edith became even more frighteningly sick; it was suspected that she might have contracted typhoid fever, the disease that killed Mittie.[103] Theodore was a man in conflict. Before him, at least in his mind, stood the great promise of military glory as well as the great devastation that Edith was on her death bed. Distraught, he began to covet the strength and solitude he had found in the West. "I long at times for the great rolling prairies of sun dried yellow," he wrote that February, obviously letting his thoughts escape to the solitude of the Badlands, the place where he found strength after Alice died.[104]

The lone holdout for peace in all of America, it seemed, was President McKinley. Though Hearst and Roosevelt had tried to push the man to war, it was a letter by Spanish Ambassador Señor Enrique Dupuy de Lome—Minister Plenipotentiary and Envoy Extraordinaire of his Catholic Majesty—that pushed McKinley to the brink. In a foolish act of epic magnitude, De Lome fired off a correspondence to a friend living in Havana that referred to McKinley as "weak and catering to the rabble; a low politician who desires to stand well with the jingoes of his party."[105] The letter was intercepted by a spy in the Havana post office and then leaked to the *Journal* which promptly published the letter on February 9th. "The worst insult to the United States in its history," the *Journal* roared. The president of America had been called out, his manhood questioned. The insult was a fighting offense.[106]

America was now a tinderbox. A spark meant war.

On the night of February 15th, 1898, the USS *Maine* exploded in Havana Harbor. 253 men died instantly.

William Hearst had been at the theater that evening when the cable came across the wire.

"Spread the story all over the page," Hearst roared upon hearing the news, "This means war!"[107]

15. USS MAINE

———————————————————◇

At dusk, the notes of "Taps" filled the serene harbor of Havana, Cuba. Most of the *Maine's* 328 enlisted men had already retired to their bunks for the evening.[1] A few of the officers settled into their quarters in the aft of the battleship, while others smoked, read, or retold the same stories to the same group of men. Captain Sigsbee, situated in the admiral's cabin, wrote a letter to his wife.

> I had laid down my pen to listen to the notes of the bugle, which were singularly beautiful in the oppressive stillness of the night. Newton [the corporal conducting "Taps"], who was rather given to fanciful effects, was evidently doing his best. During his pauses, the echoes floated back to the ship with singular distinctness, repeating the strains of the bugle fully and exactly.[2]

For almost all aboard, "Taps" was the last sound they heard on earth.

At 9:40 p.m., two massive explosions ripped through the front third of the ship, obliterating all in its path. The first sounded like a "burst of thunder," a witness recounted, followed by a "terrible mass of fire and explosion."[3] The bow of the *Maine* lifted completely off the water before a ball of orange fire blasted debris skyward, cascading fragments of wreckage on the harbor below, like defective fireworks.[4]

"Great masses of twisted and bent iron plates and beams were thrown up in confusion amidships," a witnessed recounted. "The bow had disappeared; the foremast and smokestacks had fallen; and to add to the horror and danger, the mass of wreckage amidships was on fire."[5]

Captain Sigsbee stumbled his way up to the deck and leaned over the starboard rail, his ship engulfed in flames. To prevent

Six-year-old Theodore and his younger brother Elliot (future father of Eleanor Roosevelt) view President Abraham Lincoln's funeral procession from their grandfather's mansion near Union Square.

Martha Bulloch Roosevelt, "Mittie."

Theodore Roosevelt Jr., "Teedie," about two years old.

Theodore Roosevelt Sr., "Thee."

Theodore Roosevelt's first challenge in life was to make his body strong.

Sophomore year at Harvard.

The elite men of the Harvard Porcellian Club, 1880. Theodore is sitting on the floor, second from the right.

New York State assemblymen. Left to right, back row: William O'Neil and Theodore Roosevelt; front row: Isaac Hunt, George F. Spinney, and Walter Howe.

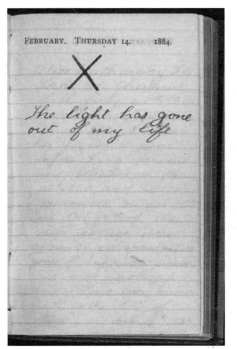

The diary entry on the day his mother and wife died. This dual tragedy haunted him his entire life; a deep melancholy settled into his being.

After Thee died, Theodore charges into the Maine wilderness. Left to right: William Sewall, Wilmot Dow (Sewall's nephew), Theodore Roosevelt.

The awkward cowboy, Theodore Roosevelt enters the western frontier.

Theodore Roosevelt, a Western cowboy.

A group of Badlands cowboys sitting in front of a home about the size of Theodore's Maltese Cross ranch house.

Photograph of three men and a wagon taken by Theodore Roosevelt.

Two men breaking in a horse, an important rite of passage on the frontier.

Roosevelt's outfit for the roundup of 1885. All of the cowboys in the county would work together; regardless of which ranch they belonged to. The roundup was crude and violent—no poser could survive it. The foreman, known as "Boss," was the leader.

A gang of cattlemen.

After the capture: A staged picture of Roosevelt keeping a watchful eye on the boat thieves.

Roosevelt in a New York studio posing in his buckskin suit, with knife and rifle prominently displayed. The backdrop is imitation grass.

Henry Cabot Lodge and Theodore would team up to create one of the most influential political friendships in American history.

The mounted policemen of New York City. The police force was entirely corrupt when Theodore became commissioner.

Board of Police Commissioners, New York City. Left to Right: Avery Andrews, Andrew Parker, Theodore Roosevelt, Frederick Grant (son of Ulysses S. Grant).

The assistant secretary of the navy at his desk.

On June 2nd, 1897 Roosevelt posed for pictures with officers of the War College. Standing on the steps of the college he is overlooking Narragansett Bay. Shortly after this picture was taken, Theodore walked into the auditorium and gave a speech that forever altered American foreign policy.

The mast and wreckage of the sunken *USS Maine* in Havana harbor.

Leonard Wood.

Admiral George Dewey.

Roosevelt in military attire.

David "Dade"
Goodrich.

Allyn Capron.

Buckey O'Neill.

Several Rough Riders.

Alexander Brodie.

Hamilton Fish.

Roosevelt, Wood, and Brodie sitting in front of camp tents, San Antonio.

The gunmen of the 1st Volunteer Cavalry.

The officers of the Rough Rider regiment, as well as the armed forces mascot, a mountain lion named Florence.

Last dinner in San Antonio: Wood and Roosevelt at the head
of the table, officers surrounding them.

From left to right: Alexander Brodie, George M.
Dunn, Joseph Wheeler, Henry A. Brown, Leonard
Wood, and Theodore Roosevelt.

Mounted horse drill.

Roosevelt giving a command
to a trooper.

Roosevelt brought the Japanese
attaché to witness the Rough
Rider drill.

General Shafter inspecting the
rail facilities. From the start of
the war, chaos reigned.

The Rough Riders took over a
coal train and rode its rails into
Port Tampa.

The convergence of trains, boats, men and equipment
choked off the docks at Tampa. "Hell won't be worse crowded
on the last day than the dock is now," a Sergeant quipped.

Aboard the *Yucatan* there was hardly any standing room.

Troopers land at Daiquiri on the rotting dock. Two soldiers from the 10th cavalry drowned.

US Army moving towards Santiago de Cuba.

A trooper is pointing towards Kettle Hill. In front of him is San Juan Heights with the blockhouse clearly visible on the bluff. Wheeler's cavalry camp setup at the base of the Heights the night the Americans seized the high ground.

Troopers crossing the River on their way to San Juan Hill.

The morning of July 1st 1898: Capron's battery firing upon the fortifications at El Caney.

William Dinwiddie's original image atop San Juan Heights.

The U.S. 10th Cavalry.

Rough Rider helping a comrade.

Roosevelt receiving the Bronco Buster statue. The surprise gift from the Rough Riders would be Theodore's most prized possession until the day he died.

Theodore and the three mascots at camp Wikoff: A dog named "Cuba" on the left, "Florence" the Mountain Lion on the right, and a War Eagle named "Teddy" atop the box.

Battle Flag of the Rough Riders held by Color-Sergeant Albert Wright.

William McKinley is shot by an estranged gunman and Roosevelt rushes to the president's bedside in Buffalo, New York.

President Roosevelt, animated and full of vigor, gives the famous Trust speech to a large crowd in Rhode Island.

A would-be assassin shot Theodore Roosevelt in the chest. A several page manuscript and a glasses case absorbed the brunt of the bullet and spared Theodore of his life (left). The shirt Theodore was wearing drenched with blood (right).

Shortly after Theodore's death in 1919, Edwin Marcus from *Life* drew this picture of Lady History trying to decide how Theodore Roosevelt should best be remembered. Lady History settled on one word: American.

another explosion, he barked an order to flood the ammunition magazine.[6] This could not be done. The forward magazine and the flames that he was looking at were already underwater, an aide shouted.[7] As Sigsbee's eyes accustomed to the horror around him, lifeless white objects began to float up to the surface. The objects, he realized, were bodies.[8]

Sigsbee cried the command for "Away all boats," though it was not needed.[9] The ship was sinking and the few who had survived the blast were already jumping into the black, shark-infested waters. Reverberating horror through the harbor were cries of "Help! Lord God, help us! Help! Help!"[10]

The complement at the time of the disaster was 355 seamen—comprising 290 sailors, 39 marines, and 26 officers. Before the debris had fallen from the sky, 178 men were dead, a full one third of their bodies never recovered. Another 75 men would perish over the next few hours.[11]

Among the men attending to the wounded was seventy-six-year-old Clara Barton, the pioneering humanitarian who created the American Red Cross during the U.S. Civil War. In July of 1897, she recommended directly to President McKinley that the Red Cross take over the relief efforts for the people of Cuba.[12] Just moments after the explosion, Barton rushed to San Ambrosio Hospital where the dead from the *Maine* were already piling up:

> They had been crushed by timbers, cut by iron, scorched by fire, and blown sometimes high in the air, sometimes driven down through the red-hot furnace room and out into the water, senseless, to be picked up by some boat and gotten ashore. Their wounds were all over them—heads and faces terribly cut, internal wounds, arms, legs, feet and hands burned to the live flesh.[13]

At 1:30 a.m., Helen Long, daughter of Secretary John Long, returned home from a dance and was startled to find a messenger lurking outside in the dead of night. The man, in a cryptic

voice, told Helen he had an important message for the secretary.[14] Helen ran upstairs to awaken her father.

"It was almost impossible to believe that it could be true, or that it was not a wild and vivid dream," Long remembered.[15]

In a daze he wrote a message to the chief of the Navy's Bureau of Navigation ordering rescue ships to set sail for Cuba, effective immediately.[16]

Next came the terrible task of notifying the president. Long sent a naval attaché to the White House who accompanied the watchmen into the family quarters. A little before two in the morning, the president, dressed in his night gown, took the call from Long.

"The *Maine* blown up, the *Maine* blown up," McKinley muttered to himself as he paced the room, head down.[17]

The burden of war had just descended upon his shoulders.

Captain Sigsbee, now safely aboard the nearby steamer the *City of Washington*, grabbed a pen and piece of Ward Line stationary. As his vessel burned and black smoke choked the harbor, he cabled a message to Washington.

Secnav, Washington, D.C.

> *Maine* blown up in Havana harbor at nine forty to-night and destroyed. Many wounded and doubtless more killed or drowned. Wounded and others aboard Spanish man-of-war and Ward Line steamer. . . No one has clothing other than that upon him. Public opinion should be suspended until further report. . .

Sigsbee[18]

Sigsbee's request that public opinion "be suspended until further report" was not at all possible.

As the sun peeked over the Havana Harbor skyline on February 16th, the light of dawn exposed the awesome horror of the scene. The *Maine* was a grotesque pile of steel and shrapnel. A lone portion of the superstructure protruded above the surface, the hull almost completely submerged. A pillar of smoke lingered indifferently above the wreckage.

As dawn broke in Washington, Roosevelt, an early riser, woke quietly so as not to disturb his dangerously ill wife. He ate a breakfast of hard-boiled eggs, before arriving at his office where he was briefed on the news reports.[19] "I would give anything if President McKinley would order the fleet to Havana tomorrow," he immediately stated, "The *Maine* was sunk by an act of dirty treachery on the part of the Spaniards."[20]

Never mind that no official details had reached Washington, and Captain Sigsbee, an eyewitness to the disaster, was pleading that public judgment be suspended. Theodore had already made up his mind.[21]

"Destruction of the Warship Maine Was the Work of an Enemy," ran the headline of Hearst's *Journal* on February 17th. Accompanying the story was an entirely premature drawing of the *Maine* peacefully anchored over a mine "wired to a Spanish fortress onshore."[22] The paper, reporting without any evidence, claimed that "Naval Officers were Unanimous That the Ship Was Destroyed on Purpose" and that a "Hidden Mine or a Sunken Torpedo Believed to Have Been the Weapon [Was] Used Against the American Man-of-War."[23] Just below the headline and in the middle of the page came a clear indication of who had become the leader for Cuban intervention: "Assistant Secretary Roosevelt Convinced the Explosion of the War Ship Was Not an Accident."[24] The article had no quotes from Roosevelt and he was surely not interviewed for the piece. Hearst had just assumed correctly.

America, like Theodore, wanted war instantly. All over the country cries of "Remember the *Maine*," were howled. Men and women shouted in the street and prayed in the church. It was an act of war; no question, it was time to fight.

McKinley still wanted peace, telling a friend, "I don't propose to be swept off my feet by the catastrophe. My duty is plain. We must learn the truth and endeavor, if possible, to fix the responsibility. The country can afford to withhold its judgment and not strike an avenging blow until the truth is known."[25] Though the president's sentiment was honorable, it was not rooted in reality. Yellow journalism and the subsequent public outcry had already crystallized the narrative of the event—it was time for action. In a last ditch effort for peace, McKinley proposed that the United States buy the island outright for $300 million. This sent Roosevelt over the top. Buy the island and not fight? Economic spinelessness was exactly the problem in America, Theodore believed. "The president," Roosevelt snarled, "has no more backbone than a chocolate éclair."[26]

The day after the explosion, Lieutenant Philip Alger, a professor at the U.S. Naval Academy and an authority on naval explosives, was quoted in the *Washington Star* that "No torpedo such as is known in modern warfare can of itself cause an explosion as powerful as that which destroyed the *Maine*. We know of no instances where the explosion of a torpedo or mine under a ship's bottom has exploded the magazine within."[27] Had the explosion been a spontaneous combustion from within the bunker of the *Maine* and not an act of war?

In order to uncover the cause of the blast, McKinley hastily appointed a Naval Court of Inquiry, which convened in Havana seven days after the explosion.

As America waited on-edge for the results of the board's investigation, Edith's health declined even more rapidly.[28] On the morning of Friday, February 25th, she was so sick that Theodore called Doctor Sir William Osler of Johns Hopkins University, the leading specialist in the country, and demanded that the doctor come check on Edith as soon as possible.

"Poor Theodore is in great distress of mind," Lodge wrote, concluding that everyone was "very anxious and depressed."[29]

Roosevelt's thoughts were heavy. His second wife was fighting off death and the court of inquiry might acquit the Spanish. In this tormented frame of mind, Roosevelt left his house on the morning of February 25th, and single-handedly prepared the country for imminent war.

Shortly before noon, Theodore received a brief note from Secretary Long stating that he would be leaving the office shortly. Long was off to get a "mechanical massage," a recently introduced technology that used an instrument to vibrate the back and legs.[30] In modern terms, he went to the spa.

Long put Roosevelt in charge, and realizing the risk that he was taking, the secretary left clear, unmistakable, instructions.

> Do not take any such step affecting the policy of the Administration without consulting with the President or me. I am not away from town and my intention was to have you look after the routine of the office while I get a quiet day off. I write to you because I am anxious to have no unnecessary occasion for a sensation in the papers.[31]

Roosevelt read the note and sprang into action. In a furious flurry of activity, Theodore alerted the navy worldwide to prepare immediately for combat, ordered ammunition and war supplies, bought tonnage of coal, sent a message to Congress asking for authority to recruit as many sailors as was required for imminent battle, and issued a strategy for redeploying ships to strike the Spanish fleet.[32] But Roosevelt's most important action was a cable to his Metropolitan lunch buddy, now commander of the Asiatic Squadron, George Dewey.

> ORDER THE SQUADRON. . . KEEP FULL OF COAL. IN THE EVENT OF DECLARATION WAR WITH SPAIN, YOUR DUTY WILL BE TO SEE THAT THE SPANISH SQUADRON DOES NOT LEAVE THE ASIATIC COAST, AND THEN OFFENSIVE OPERATION IN PHILIPPINE ISLANDS.

> KEEP OLYMPIA [Dewey's flagship] UNTIL FURTHER ORDERS.

> ROOSEVELT.[33]

The message was momentous; it was everything but the war declaration itself. The Spanish fleet, stationed in the casually defended Philippines was the perfect place for aggressive action, and Roosevelt's cable, as the acting agent in charge of the navy, gave Dewey the instructions—once war had been declared—to destroy the Spanish fleet before it could be dispatched to defend Cuba.[34]

By Theodore's side during the momentous afternoon was Henry Cabot Lodge, now the influential member of the Senate Foreign Relations Committee. Lodge, who personally vowed to president-elect McKinley that Roosevelt would not start a war, was now conspiring with Theodore to start the war.

Roosevelt's strategic sense was spot on. His actions were in lockstep with public opinion and his inclusion of Lodge got the Senate's stamp of approval. With the Senate and the public in Roosevelt's corner, President McKinley would not be able to reverse the war preparations.[35]

John Long returned to the office the next morning rested. His calm demeanor quickly turned to horror. In an urgent meeting with the president, he promised that he would never again leave Roosevelt in charge of the navy. However, it is a testament to Roosevelt's strategic actions that Long did not revoke a single order, nor did he temper the war-thirsty dispatch to Dewey. All of the Theodore's orders would stand.

"Roosevelt, in his precipitate way," Long wrote in his diary, "has come very near causing more that an explosion than happened to the *Maine*."[36] Long fretted over Roosevelt's state-of-mind, trying to make sense of his subordinate's actions.

> His wife is very ill . . . I really think he is hardly fit to be entrusted with the responsibility of the Department at this critical time. He is full of suggestions; many of which are of great value to me, and his spirited and forceful habit is a good tonic for one who is disposed to be as conservative and careful as I am. He means to be thoroughly loyal, but the very devil seemed to possess him yesterday afternoon . . .
>
> He has gone at things like a bull in a china shop, and with the best purposes in the world, has really taken what, if he could have thought, he would not have for a moment have taken, and that is the one course which is most discourteous to me, because it suggests that there had been a lack of attention which he was supplying. It shows how

the best fellow in the world and with splendid capacities is worse than of no use if he lacks a cool head and careful discretion.[37]

Long was wrong. Roosevelt's actions were neither impulsive nor without discretion. What Long did not understand, and what history has proven, is that Theodore's four-hour flurry of activity was the coherent result of over three hundred days of tactical preparation, both within the navy department and at the Metropolitan Club.[38] In fact, since he had written the *Naval War of 1812,* Roosevelt had prepared for this moment. It was not impulsive at all, it was all premeditated, and when the moment presented itself he decided to hit hard.

"I may not be supported," Theodore told his friend Leonard Wood, "but I have done what I know to be right; someday they will understand."[39]

"Few men would have dared to assume this responsibility," Wood explained some years later, "but Theodore Roosevelt knew that there were certain things that ought to be done and that delay would be fatal. He felt the responsibility was his and he took it."[40]

That weekend, Doctor Osler examined Edith and decided that emergency surgery was required to eliminate the severe swelling in her abdomen. "I held her hand until the ghastly preparations were made," Theodore wrote to Bamie.[41] Edith would survive the surgery and though she would remain wasted for over a month, the operation proved successful and a full recovery was eventually made. However, during the three weeks following the surgery, Theodore did not know whether his second wife would live or die.[42]

The inevitable happened on March 28th, when the court of inquiry determined that "the MAINE was destroyed by the explosion of a submarine mine, which caused the partial explosion of two or more of her forward magazines."[43] The findings were whitewashed, and the navy claimed they were absolved of any "fault or negligence," but that there was no evidence that the Spanish blew up the ship.[44]

To this day, the definitive explanation remains a mystery.

But in 1898, the court of inquiry's soft indictment was all that the war hungry public needed—a new war chant swept the nation: "Remember the Maine! To Hell with Spain! Remember the Maine! To Hell with Spain!"[45]

On April 11th, McKinley issued a war message to Congress.

> In the name of humanity, in the name of civilization, in behalf of endangered American interest . . . I ask the congress to authorize and empower the president to take measures to secure a full and final termination of hostilities between the government of Spain and the good people of Cuba. . . . to use the military and naval forces of the United States as may be necessary for these purposes. . .[46]

At three in the morning on April 19th, 1898 Congress passed a joint resolution for Cuban intervention.[47] America was at war. The date was especially significant to Roosevelt. It had been exactly one year to the day since he had become assistant secretary of the navy.[48]

Eleven days later and a world away, Commodore Dewey stood on the bridge of the *Olympia* and peered through his binoculars at the entrance of Manila Bay, the waterway to the Philippines' largest island.[49] After a brief war council in the late afternoon, Dewey—indeed a man of action—decided not to sweep the entrance of Manila Bay for mines, but to sail right into the Spanish stronghold under the cover of darkness. That night, the *Olympia* slithered into Manila Bay followed at a distance of four hundred yards by the *Baltimore, Raleigh, Petrel, McCulloch, Nan Shan, Zafiro, Boston,* and *Concord.*[50] As day broke, the U.S. column was met by the Spanish fleet spread in a defensive formation.[51] At 5:41 a.m.,

Dewey—in the name of duty, honor, glory, and country—turned to the commander of the *Olympia*, Charles Gridley, and in a calm unwavering voice, uttered his now famous command, "You may fire when you are ready, Gridley."[52]

Almost as quickly as it started, the battle was over. By mid-morning, Dewey's squadron had destroyed Spain's entire Pacific fleet, killing161 men and wounding another 210. Dewey had only lost one sailor, who died of heat stroke. Only nine U.S. sailors were wounded.[53] This was an extremely successful outcome, especially considering it was America's first naval action against a foreign foe since the War of 1812.

⊙⧉⊙

"Didn't Admiral Dewey do wonderfully well?" Roosevelt blasted. "I got him the position out there in Asia last year, and I had to beg hard to do it; and the reason I gave was that we might have to send him to Manila. And we sent him—and he went!"[54]

Roosevelt's begging was actually manipulation, yet his efforts to give Dewey the command had indeed paid off. Dewey had struck a lethal blow to Spain before any intervention in Cuba had taken place. Just as Roosevelt had prophesied since Harvard, it was crucial in naval warfare to strike quickly and forcefully to neutralize maritime pressure points, even if those pressure points were not in the western hemisphere. In naval operations, Theodore urged, the bees should be killed in the hive.

Commodore Dewey became an American hero overnight. Now it was Roosevelt's turn.

As part of his war declaration, President McKinley issued a call for 125,000 volunteers to supplement the roughly 30,000 men in the U.S. Regular Army. Included in McKinley's call-to-arms was appropriations for three regiments "to be composed exclusively of frontiersmen possessing special qualifications as horsemen and marksmen."[55] On the same day the summons was announced, Secretary of War Russell Alger offered Theodore Roosevelt command of an entire regiment.[56]

When Theodore declined, Alger was stunned. How could the man who played such an integral role in starting the war not want command of his own regiment now that war had been declared?

Roosevelt explained that he lacked the technical knowledge to equip and prepare an entire regiment. Illustrating great situational awareness, Theodore told Alger that he would much rather serve as Lieutenant Colonel if the leadership position went to his friend Leonard Wood. Alger thought this was rash self-abnegation on Theodore's part.[57] "Wood would do the work anyway," Alger stated, insinuating that Theodore should take the command and appoint Wood as his number two officer.[58]

"I answered that I did not wish to rise on any man's shoulders," Theodore later wrote, "that I hoped to be given every chance that my deeds and abilities warranted; but that I did not wish what I did not earn, and that above all I did not wish to hold any position where anyone else did the work."[59]

"That is foolish," Alger stated perplexingly, before consenting to Theodore's wishes.

Years later, in his autobiography, Theodore would write that his decision "was the wisest act I could have performed."[60]

Having secured the position as Lieutenant Colonel, Theodore Roosevelt sent a message to Brooks Brothers.

Washington, D.C. April 30th, 1898

Brooks Brothers,
    Twenty-second St. & Broadway, New York.
    Can you make me so I shall have it here by next Saturday a blue regular lieutenant-colonel's uniform without yellow on collar, and with leggings? If so make it.
Theodore Roosevelt[61]

He knew the importance of looking the part of the leader.

Secretary Long was still baffled by Theodore's decision to enlist in combat. "He has been of great use;" Long put to his diary, "a man of unbounded energy and force, and thoroughly honest, which is the main thing. He has lost his head in this unutterable folly of deserting the post where he is of most service and running off to ride a horse and, probably, brush mosquitoes from his neck on the Florida sands. His heart is right, and he means well, but it is one of those cases of aberration—desertion—vain glory; of which he is utterly unaware. He thinks he is following his highest ideal, whereas, in fact, as without exception, everyone of his friends advises him, he is acting like a fool."

But then, perhaps a flicker of instinct crossed the old man's mind. Long continues: "And, yet, how absurd all this will sound if, by some turn of fortune, he should accomplish some great thing and strike a very high mark."[62]

Three years later Long would return to his journal entry and in a handwritten postscript, conclude that "Roosevelt was right and we his friends were all wrong. His going into the Army led straight to the presidency."[63]

Long was only partially right. It was not Roosevelt's going into the army that drove him to the presidency. Rather, it was Roosevelt's ability to lead and unite the diverse men of his regiment that propelled him towards the White House. Theodore's unusual set of seemingly disconnected life experiences had prepared him extraordinarily well for the next 133 days. When his moment to lead presented itself, he seized it, and inspired a nation.

At a dusty outpost in San Antonio, a signboard had been pounded into the dirt.

THIS WAY TO CAMP OF ROOSEVELT'S ROUGH RIDERS.[64]

III

———◇———

LEADING

16. RAISING THE REGIMENT

⎯⎯⎯⎯⎯⎯⎯⎯⎯⎯⎯⎯⎯⎯◇

"THE HISTORY OF THE ROUGH RIDERS IS REALLY THE history of the war," journalist Edward Marshall wrote prophetically in 1899, just one year after the conflict ended.[1] Now, more than a century later, the characters and the happenings of the rag-tag regiment defined all that was splendid about the Spanish-American War. Under the leadership of Theodore Roosevelt, the Rough Riders were the first volunteers to land in Cuba, they were the first military forces to raise the American flag on Cuban soil, they were the first regiment to fire at the Spaniards, and they suffered the first tragedy of the military campaign. They led perhaps the most dramatic of charges in U.S. military history which resulted in the capture of the hill that led to victory in the war.[2] From beginning to end, the regiment lasted for less than five months, they had less than two weeks of military training, they fought in just two battles, and they had the highest casualty rate in the entire army. Over a third of them died or were wounded. They were unruly and disciplined, rowdy and effective, coarse and romantic. They were entirely American.

Immediately after meeting with Roosevelt on April 25th, Secretary of War Alger issued a declaration to the territorial governors of Oklahoma, Arizona, and New Mexico for a speedy call-up of combatants:

> The President directs that Captain Leonard Wood of the United States Army be authorized to raise a regiment of cowboys as mounted riflemen, and to be its Colonel, and has named Hon. Theodore Roosevelt as Lieutenant Colonel. All other officers will come from the vicinity where the troops are raised.

What can you do for them?
Answer Immediately.[3]

Alger's telegram was just a formality; the nation was already hot with war fever. "It was as if a mighty clarion sounded to arms throughout the Southwest: Uncle Sam needed cowboys—men accustomed to the outdoors—to fight in Cuba with Wood and Roosevelt," an account reads. "The reaction was widespread. From the ranches, the mines, the plains, the arroyos, the mountains of four territories—Arizona, New Mexico, Oklahoma, and Native American Reservations—most of them came. With rare exception, they were healthy specimens, hard and fearless and confident. To them, danger a daily matter. It was encountered from horses, the elements, and the lawless renegades of the frontier."[4]

"The difficulty in organizing was not in selecting," Theodore explained, "but in rejecting men."[5] In Arizona, a squadron had been preparing since the *Maine* exploded; they were simply awaiting word from McKinley to go to war. Arizona Governor Myron McCord, acting on his own initiative and suspecting rightly that war was imminent, had readied a regiment of over 350 men who were serving under Alexander Brodie, a mining engineer who had served during the American-Indian Wars. Brodie, a West Point graduate now living on the frontier, set rigid military conditions of enlistment. He demanded that every volunteer prove excellent horsemanship, demonstrate crack marksmanship, and exemplify excellent moral character—the latter to ensure "their qualifications for entering into the heavenly choir, in case they should by chance be killed themselves."[6] When war was finally declared, the Arizona regiment was notified that it could only send two hundred men to fight and Brodie, rather than lead an entire regiment, would instead report to Roosevelt. "This well-nigh broke Brodie's heart," a reporter recounted, probably not exaggerating.[7] Brodie, still craving the chance to fight, halved the squadron and sent out an urgent dispatch to summon the troops.

"At two o'clock on the 25th of April, I received a telegram from Brodie to leave with men on the next train to Fort Whipple," Arizona enlistee David Hughes recalled. "I was on my way to work in the mine, the Copper Queen. . . . I returned to the restaurant and left my lunch bucket. I borrowed a one-eyed pinto horse from a cow-puncher who happened to be in the 'Turf' saloon nearby and started out to round up the boys. They were mostly all working. With the aid of the officials of the mine, they were paid off and we left at five o'clock that afternoon."[8]

In Albuquerque, New Mexico, the regiment took only three days to form. "Rough riders and crack shots are wanted," Albuquerque's weekly newspaper announced, "If you want to lick Spain, come to the front."[9] On the 26th, the *Santa Fe New Mexican* announced that the regiment would "be the most noted volunteer regiment ever enlisted" before highlighting that all applicants "must be a good shot, be able to ride anything in the line of horseflesh, a rough and ready fighter, and above all must absolutely have no understanding of the word fear."[10] The *New Mexican* also promised that the lucky few who were chosen to become a Rough Rider would "teach the civilized world that America possesses a class of men who, when armed and brought face to face with an enemy, never quit fighting until victory or death comes."[11]

Miguel Otero, the governor of New Mexico, relayed a personal dispatch to various counties asking for volunteers. At a dusty outpost in Union County, telegrapher Albert Thompson received the governor's call-to-arms and moseyed into the saloon next door. Albert handed the message to a man named "Red" who was the bartender. Red called the drinking to order, cleared his throat, and read the summons aloud.

A ranch hand had but one question, "Where's Cuba at?"

"South of Texas," came the reply from someone in the back of the bar, evidently a suitable answer. Thirty men spontaneously enlisted to fight from Union County.[12]

In Oklahoma and the Native American territories, the enthusiasm was equally jingoistic. "Long before the actual declaration of war with Spain," Oklahoma Governor Cassius McDonald Barnes recounted, "I began receiving letters from patriotic citizens of the territory, offering their services in defense of the nation. . . ."[13] Barnes had no trouble selecting the best-of-the-best from Oklahoma's militia companies, and following "a rigid examination," which took place in a single afternoon, the state's quota was filled.[14]

The lure of being knighted into the frontier militia was the ultimate honor of the day. The newspapers depicted the select volunteers as "fine specimens of physical manhood," "huskiest specimens of manhood," "great, big, strapping young men," "fine riders, excellent shots."[15] The chance to have one's name published in the newspaper as "enlisted" complete with occupation and hometown, was the prize of a lifetime.

In an era when news was dispersed to the frontier by telegraph, newspaper, and word-of-mouth—usually from someone charging in from another town on horseback—it is astounding that it took less than five days to receive 20,000 applications of enlistment for a place on the 780-man roll call. The majority of the applicants came just from the frontier territories of Arizona, Oklahoma, and New Mexico. Put another way, a whopping four to eight percent of all available men of fighting age in these territories decided to impetuously suspend whatever they were doing in life to go fight in Cuba.[16] One wonders how many more would have applied had the ranks not been filled immediately.

Patriotic enthusiasm was at an apex, a lust perhaps unmatched in U.S. history. "Everywhere in this good, fair land flags were flying," Allen White, editor of the *Emporia Gazette* wrote. ". . . [E]verywhere it was flags: tattered, smoke-grimed flags in [railway] engine cabs; flags in button holes; flags on proud-poles, flags fluttering everywhere. . . ."[17]

Though President McKinley was hesitant to declare war, he quickly appreciated the drive to unite the country across the Mason–Dixon line. The charge to avenge the *Maine* could provide the rallying call to heal the still-open wound of the Civil War, and, in an effort to unite, McKinley called upon some old Confederate leaders.[18]

On April 26th, at eight thirty in the evening, Joseph "Fighting Joe" Wheeler, a West Point graduate, who held the rank of brigadier general in the Confederate cavalry at the age of twenty-six, was summoned to the White House.[19] A hero in the South, Fighting Joe was now Congressman Joe, a sixty-one-year-old politician from Alabama. Wheeler's physical presence was hardly symbolic. At five feet five inches, and barely weighing a hundred pounds, his slight build and white-haired whiskers made him look frail and little, more like an old horse jockey than a mighty military man.[20] But his reputation as a fierce fighter, who was as tough as rawhide, as well as a Confederate through-and-through, would prove intensely emblematic. By the dainty gaslight at 1600 Pennsylvania Avenue, McKinley told Wheeler that he was going to appoint the old Confederate to major general.[21]

"I am too old," Wheeler told the President.

"There must be a high officer from the South," McKinley pleaded. "There must be a symbol that the old days are gone. You are needed."[22]

The chance to mend the nation's wounds won out and Wheeler accepted, agreeing to wear the blue union uniform for the first time in almost four decades. When death finally took Fighting Joe in 1906, after a long illness, Wheeler chose to be buried in his blue uniform, the one he wore in Cuba, the one signifying a united America. An old Southern friend looked down on Wheeler's body in the coffin and smiled, "Jesus, General, I hate to think of what old Stonewall's going to say when he sees you arrivin' in that uniform!"[23]

To draw attention to the historical significance of the regiment, Theodore invited journalists into his office at the navy department to show them the fighting spirit of current Americans and the regiment's direct relation to past American warriors. A *New York Sun* article describes a scene of torrential activity in Theodore's office before drawing attention to an enormous pile of paperwork.

The bigger pile contained notes to Lieut.-Col Theo. Roosevelt asking for enlistment in his regiment of rough riders. They come from every state and Territory in the Union, and from all kinds of conditions of men. Mr. Roosevelt eyed it with mingled pride and dismay.

"They are too late," he said, regretfully. "We haven't room for another man, unless some of those we have get out. But they won't. They aren't that kind. Here is one," he said lifting from the pile, a card which bore the name of a New York journalist, "from the great-grandson of the man who led the mountain rifle men to a victory at King's Mountain in the war of the Revolution. If anyone should have the chance it is surely he. I will keep that. I know the man. To all the others I can only say I am sorry. Our ranks are full. But it is a good thing to see them come out. By George, our young Americans are all right yet."[24]

Roosevelt had not yet personally met any members of his cavalry, but was already certain they were warriors. There is no doubt that he staged the incident to advance the mythic fable of the frontier militia, purposely likening the Rough Riders to the gallant leaders of America's past who answered the call on a minute's notice. In 1898, the idea of rough-and-ready volunteers had long since been enshrined into the public conscience. The country's most epic conquests against foreign foes had all been made possible by heroic frontiersmen. The early pioneers who settled America fought frontier battles against French and Native American forces. America's greatest triumph—the American Revolution— was realized only because colonialists courageously fought against the elite British forces in the famous battles at King's Mountain, Lexington, Concord, and Bunker Hill. During the War of 1812, the frontier militia pulled off, according to general-in-command Andrew Jackson, "one of the most brilliant victories in the annals of war," by beating down seasoned European militia men who had fought at Waterloo.[25] At the battle of the Alamo in 1836, the frontiersmen, under the leadership of Davy Crockett, fought to the noble end, dying in glory and inspiring a nation to keep the Texas territory from Santa Anna's army and Mexican occupation.

Roosevelt believed that the idea of the frontiersman was not only real but transferable to each generation. Again Theodore was genuine, but purposeful. He knew that he could unite his diverse regiment around the idea of fulfilling the next link in the fabled chain of American heroic frontiersman. The men that enlisted, Theodore wrote, all "had fared hard when exploring the unknown."[26] They were the modern day frontiersman, "to a man born adventurers, in the *old* sense of the word," Theodore proclaimed.[27]

It was his honor to lead them.

Newspaper accounts featuring day-by-day updates of the cowboy regiment helped Roosevelt spread the lore of the frontier militia. Journalists from New York to San Francisco kept readers informed on who had been selected to the regiment, who had been left out, the antecedent of the fighting men, and the heroic deeds ahead of them. While Theodore promoted America's fighting spirit and set the stage for the next great act from America's frontier militia, Leonard Wood was hard at work on the technical aspects of organizing the unit.

The U.S. army was in understandable chaos. Before the war declaration, the army consisted of roughly 2,000 officers and 26,000 enlisted soldiers, mostly sprinkled along the borders of Canada and Mexico and in outposts deep in the Western interior.[28] Now, just days after the war declaration, the government was tasked with recruiting, equipping, arming, and preparing 125,000 new enlistees for an immediate war. The quintupled expansion of the army came with the inescapable consequence of confusion and disorder. There was simply not nearly enough supply warehoused to equip the surge, not enough bodies available to manage the logistics, not enough leaders who had listened to Theodore's plea that the country was ill-prepared militarily.[29] "The folly, the lack of preparation, are almost inconceivable," Theodore bemoaned; it was truly "the war of America the unready."[30] But Theodore had anticipated chaos, and it was exactly the reason why he relinquished the rank of colonel to Wood.

"To a man who knew the ground as Wood did, and who was entirely aware of our national unpreparedness," Theodore wrote, "it was evident that the ordnance and quartermaster's bureaus could not meet, for some time to come, one-tenth of the demands that would be made upon them. . . . [T]hanks to his knowledge of the situation and promptness, we immediately put in our requisitions for the articles indispensable for the equipment of the regiment."[31] Wood, acting under the premise of what he termed "first one ready, first one in," began equipping the regiment from the moment he got command on the 25th.[32] In competition with the other units in the army, Wood placed his regiment's requisitions immediately, and when the inevitable hitch occurred, he knew exactly which man in Washington to approach, the man whose single word would straighten the matter out.[33]

Wood's connections and instant actions succeeded in securing modern Krag-Jørgensen carbines, which had been reserved for the regular army. The Krag-Jørgensen, a .30-.40-caliber, five-shot, smokeless rifle, was much superior to the weapon assigned to the volunteer units, the outdated Model 1873 Springfield carbon-powder relic from the Civil War. When fired, the single-shot breechloader Model 1873 produced a cloud of smoke "the size of a cow," a private mocked, which created a floating target for enemy return fire. The old fashioned Springfields were good to "knock down two men," the private added, "the one it hit and the one who fired it."[34] Wood knew that the smoke screens were dangerous, and stormed into the office of General Flagler, the man in charge of rationing the limited supply of Krag-Jørgensens, and demanded that his regiment be outfitted with no less than one thousand of the fifteen thousand Krag-Jørgensens available.[35] Flagler consented, for his friend Leonard Wood.

Even more dangerous than the antiquated guns was the blue woolen military fatigues identical to the ones worn by the Union Army thirty years prior. Heavy, dark, and suitable for fighting in the winter, the blue uniforms had simply been stockpiled away and no one in the government had thought to prepare battle uniforms for a hot climate. Wood knew that thick wool could kill many a man in an environment of hundred plus temperatures. Having a complete grasp of military inventory, he requisitioned coarse brown canvas outfits reserved for work in horse stables, not battle.[36] The canvas fatigues were light weight, light in color, and breathed better than wool. Wood's strategic sense continued as he located a manufacturer in New England that built tools for Cuban agriculture and ordered machetes for his entire regiment. The army regulars were equipped only with sabers which could do little to remove the thick, overgrown brush along the Cuban trails. Machetes on the other hand, could not only cut thick brush but also cut down an enemy in hand-to-hand-combat.[37]

In between distribution requisitions for equipment, Wood also fired off the requirements stating that "each troop should consist of a captain, first lieutenant, second lieutenant, first sergeant, quartermaster sergeant, six sergeants, eight corporals, two farriers and blacksmiths, two trumpeters, one saddler, one wagoner, and sixty-four to seventy-eight privates."[38] The regiment would be comprised of twelve troops:

> Troops A, B, and C, from Arizona.
> Troop D, from Oklahoma.
> Troops E, F, G, H, and I, from New Mexico.
> Troop K, from Eastern colleges and cities.
> Troop L and M, from Indian Territory.[39]

In just three days, Wood ordered all the equipment that the regiment would require: tents, canteens, blankets, boots, hats, gloves, food rations, mess pans, spoons, cartridge belts, horse gear, rifles, you name it. Once finished, he put his certified papers into a single folder, walked directly into Secretary of War Alger's office and sat there for over several hours as Alger signed and authorized each document.[40] No one in the entire U.S. army had been as prepared as Leonard Wood; no one was more effective. "Wood is the ideal man for Colonel," Theodore jubilantly proclaimed to anyone that would listen, taking pride in serving under him.[41]

When the Wood-Roosevelt leadership tandem was announced to the public, the details of their power dynamic were thrown into question. Many simply could not believe that the bombastic Roosevelt could be led by another, especially by a man two years his junior. Theodore would dominate Wood, the insiders argued, just as he had done with Secretary John Long. The skeptics could not have been more wrong. "He was always thoroughly subordinate," Wood recalled. "People used to come and say, 'Well, you are going to have a good deal of trouble with Theodore as a subordinate.' There was absolutely nothing of the sort. He was the most subordinate officer you can imagine. He knew perfectly the line between subordination and servility; there was nothing of that."[42]

Theodore believed in Wood's abilities and both men shared the same vision for the regiment. Wood, a private man with a military disposition for details and structure, provided logistical and technical leadership and desired to steer clear of the limelight. Theodore was left to occupy the stage, to lead adaptively, to unite the hearts and minds of the men of the regiment. "Colonel Wood is lost sight of entirely in the effulgence of Teethadore," a press correspondent wrote shortly after the announcement.[43] Both of the men had wanted it just that way.

Wood's final act of brilliance came when he secured the fairgrounds in San Antonio, Texas, as the gathering and preparation site for the regiment. The assembly point, soon to be rechristened Camp Wood, lay on a flat and grassy six hundred acre expanse that contained an Exposition Hall, an open rodeo ground, and a large mess hall. San Antonio was hot and humid just like Cuba; it had a large supply of horses from surrounding ranches; it was close to Fort Sam Houston, a perfect training ground for cavalry; and it had railroad lines running towards the four points of the compass to bring in supplies. It was a picturesque location to raise a regiment, logistically as well as inspirationally. Just two miles from the fairgrounds sat the most hallowed and venerated of American shrines, the Alamo.

In October of 1835, American frontiersmen declared independence for Texas, launching the Texas Revolution, drove Mexican troops out of the territory. The following February, 1836, Mexican General Antonio Lopez de Santa Anna marched an army of roughly 2,000 men along the San Antonio River looking to pick a fight.[44] At a mission church nestled in a grove of cottonwood trees along the San Antonio River, General Anna launched an assault. The church—later to be baptized the Alamo, the Spanish word for cottonwood—garrisoned roughly two hundred frontier soldiers, including James Bowie, William Travis and, of course, Davy Crockett. Outnumbered at least ten-to-one, the Americans put up a vicious thirteen-day fight but when the last shot was fired, only a handful of Americans escaped alive. Overnight, news of Santa Anna's slaughter traveled throughout the countryside with the mythic vignette that there were "no less than sixteen dead Mexicans around the corpse of Colonel Crockett and one across it with the huge knife of Davy buried in the Mexican's bosom to the hilt."[45]

American adventurers ran to the countryside armed and ready, rallying to the battle cry, "Remember the Alamo!" At the Battle of San Jacinto, the following spring, April 21st, 1836, the inspired American volunteers engaged the Mexican Army in a fight that lasted just eighteen minutes. The Frontier Militia, full of patriotic vigor, kicked the Mexican army out of Texas, and America, forever.[46]

Sixty-two years and one month later, the adored battle cry, "Remember the *Maine!*" was a direct call to arms echoing the patriotic cheer, "Remember the Alamo!" The Rough Riders' training camp could not have been a better place for volunteer soldiers to prepare. To the public, to the Rough Riders, to Roosevelt, it was exactly as if a new generation of frontiersmen was charging in from the four corners of America to awaken the ghost of Davy Crockett.

On Thursday, May 5th, just ten days after war was declared on Spain, Leonard Wood arrived in San Antonio. The dusty Texas town settled by Spaniards and named after a priest from Padua, sat on the southern end of what would later be called the Texas Hill Country. Sprinkled amongst the rolling hills of wildflowers and hackberry, pecan trees and live oaks, were quaint Mexican-style adobes and Spanish cathedrals. The roughly fifty thousand residents had only a vague idea of what to expect from the motley crew that was to arrive within the week.[47]

On May 4th, the scene in Prescott, Arizona was stunning. Several thousand Arizonians lined the street from the Whipple Barracks to the train depot. The crowds, ten people deep in some places, waved flags and signs, children sat on their father's shoulders, women cheered, grown men cried. A brass band belted,

"We Won't Go Home Till Morning," as the contingent of two hundred men marched the three miles from the barracks to the town square.[48]

Lining up in columns of four in the middle of town, the men tried to stand in military order. According to one account, it was fairly disheveled, looking more like a "crowd of men in cowboy mufti—baggy pants, galluses, blanket rolls, wrinkled shirts, sweat-stained hats, and trail-scuffed boots, carrying their sparse belongings in cardboard suitcases and canvas bags."[49] If not for the red and blue hat bands, with the lettering '1st U.S. Volunteer Cavalry—Arizona Column', the men would have "been mistaken for a group of cowpunchers heading out on a trail drive."[50]

Alexander Brodie stood at the front of the column. Forty-eight years old, Brodie stood erect with medium build, broad shoulders, and a thick black mustache. He was a West Point grad before establishing a reputation as a tough-as-nails fighter during the American-Indian Wars, and most recently, he opened the Crown Point Gold Mine near Castle Creek, where his ore-quarrying business was booming. Before the *Maine* exploded, he was pulling in as much as $1,000 a ton for his ore, but with the nation at war, he pulled the pumps out of the shafts, paid off his workers, abandoned the mine, and began telegraphing "right and left to bid his friends get ready for the fight he saw impending."[51] In four years' time he would be the governor of the Arizona territory.

Standing next to Brodie was Buckey O'Neill, a man equally loved but exceptionally different in looks and personality. Patently Irish, Buckey stood six foot one, weighed two hundred pounds, had short dark hair with dark piercing eyes, and spoke with an aura of authority. A second-generation fighter, Buckey took great pride in the fact that his father had been a member of Thomas Francis Meagher's iconic Irish Brigade in the Civil War.[52] Buckey was the type of man whose reputation preceded him; the chain smoking thirty-eight-year-old was already considered "the most storied man in the territory since the departure of Wyatt Earp."[53] At odd times in his life, Buckey had been a miner, a writer of short stories, a newspaper editor, a sheriff, a cowboy, a lawyer, and was currently a politician, serving as mayor of Prescott.[54] He was also a leader of men, and therefore, appointed Captain of Troop A.

Amid the thunderous roar in the town square, Governor McCord took to the grandstand, and called the event to order. The ladies of the Women's Relief Corps at Phoenix had spent the previous night sewing the regimental colors; a blue silk ball gown was used for the field behind the white stars. Governor McCord presented the flag as the Territorial Normal School choir sang "God Be With You Till We Meet Again."[55] The elders in the audience, especially those who had lived through the previous war, wept heartily. They had never thought they would live to see such a uniting occasion.

Next, Robert Brow, a jovial and popular Prescott saloonkeeper from Whiskey Row, took to the grandstand and presented the regiment with a mascot, a mountain lion cub named Florence.[56] The cub, a striking animal with soft auburn fur and delicate eyes, had been turned over to Brow as payment for a stack of blue poker chips.[57] When a volunteer was handed the cub, he looked perplexed at what to do with the animal, before tenderly cradling the mountain lion in the nook of his arm, its head on his shoulder, as if it was a newborn.

After a few more ceremonial words, the volunteers and citizens of Prescott marched to the depot in unison. The train cars that waited to take the heroes to war were adorned in patriotic trappings, red and blue streamers hung from the railings to the chassis, everywhere in between were American flags, large and small, new and old. Two banners bore the mottoes: "Cowboy Regiment of Arizona!" and "Remember the *Maine!*"[58] in big block letters.

At seven o'clock in the evening, the train broke from the station. Children ran up and down the platform, mothers, girlfriends, and wives jumped up to get one last look at their beloved; an old maid had baked some pies and was handing them through the windows to the men.[59] On board, the mountain lion purred; she was now a part of the troop.

When the Arizona contingent passed through the station in Isleta, New Mexico, on May 6th, it decided to expedite the New Mexican troopers' departure by leaving behind an action inducing taunt:

> *Roosevelt's Troopers, Sante Fe.*
> Isleta, N.M., May 6th—Wat 'ell matter with New Mexico.
> Come running or will never get to Cuba.
>   Brodies Arizonians, 200 strong.[60]

The New Mexico troops met at the station the next day at three o'clock in the afternoon. The scene in Santa Fe was almost identical to the one in Prescott, minus the mountain lion. "The afternoon of departure was a typical Santa Fe holiday," a correspondence read. "Stores were closed, a long procession of men, women and children—almost five thousand in number—bearing food, trinkets, and mementos, marched to the station where, amid much cheering, weeping, and waving, the troops left on two sections of the long train, one at five thirty, the other, ten minutes later."[61]

Captain William H. H. Llewellyn, in command of Troop G, left on the second train. The first speaker of the house of the New Mexico territory legislature, Llewellyn was one of the "most popular and useful citizens of the area."[62] A lawyer, miner, and livestock manager, he had also served as a special agent of the Department of Justice in Montana and the Dakotas where he achieved territorial fame by leading the posse that tracked down the infamous Middleton Gang of horse thieves and murderers. Llewellyn survived a shootout on the banks of the Niobrara River, and, after taking four bullets to the body, he arrested the assassin: Doc Middleton himself.[63] Theodore Roosevelt later claimed that Llewellyn was "a good citizen, a political leader and one of the most noted peace officers in the country."[64] Llewellyn still carried the four bullets in his body and though Llewellyn was just forty-five years old, tested and tried, he was still no competition for the fighting spirit of his nineteen year old son, Morgan, also on the train.[65]

Captain Thomas P. Ledwidge was also on board. The twenty-seven-year-old leader in Troop E was a carpenter by trade and had already fought in Cuba as a filibuster during the 1896 skirmishes under rebel leader General Maximo Gomez. Ledwidge had travelled to the small island on his own accord to assist in provoking a revolution within the country. Wounded three times in action, he contracted smallpox and almost died of a hellacious fever in a Cuban hospital. Just two years later, he was ready for more.[66]

Next to Ledwidge was Charles Ballard of Roswell, a rancher and deputy U.S. marshal who had gained fame for capturing the notorious Black Jack Gang.[67] Ballard, a lawman, probably had an awkward yet colorful conversation with George Curry, a sheep trader and territorial senator who had been close friends with Billy the Kid.[68]

In Guthrie, Oklahoma, the scene was much more disciplined and tempered. In contrast to the patriotic extravaganzas in New Mexico and Arizona, the Oklahoma contingent left the depot somberly, in a businesslike manner. "The good-byes had been said early in the evening," the *Daily Oklahoma State Capital* reported, "but few relatives of the boys being present when the train left."[69]

The controlled departure from the Oklahoma contingent had a lot to do with the personality of Allyn Capron, the leader of the outfit and a fifth-generation army soldier. Tall and athletic with yellow hair and blue steely eyes, Capron, according to Theodore, was both the "archetype of the fighting man" and the "best soldier in the regiment."[70] Commanding two companies comprised of territorial natives, Capron "soon impressed himself upon the wild spirit of his followers, that he got them ahead in discipline faster than any other troop in the regiment," Theodore wrote. ". . . He required instant obedience, and tolerated not the slightest evasion of duty."[71]

Travelling with Allyn Capron was easily the most "distinct contingent" Theodore explained, with "a number of Indians—Cherokees, Chickasaws, Choctaws, and Creek"—all of whom, "lived on terms of complete equality with their white comrades."[72]

A world away in a stuffy recruiting room in the army's dispensary building in Washington DC, Theodore Roosevelt stood in the middle of some thirty-odd Easterners.[73] Orbiting the group were a least two dozen newspaper men, one of whom had dubbed the Easterners the "Fifth Avenue Boys," due to the fact that they were "the most disparate of the republic's adventurers, coming from the scholastic seclusion of Harvard, from gilded clubs of the metropolis, from splendors of millionaires' palaces."[74]

In the middle of the room Theodore cleared his throat and then paused. The room was as quiet as the inside of a cave. "Gentlemen, you have now reached the last point," he barked, then stopped. His eyes were squinted and his jaw was clenched to purposely give the appearance of a strong face.

If any one of you doesn't mean business, let him say so now. An hour from now will be too late to back out. Once in, you've got to see it through. You've got to perform without flinching whatever duty is assigned you, regardless of the difficulty or the danger attending it. If it is garrison duty, you must attend to it. If it is meeting the fever, you must be willing. If it is the closest kind of fighting, you must be anxious for it. You must know how to ride, how to shoot, how to live in the open. Absolute obedience to every command is your first lesson. No matter what comes, you mustn't squeal. Think it over—all of you. If any man wishes to withdraw he will be gladly excused, for others are ready to take his place.[75]

Not a man flinched.

Theodore let a minute pass before he reminded them that they were enlisting as nothing more than ordinary troopers, their stipend just thirteen dollars a month.[76] The train for San Antonio was leaving in two days.

The newly-minted plain troopers were men of wealth and prominence. There was Woodbury Kane, a New York playboy and cousin of John Jacob Astor, who raced yachts against the Prince of Wales[77]; Percival Gassett, the wealthy grandson of legendary naval officer "Mad Jack" Percival, commodore of the USS *Constitution*; Theodore Westwood Miller, the nephew of Thomas Edison and eventual founder of the Kappa Psi fraternity[78]; Charles and Henry Bull, sons of a well-off New York financial broker and both members of the Harvard crew team; Reginald Ronalds, a football player from Yale whose father was a tobacco tycoon; Craig Wadsworth, a wealthy society-man, former Harvard football player, and perhaps the country's best steeplechase rider; Robert Church, a physician whose father was the librarian for the U.S. Senate; Townsend Burden, a burly college football star and the son of millionaire iron-steel magnate—a young man who was said to have "money to burn, as well as diamonds to lose"; Hamilton Fish Jr., New York socialite, former captain of the Columbia crew team, and grandson of Ulysses S. Grant's secretary of state; Dade Goodrich, captain of the Harvard crew team and later, chairman of the board of B. F. Goodrich Company.[79]

There were also several athletes.

Bob Wrenn, the world's greatest tennis player and four-time U.S. singles tennis champion; Dudley Dean, the "best quarterback who ever played on a Harvard Eleven"; Horace Deveraux, a rush-end on the 1880 Princeton squad; Sumner K. Gerard and Kenneth Robinson, both national golf champions; Edward Waller, a high-jumper from Yale; Stanley Hollister, Harvard champion in the half-mile; Hal Sayre, the captain of the Harvard football team who left college a month before certain graduation; and Joseph Sampson Stevens, "the world's greatest polo player."[80]

There were also members of the New York Police Department's finest: Philip K. Sweet who fought in the Sioux Campaign in 1891; Henry H. Haywood, a former Cuban ship pilot who had already survived several bouts with yellow fever; and Henry Ebermann, a decorated sharpshooter who served in the 6th Cavalry unit in the Civil War.[81]

All of the Eastern men owed Theodore Roosevelt for the chance to fight with the 1st Volunteer Cavalry. If the war was going to unite the North and the South, Theodore Roosevelt was going to unite the East and the West. Originally, Secretary Alger had authorized an enrollment limit of 780 men, to be filled only from the Western territories. Theodore, craving to have men from the East in his regiment, stormed into Alger's office and in a single conversation the enrollment was raised to one thousand.[82] The real reason why the regiment was expanded is lost to history, but one could venture to guess that Alger simply did not want to tell Roosevelt no for fear of Theodore's reaction.

When the *New York Post* referred to the Easterners as men "with the swellest names" insinuating that they did not have the fighting stuff, Theodore snapped that everyone—absolutely everyone in the regiment—were "real Americans, going as troopers, to be exactly on the same level as cowboys. The best man is to be advanced."[83] All were "the very inspiration of young manhood"; all were ready to storm Cuba.[84]

Shortly after the Fifth Avenue boys had been sworn in, Theodore left for the exit, walking down a large stairwell, a swarm of reporters in tow.

"You're Mr. Roosevelt!" a youth shouted, running up the stairs of the dispensary building, wheezing for air, pushing aside reporters.

"Yes," Roosevelt replied, perplexed. The youth's clothes were tattered, his whole appearance disheveled. One side of his face was completely black and blue with a large swollen bruise.

"I'm Jess Langdon. I've hobo-ed by train all the way from North Dakota, and I want to join your Rough Riders," the boy shouted.

Ten years earlier, when Jess Langdon was six, his father W. C. Langdon, a Badlands veterinarian, had taken him to the Maltese Cross in Medora to inspect Theodore Roosevelt's cattle. Back then, the melancholic widower with thick glasses had picked little Jess up and hugged him, happy to hold a child, perhaps thinking of his own baby, Alice. In Theodore's arms, little Jess Langdon began to kick and scream, "Put me down! I'm no baby."

Ten years later, on the stairwell of the dispensary building, Jess again began to scream, this time shouting out his credentials, "I can ride anything that's got hair on it, I can . . ."

Theodore put up his hand, "Go upstairs and tell them I sent you," he said, grinning from ear to ear. "I'll swear you in personally when I get to San Antonio."

As for the bruise on Jess Langdon's face, he had mistimed his jump while leaping from the train at the Washington yards and smacked into a railroad tie, face first.[85]

Two days later, on May 7th, at ten o'clock at night, the Eastern contingent left Washington on the Baltimore & Ohio Railroad. On board were several millionaires, members of the Knickerbocker and Somerset Clubs, numerous ivy leaguers, many of the nation's best athletes, four policemen, and one hobo teenager from North Dakota.

Theodore was not on the train. He had work left to do in Washington.

While organizing the training grounds in San Antonio, Wood demanded that Theodore stay in Washington. It was Wood's desire to have his second in command in the heart of the war preparations for as long as possible, because Theodore, Wood knew, could forcefully smooth out any hiccups in the equipment appropriations through nothing more than sheer force of personality.

It took everything Theodore had to be subordinate. He wanted action; he wanted to be in San Antonio with the men, drilling, riding, being seen near the Alamo, leading. He gritted his teeth, wholly subservient, and worked at his desk, around the clock. "We had two such human reservoirs of kinetic energy at either end of the line as Wood and Roosevelt," recounted Tom Hall, a West Point adjutant stationed in San Antonio and charged with securing the supplies that Wood had ordered. "I will not attempt to say how much wire was burned off the telegraph terminals by the telegrams sent by these two officers, or how many instruments were damaged; but the total destruction must have been considerable. . . . [T]he wheels began to move, and in a few days the equipment began arriving, in small and varied carloads at first, but eventually with a rush."[86]

Theodore was beside himself at the unpreparedness of the U.S. government. He learned, much to his dismay, that the army had been issued wool winter uniforms, because, according to official government regulations, all clothing procured in the summer months had to be winter clothing, as it allowed ample time for the uniforms to be shipped before the cold winter weather settled in. In other words, wool clothing was issued because protocol held that it was the right course of action for past military conflicts, never mind that the fight was taking place on a Caribbean island and the fighting would begin in sixty days in the middle of summer.[87] The lack of pragmatism only got worse. A senior military official told Theodore that Wood's request for the smokeless Krag-Jørgensens was a foolish mistake. "There was a good deal to be said about having smoke conceal us from the enemy," the superior officer told Theodore, who was no doubt about to erupt.[88] But what about the floating target, what about the fact that our men would be blinded behind a curtain of white? Would the white smoke stop an enemy bullet?

Theodore also learned that before the one thousand horses could be purchased, it was standard regulation that "advertisements had to be run in various journals over a period of thirty days," to ensure fair competition. "The whole damn war could be over in thirty days," Theodore barked to the bureaucrat in charge of horse procurement. "Oh, dear!" was the bureaucrat's response, "I had this office running in such good shape—and then along came the war and upset everything!"[89]

Theodore detested red tape for the entirety of his life; he believed that results mattered, not bureaucracy.

The fact that Roosevelt was second in command and stayed in Washington under Wood's orders had little effect on the public or the newspapers. "The belief of the people [was], that Roosevelt was the colonel;" a reporter for the *Journal* wrote, "that Roosevelt was the organizer; and that Roosevelt would carry the regiment through to victory. . . ."[90] The adoring press, which had more members following the 1st Cavalry than all the other regiments combined, penned numerous articles in an attempt to give the regiment a name. Almost all of them were alliterations to the Lieutenant Colonel: "Teddy's Terror," "Teddy's Holy Terrors," "Roosevelt's Rough 'Uns," "Teddy's Gilded Gang," "Teddy's Cowboy Contingent," "Teddy's Riotous Rounders," "Teddy's Canvasbacks." Eventually, the press and subsequent history books, settled on "Roosevelt's Rough Riders," derived from the popular "Congress of Rough Riders" in Buffalo Bill Cody's world famous Wild West Show.[91]

Theodore hated the name. "The objection to that term," he snarled to a reporter from his desk in Washington, "is that people who read it may get the impression that the regiment is to be a hippodrome affair. Those who get that idea will discover that it is a mistake. The regiment may be one of rough riders, but they will be as orderly, obedient, and generally well disciplined a body as any equal number of men in any branch of the service."[92] All of the men, Theodore urged, had calculated the price of war. They had no doubt read the government's report in April—retold in almost every newspaper—that predicted that at least a full third of the regiment could die from heat stroke or the dreaded yellow fever. The other roughly sixty-percent—those lucky enough to survive the sun and mosquitoes—would have the privilege of dodging Spanish bullets, the smokeless Mausers.

The year following the war, in a significant insight into why his regiment proved so successful, Theodore explains that his followers "all sought entry into the ranks of the Rough Riders as eagerly as if it meant something widely different from hard work, rough fare, and the possibility of death; and the reason why they turned out to be such good soldiers lay largely in the fact that they were men who had thoroughly *counted the cost* before entering, and who went into the regiment because they believed that this offered the best chance for seeing hard and dangerous service."[93]

As for Roosevelt, he went to war knowing he had done his part, or, as he put to his diary, "I have the navy in good shape."[94] On May 12th, at ten o'clock at night, to no fanfare, he left on a train bound for Texas.[95]

By May 11th, just sixteen days after war had officially been declared, almost all of the one thousand troopers had arrived in San Antonio.[96] The scene was historic. At no moment in U.S. history had so many diverse sets of individuals come together in the name of anything. It was chaos, exactly the hippodrome affair that Theodore feared.

"It was the society page, financial column and Wild West Show all wrapped up in one," a reporter quipped.[97]

The diversity was accentuated by the different habiliments of fashion. Some wore dude rags, standing collars, patent leather shoes, and hard-boiled hats. The millionaires and Fifth Avenue dandies were dressed in suits accompanied by "wagon loads each of solid leather trunks and hat boxes."[98] The cowboys adorned chaps, high-heeled boots, and spurs. A few of the athletes, dressed casually in khakis and polo shirts, swung golf clubs or threw around a football. The miners and down-and-out's wore soiled and tattered blue denim overall jumpers. The musicians had their drums, guitars, fifes, cornets, and violins. The gamblers had dice, cards, faro, and crap lay-outs. Florence, the Arizona mountain lion, now the mascot of the entire Camp Wood, was on the prowl lurking through the luggage for loose food. One rough rider recalled that through all the commotion, he even remembered seeing a few Bibles.[99]

The clash of cultures, personalities, antecedents, and wealth symbolized the greatest asset for a country on the rim of a new frontier: diversity. The ivy leaguers with rosy cheeks stood beside cowboys, whose gristly faces had been leathered by the sun and the wind and the snow. The yachtsmen shook hands with the Cherokees. A Cree stared at a Scottish laird trying to figure out what planet the man had come from. Charles Younger, son of Bob Younger of Jesse James's gang, watched the Texas rangers with steely eyes. William Tiffany, the fair-faced, wealthy societal chap noticed that the Marshal of Dodge City was missing an ear, "bitten off in a bar fight," it was later explained. The nation's tennis champion stood gracefully next to the hardened teamster from the steel mill. The world's greatest polo player was perplexed on just how to go about mingling with the fugitive mountain-man who was running from the law and asked everyone just to call him "Mr. Smith," because, as Mr. Smith later explained: "I had a little trouble with a gentleman, and—er—well, in fact, I had to kill him."[100]

Under the scorching Texas sun stood millionaires who never held a job, as well as lawyers, stockmen, doctors, farmers, college professors, miners, adventurers, preachers, prospectors, socialists, journalists, clerks, artists, writers, grocers, linemen, jockeys, insurance agents, a cigar maker, four low-life congressmen, two mechanics, four watchmakers, eight marshals of the law, a publicist, several Jews, some Gentiles, many professed Christians, several Native Americans, a hundred and sixty cowboys, forty-four ranchers, several West Point graduates, ten football players, a few professed thinkers, eight plumbers, four electricians, one weatherman, two singers, one songwriter, five salesmen, thirty-one railroad men, an agent of the Internal Revenue Service, an architect, and two actors.[101] They had come from forty-two states and four unnamed territories.[102]

One man, who was being held for murder, was paroled by a federal judge so that he could enlist with the regiment. He joined the Rough Riders, fought in Cuba, returned to America and was acquitted, not for lack of evidence but because he came home a war hero.[103]

The muster was created on May 17th, and was equally as diverse.[104] The Easterners had wealthy names like Reginald, Winthrop, Townsend, Percival. From the West there was "Hell-Roarer," an unusually shy and quiet man; "Metropolitan Bill," who got the nickname because he boasted his worldly adventures by telling people he had an aunt who at one time had lived in New York; "Rocky Mountain Bill," distinguishable by a huge scar above his right eye made by the claw of a bear—not to be confused with "Smoky Mountain Bill," another man; "Dead Shot Jim," who as he claimed, could shoot a jackrabbit in the eye at a thousand yards from the back of a galloping stallion; "Prayerful James," who only knew profanity; "Sheeney Solomon," a huge redheaded Irishman; "Lariat Ned," who claimed he could lasso a squirrel; "Pork-Chop," a Jew; "Rattlesnake Pete," who had lived with the Moquis tribe and was a snake-whisperer; "Smoky Moore," who tamed vicious horses, known in the frontier as "smoky horses"; "Happy Jack," the only name he would give as it was still uncertain whether he had actually been paroled from McAlester penitentiary; and "Hells Bells," Happy Jack's bunkmate, a Baptist minister.[105]

The mixture of backgrounds perplexed them all for the first few days. "The bizarre make-up of the regiment gave me some queer experiences," Rough Rider Tom Hall wrote. "It is not often that the adjutant of a regiment of soldiers has a millionaire for an orderly one day, a cotillion leader the next, an Arctic explorer the next, an African traveler the next and, so on through the roster. . . . [F]or a short time we even had an opium fiend. We soon got rid of him."[106]

Even the mascots were diverse. There was, of course, Florence, but there was also a majestic war eagle brought by the New Mexico troopers, as well as a stray dog that had been found in San Antonio and named Cuba. Not to be outdone, the Native contingent provided by far the scariest mascot, an invisible rattlesnake. The Natives took such great care of their mascot that the Easterners were too scared to even joke about it.[107]

Amidst the chaotic sea of characters and happenings, a reporter for the *New York World*, recognized a single commonality:

> In many ways the regiment is an elaborate photograph of the character of its founder, Theodore Roosevelt. At odd times he is a ranchman, hunter, politician, reformer, society man, athlete, litterateur, and statesman. Only in his complex brain, with its intense versatility, could the idea of forming such a regiment have been born. But its wide knowledge of the ramifications of the social scale told him that the men he wanted were working upon every round of the ladder from the bottom to the top. He knew that the Fifth Avenue clubman had the genuine fighting stuff, as well as the plainsman who carried a dozen notches on his gun. It only needed opportunity to bring it all out.[108]

The four days from May 11th, when the majority of the regiment had arrived, until May 15th, when Theodore arrived, were chaotic and rowdy. Wood was trying his damnedest to open boxes, count supplies, and disperse training manuals, but the integration of such a diverse set of men, coupled with the triumphant scene in San Antonio, proved to be too much. The volunteers were viewed as celebrities and were treated accordingly; it hardly seemed as if they were there to get ready for a war. The scene was a carnival.

"Thousands of visitors came every day," Rough Rider David Hughes reminisced. ". . . [T]here would be probably 10,000 to 15,000 visitors. Some days the girls would come out and bring a lot of cakes. Everyone selected their partners, and would then sit down and eat alongside each other. We had beans, coffee, and bread. . . ."[109] Surrounding the entrance into the fairgrounds was a beer garden, a stand that sold popcorn, peanuts, and chewing gum, as well as a make-shift stage where local bands boomed "Yankee Doodle" and "There'll be a Hot Time in The Old Town."[110] Curious sightseers from out of town boarded trolley cars with canvas signs that read: Take This Car for the Exposition Grounds Where Roosevelt's Famous Rough Riders Are Camped.[111] To impress the tourists and the ladies, carefree cowboys rode bareback, providing "exhibitions equal to anything Buffalo Bill's Wild West Show put on for $1.00."[112]

The tough men also wanted to prove that they were indeed tough enough. "At the first company mess," a trooper nicknamed Maverick recalled, "one man refused to pass another man the beans. The second man jabbed him with his fork whereupon the first man slashed the other man's cheek with his case-knife, laying open a long gash."

"Jesus!" Maverick said to himself, "Here is where they make fricassee of me."[113]

The newspaper accounts—like the ones stating that the Rough Riders were "all carefully picked men. . .they have hearts of flint, muscles of iron. Every man of them means to return wreathed in laurels"—had clearly gone straight to the troopers' heads.[114] With no guns, horses, or tents, and armed with an inflated sense of self, the Rough Riders went to town hard. Drinking profoundly, they shot out street lights, fired their weapons in bars, and roughed up the locals. "The men," Rough Rider Fred Herrig recounts, "by drunkenness and wildness, terrorized the citizens of San Antonio."[115]

At night, two guards had been placed on duty to keep the men on the grounds and instill some semblance of order. Both guards were incompetent.

At an early morning hour, a group of fifty or so troopers came stumbling back to the fairgrounds. Noticing the two sentries on duty, one drunken soldier came up with a genius plan. The intoxicated ringleader acted as an officer of the detail and formed his men into two columns and marched right up to the main entrance of the grounds. The guards crossed their carbines and halted the detail.

"Our temporary officer demanded a salute and ordered the detail forward," trooper Dick Stanton recalled.

The guards looked at one another and, suspecting that they were outranked, simply let the men enter.

"[We] dispersed very promptly, after it, having gained entrance," Stanton concluded.[116]

Other troopers had less discretion but were equally clever. In the early morning hours, a party of drunken soldiers returned to the barracks in a coach, and was halted by the same two guards. Instantly a head was thrust out of the window.

"Stand by, fellow, and let Colonel Roosevelt and his staff pass!" an intoxicated trooper slurred.

The sentry scrambled to open the gate and stood at attention as the wagon rolled into the grounds. The guards obviously did not question why Theodore Roosevelt was making his entrance to camp drunk at four in the morning.[117]

The conductor of the Southern Pacific told Theodore that the train would arrive in San Antonio with the sun, around seven in the morning. Too anxious to sleep, Roosevelt had spent the pre-dawn hours poring through a slim book, *Drill Regulations for Cavalry, United States Army, 1896.*[118]

He had received the report from McKinley that American forces could embark for Cuba in as little as ten days, probably no more than twenty.

As the light of the world snuck over the horizon, Theodore stared out into the tanned countryside of south-central Texas. He knew he was about to embark on the adventure of his lifetime.

But questions remained. How could he unite the widely diverse men in such a short period of time? How should he discipline men accustomed to life on the free range? How could he lead captains that were all more experienced militarily? What leadership lessons should he draw upon?

The conductor barked into the train car, it was fifteen minutes until San Antonio.

Theodore leaned back in his seat. From here forward the world would be told of his every move; failure and death a distinct possibility. He was now truly a frontiersman fighter, straight out of a Mayne Reid novel. It was all so perfect.

When the train arrived, the band at the depot started into "It'll be a Hot Time in the Old Town."[119] Theodore hit the platform sprinting, charging towards the throng of city notables and newspapermen awaiting his arrival. He was energetic and vigorous, and he looked the part: "His khaki trousers stuffed into spit-polished cordovan boots, the stiff collar of his epauletted, fawn-colored, khaki jacket bearing the initials U.S.V. beside embroidered crossed sabers surmounted by the number 1, the brim of his shapeless campaign hat rakishly pinned up on the side with a huge crossed-sabers badge."[120]

Roosevelt went directly to the officers' headquarters at the Menger Hotel where he freshened up, ate a hearty breakfast, and collected his thoughts one last time. When he left for the fairgrounds, he knew he was going on stage.

Five years and five months later, Theodore Roosevelt wrote a private letter, on White House stationary, to his son Ted.

> A man must develop his physical prowess up to a certain point; but after he has reached that point there are other things that count more. In my regiment nine-tenths of the men were better horsemen than I was, and probably two-thirds of them better shots than I was, while on the average they were certainly hardier and more enduring. Yet after I had had them a very short while they all knew, and I knew too, that nobody else could command them as I could.[121]

17. UNITING THE FRONTIERSMEN

BOUNCING ALONG TOGETHER IN A CARRIAGE, LEONARD WOOD shows Theodore Roosevelt the lay of the San Antonio fairgrounds while complaining that the tents, rifles, and fatigues had all yet to arrive. The majority of the men had been forced to sleep in the grandstand bleachers or on the floor of the exposition building, which was covered with dust and crawling with scorpions.[1]

Above the creak of the carriage wheels, Wood and Roosevelt spoke of the challenge that lay ahead. Wood would focus on the technical and military aspects of organizing. Roosevelt would manage the adaptive aspects of leadership, uniting, and inspiring.

When the carriage stopped at the headquarters tent, several hundred troopers had already lined up along the narrow stretch of road to get the first glimpse of Theodore Roosevelt. Regiment trumpeter Emilio Cassi, on cue, sounded the officers' call which sent several hundred more men running in from all over the grounds.[2]

"Upon his arrival, believe me, there was a grand rush on the part of everyone to get a look at the man who was the prime mover of the organization," trooper George Sands recalled.[3]

As Theodore stepped out of the carriage, a trooper bounded toward him with a wooden box. "Speech, Colonel Roosevelt! Speech!"[4] All of the men were giddy and celebratory; everyone was cheerily carefree.

Theodore smiled, nodding his head in approval and stepped onto the wooden crate. Then his demeanor changed, he began to glare.

I haven't much to say at this time. When we come back from Cuba I'll say more. I have heard about your carousals in San Antonio and from now on it must stop. Pay strict attention to your officers, work hard, and drill. If you do, this regiment will be a regiment. As it is now, you are a mob, and are worthless to me as soldiers! The man who doesn't obey his officers and maintain perfect discipline will be fired out of the Army.[5]

Then he paused, his expression something of a contorted scowl.

"Men," he concluded abruptly, snapping off his words, "I shall not hesitate to spend your lives as I spend my own."[6] Turning on his heel, he jumped off the box and bounded into the tent. The festive carefree mood had been obliterated, his audience left stunned.

As disappointed as Theodore had been of his men's late-night antics, they were more disappointed in the way their lieutenant colonel looked. He was a far cry from the gallant warrior that the newspapers depicted. He was short, squat, with huge white teeth. When he spoke, his eastern accent was almost comical in its high-pitched squeal. Worse, he had round funny little eyeglasses attached to a black ribbon. Not exactly the look of a warrior.

"Colonel Roosevelt was not popular among the men at first, as we did not know him," rough rider Cliff Scott later explained, "and as we were told by rumor, he was a New York cop with lots of money, but as we talked it over among ourselves, we wanted somebody that would scrap . . . when the time arrived, the bunch was lined up to see him. There was a noticeable wave of disappointment. You could hear different groups discussing him, but the big objection was that he wore glasses, and he was a New Yorker. He was very unpopular among us cowpunchers who did not know him."[7]

Kenneth Harris, a disappointed trooper, was also not impressed, "When I seen him in San Antonio I figgered he was raised a pet an' wouldn't kick if you tickled his heels with a toothpick."[8]

"[He is a] banty rooster with funny eyeglasses," Bill Owens told another trooper after seeing Roosevelt for the first time. ". . . I don't like the way he skins his teeth back when he talks to a fellow."[9]

Theodore expected this. It was the same thing that happened when he arrived in Medora, North Dakota a decade earlier. To prepare his men for battle and win their favor, Theodore began a two-pronged strategy. First, he had to implement structure so that discipline could prevail. Then, he would have to increase his individual informal authority and gain respect. Only if he could be successful in both of those endeavors could he begin to unite the men around the collective goal of becoming the next link on the proverbial chain of American frontier heroes.

To create a holding environment—that is to say, generate circumstances where leadership can function—Theodore forbade everyone to leave the grounds at night unless they had a pass. "Rigid guard duty was established at once, and everyone was impressed with the necessity for vigilance and watchfulness," he explained. "The policing of the camp was likewise attended to with the utmost vigor."[10] To emphasize vigilance and prove that "short work will be made to the saloon cowboy, the bad man who wants to be a terror," Roosevelt placed an astounding one hundred and twenty-eight men on guard duty—over ten percent of the regiment total.[11] Just one day after Theodore's declaration that the men were just a mob, three troopers got drunk, snuck out, and shot up the town. Theodore discharged them the next morning. Word travelled fast; the Lieutenant Colonel meant business. Not another man was fired for misconduct the entire time in San Antonio.[12]

To supplement the structure of discipline, Theodore instituted a strict regimen of drilling. "The first ten days broke the back of the difficulty of organizing," a trooper writes, before adding that it was a ten days that he "never wishes to see again."[13] The drills implemented a semblance of order to camp and made the men too tired to leave at night.

"For the first time in their lives they were subjected to military drill," a newspaper recounted. ". . . [T]hey were drilled from sunrise to sunset, moonrise to sun up again."[14]

The schedule was appropriately grueling.

Reveille sounded at 0530 hours, a roll call followed, and at 0610 was stable duty where troopers had twenty minutes to feed and ready the horses. After that, breakfast in the mess hall, and by 0830 the horses were led to the river and watered.

From 0900 until 1300 the undisciplined and individualistic men—"accustomed to the freedom of polo hunting, and the open range"—were drilled in the nuances of advancing, flanking, wheeling in, wheeling out, fanning in, fanning out, fanning back, and maintaining columns.[15]

Lunch was at 1330 and after that, in the heat of the day, the horses were returned to the stables and the men were drilled on foot. The cowpuncher, who stood with his legs wide apart and his back hunched, was now made to stand erect with his heels together, his shoulders thrown back, his head straight.[16] The men were taught to present arms and military lingo was tested. Officers barked orders; volunteers swore under their breath. Never mind that the guns had not arrived. Broomsticks and tree limbs were used to simulate weapons.

The San Antonio afternoons were vicious; the sun mercilessly beat down on the men. The mercury in a thermometer signaled over a hundred degrees in the shade. By the late afternoon, dust and sweat covered everything. The easterner covered in mud, and a new tan, was as bronzed as the Native; the yachtsman from New York indistinguishable from the fugitive from parts unknown. Only two showers were operable on the entire fairgrounds, both of which spewed dark brown water.[17] To become distinguishable again, the men, by the hundreds, took their soap to the river to bathe.

At 1600, another stable call was commenced and then more drills. After that, an hour-long dress parade followed, where the men looked "exactly as a body of cowboy cavalry should look," according to Theodore. Supper was from 1900 to 1930 before a brief service from the chaplain Henry W. Brown. Next, there was night school for the officers, before final roll call after tattoo, which sounded a 2030. Thirty minutes later, "Taps" sounded, lights out.[18]

"It was hard work," a trooper remembered, "the hardest that ever fell to me."[19]

As the days rolled along, attention to details became paramount, and emphasized in every action. "[After Theodore] had arrived," a trooper recalled, ". . . he went right into administering his duties in the regiment in a very businesslike manner . . . it was the small details that he seemed to be more careful about."[20]

Cleanliness in camp, in the stables, and in the mess room brooked no laxity. A focus on hygienic conditions meant that no detail was too small. Everyone had to take care of his own area, the non-conformist easily identified. It was the attention to details, Theodore urged, that illustrated a readiness to fight. Frank Brito, of Troop H, was frustrated. "We were young and full of vigor, and it was tough trying to fill twenty-four hours in camp with a war going on. We were sure it would be over while we were drilling out there at Camp Wood."[21] The men did not want to drill, did not care about details; they just wanted to fight, to become famous. Drilling is what mattered, Theodore insisted to the mob; the U.S. Army would not let them fight the Spanish if they were not prepared. Details, details, details—if you wanted to be a hero, you must first be organized.

The first week of camp was brutal. "It was the wise policy of our colonel to break the men into discipline by degrees," a Rough Rider later wrote, "and gradually tighten the bonds."[22] Each night, as the fairgrounds descended into darkness, the exhausted soldiers were too tired to raise hell, falling asleep sore and beat.

At night, the guards on duty were the only ones stirring about. Over at the headquarters tent, a soft light shone deep into the small hours of the morning. "Lieutenant Colonel Roosevelt burned the midnight oil in studying tactics," Sergeant Ledwidge vividly remembered, "and what he learned one night he practiced on us the next day."[23]

Theodore Roosevelt was in heaven. During the first week of camp he bounded about, jovial as a carefree boy; a bundle of energy that never seemed to tire.[24] The contrast of Wood's and Roosevelt's leadership styles was obvious to the volunteers. "Colonel Roosevelt was the 'whole cheese,' so to speak," a trooper explained. "He was everywhere and everybody went to him. He was the busy man of the busy bunch. If anything had to be done, he was the man to do it. Colonel Wood, of course, was working too, but he was organizing the regiment and had a good deal of clerical work to do, which kept him more or less inside, while Roosevelt did the outside work, or what they termed 'rustling,' and he was some rustler too."[25]

When the dog tents—two pieces of canvas four feet wide and six and a half feet long, buttoned to a pole standing three feet tall—finally arrived on May 20th, Wood's militarily-precise layout of the fairground was noticeable. The meticulously positioned tents, coupled with the clean pathways and the sanitary mess hall were all noticeable indicators of Wood's management ability.[26] Onlookers could visibly see what Colonel Wood was doing for the regiment.

Those in camp were beginning to feel the Theodore Roosevelt effect.

From his time in the Badlands, Roosevelt had learned that those with formal authority—those who held positions of power that were given, not gained—were not automatically respected by the westerner. The wealthy ranch owner that barked orders but did not do work himself was shunned; the local sheriff who hid behind his badge was disregarded as a phony. On the open range, trust was only given informally, that is to say, it was earned through respect. To gain informal authority, Theodore just acted, as he put it, "like being on the roundup again."[27]

"Colonel Roosevelt quickly won the love and confidence of the men who were under him, by refusing to accept for himself any conveniences which he could not offer to his men," a reporter for the *Journal* noticed. "He slept as they slept, and ate what they ate."[28]

He used the same mess kit issued to the troopers, he fraternized with the men, he labored with them under the raging Texas sun, and he laughed with them—the Indians called him Laughing Horse.[29] And on May 19th, he just wowed them.

Shortly after the break of dawn, the first mounted drill was held, and the horses that Wood had purchased from local ranchers were drawn by lots—the same protocol as was done on the round-up.[30] Several hundred soldiers were arranged in a semi-circle in the fairgrounds, timidly holding the reins of wild, snorting horses that were almost all unbroken.[31]

When the command to mount was given, all hell broke loose. "Instantly, around three hundred to four hundred horses started to 'Buck,' all at the same time," a Rough Rider chuckled in remembrance. "It is a picture I never expect to see again!"[32] Men, saddles, horses, and dirt shot heavenward. Half of the Rough Riders were bucked off, several men were kicked, numerous soldiers were sent off to the field hospital, limping. It was very dangerous work.

"It was here that the men first got a glimpse of Roosevelt's horsemanship," a Rough Rider later stated in amazement.[33] Theodore, sensing an opportunity, took to the stage, demanding right in front of his men, to ride the largest and wildest horse in the bunch, a ferociously rough iron-gray.

Rough Rider Cliff Scott recounted the scene.

When Colonel Roosevelt saw the horse, he said, "That one is mine, I want that one!" A number of us smiled, for here is where we figured that we would lose our colonel if he ever tried to ride that one, even after someone had broke him, but he picked up a rope and started out to rope him and I wondered what kind of a fool he was, because anyone who ever saw this horse would know that this fellow would fight; but he made a clean throw and got him, and it was done in the correct way, and it rather surprised us, but when he saddled that brute without any help, (He would not let us help him down) and mounted him and took off his hat and slapped him over both rumps. . . we were thunderstruck, and wondered who was responsible for that story that he was a New York cop.[34]

Theodore's actions were genuine, yet purposeful. He knew what he was doing. A measure of a person's competency on the frontier, Theodore already knew, was weighed on a horse. He had already learned this on the roundup in Medora, and now, a decade later, he knew how to prove that he was capable, unafraid, worthy of respect.

Later in the same day, sixty officers who had been issued blank cartridges for their six shooters, ran their horses towards the squadron at full speed, firing their weapons as fast as they could. The idea was to accustom the previously free-range horses to stand fire in battle. "The consequence," a trooper recalled, "was that we stampeded nearly the entire outfit . . . you could see many of the horses going at full speed, dragging a trooper with him, the trooper doing everything possible to regain his feet."[35] The scene was hazardous and loud, forceful and precarious. Just like Theodore.

"[He rode] a high spirited horse, full of action," a trooper relived the scene, "and he put him [the horse] through all the paces, jumps, and quick turns and would 'set' his horse in the shortest kind of space. He joined the non-coms in firing his pistol at full speed and cutting up all sorts of antics while horses were pitching all around him."[36] The effect was instant and profound. As Theodore charged and raced in the sweltering sun, "the men immediately recognized their Master Leader," the trooper confirmed, "and after their talks, in groups, that night after supper, they were ready to go anywhere at his command. I repeat again, 'anywhere!'"[37]

The following day, Theodore again embraced the stage, orchestrating a conflict to prove a point.

Henry Bardshar, from the Arizona cowboy contingent, was Roosevelt's point-man for errands. In the inferno that was the San Antonio afternoon, Roosevelt sent Bardshar to the telegraph office downtown and Bardshar had no more than arrived at the office when an important telegraph for Roosevelt came in over the wire. Bardshar instantly remounted his horse and charged back to camp at full tilt, message in hand. He flung himself off his horse just as Tom Hall, the regiment adjutant, came into view. Hall, a by-the-book military man from West Point hired by Wood to procure supplies, was insulted.

"What do you mean by brushing past me in this manner without saluting!?" barked Hall, referring to military protocol to salute a ranking officer.

"I am in too much of a hurry," responded Bardshar, holding up the telegram.

"Why haven't you got your coat on?" snapped the adjutant, referring to the standard issued jacket that Bardshar had taken off on account of the heat and had noticeably fastened to the back of his saddle.

"Aw you go plum to Hell," cried Bardshar.

"You are under arrest!" shrieked Hall, "go to the guard house!"

Roosevelt heard the commotion and blasted out of his tent. Several nearby troopers heard the row and listened intently, exceptionally interested in what Roosevelt had to say on the matter.

"I put him under arrest for subordination, and for not wearing his coat," Hall explained as Theodore charged forward, fully expecting the Lieutenant Colonel's support.

"Forget it, Hall," shouted Roosevelt. "I heard what passed between you. As for the coat, it's a hot day and I think that Trooper Bardshar was entirely right in taking it off."[38]

Hall bristled and snorted about military decorum, but it did no good. Roosevelt had made up his mind and had made Hall look small. The troopers who had witnessed the event were impressed; the encounter became *the* news of the day. Roosevelt was one of us, they whispered to each other in the barracks that night.

But why would Roosevelt downplay military hierarchy when he was trying to instill military detail and discipline? Was this not counterintuitive, even contradictory?

The reason for Roosevelt's actions is best described by another trooper. "We sure had a lot more respect for him [Roosevelt] from then on [after the coat incident]. In fact we recognized him as the boss. . . . [T]here were a lot of us that could not tell a lieutenant from a colonel, and we had never had any military training, and the rule with most of us was that one man is as good as another if he can do his work, and none of us ever took an order very seriously unless it came from the Boss."[39]

The title "The Boss" is a reference to the foreman of the round-up, the man who had to prove his competency—informal authority—by leading ranch hands from all over the region, from all sorts of different outfits. Each spring during the cattle drive, "The Boss" had to prove himself to a new set of ranchmen before expecting to be followed. The Boss was capable, tough, and egalitarian to a point.

Almost three decades after the regiment disbanded, Roosevelt historian Hermann Hagedorn wrote a sensationalist account of the feats of the regiment in a book titled *The Rough Riders*, published in 1927. For source material, much of which he did not use in his book, Hagedorn interviewed several members of the regiment, now in the twilight of their lives. The surviving interview notes are littered with disrespectful remarks towards adjutant Tom Hall, and it is almost comically absurd—even thirty years after the regiment disbanded—how sore the men were towards Hall: "He knew everything pertaining to the army backwards and forwards, but he did not know how to get along with the men, and in the matter of discipline, he was just a plain 'Jack-ass'"; "practically kicked out of the regiment"; "overbearing"; "made many enemies in the regiment"; "would have shot him if they had half a chance"; "particularly disagreeable"; "I'd smash my face in [if he were my troop leader]."[40]

In 1899, when Tom Hall wrote a book, *Fun and Fighting of the Rough Riders,* another trooper, A. F. Cosby, took out a column in the *New York Times* to refute Hall's claims, highlighting its inaccuracies, and lambasting Tom Hall's contribution to the regiment.

In battle, Tom Hall would indeed prove to be a runaway and a liar. During the very first sound of enemy fire in Cuba, he sprinted back to headquarters camp shouting that the Rough Riders were getting annihilated and that he carried with him "Wood's dying message to his wife."[41] Neither of which were true. The Rough Riders had not been routed, nor had Wood even been shot, let alone dispatched final words to his wife. But what is telling about the surviving Rough Riders interview notes is that they do not focus on Hall's cowardice or his dodging to the rear during battle. The men were more offended—a third of a century later—that Tom Hall had the audacity to believe that he was entitled to lead them because of his rank; that he was authorized to lead because he had a fancy title.

After the coat incident, Roosevelt sent Captain Brodie, also a West Point graduate, to speak with Hall. "You don't know these men, Hall," Brodie said, "and I do. They are not as ignorant as they look. They may not know things that you and I know perhaps, but they know a lot of other things that may be just as valuable. You and I have been through West Point. Remember it took us four years to learn the rudiments of soldiering, and here you are expecting these men to know everything that you know within a week. You are unreasonable."[42]

Hall refused to listen to Brodie, and the men refused to be led by Hall.

Theodore's greatest leadership feat, and much more impressive than his charge on San Juan Heights, was that he understood where his followers were, and led them from there. He would have loved to implement military hierarchy, but with just a few days to train, he could not force the cowboys and Western men to unlearn something so deeply engrained into their belief system. The men from the frontier believed that the "leader" must be willing to serve the "follower"; the leader must look them in the eye, be authentic, be capable, be tough, be competent. Leadership was earned, not given.

Sergeant Thomas P. Ledwidge, who, like all of the men, detested Tom Hall and loved Theodore Roosevelt, was impressed that Theodore understood "the kind of men we had . . . ready to serve under another man, but never yielding their personal equality with him. Equality as comrades in arms, no matter what the rank, was a distinguishing characteristic of the mental attitude of these men—a quality just a bit hard to portray without overdrawing."[43]

It had become clear, fourteen years after the fact, that the forlorn and melancholic young man from the East had introspectively internalized how "The Boss" in the Badlands became a leader.

The thorny issue of uniting men from such diverse backgrounds was Theodore's next obstacle to conquor. He knew well the stigma associated with the outsider. He had experienced the funny looks, the jeers, the taunts of "four-eyes!" from the townsfolk in Medora. He knew that many of the Western troopers had never met a man from the East, and they already distrusted him.

"When they [the Easterners] arrived we were a little abashed, for they all wore fine clothes, and looked like they had just stepped out of a band box, and we were all dressed in old clothes that we could throw away," a cowpuncher recalled, sheepishly jealous.[44]

"We always considered the eastern man as a 'tender-foot,'" another proclaimed.[45] "There was considerable fighting among us," confirms another.[46]

The *San Antonio Express* was no help, claiming that "ninety percent of them [the easterners] carry a large wad in their side pockets with which to play a little game of draw and large bank accounts behind them. Some of them have their 'men' with them to care for their uniforms and top boots at a salary of $60 a month, also to cook at $100 a month."[47]

Despite what anybody said or thought, Theodore knew that all the men in the regiment were not that different from one another. They just needed to embrace their similarities, and to do so before they killed one another.

Shortly after the drill regimen started, a report reached Theodore that the Westerners had planned to make life tough for the eastern tenderfoot. "We didn't want a lot of dudes to have to take care of," a cowpuncher recalled, "and it was decided among a bunch of us that we would make it too unpleasant for them to stay."[48]

"Colonel Roosevelt, however, was always on the job, and heard of it and scented trouble," a soldier remembered. ". . .[H]e gave us a short talk, and told us to give them a fair trial, that they were good sports, and that he would personally stand sponsor for them. The following morning, Roosevelt asked us to line up when the New Yorkers came [by] and give them a good old cowboy yell." The Westerner then admitted that he only gave the easterners a "good old cowboy yell" because "we had learned to love the colonel by this time and I don't think there was a man that wouldn't have climbed a tree and jumped out if Roosevelt had told him to."[49]

Roosevelt knew that he must put the work of uniting the troopers back to the men themselves. That is to say, he could not force them to like each other; they must unite on their own. He decided to bunk the Easterner aristocrat with the cowpuncher and scattered men from different geographic locations into different troops. Collusion with only like-minded troopers became impossible. The result was exactly what Theodore expected.

"They were good mixers," a cowboy said of the Easterners, "and seemed to take a real interest in us, and it was only a short time until we found out that they were real he-men, and would fight as quick for us as we learned to fight for them."[50] One Westerner, David Hughes, remembered that he distrusted the Eastern man until he was forced to do laundry with him. "I never will forget the time young William Tiffany, of New York, and myself boiled the cooties out of our clothes together in the same oil can and washed our clothes out and waited around exchanging little experiences we had passed through until our clothes dried so we could put them on."[51]

Another great equalizer was horsemanship, and in the early days of camp, a rumor spread from tent to tent that a city-slicker was about to break in a "Roman-nosed claybank with a retrospective eye" at the entrance of the exposition hall. A crowd of Westerners gathered, quietly snickering in unison. The tenderfoot was going to break his neck, they chortled under their breath. This should be fun to watch. An account captures the scene:

> The crowd gathered, ready to watch the departure—or downfall. In time, the "tenderfoot" came out. . .
>
> Anyone could see the critter tethered near the Hall was wild and that it would become a volcano of action the moment a foot was put in the stirrup. But apparently not the slicker who had chosen it.
>
> The moment came. With rhythmic ease, he [the "tenderfoot"] gathered up the reins and swung into the saddle. A practiced heel touched the claybank ever so lightly, quick and commanding. The animal tensed, as though ready to go into a tantrum, but the rider held its head high, signaling authority with a pull of the reins. Instantly there was recognition of the master in the animal's eyes. A hint of a lunge to the side, the slightest bit of a jog with its hind legs, and off it went in a gentle canter.
>
> The horseman raised his sombrero and tipped it gracefully as he moved away. Westerners stared in amazement—and with some degree of disappointment.[52]

The tenderfoot easterner was actually Craig Wadsworth, described as a "crack polo player and perhaps best cross-country rider in America."[53] Wadsworth was theatrically proving what Theodore was telling everyone: the foxhunters and polo players of the East could ride as well as the cowboys and ranchers of the West. They just needed a chance to prove it.

To promote equality Theodore urged his captains to treat everyone equally. Sergeant Ledwidge, heeding Theodore's wishes, gave orders to a couple dozen easterners to fill in the filthy latrines west of the officers' tents. Symbolically, it was a gem of an order. The sight of the wealthy nobles sweating in the sun covering fecal matter was humbling for everyone. "The New York swells turned to it with a will; not one of them flinched," a rough rider remembered, "Seeing the stuff they were made of, Ledwidge himself took up a spade and did his share of the work even though he was supposed to do nothing but boss the job."

"Even the boss works on a western outfit!" Ledwidge said aloud for all to hear.[54]

The smell was rancid, the sight uniting. Twenty rich aristocrats and one of the highest ranking captains from the New Mexico contingent covered in fecal matter, together, as one.

To further the principle of equality, Theodore placed several of the Fifth Avenue boys on meager chore duty. Millionaire Easterners like Woodbury Kane, were in charge of cooking and serving for the New Mexican cowpunchers. A polo champ was ordered to chop wood for the cooking stove. Dade Goodrich dug a ditch near the entrance.

Theodore also introduced a rule that if one man complained about another man's work, then the complainer must take over the detail himself. Woodbury Kane, who barely knew how to boil water, had put equal amounts salt and rice in the cauldron. Jack Amrine, from the Indian territory, took one bite and balled out, "Who in the Hell salted this rice," before catching himself and guiltily adding, "but that is just the way I like it!"[55]

The Westerners soon found out that just because an Easterner had money or a college education, it did not mean that he would "shirk his tasks nor fall off his horse."[56] The little experiences born of doing laundry, breaking in horses, cooking, serving one another, and digging holes, proved to unify the men. "It only took a short time after we began working together to understand one another," a trooper claimed, ". . . [and] we became welded into one large family."[57]

One week into Theodore's drill and unity campaign, Camp Wood was humming right along. The question on everyone's mind turned to whether the regiment would see action in the war. Would Secretary Alger select the Rough Riders to fight? Would the war be over before the 1st Volunteer Cavalry could get to it? Unsettling newspaper accounts from Havana told that the U.S. navy might just end the war before the army could land forces onto the island.[58]

The uncertainty in Havana coupled with the strict, now perhaps futile drilling, made everyone nervous. The men were sunburned and impatient, tired and worried. Theodore knew this. "Most of the men had simple souls," he explained. "They could relate facts but they said very little about what they simply felt."[59] It was his job, as he saw it, to know what they felt, to manage their emotions.

An Indian named Colbert retold a story years later that illustrates just how well Theodore monitored the pulse of his men.

"The sun was hot, it was hell! . . .we had more trouble than you ever saw keeping in line and step," Colbert explained about the mid-afternoon foot drills. "Couldn't seem to improve much either no matter how hard we tried. Oh, but we wished we could get into the saddle again!"

The New Mexican troopers knew that Theodore was on his way to inspect them, look at the details, judge improvement. The contingent was exhausted, the San Antonio heat miserable. But it was the rumor that they might not get the opportunity to fight in Cuba that was downright demoralizing. The result was a drill that was a hot mess.

> . . . the same old trouble! Out of step, out of line—irregular. We knew it. [Colbert continued]
>
> Then Roosevelt appeared . . . filed by several times, wheeled, marched again, filed by, wheeled, marched again. Then he halted.

Roosevelt watched us during those memorable moments! And we watched him! We wondered what he would say— what he could say!

He smiled. He grinned. Finally he beamed on us as we stood at attention before him.

"'Well,' said he, 'boys, I've seen better marching than that, but I'd be damned if I ever saw any worse!'"

The relief was instantaneous. We lost all order, threw up our hats, attempted to straighten out our legs and laughed with him. From that moment he had us![60]

Theodore sensed the mood of his men and acted accordingly. He did not beat his men when they were down. His informal authority skyrocketed.

But as insightful as Theodore acted, he also went too far in his effort to build his informal authority. Just a few days later and just minutes after a four-hour drilling session in the mesquite of San Antonio, Roosevelt was leading a team of haggard troopers back to camp when they passed a beer garden near Riverside Park. Theodore halted the squadron and lined them up on the road. The mud on Roosevelt's spectacles was, according to a trooper, "almost as thick as the glasses he wore."[61]

"Captains will dismount their troops and the men can go in and drink all the beer they want, which I will pay for," Theodore shouted. Clinching his teeth and shaking his fist in the face of the line, he added, "But if any man drinks more beer than is good for him, I will cinch him."[62]

The tactic of buying the men beer had worked wonders for Theodore in Medora. Often, he would walk into the saloon, open up a tab, let his men drink up, and then as the night ended shout "last drink, move it on out."[63] It gained him respect—it made Theodore more like "The Boss," rather than the wealthy ranch owner from the East.

But this instance was different. Theodore was now a member of the U.S. military. His men were not ranch hands, they were soldiers.

Back at headquarters, Wood got wind of the beer incident. He did not let on that he knew which high-ranking officer had taken his men to get beer. Instead he simply addressed the broad rumor of "officers drinking with their men." Wood confesses that he "painted it in the most dreadful fashion possible and ended up by saying that of course an officer who would go out with a large batch of men and drink with them was quite unfit to hold a commission."[64] When Wood finished his stern lecture to all of his officers, the room was dead silent.

"I went up to my tent," Wood recalled later. "In a few minutes I heard this quick pattering walk of the colonel coming up, and he scratched on the tent and said, 'I would like to speak with the Colonel. I want to talk with you, sir. I listened to what you said this afternoon. I agree with every word you said. You are quite right, quite proper.'"

Theodore drew a long breath. "I wish to tell you, sir, that I took the squadron, without thinking about this question of officers drinking with their men, and I gave them all a schooner of beer. I wish to say, sir, that I agree with what you said. I consider myself the damnedest ass within ten miles of this camp. Good night."[65]

And off Theodore went, humbled.

Theodore's response to Wood, in many ways, exemplifies the personal authenticity that made Roosevelt's men love him. In San Antonio, Theodore never pretended to be something he was not; he freely admitted mistakes and never tried to hide his weaknesses. During the few little pockets of down time at camp, Theodore would take to an open field, in front of everyone, and practice leading. He would scan the *Drill Regulations,* then put the book behind his back, ponder what he had read, and then shout out orders to invisible troopers. He was literally practicing his commands right in front of the men he was already supposed to know how to lead.[66] Worse, in his first attempt to conduct a mounted drill and apply what he learned, he failed miserably. Mixing up the commands for different drills, he shouted out a series of contradictory orders which resulted in a tangled knot of a hundred men and horses. Cuss words were thrown out by the troopers, captains were annoyed. Roosevelt owned the mistake, quickly apologized, and called in the major of the squadron to take over the drill. He himself retreated to the side.[67]

Why then did the troopers never dissent against Theodore's lack of competency in military drill? The soldiers were entrusting this man with their lives and he did not seem to know how to set-up cavalry columns or how to give simple orders. Yet the men never rebelled, complained to their captains, or ever seemed to question Theodore at all. A Rough Rider who Theodore out-ranked, actually took pride in helping the second-in-command of the entire regiment learn how to conduct straightforward drills, proudly boasting that he "was the one" who "had the honor" of drilling Colonel Roosevelt in the Manual of Arms "down behind the grandstand."[68]

It seems that it all came down to Theodore's authenticity. The men empathized with him. Roosevelt was trying his best to learn, not afraid to show his deficiencies. His mock-drill practice and his willingness to admit mistakes went far with the men who were also trying to learn drills for the first time in their lives. "The more they [the western men] saw him and heard him, the more they liked him," a trooper explained, "His everlasting energy, his quick decision with a shriek of 'yes' or 'no,' *and he meant just what he said.*"[69]

It was Theodore's enthusiasm that trumped all. Every day, under the scorching sun, he was an engine of energy: running, jumping, laughing, smiling, helping his men, shouting quick com-mands, apologizing, asking questions, firing off his six-shooter, hopping on his horse, hopping off his horse, slapping troopers on the back, running from tent to tent, asking a grunt about his family's history, then leaning forward to intently listen to every detail of that man's life.

In every action, it was clear to the troopers that Roosevelt enjoyed leading them. As his correspondence in San Antonio suggests, it was also clear that Theodore harbored great respect for his men: "I really doubt if there ever has been a regiment quite like this"—"I cannot help but being a little enthusiastic about it"—"they are intelligent as well as game, and they study the tactics"—"[they] could whip Caesar's Tenth Legion"—"the way these men have got their wild half-broken horses into order is something marvelous."[70]

He believed in them so much that they were almost forced to believe in him.

"The colonel was always as ready to listen to a private as to a major-general,"[71] said a trooper. Theodore, for his part, explained that leaders "must not be over-familiar with their men, and yet that they must care for them in every way."[72]

"They [Rough Riders] would be willing to go into the jaws of death to serve him," Sergeant Ledwidge stated frankly, "because he would do the same for them."[73]

On Sunday, May 22nd, a full week after Theodore arrived, Captain Llewellyn of the New Mexico contingent called attention to the leadership in the headquarters' tent that the Articles of War had not been read to the soldiers.[74] The articles should have already been recited to each trooper, and in the race to get to war, no one had remembered to do so.[75] Rather than make the reading the usual "red taped affair on a troop by troop basis," the entire regiment was brought together in a grand ceremony of patriotic accord. Though it is not known who came up with the idea, it is hard to imagine that Mittie Roosevelt's son did not have a hand in the decision for pomp and pageantry.[76]

"Perhaps the most impressive day in San Antonio was Sunday, May 22nd" a reporter for the *Journal* wrote. "The whole regiment, fully uniformed, was arrayed in squadron formation before Colonel Wood's tent early in the morning. The object was the reading of the articles of war, and the ceremony lasted nearly an hour and a half. The stately passages were pronounced in solemn sentences by the captains of troops, and the men were much impressed."[77] The scene was moving; it brought the gravity of the situation that much closer to the men's hearts. It was also the Lord's Day and drill was called off. Shortly after breakfast, the harmony of the cowboy choir "was plainly heard in San Antonio, a mile away," a journalist proclaimed.[78] The cowpunchers and the millionaires, the Indians and the foxhunters, the outlaws and the minister, all sang patriotic melodies, together.

A. R. Perry—"the best bronco buster of them all"—stood up and sang "Onward, Christian Soldiers" by himself. He had no singing talent, but he gave the song everything in him. When

Perry sat down, his comrades of different rank, heritage, wealth, and skin color were all seen wiping away tears.[79]

Eighteen hundred miles away, at an off-the-cuff meeting with a few journalists, Thomas Platt, the sixty-five-year-old kingpin of the New York Republican machine, stated laconically that the Republican nominee for governor of New York was still undecided, though the election was just six months away. "That war may develop a hero," Platt said nonchalantly pointing off to somewhere in the distance. "Popular sentiment may force the nomination of that hero for governor of New York. Theodore Roosevelt has just resigned as assistant secretary of the navy and is drilling his Rough Riders in the West. . . ."[80]

It was not until May 23rd that the rifles, as well as the rest of the supplies, finally arrived. The equipment list for each soldier was impressive:

> A McClelland saddle, bridle, water bridle, halter, saddle bags, surcingle, picket pin and rope, nose bag, curry-comb and brush, spurs, canteen, mess pan and tin cup, knife, fork and spoon, poncho, body blanket, horse blanket, one-half shelter tent, service belt, machete and scabbard, Krag-Jørgensen .30–30 carbine and scabbard, .44-caliber single-action Colt revolver and scabbard, and cartridge belt.[81]

Leonard Wood and adjutant Tom Hall had come through in securing the equipment and getting it to San Antonio. Theodore got the credit. Roosevelt had been the one with the men when they were drilling, when they were sweating, when they were cussing, when they prayed. He was also front-and-center when the Krag-Jørgensens were handed out, reminding the troopers that the exclusive club of Rough Riders had the most modern rifle available, as well as machetes. The regulars in the army were lucky to have one of the weapons, the majority of them had neither. It was appreciated by all that the leader of the Rough Riders would take care of his men.

The equipment arrived just in time. The same afternoon the rifles arrived, so did a telegram from the War Department inquiring when the regiment would be ready to embark for Tampa, Florida, to join the Fifth Corps for immediate action. "Lieutenant-Colonel Roosevelt read the message," a correspondent wrote, "and then he and Colonel Wood embraced like schoolboys."[82] The troopers, who ran to see what the fuss was all about, were greeted with an unusual display as Roosevelt shouted and danced in front of Wood, his hat in his right hand high above his head, his body convulsing, his left hand slapping his knee.[83] As the good word passed throughout camp, the entire fairground exploded in cheers, as if there was dynamite along a wire.[84] The roar continued for several minutes.

Wood sent a message back to Washington. The regiment would be ready to move "AT ONCE."[85]

There would be no time to test the equipment or fire the guns. The Rough Riders were off to war.

On May 24th, the mayor of San Antonio, expecting the Rough Riders to depart within a day, invited the entire regiment to Riverside Park for a send-off concert in their honor. Professor Carl Beck, the conductor of the Beethoven Männerchor in San Antonio, was in charge of the music. The highlight of the evening was reserved for the last number, "The Cavalry Charge," and Beck recruited the help of twelve troopers to fire blank cartridges into the air on his cue. The crescendo chorus, coupled with the twelve gun salute, would provide for a grand and memorable ending, the conductor thought. Turns out that Beck was more correct than he knew.

Under a blanket of bright Texas stars on a sticky night, the concert started without a hitch. The Rough Riders were well behaved, Beck's music a smashing success. And then came the finale. "There was frantic rhythm," an account retells. "Notes came out in a whirlwind of harmony, quick and ecstatic, fast, fast, faster. Beck's eyes danced. He reared on tiptoe and fell back upon his heels, swayed by the enthusiasm of the bumptitty-ta-ta beat. He waited for the moment, the moment to start the shooting. It arrived, and he grandiloquently gave the signal with his baton."[86] Twelve shots were fired. Then the rest of the Rough Riders reacted instinctively, firing skyward, almost in unison. Then the men reloaded and fired again. Then again. And then again.

Over two thousand shots were said to have been blasted into the balmy San Antonio night.[87] One unlucky bullet sheared the only electrical wire into the park and the whole place went dark. A stampede ensued, and though nobody was hurt, the incident provided horrible press.

"Prof. Beck's Band Played the Cavalry Charge and the Rough Riders Played Hell," the headline of the *San Antonio Light* blared the next day.[88]

Roosevelt, anxious to soothe matters—just as he had done with Secretary Long—sent a calming letter to President McKinley, indicating that everything was under control at camp.

San Antonio, May 25th, 1898

My dear Mr. President,

This is just a line to tell you that we are in fine shape. Wood is a dandy Colonel, and I really think the rank and file of this regiment are better than you would find in any other regiment anywhere. In fact, in all the world there is not a regiment I would so soon belong to. The men are picking up the drill wonderfully. They are very intelligent, and, rather to my surprise, they are very orderly—and they mean business. We are ready to leave at any moment, and we hope we will be put into Cuba with the very first troops; the sooner the better; at any rate, we do want to see active service against the enemy.

With great respect. Faithfully yours.

Theodore Roosevelt[89]

President McKinley did not care about the shooting incident in San Antonio. He had the much more momentous issue of war to worry about. Word was trickling back to the White House that Tampa was a port of confusion. Transports, men, supplies, horses, luggage and boats were converging into a quagmire of chaos. It was apparent to the president that America was not at all prepared for the undertaking she had started.

It was not until two days after the riot at Riverside that the order to move was officially received on May 26th.[90] Wood notified the Southern Pacific that the transport "needed twenty-five day coaches, two Pullman cars, five baggage cars, eight box cars, and sixty livestock cars."[91] Wood then set his sights on readying the Union Stockyard, three miles from camp, for the transportation of roughly 1,000 men and 1,300 horses and mules, as well as all of the arms and equipment.[92]

Theodore readied the men. On the evening before departure, he called the troopers together.[93]

> Boys, as you know, we are breaking camp tonight and will start on our trip to Cuba; we are going to get close to the enemy, which means that a great many of us will be wounded, followed by much suffering and some of us will make the supreme sacrifice. I don't think we have, and we don't want, anyone to whine or complain as a result of these hardships, so now, if any one of you has a mother, wife or sweetheart that you feel you cannot afford to leave and take the chance of being lost to these dear ones, I want you to step forward, now, and you will be released, otherwise, I ask you to forever keep your peace.[94]

No one moved a muscle.

At three in the morning, on May 29th, reveille was sounded. Working under lantern light in the cool dawn, the men attended to the last of the particulars. Around 9 a.m. the first of three squadrons, under the direction of Major Brodie, was given orders to move out.[95]

At the stockyard, frustration compounded confusion. There were no ramps to load the horses and mules, no water or food for the animals, and several passenger cars had not arrived. It was not until dusk, almost fifteen hours later, that Theodore, in the final squadron, marched the last file of dusty troopers into the station yard. Again, there were no passenger cars to be found. Leonard Wood, and two-thirds of the Rough Riders, had already embarked for Tampa, and now Theodore was told that the trains to transport the final squadron would not be arriving until much later that night, perhaps as late as the following morning. With nothing to do, the men grew bored and restless, drifting off, as Theodore put it, "to the vile drinking-booths around the stockyards."[96]

Summoning the trumpeter, Theodore snarled an order to blare the call to round-up the men for roll call. Theodore told the men to hunker in for the night, to fall out "by the tracks and in the brush, to sleep until morning."[97] Any man who went to the tavern would be left behind.

In the brush by the tracks, Theodore rolled out his bedroll. He did not have a blanket; his horse's nosebag was his pillow. Not lost on the men was the fact that as the senior officer, Roosevelt could have taken up a room at any one of the many hotels surrounding the stockyard. The light from the hotels was warmly visible through the graying night. Theodore slept on the ground, just as he had done in the Badlands.[98]

Shortly after dawn, the passenger cars finally arrived and the last of the Rough Riders left San Antonio. As the train charged out of the city limits, the men began to sing heartily.

We thud-thud down the dusty pike,
We jingle across the plain,
We cut and thrust, we lunge and strike,
We throttle the sons of Spain,
Going to Cuba with Roosevelt![99]

Only fifteen days prior, the regiment was an assorted set of individuals from every walk of life, a mob of characters clinging to their own factions, speaking and acting in partisan terms. Now, as the train charged east, they were wholly united, the latest incarnation of the American frontiersman. They were still wild and unruly, rowdy and boisterous—prone to extraordinary insubordination. But now they trusted one another and wanted to fight together. They were not a mob; they were frontiersmen.

"We had enjoyed San Antonio," Theodore wrote revealingly about the values that united the men, "and [we] were glad that our regiment had been organized in the city where the Alamo commemorates the death fight of Crockett, Bowie, and their famous band of frontier heroes."[100]

18. OFF TO WAR

———————————————————————◇

On Monday, May 30th, 1898, the last of the Rough Riders left San Antonio traveling along the gulf route through Houston, New Orleans, Mobile, and Tallahassee. The rail company had promised that the regiment would arrive in Tampa in less than forty-eight hours. It took almost five days.

The Southern Pacific Railroad, perhaps rightly expecting that the Rough Riders would trash the transport, supplied the oldest and most dilapidated railcars in their fleet. The pace was sluggish, the cars dirty and hot. When the heat became insufferable, the troopers opened the windows and were blasted with cinders from the smokestacks. The large black flakes, the size of half-dollars, gusted into the men's faces, burning their skin and blackening everything in the car. The endless cycle of closing and opening the windows, alternating between hundred plus temperatures and a thick cloud of black smoke, took its toll on the men. All aboard were filthy, hot, and starved. Roosevelt was right there with them, his face marred with sweat and smoke. Even before the train left San Antonio, he had given up his cabin to Private Charles Nicholson of K Troop who had the measles. Nobody could whine aloud about the conditions. Everyone was in it together.[1]

After a series of unaccountable delays, the troopers finally pulled into Houston after nightfall, the first planned stop on the itinerary. In half of one day they had travelled only two hundred miles.[2]

To the chagrin of all aboard, the depot in Houston was shut down. The throng of onlookers and the state of confusion at the yard kept trains from advancing. Sensing the growing fury of his troopers, Theodore decided it was time to take charge of the trains himself. As soon as his boots hit the platform, he charged the brakeman, a big, burly, red-faced mountain of a man.

"Have this train, all trains, proceed at once, understand me, these are my orders!" Theodore shouted.

"This train don't go, damn you, until I get good and ready," the brakeman shouted back, "I am running this caboose, not you, and you mind your own business, damn you, these are my orders, who in the hell are you anyway?"[3]

Without a word, Hamilton Fish—the New York aristocratic tough guy—lurched forward and punched the railroad operator under the jaw, knocking him clean to the ground.

"Do you know who you're talking to?" Fish snapped at the brakeman, whose boots were now pointing skyward.

Hayes recounted, "Fish enlightened him. Roosevelt went on, with a grim smile."[4]

With the brakeman unconscious, Theodore put the Rough Riders in charge. "Colonel Roosevelt, believing that he had men in his regiment that could do anything, called for volunteer train men," Trooper Colbert, a descendant of Chickasaw chiefs recalled. "Several men stepped forward and he selected a yard crew composed of an engineer, fireman, switchman and telegraph operator who proceeded to switch the cars into place, telegraphic orders were obtained and without further delay we were on our way."[5]

When the train finally began to move, the story of Hamilton's punch, Roosevelt's grim smile, and how the Rough Riders took control of the entire railroad system, passed through the railcars along with buckets full of coffee. Roosevelt's tenacity and no-nonsense attitude inspired them. "Red tape was nonexistent," a Rough Rider confirmed, insinuating that it was all about results.[6] Soon someone asked where the treasured coffee had come from. It was a pleasant surprise to the exhausted travelers. Roosevelt ordered it, was the response. He had paid for it out of his own pocket, someone added.[7]

At two in the morning the following day, the train pulled into New Orleans and had not so much as stopped when Theodore climbed to the top of the rail car—some eleven feet off of the ground—and began barking orders. In an uproar of commotion he shouted commands to his men, workers on the platform, the brakeman, and even civilians.[8] Atop the railcar, it was clear that nothing was going to stop Roosevelt or his regiment from getting to Tampa. Theodore sounded like Thee: "Quicker! Faster! Seize the moment! Get Action! Move! Move! Move! Now! Now! You over there, Move! Quicker!"

The two-in-the-morning scene on the platform was electric, pure theater. At that hour the men should have been exhausted and grumbling. Instead they caught Roosevelt's spirit and a chant broke out: "Rough! Tough! We're the stuff! We're the scrappers; never get enough! W-h-e-e-e-e-!" The chant was said to be heard from over a mile away.[9]

Although the train ride through the southern part of America "had no superior in misery," A. F. Cosby of K Troop explained, "it was [still] a triumphal procession."[10] Throngs of citizens stood for hours along the tracks just trying to get a glimpse of the romantic regiment. At the station platforms, the energetic outpouring was profoundly patriotic, a clear sign of the new united state of America.

Only thirty years of time separated us from the bitterness of the Civil War [A. F. Cosby writes]. Yet, there we were traveling across 2,000 miles of the deepest South. . . . the people in all of these states greeted us with cheers and gifts. Everywhere, we saw the Stars and Stripes being flown or held aloft by persons in the crowds. Maybe I was especially conscious of this because of my own family's role in this war. My father had served as a Union Naval officer. His brother was a Confederate general. My mother's brother had left his studies at Princeton to fight for the South. He was killed at the second battle of Manassas. I watched the station coming—the older men and their women who smiled solemnly [they knew what war was like]—and their children who must have heard the tragic stories of the South's collapse—yet there they were enthusiastically welcoming us. . . . [I]ts parts were coming together . . .[11]

Tampa, Florida, was selected as the point of concentration for the U.S. army because of its secure harbor, as well as its dock and rail facilities. Inhabited from 900 to 1700 by indigenous peoples of the aptly named Safety Harbor Culture, the port at Tampa lay deep inside a thirty-mile channel to the Gulf of Mexico; a God-made safe haven from a naval attack.

If the secure geographic location was the work of God, the creation of the city was the work of one man: Henry Bradley Plant. Plant, a railroad magnate, envisioned that the U.S. global economic expansion would necessitate a harbor on Florida's Gulf coast to facilitate trade to and from Central and South America. Plant also subscribed to the novel thought that more disposable income in the economy might mean that northerners would tour down south to enjoy Florida's surf and sun.

Plant's vision and money made Tampa cosmopolitan almost overnight. The tycoon built eight hotels, an amusement park named Picnic Island, and an enormous wharf with ample walkways. He laid the railroad tracks next to paved streets that he lit with the technological gem of the era, electricity.[12] Plant's grand triumph was reserved for the Tampa Bay Hotel, a five story behemoth of a building with over five hundred rooms spread out over five acres. Described by a newspaperman as larger than "the palace which Ismail Pasha built overnight at Cairo,"[13] the hotel encapsulated the "spirit of the gay nineties," complete with a casino, an auditorium, a swimming pool with a retractable floor above it, a golf expert from Scotland, exotic plants, peacocks, and a plethora of gaudy ebony and gold furniture.[14]

Plant's creation, finished in 1888, was waiting for tourists. Instead it got a war. Overnight, the 26,000 residents of Tampa were flooded with 30,000 U.S. soldiers, as well as tens of thousands of other personnel: military attachés, postal workers, railroad workers. The sawgrass flats on the outskirts of town with the unspoiled moss-hung pines and palmetto groves, were turned into base camps now filled with platoons of men. There were tents, artillery batteries, boxes of supplies, horses, and mules as far as the eye could see. The crystal blue waters of the harbor were now packed with naval gunboats; lavish yachts were now military transports. A vibrant Red Light District sprouted up. Prices in the city quadrupled overnight.

The traffic jam was mind-boggling. Thousands of freight cars, unable to move into Tampa, had backed up all the way to Columbia, South Carolina, a full five hundred miles north. Boxcar after boxcar of unmarked supplies lined the sidings of the tracks. Soldiers went scrounging, forced to open each car, just to discover what they contained. Boxes of food spoiled in the hot sun, the stench reeked for miles.

At the center of the confusion was General William Rufus Shafter, a sixty-two-year-old major general whom President McKinley selected to lead the entire Cuban expedition. A veteran of the Civil War and the Indian Campaigns, Shafter had received the Medal of Honor for his open-field charge at Fair Oaks in 1862.[15] The old general was a military hero of the past war, proving then to be competent in leading men. But Shafter was certainly not the dynamic leader required to lead an unprepared country engaged in a spontaneous war. To be fair, no American officer had ever managed an overseas expedition of this scale, nor urgency.

But Shafter was coarse, slow, and the opposite of energetic. Standing six feet tall, he weighed well north of three hundred pounds. His massive head of grey hair was parted in the middle and he had a matching mustache that wilted downward at both ends. His large belly made it seem as if he was concealing a whiskey barrel under his shirt; the buttons of his coat perpetually ready to pop off under intense pressure. Described as "beastly obese" by one officer and a "floating tent" by another, Shafter moved at the speed of syrup on account of his gout.[16]

When Shafter arrived in Tampa in early May, his original war plan did not included the Rough Riders.[17] Perhaps he found Roosevelt and Wood too green, perhaps he viewed the western fighters too wild, or perhaps he wanted to minimize the presence of volunteers in Cuba. But as Shafter lumbered like a bear through the Army encampment, he discovered a serious lack of soldiers prepared with appropriate supplies. On account of the logistical quagmire, Shafter decided to call for more soldiers, as if to concede that if a regiment could navigate their way to Tampa with their equipment in hand, then they would be sent to the fight.[18]

The last train bearing Theodore Roosevelt and the rest of the regiment finally arrived in Tampa on the afternoon of June 3rd, to a scene that was, as Theodore put it, "a perfect welter of confusion . . . everything connected with both military and railroad matters was in an almost inextricable tangle. There was no one to meet us or to tell us where we were to camp, and no one to issue us food for the first twenty-four hours."[19] The train conductor, refusing to venture any closer to Tampa, dumped the entire regiment off in Ybor City, a full eight miles away from the rendezvous point.[20] "No words can paint the confusion," Theodore wrote angrily in his diary, "No *head*; a breakdown of both the railroad and military system of the country."[21]

Though livid, Theodore did not dwell in front of the troopers and quickly demanded that horses be unloaded and fed, and the supplies unpacked. Several hours later, the whole company— dispirited, tired, and hungry—began marching in the general direction of where they believed the rest of the regiment had set up camp. They did not stumble upon the other Rough Riders until long after nightfall.

After a brief meeting, Wood and Roosevelt agreed that it was absolutely paramount to get order out of confusion. "Under Wood's eye," Theodore explained, "the tents were put up in long streets, the picket-line of each troop stretching down its side of each street. The officers' quarters were at the upper ends of the streets, the company kitchens and sinks at the opposite ends." As for Theodore, he made certain that "camp was strictly policed, and drill promptly begun."[22]

"Our day begins at 5 with 1st call reveille at 5:10," Arthur F. Cosby wrote in a letter to his mother on June 6th; "breakfast 5:30, watering horses at 'stables' at six. This is hard as we ride them a mile, feed them, groom them. Guard mount at 7. Regimental drill 8:25 to about 10:25, dinner [lunch in today's terms] at 12, drill again at 3:00, 'stables' again at 5, supper at six and taps at 9."[23]

On June 6th, one of the last great cavalry drills in American history took place. It was a site to behold. Nearly 2,000 mounted army regulars swept across the sawgrass, advancing in columns that stretched as far as two miles wide. The drill was crisp, run with military precision.

In contrast, the Rough Rider volunteers were ragged, their drills were abysmal. They had left all of their confidence in San Antonio. Men were missing orders, horses were out of control, and the columns were a tangled mess. "The difficulty," a trooper explained, "[was that we] were in the presence of the regulars and had a wholesale attack of stage fright."[24] The cocky volunteers had seen the professional soldiers drill, and lost their mojo.

The trooper's lack of confidence was not lost on Theodore. He immediately began shouting to newspaper correspondents that his "men are good men, all of them, and I expect great things from them!"[25] He then added that he felt that they were "doing as well as the regular regiments."[26] To supplement his rhetorical praise, Theodore showed up for an afternoon drill with the foreign military attachés from England, Germany, France, Russia, and Japan.[27] The military attachés—conspicuously dressed in the colors of their home country—proved to be a startling sight for the Rough Riders who were already struggling with confidence. Instantly, the Rough Rider moxie returned. If their leader had the confidence to bring the highest ranking military diplomats from around the world to inspect their drill, then why should they not believe in themselves? Throughout the entire drill, it was said that Theodore bragged loudly to anyone that would listen.

By the time the Rough Riders arrived in Tampa, the Army was in the latter phase of what Richard Harding Davis coined the "rocking chair period of the war."[28] "It was an army of occupation, but it occupied the piazza of a big hotel," trooper A. F. Cosby quipped, referring to the Army's makeshift headquarters at Plant's lavish Tampa Bay Hotel.[29] As for the Rough Riders, they were there for business, or that is at least what Wood and Roosevelt preached from the start.

The antics of the regiment's hell-bent nights in San Antonio had preceded their arrival in Tampa. A committee of local civic leaders had come together and asked the army paymaster to withhold the Rough Riders' stipend payment for several days. The very real fear was that the Rough Riders, fresh with cash, would go to town in pursuit of faro, whiskey, and women.[30] For a leader that did everything for his men, it is telling that Roosevelt took only minimal action to get his men paid on arrival. Instead, the Rough Riders were not given their stipend until the evening of June 6th, the day before they left for Cuba.[31] So rather than drink, chase women, and shoot up the town, the men spent their evenings in Ybor City roping alligators from the nearby swamp.[32] It was cheaper and less dangerous.

⊗⅏

On the evening of June 7th, Shafter was summoned off of the rocking chair on the piazza of the Tampa Bay Hotel to the nearby Western Union office. On the other end of the direct line was President McKinley. For the next forty minutes, keys clicked back and forth; the monumental movements of war were set into motion.

"Time is the essence of the situation. Early departure of first importance," McKinley messaged to Shafter.

"I will sail tomorrow morning. Steam cannot be gotten up earlier. . ." Shafter replied, while sitting on a three-legged stool in a dirty office, wiping sweat from his brow. He looked hot and uncomfortable; he seemed nervous.[33]

"You will sail immediately as you are needed at destination," came the cable from Washington.

"Will sail then," Shafter told the President tellingly, "[with] whatever I have on board."[34]

At 10:00 p.m. the Rough Riders got their orders to break camp. Their spirit was dampened. Shafter, on account of the transport shortage, had given official notice that only eight of the twelve troops in the regiment would be sent to Cuba, and all the horses, except those of the top officers, were to be left behind.

"I saw more than one, both among the officers and privates, burst into tears when he found he could not go," Theodore later wrote. "No outsider can appreciate the bitterness of the disappointment."[35]

"That almost took the starch out of the boys," a Rough Rider remembered upon learning that he would fight on foot. "A cowboy is almost as helpless on foot as a fish is out of water."[36]

Theodore had a message for those left behind: "each man was doing his duty, and much the hardest and most disagreeable duty was to stay."[37] To the men who would get the chance to fight, but not on horseback, Theodore had a message for them as well: "we would rather crawl on all fours than not go."[38]

Roosevelt turned his attention to getting his regiment of approximately 560 men to Port Tampa, eight miles away.[39] The ship was leaving at daybreak, he was told, "and that if we were not aboard our transport by that time we could not go."[40] Theodore also received word from the quartermaster that the army had wagons en route to "move the regiment's heavy equipment and supplies."[41] Theodore was skeptical. Everything about Tampa demonstrated confusion, and he knew that if his men were separated from their supplies, their chance of getting to Cuba was shot. So he reached into his pockets and gave three officers money to procure wagons to move the heavy equipment. Roosevelt's foresight proved monumental when the army transports never arrived.[42] One is left to wonder if Theodore's seemingly small administrative action enabled his men to get on the transport, which afforded him the chance to get to Cuba and become a military hero.

The Rough Riders arrived trackside at midnight, equipment in tow by Theodore's hired mercenaries. Their train, again, was nowhere to be found. Theodore hastily tracked down a brigadier-general and then a major general, but nobody seemed to know anything. Several hours later, a train finally showed up, only to leave with regulars onboard. At three o'clock in the morning, an order was received to march to an entirely different track. The Rough Riders hurried over to the new track. Again, there was no train.[43]

"In the darkness we could hear the shuffle of many feet, the talk of many soldiers, the orders of many perplexed officers, sergeants and corporals," A. F. Cosby remembered. "I realized that almost the *whole* army was stumbling about in the darkness."[44]

Theodore was frantic. It was not until six in the morning—just a few hours before the scheduled departure of the entire expedition force—that another train finally showed up. Hopes spiraled and then plummeted. The train was not for the Rough Riders, but rather an old engine dragging several empty coal cars that it had just dropped off at the dock in Tampa. The train was heading out of town and the conductor had no desire to go back to Tampa; the port was in chaos and his train could get stuck for hours, if not days. For the second time in his life, Theodore decided to hijack a train and jumped aboard. Roosevelt demanded that the conductor reverse eight miles back to the dock, and while the engineer was still thinking about Theodore's brashness, Roosevelt turned and ordered all of his men to board. Had the conductor had the gumption to continue forward, he would have taken the entire regiment inland, away from the war.

The 71st New York Volunteers were sitting on flatcars wharf side when they heard the commotion of the Rough Riders' arrival. It was a sight they would never forget. The coal transports, traveling in reverse, were too deep to stand in so the Rough Riders, caked in coal dust, were squatting on the thin top rails, riding the side-rail as if it were a steel horse. Seeing the port for the first time, the Rough Riders began rocking on the cars, waving their hats above their heads as if it were a rodeo. Then they began to sing in unison: *Rough! Tough! We're the stuff! We want to fight! And we can't get enough!* [45]

It was a hell of an entrance. Roosevelt, standing in an open door of the coal car, grinned from ear-to-ear, his blue bandanna waving in the wind.[46] The 71st New York Volunteers, upon seeing their home-state hero, erupted into a lusty cheer. Theodore bowed his head ever so slightly in acknowledgement of the 71st. And then he proceeded to steal their boat.

Once at port, Wood and Roosevelt started on a frantic hunt for sea transport. "From the highest General down, nobody could tell us where to go," Theodore recalled in disgust.[47] The wharf was an "ant-heap of humanity" according to Theodore, a scene of complete pandemonium.[48] The docks, smothered with equipment stacked ten feet high, were impassable in parts. Ten thousand men, all dressed for war, had no place to move, and were standing elbow-to-elbow trying to make sense of the upheaval around them. "Hell won't be worse crowded on the last day than the dock is now," a Sergeant quipped in disgust.[49]

Rough Rider Sherrard Coleman tracked down General Shafter to find out which boat was reserved for the Rough Riders.

"Damned if I know," was the Commanding General's articulate response.[50]

"A good deal of higglety-pigglety business," Roosevelt exclaimed.[51] "No plans, no staff officers, no instructions to us. Each officer finds out for himself and takes his chances."[52] It was a free-for-all, and it needed decisive action.

Almost by accident, Wood and Roosevelt bumped into Colonel Humphrey who told them that he thought that the *Yucatan* had been allotted for the Rough Riders. The only problem was that the *Yucatan* was out in the bay at anchor, rocking lazily to and fro. Wood promptly seized a stray launch and paddled to the boat. Roosevelt returned to round up the troops.[53]

On his way back to the track, Roosevelt was informed by a superior officer that the *Yucatan* had actually been allotted to the Second Regular Infantry and the 71st New York Volunteers—the Rough Riders were out of luck. Armed with this news, Theodore broke into a sprint. "I ran at full speed to our train; and leaving a strong guard with the baggage, I double-quicked the rest of the regiment up to the boat, just in time. . ."[54] As Roosevelt rushed the men down the waterfront, weaving through cartons and soldiers, he saw Wood out on the bow of the *Yucatan* pointing in the direction of open dock space.[55]

When Roosevelt and his men reached the gangplank of the *Yucatan*, another officer stepped forward.

"This transport has been set aside for another regiment!" the other officer barked, referring to the 71st.

"All right," said Roosevelt, "Where are we to go?"

The officer did not know, "You will have to find a ship as best you can," he replied tersely.

"It is just as easy for the other outfit to find a ship as it is for me," Roosevelt retorted. The officer was trying to make up his mind on how to respond, when Theodore turned on his heel and ordered his men to march aboard.[56]

Captain Anthony J. Bleecker, commanding officer of the 71st, stormed towards Roosevelt, who was standing on the gangplank, letting only Rough Riders pass.

"Hello, what can I do for you?" Theodore asked snarkily.

"That's our ship," Bleecker shouted.

"Well, we seem to have it," Roosevelt replied.

"71st Regiment, New York. We have been assigned to this ship," came the reply.

"Sorry, not this ship," Roosevelt responded, holding up a piece of paper, "I have my assignment."

"I have my assignment, too," Bleecker said tersely, holding up a piece of paper of his own, an official document.

Theodore's paper was blank, so he pocketed it. "We were here first, and we expect to stay," he responded with a grin.[57] Standing dockside with the Westerners and armed guards behind him, Roosevelt seemed indomitable. He had a wild look in his eye.

Bleecker ordered his men off the dock. The Rough Riders could have the ship.

Listening to the exchange were Albert Smith and Jim Blackton, journalists assigned to follow the 71st. Loaded with cameras, tripods, and tin wheels, they did not want to continue their search for another transport.

"We are the Vitagraph Company," Smith blurted as Theodore began to march away. "We are going to Cuba to take moving pictures of the war."

Theodore had heard of this new invention, pictures that moved. What better way to show history in the making than with moving images?

". . . I might be able to handle you two," Theodore replied, summoning the men aboard.[58]

Roosevelt's actions in stealing the *Yucatan* were later the subject of interest to a committee charged with investigating the conduct of the war. It was one thing to steal a train; it was another to defy official army orders and rip-off a transport on its way to battle. But by the time the report was published its indictments were meek.[59] After all, America had won the war and Roosevelt was the national hero of the entire thing. Never one to worry about disobeying authority, Theodore did not hide the fact that he stole the boat. Instead he boasted proudly and publicly that "the 71st arrived a little too late, being a shade less ready in individual initiative."[60]

Frank Hughes, a farmer who joined the Rough Riders in Muskogee, Oklahoma, confirmed what all the men aboard the

Yucatan were thinking, "Had it not been for the untiring efforts of Roosevelt, we would have been left at Tampa."[61]

Shortly before two in the afternoon on June 8th, the *Yucatan* moved out into the bay, ready to sail for glory. As the last transport door closed, it was said that the streets of Port Tampa resembled "the day after a carnival."[62]

The largest invading force America had ever seen was sitting in the harbor. Consisting of thirty-six ships, both naval gunboats as well as converted millionaires' yachts, the armada carried 819 officers, 16,058 enlisted men, 30 civilian clerks, 272 teamsters and packers, 107 stevedores, and eighty-nine newspaper and magazine correspondents.[63] In the cargo holds, there were 2,295 horses and mules, some one hundred wagons, and seven ambulances. The artillery arsenal consisted of sixteen light batteries, one Hotchkiss revolving cannon, one pneumatic dynamite gun, four 5-inch siege rifles, four 7-inch howitzers, eight 3.6-inch field mortars, and what would prove to be the most important weapon of all, four Gatling machine guns.[64]

A raucous cheer erupted when the lead ship, the *Seguranca*, transporting the military brass, including General Shafter, headed out into the bay.

America was off to war.

Not ten minutes after leaving the dock, the *Seguranca* was overtaken by a tug. A telegram had arrived from Washington. Someone took the summons below to awaken Shafter, the big man having had laid down for a nap.[65]

Washington had received intelligence that a torpedo boat was lurking at the entrance of Tampa Bay. "Wait until you get further orders before you sail. Answer quick," the cable from Secretary of War Alger read.[66]

All transports were halted and Shafter ordered the gunboats *Castine, Annapolis, Hornet,* and *Helena* to the entrance of the bay—some thirty miles away—to fortify against an invasion.[67]

The potential invading fleet never existed. The scare was the product of a nervous naval officer who had a quick trigger finger on the telegraph machine. But in that moment the torpedo threat was real, and for the next five days the army wilted under the ripe Florida sun, unable to move.[68] The boat captains were under strict orders to not let the troopers ashore for fear that it would take another full day to reload the men and equipment. For the next one hundred and twenty hours, the entire army expedition fleet indolently swung on the anchor of their transport, forced into inaction on what they had believed was the eve of battle.

The soldiers onboard had nothing to do. The stench soon became unbearable.

"We are in a sewer," Roosevelt wrote angrily.[69] "The transport was overloaded, the men being packed like sardines, not only below but upon the decks; so that at night it was only possible to walk about by continually stepping over the bodies of the sleepers."[70]

The *Yucatan* had formerly been a freight vessel converted to a transport ship sometime after war was declared. Contractors had built make-shift berths in the hull which had last been used for carrying coal. The black grime of coal dust was still everywhere. Several of the bunks, built of rough lumber, fell off of the walls the first time a man laid on them.[71] The men referred to the dungeon below as the Black Hole of Calcutta.

Above the waterline, it was not any better. The decks were so crowded that the men were forced to stand all day. As there were not enough beds below, the men lay crisscrossed on the deck at night, as if they were fish packed in a can. Someone hung a sign over the railing, "Standing Room Only." A short while later, another more disgruntled sign was added, "And damn little of that!"[72]

Theodore's chief concern was for the well-being of his men and he set up a tight schedule. The mornings and evenings were for swimming—to reduce the spread of communicable disease—and the days were spent studying the manual of arms. "Every book of tactics in the regiment was in use from morning until night, and the officers and non-commissioned officers were always studying the problems presented at the schools."[73] Everything was done to keep his troopers occupied, including time allotted for cards, two daily concerts by the Second Infantry band, and a daily Bible study.[74] Though stuck on the ship, inspection, roll call, reveille, and tattoo were all administered, just to occupy time.

As the days passed by, the water channel began to fill with human waste. The stench was horrendous, the mood on board equally pungent.

Rumors were rampant. Would the war end before the Rough Riders even arrived? Was McKinley brokering for peace at the eleventh hour? Why in the hell are we not moving?

"What this meant none of us could understand," Theodore wrote of the conflicting reports coming aboard.[75]

Aside from the uncertainty and the smell of fecal matter, the chief complaint among the men was the food rations, which were vile. Each trooper had been rationed hardtack and a can of tomatoes. There was no ice, no water, no fresh fruits or vegetables. The only meat was Government issued "canned fresh beef," which turned out to be neither fresh nor beef. Canned for the Sino-Japanese War of 1894, the contents had spoiled on the docks of Tampa.[76]

Alvin Ash, a cowpoke from New Mexico, opened one of the cans, smelled it, and passed it around for inspection amid a cackle of profanity. Roosevelt, walking amongst his men rather than playing cards in the shade of the officers den, heard the profanity and ran towards the swearing.

"Are you complaining already?" Theodore ejaculated, running up behind Ash. "This is war, not a pink tea! You've got to expect hardships!"

Ash turned slowly. "That's all right, Colonel," he drawled, "I've been used to hardships all my life, but I've always been fed right. An' this canned carcass ain't right."[77]

Roosevelt grabbed the can and smelled it. He cringed, skinned his teeth and then agreed with Ash. Roosevelt ordered several more cans opened for inspection. All were spoiled.

It is hard to imagine that there was a time when American soldiers had to pay for reasonable food while on a combat mission. Such was the case onboard the *Yucatan*. Much like a modern day ferry ride, the Ward Line had placed a cook in charge of meals, which cost a dollar a day. The officers and the Fifth

Avenue boys—those who could afford the meals—were eating soups, meats, bread and butter, cookies and desserts served on nice dishes.[78] Everyone else was eating canned fresh beef, or as troopers called it, "shark poison."[79]

The dollar a day for meals was twice the amount that the Rough Rider made a day for his service to the country; it would have been equivalent to an American soldier paying something like $150 in today's constant dollars just for three square meals.[80]

To Theodore, this was not equality in arms and he stormed down to the officer's saloon and demanded that the cook feed the entire regiment. "The ship's steward did not want to feed [us]," Lyman F. Beard recounted, ". . . [W]hen the colonel learned of this he came down, pointed his finger at the steward and said, 'These are my boys, feed them!' We all got everything we ordered, and the Colonel gained the undying love of a troop of hungry men."[81] It is uncertain whether Theodore paid to feed the entire regiment, or whether he had just scared the cook into doing so. Regardless, the Rough Riders had edible food, and again, Roosevelt had come through.

In the heat of one afternoon, William "Jimmie" Shields, a cowpuncher and former round-up cook from Arizona, snapped. Prone to bouts of anger, Shields had told a comrade that he "would go thru hell and breakfast for Colonel Roosevelt, but he would be damned if he would obey or even listen to any other officer."[82] Sitting deck side in the sweltering heat, Shields lived up to his promise and told an officer to "go to hell."

"Consider yourself under arrest," returned the officer.

Shields smiled and then, without any warning, jumped the officer. Amidst swinging, punching, and clawing, Shields drew his revolver and threatened to kill his superior.

"That meant of course, the brig straightway and a summary court-martial," a trooper recalled.

"We were on the transport," Roosevelt explained. "[T]here was no hard labor to do; and the prison consisted solely of another cow-puncher who kept guard over him [Shields] with his carbine, evidently divided in his feelings as to whether he would like most to shoot him or let him go."[83]

Adjutant Tom Hall, acting as judge advocate, wrote up Shields' charges, which included a sentence of one year hard labor and dishonorable discharge. Under Hall's urging, the major-general commanding the division approved the sentence and Jimmie Shields was banned from fighting, destined for prison when the war ended.

When the regiment finally landed in Cuba, Roosevelt ordered Shields to stay with the equipment in the rear.

"Colonel, they say you're going to leave me with the baggage when the fight is on," Shields pleaded to Roosevelt. "Colonel, if you do that, I'll never show my face in Arizona again. Colonel, if you will let me go to the front, I promise I will obey any one you say—any one you say, Colonel."

"Shields," said Roosevelt, thinking the matter over, head tilted to the side, "there is no one in this regiment more entitled to be shot than you are, and you shall get to the front."

"I'll never forget this, Colonel, never," returned Shields gratefully.

In battle, Shields proved himself courageously and after the war, Theodore, impressed with the man's valor, remitted the court-martial and let Shields go free. But Theodore did not have the authority to set Shields free, and worse, he did not tell anybody, let alone use correct military procedure.

On the day the Rough Riders mustered out, a regular officer came to take Shields to jail.

"Where is the prisoner?" the officer asked.

"What prisoner?" replied Roosevelt.

"The prisoner, the man who was sentenced to a year's imprisonment with hard labor and dishonorable discharge."

"Oh!" said Roosevelt, "I pardoned him."

"I beg your pardon; you did what?"

"Well, I did pardon him," repeated Roosevelt, "and he has gone with the rest."

"He was sentenced by a court martial, and the sentence was approved by the major-general commanding the division" the officer shouted. "You were a lieutenant-colonel, and you pardoned him?"

The arresting officer paused,unsure of what action to take. "Well, it was nervy, that's all I'll say!" Then he walked away shaking his head, uncertain of what to tell his superior.

Already on a train heading back to Arizona was Jimmie Shields, the honorable war hero.[84]

On the afternoon of June 13th, President McKinley, now certain that no torpedo boats were lurking outside of Tampa Bay, cabled orders to proceed. The next day the fleet left for Cuba. It was said that upon hearing the orders to set sail, the Rough Riders picked up anchor so fast the crew "had to play the hose on the hawser ropes to keep them from catching fire."[85] Amidst a chorus of cheers, the 2nd Infantry started into the "Star Spangled Banner."

Leaving Tampa, the armada aligned in three columns, each with twelve ships. At the front were with the gunboats.[86]

19. CUBA

$\diamond$

FOR FIVE DAYS THE EXPEDITION FORCES STEAMED SOUTH-southeast across a sapphire sea, at an average speed of four knots. Under a cloudless sky, the cool ocean breeze rippled the flags above. Looking seaward, it had the feel of a cruise. On board, Theodore was adamant that the daily schedule remain. Dismounted cavalry schooling was conducted during the day, officers' school in the afternoon, and a Bible study in the early evening. Inspection, roll call, reveille, and tattoo all continued. Deep into the evenings, the concert band thundered tune after tune, as the men sang along, their voices reverberating deep into the sultry night. Only the morning and afternoon bathing requirements had been canceled, for obvious reasons.

On Sunday, June 19th, the U.S. transports sailed around Punta Maisi, the eastern-most point on the island of Cuba, before turning hard starboard. Passing Guantanamo Bay en route to the port town of Santiago, the Cuban island was picturesque.[1] The long water's edge of crystal blue flowed gently into the rolling hills of sawgrass. At the foothills, the thick dense jungle, overgrown with coconut palms and manigua bushes, blended into the dark and limitless Sierra Maestro Mountains, which, at a distance, looked to Theodore as if they belonged in Montana, not the Caribbean.[2]

On June 21st, the convoy came to a stop some ten miles off the coast of Daiquiri, powering down steam, drifting lazily at sea. The *Seguranca* charged Shafter ashore to meet with U.S. Marines and Cuban rebels to finalize a strategy for landing on Daiquiri, a fishing village with a beachhead wide enough for the entire U.S. expedition.[3]

"Far off on shore," Theodore wrote, "we can see the frowning Spanish batteries, and around us the great warships steam slowly, sullen and majestic."[4]

The scars of war on the Cuban soil were noticeable to everyone aboard the *Yucatan*. Small discreet trails—carved by a century of guerrilla warfare—cut harshly through the dense brush. Wisps of black smoke rose from entrenched palm-thatched huts, undoubtedly housing Spanish combatants who were glaring down upon the U.S. convoy. The foliage of the jungle was heavy, dark, and seemed impenetrable. Every tree, every bush, every rock, could conceal a sharpshooter; every grove could conceal an entire platoon of Spanish fighters.

The site of the dark jungle and the open beachhead cast a morbid spell over the boat.

"We had heard so much about Cuba—it had punctuated our talk, it had evoked many daydreams," A. F. Cosby wrote. "But while we were in camp at San Antonio and Tampa, Cuba had seemed a long way off. At sea there had been a sense of unreality with nothing but the sea and ships in sight. But now our senses—our eyes had seen the land where we were to fight. Our dreams turned to questions of an immediate concern—what was the enemy like? Would he show much resistance? How good was he in battle?"[5]

A Rough Rider from Harvard was reflective, "I cannot help but wonder what the barren shore has in store for me."[6]

The monumental questions of war were heavy on the minds of the Rough Riders—will the battle be hot? Is there a heaven? Am I brave enough to go through with this?—When the gunner *Castine*, flying the signal halyards, sailed towards the *Yucatan*.[7] An officer of the *Castine* put a foot on the gunwale and began shouting through a megaphone. "Be ready . . ." the officer started, the rest of his words too faint to be heard.

"What did he say?" the Rough Riders asked each other, leaning over the side of the ship. "Be ready . . ." the man shouted, again his words still too faint. The *Castine* sailed nearer and nearer ". . . to land at daybreak! Be ready to land at daybreak! The *Castine* will lead the column!"[8]

Silence arrested the ship. The time of reckoning was upon them. The war was here.

Theodore took off his hat, then smiled, then started to dance. He whirled his body in excitement, his hat clenched in his hand high above his head. He started to shout a patriotic Irish folksong:

"Shout hurrah for Erin go Bragh! And all the Yankee nation!"
"Shout hurrah for Erin go Bragh! And all the Yankee nation!"

The *Yucatan* erupted in cheers.[9]

General Shafter's strategy for victory concentrated on the U.S. occupation of Santiago, a city eighteen miles west of the beachhead at Daiquiri. At dawn on June 22nd, 1898, the army would land at Daiquiri under cover fire from naval gunboats. Once on Cuban soil, the expedition would intersect the jungle to the fishing port at Siboney, seven miles to the west. Once Siboney had fallen, the army would swing northwest and march eleven miles along the Camino Real—the King's Road—over a dense, rolling terrain towards Santiago. Ambushes were expected in the hills along the Camino Real, but the big fight would occur at the ridgeline above Santiago where fortifications were heavy. Entrenched in the highland above Santiago was the Spanish army. The key to victory in the war—or rather the key to American world supremacy—required that the army take the hills overlooking Santiago.[10]

The hills overlooking Santiago were called San Juan Heights.

Reveille broke the silence of the tropical still at 3:30 a.m. The men rose and dressed in quiet whispers. Solemnity governed. The somberness of the situation arrested the men's thoughts—is this the last morning I awake on earth?

The entire landing point was wreathed in a predawn mist; the outline of the dark mountain range above was barely visible.

Along the hillside, small fires of flickering auburn were scattered across the low lands, a clear indication to those on the boat that the enemy awaited.

The Rough Riders scurried in the darkness gathering three days rations, a single canteen, a bedroll and one hundred rounds of ammunition.[11] Theodore, it was said, jumped around the bridge all morning.[12]

Breakfast was served at five o'clock, shortly before the sun rose. First light revealed that the U.S. naval transports had aligned in a semicircle, five miles offshore.[13] Several American warships had broken off from the convoy, stretching the horizon from Daiquiri to Santiago, ready to fire on the fortified hillside. For the next four hours, the men waited for the roar of the guns, their eyes fixated on the beachhead.

The *Vixen*, commanded by Theodore's former colleague at the naval department, Lieutenant Sharp, sailed alongside the *Yucatan*. The operation to land had not yet been explained, let alone practiced. Sharp offered to lead Roosevelt and his men closer toward the shore, ensuring that they were to be among the first troopers on land. Theodore smiled at his old friend and accepted the offer.[14]

At 9:40 a.m., the bombardment began. It sounded like thunder. The entire island seemed to shake; trees were sawed in half, and palmed huts obliterated. Grey smoke from the warships hovered just above the water, before an ocean breeze picked up and blew the haze out to sea.[15]

At 10:10 a.m., General Henry Lawton's infantry division started the invasion. Climbing down cargo nets, the men then jumped into small boats that held sixteen soldiers.[16]

"We held our breath. We expected a most desperate fight for the landing," a journalist wrote.[17]

About half an hour later, and following the lead of the *Vixen*, the *Yucatan* sailed to within a few hundred yards of the shore.[18] "We did the landing as we had done everything else—that is, in a scramble," Theodore recalled angrily.[19] The awesome confusion sent army boats racing for the open beach, or for the pier, or for the dense seashore where coconut leaves bent down, almost touching the water. It was a free-for-all.

To everyone's surprise, there was no return fire from the Spaniards.

Wood ordered the *Yucatan's* lifeboats to draw down. Roosevelt shouted that he would lead the first expedition of Rough Riders on shore and pointed to the pier, his destination. Descending down the cargo ladder, he leapt into the life boat. With him he had a yellow mackintosh, a toothbrush stuck in the twine of his hat and eight pairs of glasses, all sewn into the lining of his jacket.[20]

The bulging ocean swells made rowing a challenge. Many of the cutters, weighed down with too many men and supplies, took on water, the bow careening into the heavy swells. Several boats soon capsized, spewing soldiers into the ocean and sending them swimming for their lives.[21] Those whose boats made it to the pier were not much better off. They had to wait until the swell lifted their crafts above the dock line, and then time their jump onto the rotting wood of the pier. Two members of the 10th cavalry—the Buffalo Soldiers—got caught in a swell and were helplessly thrown against the pilings before being pulled down by the undertow. Rough Rider Buckey O'Neill, in full uniform, jumped headfirst into the waves to save them. It was heroic but useless; the sea had swallowed the two soldiers instantly.[22] But Buckey's valiant attempt made headlines across America. Equality in arms is what mattered to the Rough Riders, not skin color, the newspapers preached. What came instinctually to Buckey, the frontiersman from Arizona, would take the U.S. Army another half century to figure out. Not until President Harry Truman signed an executive order in 1948 was the American army finally desegregated.[23]

Dockside, Theodore managed the landing of the regiment, standing out in the open, barking orders. To his astonishment, he looked up to find that the *Yucatan* was steaming back to sea. After the men had disembarked, the boat's captain, nervous of his proximity to shore, decided to sail out to safety, taking with him all of the regiment's supplies.[24] Theodore sent a dispatch boat to stop the *Yucatan,* and then turned his attention to establishing a command center to round up the Rough Riders.

With the Spanish not returning fire, Theodore and Wood got word that the invading army would spend the remainder of the day and that night beachside, before leaving the following morning for Siboney. The Rough Riders were ordered to set up camp, which they did "on a dusty, brush-covered flat, with jungle on one side, and on the other a shallow, fetid pool fringed with palm-trees."[25] Wood administered the layout of the dog tents while Theodore cut down palm thatches for impromptu roofs, should it rain. "Colonel Wood and Colonel Roosevelt did not maintain such military discipline in the construction of their camp as did some of the other commanding officers," a war correspondent wrote. But after watching Theodore and Wood bound through camp helping their troopers, the reporter concluded that "probably no officers ever looked more carefully after the comfort of their men. . . ."[26]

The scene dockside had the uncanny feeling of a day at the beach. The men, who had not showered in seven days, stripped to the nude and washed themselves. Two Rough Riders, Charles Knoblauch, a former water polo player and member of the New York Stock Exchange, and Alfred Judson, a New York broker, were diving off the dock, in their skives, to retrieve guns and equipment from capsized boats that now lay on the floor of the bay.[27] Every time the New York financiers came to the surface with a gun in their hands the men on the dock would cheer lavishly, as if it were a contest.

"It was evident that the Spaniards had left their trenches up there with considerable haste," Edward Marshall, a correspondent for the *World* wrote, "for behind them remained many abandoned trappings."[28] On a bluff overlooking the bay stood a dilapidated blockhouse, a Spanish fort that was abandoned during the morning barrage. Edward Marshall thought aloud that an American flag hoisted above the Spanish fort would be emblematic. Three Rough Riders jumped at the suggestion and immediately stormed the hillside to raise the handmade flag given to them by the Women's Relief Corps of Prescott, Arizona.[29] Marshall recounted the patriotic sight from atop the Spanish fort.

> The little bay in which the transports were anchored lay like a sheet of silver in front of us. Between it and the foot of our hill the coast of Cuba stretched like a map. The ships looked like toy ships from our point of vantage, and our soldiers looked like toy soldiers. The flag had been waving in the breeze perhaps a minute before these toy soldiers

and the men on those toy ships got sight of it. And when they did, bedlam broke loose. Every steam whistle on the warships screamed its loudest, every soldier in the invading thousands yelled his hoarsest, and the Cubans, proud of the new Lee rifles which had been distributed among them by the navy, fired them off in greeting volleys to the bit of red, white, and blue which fluttered brightly at the top of Mount Losiltires.[30]

By six o'clock in the evening, some six thousand U.S. soldiers and all the animals had landed at Daiquiri. Not a single shot had been fired by the Spanish. General Shafter was perplexed, unaware that this was strategy, not cowardice. The Spanish methodology, which became clear in a matter of days, was that it did not believe that it had enough men to beat the Americans in head-to-head battle so it was decided to draw the invading force onto the island and buy time through sporadic firefights in the jungle. The Spanish Generals knew that their most dangerous weapon was dysentery and yellow fever, which could wipe out an entire U.S. army within two weeks.

That night, the Rough Riders slept on their bedrolls, their rifles an arm's reach away. After a brief meeting with the officers Theodore took out his diary, "June 22nd—landed," was all he wrote.[31]

The following day, around 1:00 p.m., the Rough Riders broke their make-shift camp on the Daiquiri beachhead and began marching the eight miles to Siboney, the waterfront port on the road to Santiago. Along the trail, with sweat pouring into their eyes, the troopers got their first glimpse of the people they were there to liberate when a few naked Cuban soldiers meandered out of a palmetto grove, rifles in hand. "In all my travels, I never saw such a dilapidated, hungry, undressed group of men in my life as these Cuban soldiers were," a trooper recalled.[32]

"I am going to dress this bird right now," a Rough Rider shouted before unrolling his pack, grabbing an extra pair of underwear and tossing it to the Cuban.[33] Other soldiers followed suit, handing over clothes, food, and any extras in their pack. Had the Rough Riders known they would not be able to change their clothes for the next four weeks, they might not have been so generous.

The sun lay flat on the horizon by the time the lead squadron came across the first sight of war. Several dead Cuban soldiers, killed that afternoon, grotesquely lay along the trail. The bodies—left out in the open as a warning to the Americans—had already begun to decompose in the heat. A swarm of land crabs, some of them a foot and a half long, had ripped apart the corpses; eyes and chunks of flesh were missing from the bodies.[34]

It was long after nightfall when the first of the Rough Riders reached Siboney. Burr McIntosh, a war correspondent from *Leslie's Magazine* standing near the rear of the perimeter, watched in amazement as Wood and Roosevelt led the Rough Riders right through camp, not pausing, marching onward to the front. McIntosh turned to Brigadier General Bates, inquiring where the regiment was headed. "I don't know," Bates shrugged; "they have not had any orders to go beyond us."[35]

At the extreme front of the American line, Roosevelt and Wood drew the men into columns and ordered them to fall where they lay.

That night Theodore sat around the campfire. He ate hardtack and boiled coffee and fellowshipped with the men. He put to his diary, "June 23th—Marched."

By the campfire, Ed Culver, a Cherokee from the Indian territory talked with Hamilton Fish, the New York City playboy. Both men complained about the day's hike, both men apprehensive about what the next morning would bring.[36] The conversation turned to death.

"I suppose the people at home are thinking about us now," Hamilton Fish stated gravely, staring out into the black of the night. "It would be just my luck to be put out of the way in the first scrap and not see any of the war."[37]

Hamilton Fish would be killed the following morning. The son of a U.S. diplomat and wealthy banker, and the grandson of the twenty-sixth secretary of state, was the first combat casualty of the campaign.

Cuban rebel intelligence told that the Spanish army lay in waiting—some two thousand soldiers strong—entrenched on a ridge overlooking the El Camino Real, near the village of Las Guasimas.[38] It was decided that Brigadier General Samuel Young would take his 470 Regulars up the El Camino Real and engage the Spanish fortification head-on. A Rough Rider squadron and a squadron from the Buffalo soldiers—420 men in total—would leave Siboney along a guerrilla trail, head straight up a large rocky hillside, heading due west along the Cuban coastline. After three thousand yards, and once atop the plateau of the ridge, the column would pivot north-northwest and drive deep into the jungle in an effort to outflank the Spaniard position on the left.[39] Fighting Joe Wheeler made the objective of the battle clear: "hit the Spaniards . . . as soon after daybreak as possible."[40]

20. BATTLE OF LAS GUASIMAS

—————————◇

AT 5:40 A.M., THE ROUGH RIDERS ADVANCED IN A LONG COL-
umn 250 yards behind the reconnaissance leaders, Sergeant
Hamilton Fish and Captain Allyn Capron.[1] Behind the point men
was Troop L, and then Leonard Wood with his three aides, and
then Roosevelt, flanked by news correspondents Richard Harding
Davis and Edward Marshall. Davis, perhaps the most famous newspaper man in all of America, was adorned in full regalia: "felt hat
with white puggaree, high, white composition collar, blue coat,
trousers tucked into field boots, and field glasses slung over his
shoulder."[2] The sight of the inappropriately dressed newspaper
man at the front of a combat march was not the oddest peculiar-
ity of the moment. Wood had to remind the regiment chaplain,
dressed in a black coat and white collar, that it was against military
regulations for him to be carrying a rifle and stalking the enemy.
Chaplain Henry W. Brown reluctantly agreed, turned over his
rifle and fell to the back of the column, armed only with the Bible
in his breast pocket.[3]

Dawn broke over Cuba as "quick as the crack of an egg,"
Edward Marshall explained. "And so as the first heat of the
Cuban day began to beat down upon the side of that precip-
itous hill, the Rough Riders commenced to crawl slowly up it
like great brown flies. The trail was miserable. . . . I had to pull
myself up by clinging to rocks and shrubs."[4]

Once atop the ridgeline, the advancing Americans received a
straightforward message from the 22nd infantry who had spent
the night on patrol: "the Spaniards were definitely at Las Guasimas, for they had been heard during the night felling trees and
strengthening their fortifications."[5] The land between the Rough

Riders and the yet-to-be-seen Spanish army was ominous. The pockets of open grassy glades that led into the jungle seemed to get swallowed whole by the dense tropical palms. The guerrilla trail narrowed down to a mere path, abutted on each side by impenetrable, tangled bush. Land crabs scuttled unseen.[6]

"The jungle had a kind of hot, sullen beauty," a trooper wrote. "We had the feeling that it resented our intrusion—that, if we penetrated too far, it would rise up in anger, and smother us."[7]

The sharp call of a brush cuckoo caught the bird lover's ear. Theodore peered through the canopy, squinting through his spectacles, trying to get a glimpse of the cuckoo in flight. He never saw one take wing. "They [the cuckoos] apparently receded as the regiment advanced," a trooper recalled thinking.[8]

Stealthily suspended in the trees above were Spanish sharpshooters, mimicking the call of the cuckoo, relaying ahead the size and movements of the Rough Riders. The Spanish sharpshooter, wearing a gingham uniform with hemp sandals, was accustomed to guerrilla warfare. He sat on a bamboo swing covered in grass. A small bundle of palm leaves held his food. Tied to the tree next to him was a hollowed-out bamboo shoot, approximately two inches wide and four feet long, which served as his canteen. He could remain in the tree, invisible, for a week at a time.[9]

Shortly before eight in the morning a Cuban scout ran towards Capron and Fish, explaining that the landmark of the mission was five-hundred yards further down the trail. Capron sent a message to Wood who demanded silence in the ranks, followed by the order to fill their magazines.[10]

Only the sound of the brush cuckoo broke the quiet of the front.

A mile and a quarter to the right, and approximately three-hundred feet below, Young's column advanced on the Camino Real. Separated by thick jungle, communication was impossible.[11] Each regiment was on its own.

"The men were totally unconcerned," Roosevelt wrote of Wood's orders. "I do not think they realized that any fighting was at hand."[12] The Rough Riders had yet to see a single Spaniard. The landing at Daiquiri was more of a boat race than an army invasion. The port town of Siboney had been taken without a shot fired. This entire generation of American soldiers on the guerrilla trail had grown up hearing about the epic Civil War clashes, which took place on open fields of battle, enemies fighting eye-to-eye.

When Wood's order to fill magazines was received, the men fell out and hunkered along the trail. Haphazardly, one man began throwing stones at his fellow troopers. Another blew paste balls. One trooper quipped that Happy Jack, with his now loaded gun, was more of a cause for worry than the entire Spanish army.[13] A private of Troop B stared up to the sun and sighed loudly, "By God! How would you like a glass of cold beer?"[14]

Theodore was no exception. He sat on the edge of the jungle, with no sign of the enemy anywhere, and began talking with journalist Edward Marshall regarding a luncheon in the Astor House that they both had attended a few months prior.[15]

Several vultures portentously circled above.

"We had stopped near the end of a beautiful lane, carpeted with grass almost as soft as the turn in the garden of an old English country house," Marshall writes. "The tropical growth on our right shot up, rank and strong for ten or fifteen feet, and then arched over until our resting place was almost embowered. On the left was a narrow, treeless slope on which tall Cuban grass waved lazily."[16]

Another ten minutes passed.

Theodore got up to stretch his legs, walking towards a barbed wire fence just off the trail. He picked up one end of the strand that lay curled on the ground at the foot of the post.

"My God!" the former ranchman exclaimed, "this wire has been cut today."

"What makes you think so?" Marshall asked.

"The end is bright, and there has been enough dew, even since sunrise, to put a light rust on it, had it not been cut lately."[17]

The cut barbed wire, the vultures above, the mysterious cuckoo calls.

Behind Roosevelt the regimental surgeon came up the trail, noisily riding a mule. Theodore leapt towards him. "Get down, be quiet," Theodore barked.[18]

The first shot came seconds later. It was 8:15 a.m.

"Bullets began to whistle among the branches and nip at the trees," Stephen Crane remembered. "Twigs and leaves came sailing down. It was as if a thousand axes, wee and invisible, were being wielded."[19]

The Spanish shooters were completely invisible. They knew the trails that the Rough Riders were advancing along, they knew the range of fire from their entrenchments to any number of landmarks and, most efficiently, the Mauser bullets they shot were smokeless. The effect was remarkable. "The jungle covered everything, and not the faintest trace of smoke was to be seen in any direction to indicate from whence the bullets came," Theodore expounded.[20] There was no enemy to shoot back at; there was nowhere to safely run. All surviving accounts of the battle indicate that that first few minutes were fought entirely blind: "Somewhere in front of us," "well concealed," "totally hidden," "unseen," "entirely invisible,"[21] "the worst kind of guerrilla warfare."[22]

"Nothing stirred. Not an enemy was in sight. There was no smoke, or any other visible sign of battle." Marshall, an eyewitness, explained. "And yet from nowhere came the shrieking little Mausers, and from everywhere we heard the popping of the guns that sent them."[23]

"The Mauser's noise," it was explained, ". . .is like 'z-z-z-z-z-eu.' It begins low, goes up high, and then drops, and stops suddenly on the 'eu.'"[24] Those that got hit "went down in a lump without cries, without jumping up in the air, without throwing up hands," a newspaperman recalled, "they just went down like clods in the grass."[25]

It was the sound of "chug"—the bullets ripping flesh—that was the most sickening and gruesome sound imaginable.

At the front Allyn Capron and Hamilton Fish lay dead from bullet wounds. Another six Rough Riders would die in the firefight that ensued; thirty-four men badly wounded, many shot multiple times. Captain John Thomas was shocked to see Private Thomas Isbell wobbling back to the rear, covered in blood from seven gunshot wounds; four to the head and neck, three to the hands. His thumb had been blown almost clean off.[26]

Roosevelt was panicky and it showed. He ran back and forth along the trail, uncertain of what action to take. At one point in his mad scramble, the sword attached to his belt—which was worn for pomp—got caught between his legs and sent him sprawling forward to the ground. He discarded the sword and moved for cover. While standing next to a large palm, a bullet exploded into the bark of the tree, blasting splinters into his left eye and ear.[27]

For a man who coveted attention, and wanted nothing more than to be *the* symbol of frontiersman-like strength and vitality, Theodore is surprisingly open about the confusion that engulfed him in his first battle. He admitted freely in his autobiography that he "had an awful time trying to get into the fight" and was uncertain about "trying to do what was right when in it."[28] Putting authenticity over valor he admits confusion several times during his battle narrative: "what to do then I had not an idea," "I was never more puzzled to know what to do," and "I had not the faintest idea what had happened."[29]

Theodore's edginess shocked reporter Edward Marshall. "Colonel Wood was as cool a man as I ever saw. . . . Roosevelt, on the contrary, jumped up and down, literally, I mean, with emotions evidently divided between joy and a tendency to run," Marshall retold.[30] Wood, who showed "not one sign of undue excitement," ordered Theodore to command troops G, K, and A into the jungle to the right, in an effort to connect with Young's regulars storming up the ridge from the El Camino Real.[31] The faint reports of Young's Hotchkiss guns could now be heard from below. Both U.S. columns had engaged the enemy.

"Perhaps a dozen of Roosevelt's men had passed into the thicket [after the enemy] before he did," Marshall confirmed.[32] One gets the sense, both from Theodore's accounts and the witnesses on the scene, that Roosevelt was dazed, if not stunned. It was almost as if he had to repeatedly remind himself to not be afraid.

"Then he stepped across the wire himself, and, from that instant, became the most magnificent soldier I have ever seen," Marshall recalled.

> It was as if that barbed-wire strand had formed a dividing line in his life, and that when he stepped across it he left behind him in the bridle path all those unadmirable and conspicuous traits which have so often caused him to

be justly criticized in civic life, and . . . found on the other side of it, in that Cuban thicket, the coolness, the calm judgment, the towering heroism, which made him, perhaps, the most admired and best loved of all Americans in Cuba.[33]

"It's up to us, boys!" Theodore boomed as he ran into the jungle. "[S]catter out to the right there, quick, you! Scatter to the right! Look alive!"[34]

"I took the men forward," Theodore explained his actions. "I could not see where the rest of my regiment was and I could not see the Spaniards. I did not know what to do. Fortunately, I knew that if you were in doubt, go towards the guns. I was uncertain, but I knew it could not be wrong to go forward."[35]

Cliff Scott followed Theodore into the thicket. "Colonel Roosevelt seemed to be everywhere, and he only had one idea, and that was to smash through them [the Spanish], and that is what happened."[36]

As comrades dropped around him, all that Theodore could think about was a fox-hunting jingle: "here's to every friend who struggled to the end . . . here's to every friend who struggled to the end . . . here's to every friend . . ."[37] He continued to charge ahead, the enemy nowhere in sight.

After a series of mad dashes through the thick jungle—sometimes on hands and knees—the tropical forest parted up into an open meadow. Roosevelt found himself "gazing out over the Santiago road to a razorback ridge on the opposite side of the valley."[38] Theodore was still confused. Peering through his sweaty spectacles at the clearing, he saw nothing. Where were the Spaniards? Where were Young's men?[39]

Of the several hundred military men present in the battle, it was a newspaper correspondent who played the largest role in the engagement. Richard Harding Davis, having long since discarded his notebook and now carrying a rifle that he seized from among the dead, looked out into the grassy knoll a few hundred yards away. "There they are, Colonel; look over there; I can see their hats near that glade."[40] Theodore whipped his head around, and for the first time since the battle started, some forty minutes prior, he saw the enemy. "In a minute I, too, made out the hats, and then pointed them out to three or four of our best shots," he recounted.[41] Spaniards suddenly sprang out of their cover, retreating back up over the hill on which they had been entrenched. At the first return fire from the Americans, the Spanish were on the run.

Now on the edge of the jungle, Theodore was contemplating an advance, when he caught sight of the U.S. regulars charging up the ravine to his right. In the fog of war—rather, the obscurity of the jungle—the regulars spotted the movement of the Rough Riders, and, expecting that no American troopers had advanced so far northwest along the ridgeline, fired a volley into them. Theodore ordered a first sergeant up a tree to wave a guidon, which ceased the friendly fire.[42]

With the Spanish on the run, and the American troops united in a dense palm thicket, a new attack plan was decided upon. The landscape before the Americans was a succession of grassy knobs with a series of red-tiled ranch buildings perched on an open hillside; the ground before them was open to charge.

With Roosevelt on the left, Wood in the center, and General Fightin' Joe Wheeler commanding the far right, orders to storm the meadow were given.

"About nine hundred men broke out into the open and ran up the valley," an account retells. "[T]heir rifle-cracks drowned in the booming of four Hotchkiss mountain-guns. Like ants shaken from a biscuit, some fifteen-hundred Spaniards leaped from their rock-forts along the ridge and scattered in the direction of Santiago."[43]

"Come on!" Fighting Joe Wheeler cried as he charged through the meadow, seeming to forget what war he was fighting, "We've got the *damn Yankees* on the run!"[44]

By 9:30 a.m. the battle of Las Guasimas had ended. About 1,000 Americans had driven back 1,500 Spanish soldiers.[45] In total, sixteen Americans were dead, another fifty-two wounded. Initial reports held that the bodies of forty-two Spanish soldiers had been discovered.[46]

As news of the skirmish reached stateside, Roosevelt critics would claim that Theodore led his men into an ambush, proof that he was unfit to lead. Over time, the accounts of the battle would show that the Rough Riders had found the Spaniards where they expected them and, ambush or not, they had not only stood their ground but charged and sent the enemy receding.

The Rough Riders had demonstrated extraordinary courage. Until the fight at Las Guasimas, they had only proven to be out of shape and undisciplined; adept at raising hell, getting drunk and terrorizing civilians. But when the bullets flew they were magnificent. They charged into battle with such a passion that Wood had to order the bugle call "cease fire" as the Spanish retreated. Running after his men, Wood was heard to shout repeatedly, "Don't shoot at retreating men! Don't shoot at retreating men!"[47]

"Every man behaved well; there was no flinching," Theodore recalled matter-of-factly, not surprised in the least.[48]

The finest compliment came from the enemy. "The Americans were beaten," a Spanish combatant stated bluntly, "but persisted in fighting."[49]

"They tried to catch us with their hands," added another.[50]

The following day at eleven o'clock, the eight dead Rough Riders were put to the earth upon a bed of guinea grass and palm leaves, their feet facing east. The eight crudely dug trenches rested near the intersection of the guerilla trail and the Camino Real. "Nearer, My God, to Thee," was hymned. Vultures circled somberly ahead, hovering in long drawn out circles, casting transient shadows on the men below. After a brief ceremony the mournful notes of "Taps" cascaded towards the distant Sierra Maestra, marking the end.[51]

Theodore, as he always had done when surrounded by death, decided to take action. The men that survived the battle were exhausted and hungry. Their nerves had been rattled. Roosevelt's duty, as he knew it, was to take care of the living, or as he so often put it over the next several days, "take care of my boys."[52] The dead could bury the dead.

During the six days after the battle of Las Guasimas nothing of historical importance happened. No battles, no heroic deeds, no courageous feats. But to the men who lived it, it was the most important part of the campaign, if not pure misery to get through. Since they had landed on Cuban soil, all they had to eat was hardtack and pork rinds. "General Shafter ignored appeals for food, declaring that the transportation facilities, such as they were, had to be used for ammunition," a trooper remembered in disgust. "There was plenty of ammunition at the front all the time, but never anywhere near enough food."[53]

On the morning of the 26th, Theodore took matters into his own hands and charged a squadron back towards Siboney to procure food. Storming up on a commissary officer, Theodore ordered eleven hundred pounds of beans.

The commissary reached for a book of regulations and handed it to Theodore, "under sub section B of Section C of article 4 . . . beans were issued only for the officers' mess."[54]

Theodore, without hesitation, barked that he wanted "eleven hundred pounds of beans for the officer's mess."

"Why Colonel, your officers can't eat eleven hundred pounds of beans!" came the response.

"You don't know what appetite my officers have!" Roosevelt retorted.

The commissary claimed it would require a requisition to Washington and the price of the beans would come out of Theodore's salary.[55]

"That will be all right, only give me the beans!"[56]

The cheer that went up from the Rough Riders when the dozen mules arrived with the beans was, according to one trooper, "the most enthusiastic outburst . . . during their whole stay in Cuba."[57]

Theodore was far from finished. His intuition led him to believe that several tons of food remained in the hulls of the ships at bay, and he again marched back to Siboney. "[I] bought all that an elastic stretch of my conscience would allow me to say could be used for the officers," he admits, "and then I got a boat and went out to the transport and brought in about 500 pounds of beans, and I got all the tomatoes I wished, and put them on horses and the backs of the men, and marched back, and it was a great thing for the men."[58]

With the army commissaries now suspicious of Theodore's mere presence, he decided to try his luck at the Red Cross headquarters.

"I hear that you have supplies here," Theodore stated frankly. "I want to buy some. My men are out in the jungle and they are starving."

"We can't sell anything, sir," said Miss Jennings, Clara Barton's assistant.

"My men can't wait," Theodore persisted. "There's no time to get an order thru. I'll pay for what I get myself."

"The Red Cross does not sell supplies," replied Miss Jennings.

"Oh, so that's how it is—is it? Got a sack around here?" Theodore retorted, picking up a large haversack and loading it himself with flour, coffee, beans, hardtack, bacon—everything he could find. Throwing the heavy bag across his shoulder he stormed back to the countryside, as if he were Santa Claus.[59]

Soon Theodore's spirit of taking care of the men influenced Chaplain Brown. Henry Bardshar recalled Roosevelt complaining aloud to his officers that the men were still starving "but I have already stretched my authority to the limit. Where can we get any?"

"I'll find something," said the chaplain, with a smirk.

"Where?" Theodore retored.

"Will you leave it to me?" came the godly man's response.

Some three hours later the Chaplain returned with a wagon-load chock-full of eats.

"Now where in Sam Hill, Chaplain, did you get it?" Roosevelt cried enthusiastically.

"God put it down there and kept it for me," said the Chaplain, sheepishly, before coming clean. "When I reached Siboney, I found a great body of men packing supplies into a number of wagons. One wagon which was entirely loaded, was without a driver. I supplied the deficiency and drove away."[60]

Though Roosevelt was providing for his men at the expense of the army as a whole, the effect was magical. Theodore Roosevelt was the one who could "cut the Gordian knot," a trooper stated in astonishment. Theodore was the one who endured all hardships, put his men first, got results, got food.

What little emotion Theodore had shown for the dead stood in contrast to his actions for the sick. During one of his bean raids, word reached Theodore that a trooper, who was suspected of having malaria, was not being properly cared for in the field hospital. Theodore went to investigate.

"The young surgeon in charge did not know him and did not know his rank, since Roosevelt had his tunic off," Frank Hayes recalled. "Roosevelt was intent on his purpose and beyond a nod, paid no attention to the surgeon."

"What do you mean by not saluting me?" cried the young doctor.

Roosevelt lost it. "Your job is to take care of my wounded and not to bother about salutes. Besides, I am Colonel Roosevelt and if anybody is to do any saluting, you are the man!"

The surgeon snapped into a salute. With a look of contempt Roosevelt continued to shout.

"I sent a sick man down here some time ago to be taken care of and my men say you have done nothing for him!"

"There is nothing the matter with him," replied the doctor in defiance.

"Very well, we'll see." Theodore shouted, turning and walking over to another medical tent, returning a few moments later with two different surgeons in tow.

"He is a very sick man," one of the new doctors proclaimed, after examining the sick Rough Rider.

Theodore, now as mad as a bull moose, turned and stormed the original doctor, who was back-peddling as fast as he could. According to a witness, Theodore proceeded to dole out "the greatest tongue lashing" that the world had ever seen.[61]

"A thousand pardons, Colonel Roosevelt . . ." the doctor tried to reply before Theodore cut him off.

"My boys are all good soldiers, every one of them, and they must be taken care of if I have to look after them myself!" Theodore boomed so loudly that everyone in the vicinity had to hear him.

"Before he left the piazza," a Rough Rider remembered, "he [then] came over and spoke to a big rough Irishman with a beard, who was lying near me. I think he called him 'Jim' and asked him how his rheumatism was. He seemed to know *all his men by name*, which is not usual with the commanding officer of a regiment. Who can wonder that his men would have followed him anywhere!"[62]

Fred Herrig, a Rough Rider from the Badlands, was interviewed twenty years after the war ended and recalled that it was Theodore's personal touch which made him so loved. During the intense battle at Las Guasimas, a packer who was in charge of moving the rapid fire machine guns up the trail lost his nerve and let the mules loose. Roosevelt, worried that the weapons still attached to the pack mules would fall into enemy arms, sent Fred Herrig, a back-country hunting guide from Kalispell, Montana, into the jungle to track the animals down. Cutting tracks into a ravine, Herrig found the mules none the wiser and a bit shell shocked.

Back at camp, Herrig was rightfully proud of recovering the machine guns, but he was absolutely honored how Theodore reacted.

"I reported to Roosevelt." Herrig beamed as he retold the story, "Roosevelt turned to Wood and said, 'Didn't I tell you! Didn't I tell you, Wood, [that] Fred would find those guns?! Didn't I tell you, didn't I tell you . . .'"[63] Theodore was as excited as a boy, slapping Herrig upside the shoulder, smiling from ear to ear.

For six days, the Rough Riders camped in a small grove near Las Guasimas, awaiting their next orders. Around them the arrangement slowly began to look official, as supplies and men began to trickle to the front. "The troops, the pack trains, the lines of toiling porters, so inextricably tangled along the single wagon road, magically unsnarled themselves," Rough Rider Thomas Ledwidge recounted, ". . . and dropped into the orderly array of a military encampment . . . it was like the crouching of a great tiger, gathering all his energies to spring upon his prey."[64]

The entire U.S. military expedition was on land, and now, amazingly, so too was General Shafter. A pack of mules had pulled him up the Camino Real on a buckboard.[65] Trooper J. W. Lee was unimpressed when he saw Shafter for the first time: "Enormous, panting. . . fanned by two orderlies."[66]

On the morning of June 30th, Shafter rode a mule—"the army's stoutest mule"—four miles outside of Las Guasimas along the Camino Real to a tall narrow hill appropriately named El Pozo, or the Fountain.[67] For the first time, the man in charge of the entire operation glassed the terrain that the Rough Riders had known intimately.

Atop El Pozo, the entire war came into focus.

Four miles ahead, along the Camino Real, was the city of Santiago, the prize. Its red-tiled roof buildings were clearly visible to the naked eye.

Four miles to Shafter's left, to the Southwest, the U.S. Navy under the command of Rear Admiral William T. Sampson, had established a naval blockade at the mouth of Santiago Harbor. The Spanish fleet was trapped in port, staring down the gunnels of the entire U.S. Expedition fleet. The *Oregon, Iowa, Texas, Brooklyn, Vixen, New York,* and *Indiana* slowly patrolled the small exit to the sea. Admiral Sampson dared not enter the fortified waterway for fear of mines and land forts, but he simply did not have to. The Spanish navy was imprisoned in port. If it tried to set sail for the open sea it would be almost certain suicide.[68]

Four miles northeast, to Shafter's right, was El Caney, a small village nestled into the foothills of the Sierra Maestra. Though Santiago's main water supply ran through the village, its strategic importance, as Shafter saw it, was its formidable entrenchments— six wooden blockhouses, a stone building, and a church—that could pose a high-altitude threat to the eastern flank of an American advancement into Santiago.[69] The town had to be neutralized, Shafter thought to himself.

Ahead of Shafter, northwest some 2,500 yards, and equidistant from the town of El Caney and the U.S. naval blockade outside Santiago Harbor, stood San Juan Heights. Only the Heights separated the U.S. army from Santiago de Cuba. More or less a series of hills, the Heights looked, according to Richard Harding Davis who stood next to Shafter, "so quiet and sunny and well-kept that they reminded one of a New England orchard."[70]

Since the skirmish at Las Guasimas, the Spanish forces had spent six furious days and nights fortifying the Heights. It was extraordinary trench work, some two miles long, snaking crudely across the hillside, looking like a jagged scar. The flanks of the ridgeline were also lined with ditches covered with barbed wire and gun pits.[71]

A not-so-prominent feature of San Juan Heights was a knob on the northernmost rise of the chain of hills, roughly four-hundred yards from the main fortification. Approximately one-hundred feet high and dotted with sparse shrubbery, but otherwise an open landscape, its grassy peak was separated from San Juan Hill only by a small depression, which contained a shallow pond.[72] General Shafter, not worried about the smaller hill, decided not to include it in his hand-drawn battle plans. Simply for the sake of a landmark, it was called Kettle Hill, because several large black sugar kettles surrounded a single blockhouse.[73]

From the top of El Pozo, the Camino Real road to San Juan and Kettle Hill dropped from Shafter's feet into a jungle basin three quarters of a mile long. At the bottom of the valley the Aguadores River meandered south-southwest before fording into Las Guasimas creek. About where the trail intersected the river and the creek, the landscape opened up into a grassy meadowland that was the length of two football fields. The open grassland shot heavenward, up the valley to the San Juan Heights, which stood approximately ten stories above the river bottom. Any attempt to take the hill meant a descent into the jungle below, a trek across the river bottom, and then an undoubtedly deadly charge up the open hillside mutilated with trenches and barbed wired.

Back at the makeshift headquarters tent on the afternoon of June 30th, Shafter sat in a wilted chair and looked disheveled. His wrinkled shirt was soaked with sweat, his swollen foot wrapped in a burlap sack.[74] He explained his battle plan, which was ferociously simple. "There was no attempt at strategy," Shafter coldly admitted, "and no attempt at turning their flanks. It was simply [a matter of] going straight for them."[75]

The deployment plan resembled a pitchfork. The long handle was the only trail into the jungle, the Camino Real, where the entire army would march, single file, and then arrange along the river bottom under the cover of the jungle. The far right prong was the town of El Caney, the middle prong was pointed directly at Kettle Hill, the far left prong was San Juan Hill. General Lawton would follow the right prong and take El Caney, which was suspected to topple in just two hours. Lawton would then march his men two miles along the hillside towards Kettle Hill—the middle prong—where, like the coming of the ocean tide, he would meet up with General Wheeler's Cavalry division at the base of the Heights. With El Caney under American occupation and the entire combat force in the valley between San Juan Heights and El Pozo, a frontal assault on the Heights would win the day while being covered by General Grimes' artillery stationed atop El Pozo Hill.[76]

That was the plan anyway.

The battle strategy had just been authorized when a staff officer rushed to the Rough Rider camp. Both General Young and General Wheeler had taken ill with fever; malaria was the suspected culprit. Brigadier General Samuel Sumner would take over Wheeler's Cavalry Division and Colonel Wood was now in command of Young's 2nd Brigade. Someone notified Theodore that he was now the colonel in command of the Rough Riders. On the eve of battle, he finally had the formal title as the leader of his men.

21. THE CHARGE

July 1st, 1898, "The great day of my life. . ."[1]

4:00 a.m.

The Rough Riders were awakened by voice and shove; too close to the enemy for a bugle call.

Theodore spent the night under a raincoat, on top of a saddle blanket. His pre-battle state of mind was a "feeling of uneasy excitement."[2]

In the quiet of the morning, Rough Rider A. F. Cosby found comfort. About twenty feet away from Arthur, Theodore began to shave; a mug in one hand, his face lathered with soap. "It was a strangely reassuring sight," Cosby thought to himself, "to see a man—especially our commanding officer—on the dawn of a great battle performing an everyday function as though we were simply on an enjoyable camping trip."[3]

Dressed in a dark blue shirt, brown pants, and yellow suspenders that match the "U.S.V." embodied into his collar, Theodore tied a blue polka-dot bandanna handkerchief around his neck.[4] At his hip was a Colt Army-Navy Model 1892 double action revolver, which had been salvaged from the sunken *Maine* and given to him as a gift.[5]

Theodore breakfasted with Leonard Wood, eating a handful of beans, hardtack, and a slab of bacon. They do not talk much.

6:00 a.m.

La Rojigualda—the Flag of Spain—was defiantly hoisted up the flagpole on the main fortification at El Caney. The bright yellow flag, bordered with red bars was distinctive to the Americans on the opposite hillside.[6]

6:15 a.m.

Along the eastern slope of El Pozo, near an abandoned sugar mill, Theodore called for his men to fall into order. On top of the hill above them, through exhaustive grunts, a team of horses pulled Captain George Grime's batteries onto the brow overlooking the Spanish-held hillside. Below the Rough Riders, hundreds of regulars were still washing themselves in the stream. Little wisps of smoke curled up from the valley, the smell of bacon pervaded.

In the cool of the tropic dawn, Theodore led his men to the top of El Pozo, through a clearing that had been cut the previous night. The Rough Riders stared out onto San Juan valley. The canopy below them was blanketed in a veil of morning vapor, the fortified Heights across the basin were clearly marred with long trenches and infrequent rifle pits. Off to the right, as far as the eye could see, a dilapidated church atop El Caney is visible in the gray of the morning; it seems to suspended above the earth, a beacon of white engulfed in dark. The entire scene was hushed, expectant. An easterner commented that it felt like he was sitting in the "royal box at the opera on a gala night."[7] To Theodore it looked like an "amphitheater for the battle."[8]

6:35 a.m.

The first report of American cannon fire from El Caney thundered down the valley. The Spanish soldiers came alive. Rows of straw hats sprouted up, scurrying towards rifle-pits and trenches contiguous to the village.[9]

General Lawton's artillery was under the command of Captain Allyn Capron—whose Rough Rider son, with the same name, died at Las Guasimas. In two hours' time, if the plans held, the entire division would take the village and head down the valley towards the Heights en route to Santiago.

For twenty minutes, Capron's batteries blasted away at the village with unremarkable results. The artillery, four light guns firing from a distance of over 2,000 yards, has no effect on the targets.

Someone began to wonder whether the little white hats, visible through eyeglasses, were actually dummies.[10]

A realization seized General Lawton. The antiquated U.S. artillery batteries would not provide the heavy fire required to dislodge the Spanish troops. Lawton ordered the infantry, Chaffee's Brigade, to the front. For the next three hours, the battle was an infantry gunfight, the range between enemies was no more than six hundred yards.[11]

It was now clear that Lawton's division would arrive late to the Heights. How late was unknown.

8:20 a.m.

Captain Grimes took out his pocket watch. Lawton has taken El Caney by now, he thinks to himself, before clearing a small area around his batteries where newspapermen and orderlies had congregated.

"Number one, ready! Fire!"

Eyeglasses and binoculars were raised to the blockhouse over a mile away on San Juan Heights. The powder of the American artillery belched a large cloud of smoke, now hovering on top of El Pozo.

The shot sailed long.

"Number two, ready! Fire!"

Again, long, perhaps by a hundred yards.

"Number three, ready! Fire!"

Missed again.

"Number four, ready! Fire!"

"Struck block house number one!" someone shouted, seconds after the shell burst through the roof of the blockhouse, sending tile and cement skyward. A loud cheer erupted behind the American batteries. Men clapped, shook hands, grinned.[12]

Leonard Wood turned to Theodore and remarked that he wished he could move his men off the hill. There would be "hell to pay" if the Spanish returned fire.[13]

"You can bet your life," a Rough Rider speculated aloud. "Those Spaniards know the exact distance to this hill."[14]

A faint boom came from the Spanish entrenchment, a whistling screech pierced through the air, growing in intensity. Seconds later, a loud explosion overhead sent foreign military attachés, staff, and journalists diving for cover. The Rough Riders stormed over the crest of the ridge. A journalist, hovering near a tree, turned back towards Grimes's batteries and looked at an abandoned block house. Several more shots roared across the valley.

> Instantly another shell came, which burst in front of the building and in the ranks of the troops gathered there. Several men were wounded; one poor fellow had his leg torn off. Another shell penetrated the roof and exploded inside, where several Cubans were hiding. They were literally blown through the windows and door . . .[15]

"Get out of this hell spot!" boomed Captain Grimes before ordering a bugle call, which sent horses charging from the covered timber up the hillside.[16] A few artillery men franticly hitched the batteries to the mounts, and sent the animals and weapons galloping down the hill, over brush and rocks to safety.

The quieting of Grimes's batteries indicated to all in the valley—both friend and foe alike—that the U.S. army would have to proceed without cover fire from El Pozo.

Theodore jumped on his horse, Texas, and rides for the ridge-line opposite Santiago. Another shell explodes almost on top of him, sending shrapnel into his arm, "raising a bump about as big as a hickory nut."[17] He shouted orders to the Rough Riders to take cover in the thick underbrush. Another shell exploded, the horse Wood was riding tumbled to the ground, a large piece of shrapnel had pierced through its lungs.[18]

Theodore looked down at his throbbing hand. "Well, that's the first one," he belted loudly, "They'll have to do better next time."[19]

A courier from headquarters rode up to Theodore and tells him that the Rough Riders were to proceed into the valley, cross the river, and then turn right to support Lawton's division as it came down from El Caney. The Rough Riders were not to attack the Heights under any circumstances.[20] They must maintain a presence in the valley to prevent any attempt by the Spanish to surround Lawton and attack him from the rear. The Rough Riders were only needed for support, it was urged. Theodore listened intently, finding the orders to be of the "vaguest kind."[21]

"Now!" Roosevelt shouted turning back to the Rough Riders after he got his orders, "get ready to march down the road."[22]

9:00 a.m.
The Spanish ceased artillery fire.[23] The quiet puzzled the Americans. The Spanish repositioned their guns at the trailhead of the basin.

9:30 a.m.
Theodore stood at the front of his column on the slope of the hill and ordered the troopers to strip for combat. Tents, blanket rolls, and rations were stacked in orderly piles. Each man kept only his carbine, ammunition, and canteen.[24]

The entire army was moving forward on a single lane down the trailhead on the Camino Real—the handle of the pitchfork. The Rough Riders were the last in, forced to watch as the 1st, 3rd, 6th, 9th, and 10th cavalries all tramped down the muddy, overcrowded trail ahead of them.[25] The road looked more like "the chute of death," a journalist noted.[26]

Why had the army, with six days to prepare, not cut new trails into the jungle, everyone waiting in line must have thought?

General Chaffee had asked during the war council briefing the previous day if the enemy would train its guns along the only serviceable trail into the valley.[27] The question was dismissed. It was the only way in, Chaffee was told. Several thousand men would descend down a path not ten feet wide.[28]

Some forty minutes passed before the Rough Riders started down the trail, into Hell's Pocket.[29] Theodore mounted his horse, believing that on a perch he would be easier to see, easier to follow. In columns two abreast he led the men into the jungle below, advancing slowly.[30]

At the bottom of the basin, later to be renamed Bloody Bend, Private Benjamin Post heard "clicking and buzzing noises" above.[31] He looked up as a wave of bullets poured down; leaves, twigs, and branches rained down on the men.[32] "Someone was trying to kill us," Post thought of the desultory fire, "each one of us individually, and in a highly impersonal way."[33]

A. F. Cosby felt tense, mad as hell. He wanted to shoot back, to fight for his life. But where were the shots coming from? Snipers in the trees, Spaniards entrenched on the valley floor, volleys from the opposite hillside?

The Rough Riders marched into the basin. The trail narrowed, buffered on either side by discarded supplies as well as the bodies of horses and men. Theodore ordered his regiment into a single file, making room for the stretchers carrying the severely wounded to the field hospital at the rear. The soldiers who were barely wounded—those lucky to be alive—hobbled back up the trail.

Rough Rider Thomas Ledwidge scoffed at a thought that passed through his mind at that moment. How different this march, the one into enemy fire in the jungle, was from the brave march that the New Mexican contingent performed on the paved streets of Santa Fe just a month prior. In Santa Fe, patriotic heads were held high as men marched towards a train bound for glory. How naive that all seemed, Ledwidge thought.[34]

10:20 a.m.

The battle at El Caney was entering its fifth hour. Lawton's division was at a standstill, halted in a withering barrage of return fire.

10:50 a.m.

The Rough Riders were stopped several hundred yards up from the bottom of the valley where the Camino Real and the Aguadores River meet. The mass of soldiers—infantry marching forward, the wounded marching out—had choked off the trail.[35] The ground "underfoot was slippery" a trooper noticed, "mud made by the blood of the dead and wounded."[36] A courier rode towards Theodore with new orders: cross the ford, march half a mile to the right, and remain in reserve near the creek in a forested lane beneath Kettle Hill.

Theodore relayed the orders. The regiment waded through the Aguadores River, passing into an open field in full view of the enemy trenches some six hundred yards away.

"Colonel, better get down, or they'll pot you," Lieutenant Miley shouted while hiding in a thicket.[37]

"I'm not going to lie down for any confounded Spaniard!" Roosevelt snorted.[38]

10:55 a.m.

The entire United States air force, consisting of a single hot air balloon, took to the sky. The plan, according to the pre-battle strategy, was for the Signal Corps to follow the inflatable balloon, which was attached to the ground with coils of rope. Two troopers in the balloon's basket would relay the movements of the Spanish army by dropping little white maps that would flutter to the ground. The white notes, in theory, would alert those below of enemy movements.[39]

The balloon drifted directly over the bottleneck of humanity at Bloody Bend. To the mortification of everyone below, the balloon's guide ropes got entangled in the trees and stalled out some fifty feet above the jungle.

Every Spanish weapon in the valley was now aimed at the novelty.

"Like the first drops of a rainstorm," a Rough Rider recalled. "We heard each bullet as it sang over our heads."[40]

It seemed as if "the gates of hell had opened," a trooper stated.[41] Everything was thrown into confusion. Remaining on horseback, Theodore shouted at the men to take cover. Troopers dove into the grass along the lane on the river bottom. Others, still crossing the river, swam furiously to the side; several lay in mosquito bogs along the embankments, clinging to shrubs, heads down.

Seconds later, a bullet smashed into the stomach of Henry Haywood, the New York policeman, sounding as if someone had jammed a "fist into a pillow."[42] Haywood crumpled over, dead.[43]

"Remaining there under this galling fire of exploding shrapnel and deadly Mauser volleys the minutes seemed like hours," thirty-seven-year-old John "Black Jack" Pershing remembered. Pershing—the future mentor of World War II General Eisenhower, Bradley, and Patton—decided to get his men across the river over to safety, and in doing so spotted General Wheeler, who at the sound of the battle had lept off of his sick bed and rode to the front. Pershing and Wheeler met in the middle of the river, directly below the balloon. "We've got to get that damn thing out of the air!" they shouted to one another. A Spanish shell exploded in the river next to them, splashing water over their heads.[44]

"The shelling seems quite lively," General Wheeler said with a smirk and a crazy look in his eye. Both men charged for cover.[45]

Theodore ran to the front of his men's position, taking cover in the grass at the foot of the hillside. Through the sweat pouring down his brow, he made out a few large black kettles above him on the open hillside, some five hundred yards away. This must be Kettle Hill, he thought.

Where was Lawton? What were the next orders?

11:15 a.m.

The balloon, riddled with holes, finally fell from the sky. In the line of fire of the Spanish entrenchment atop San Juan Heights to the Camino Real—through the path of the balloon—several hundred men lay dead or wounded in an area one city block in length and no wider than ten feet.[46]

A dispatch was sent back up the hill to Captain Grimes. It was slaughter in the valley; the men needed cover fire if only to draw artillery shells away from the troopers below.

"For a time," Richard Harding Davis thought, "it seemed as though every second man was either killed or wounded."[47]

A new report came to the front.

Spanish snipers, invisible in the palm leaves above, had let the Americans march into the valley and were now firing at the wounded as they treaded back to the field hospital.[48]

It was beginning to look like a turkey shoot.[49]

11:40 a.m.

At El Caney, Captain Lee crawled over the ridgeline and looked down at the battle below. He saw roughly one hundred Americans lying in the grass.

"Are those your reserves?" he asked an officer, squinting his eyes.

"No, sir, by God, they are casualties!" the officer retorted.

Lawton's division was still halted at El Caney, not on its way to the Heights. The entire army in the valley, including Roosevelt, did not know this. They expected Lawton's men to enter the basin at any moment.

Theodore got back on his horse, trying to set an example of courage.[50]

11:50 a.m.

The American army was now stretched a thousand yards along the bottom of San Juan Heights. The 1st brigade, to the far left of the valley, was positioned directly under San Juan Hill. The 2nd brigade commanded the position directly under Kettle Hill. At the rear of the 2nd brigade and pinned in the back on the extreme western flank, the Rough Riders lay in the grass behind the 3rd, 6th, and 9th cavalries.

At the bottom of Kettle Hill a trooper looked perplexingly at the field between the last of the jungle cover and open grass up to the Heights. Why did the tall grass, where several men lay, flutter as if in a gust of wind? Then a horrible realization hit him. It was the volley of bullets that stirred the grass into movement, not a breeze. "It was a steady deathly static," he described.[51]

From the grass a chorus of cries emanated: *I'm hit . . . I'm done . . . They got me . . . Help!*[52] A man would get hit and then crumple over. And then another.

Smoking a cigarette and walking upright in front of his men was Buckey O'Neill, the captain of the Arizona contingent. He wanted to stand tall, exude courage, lead under the faulty premise that an officer ought never to take cover.[53]

"Captain, a bullet is sure to hit you," someone shouted at Buckey.

"Sergeant, the Spanish bullet isn't made that will kill me," Buckey replied, a cigarette hanging limply at the corner of his smiling mouth.[54]

When Buckey opens his mouth to speak again, a bullet ripped clean through his face, blowing out the back of his head.

"He was dead before he hit the ground," recalled a trooper who was hunkered in the grass near Buckey. Theodore, only a few feet away from Buckey, was a bit more romantic in his description, "even before he fell his wild and gallant soul had gone into the darkness."[55]

With Buckey dead, Theodore took cover in the grass. The bullets continued to rain down. A man next to Theodore was hit—*chug,*—then another—*chug,*—then another—*chug, chug, chug.*

The regiment could not retreat and it could not remain. There was only one option: charge the guns fortified on top of the hill.[56]

Theodore summoned a trooper.

"Go to the back and ask whatever general you come across for permission to advance—my men are being cut up!"[57]

The trooper stood up, saluted, and pitched forward across Roosevelt's knees. A bullet had ripped through his neck, obliterating the carotid artery, killing him instantly. Blood was everywhere.[58]

Noon

The Rough Riders had been pinned down at Bloody Bend on the Aguadores River for over an hour. Crouched in tall grass in hundred-plus-degree weather, the scene was entirely grotesque. "Men gasped on their backs, like fishes in the bottom of a boat," a witness wrote, ". . their tongues sticking out and their eyes rolling."[59]

There were still no orders from General Shafter, no sight of Lawton's men. Along the river bottom officers trampled back and forth, looking for instructions. It seemed is if nobody was in charge.

Theodore sent messenger after messenger to get permission to advance. He received no response.[60]

Medical corpsmen, finally reaching the river bottom, stand over wounded soldiers tagging the fallen where they lay: white tags for the wounded; blue tags for the seriously wounded; red tags, all but dead; no tags, dead.[61]

"Cover him up! He's an officer!" someone screamed, standing near a corpse. "Cover him up, goddammit!"[62]

"We ought to take that hill," Theodore shouted, preparing his men for what he believed was inevitable, "We ought to take that hill! We ought to take . . ."[63]

12:10 p.m.

Colonel Charles A. Wikoff, in charge of the 22nd Infantry, was shot and killed. Lieutenant-Colonel Worth was then put in command.[64]

12:15 p.m.

Worth went down and Lieutenant Colonel Liscum took command.[65]

12:20 p.m.

Liscum went down and Lieutenant Colonel Ezra Ewers took command.[66]

12:30 p.m.

Theodore, his face marred with blood and sweat, ran up and down the line, trying to project confidence. "Boys, this is the day we have trained for. You know we are being watched by the regulars. Don't forget you are a Rough Rider. Don't forget, boys, that we must get through this battle so your reward can come in the future."[67]

Theodore desperately tried to keep the men focused on the task at hand. "I had been joking with some and swearing at others," he explained later, "as the exigencies of the case seemed to demand."[68]

A private recalled having "a tenseness in [his] throat, a dryness that was not a thirst, and little chilly surges in [his] stomach."[69] *Something had to give,* the trooper thought, *something must happen.* It was all just a hideous blur of carnage.

12:55 p.m.

General Shafter's aide-de camp, Lieutenant John D. Miley, paced anxiously along the Camino Real. Miley was visibly nervous. Generals and colonels surrounded him, everyone peering down the trail for the mounted messenger to return from El Pozo with Shafter's command. Shafter—who had fallen ill and was lying on a door that had been unhinged from the field hospital—was unaware of the situation on the ground and did not have a clear line of communication to the front of the battle. It became clear that someone was going to have to make a decision. As the spokesperson for the man in charge, it began to dawn on Miley that the responsibility might default to him.

As rifle shots reverberated all around him, Miley "swallowed hard" and faced the men that outranked him. "The heights must be taken at all hazards," Miley told the colonels, brigadiers, and major generals. "A retreat now would be a disastrous defeat."

And so with that, the inevitable order had finally come. Not from General Shafter, but from a Lieutenant.[70]

12:57 p.m.

General Shafter, unaware of Miley's order, rose and put on his pants. He sent an order to disengage American forces at El Caney and retreat. When General Lawton received the order he ignored it.[71]

1:00 p.m.

Through a hail of bullets, Lieutenant Colonel Joseph Haddox Dorst charged to the rear of the cavalry flank. He found Theodore Roosevelt and gave the command: "Move forward and support the regulars in the assault on the hills in front."[72]

"The instant I received the order I sprang on my horse," Theodore recalled, "and then my 'crowded hour' began."[73]

Galloping back and forth, Roosevelt began to shout, "Men, we must advance! Rough Riders Forward, Come On!"[74]

The distinction between "Come on!" and "Go on!" was not lost on the men.[75]

The Rough Riders leapt from their trenches at the rear flank and ran in spurts of ten to fifteen yards, diving into cover behind brush and grass, at times crawling on hands and knees to the front. Soon the regiment was crowding the 9th cavalry, who had not yet received the official order to charge.

Theodore saw a man lying in the grass, not moving ahead.

"Are you afraid to stand up when I am on horseback?" Theodore shouted.

The soldier got up and fell forward on his face, a bullet striking him lengthwise, killing him instantly.

"I suppose the bullet had been aimed at me," Theodore thought, describing it later as a "curious incident."[76]

Roosevelt rode on. "Charge, boys, charge," he shouted.

The captain of the 9th cavalry ordered his men not to move, to await official orders.

"Where is your colonel?" Theodore shouted.

The captain did not know and shrugged.

"Then I am the ranking officer here and I give the order to charge!"

The captain hesitated.

"Then let my men through!" Roosevelt blasted from atop his horse. At this moment, he looked "like a Sioux."[77]

The Rough Riders erupted into wild animalistic cheers; it was pure "patriotic insanity."[78] A Pawnee Indian, the son of Chief Big Eagle, let out a native war cry.[79]

The captain from the 9th cavalry caught the spirit of the thing and began to shout, "Don't let those volunteers beat you to it! Don't let those volunteers . . ."

At the extreme front of the tree line, Theodore stopped one last time. With Kettle Hill as his backdrop—the summit no more than ninety yards away through an open field, ascending at a forty-five degree angle—he turned back to his men. The 3rd, 6th, 9th, and 10th cavalries, as well as his Rough Riders, had all intermingled. There was no formation, no structure. Theodore looked down at the regulars and the volunteers, the blacks, the natives, the whites, the rich, and the poor.

"Our cause is just and God is with us, let all brave men follow me,"[80] he shouted.

"Gentlemen, charge!"

1:05 p.m.

"By God, there go our boys up the hill!" someone yelled from the military attaché a mile and a half away atop El Pozo. "They can't take it," another moaned, "It's impossible!"

"Never in the world. It is slaughter, absolute slaughter," someone cried in horror.[81] The Japanese diplomat just dropped his head to his chest, speechless, mortified.[82]

Theodore Roosevelt broke out into the open, charging up the hillside.[83]

"Mounted high on horseback and charging the rifle-pits at a gallop and quite alone, [he] made you feel that you would like to cheer," an eye witness wrote. "[His] blue polka-dot handkerchief . . . floated out straight behind his head like a guidon."[84]

It was as if this was "the flying wedge in football," trooper Ray Clark thought to himself, "with the Colonel at the point."[85]

It seemed as if someone had made an awful and terrible mistake [Richard Harding Davis wrote]. One's instinct was to call them to come back. You felt that someone had blundered . . .it was not heroic then, it seemed merely terribly pathetic. The pity of it, the folly of such a sacrifice was what held you.[86]

"No man who saw Roosevelt take that ride expected he would finish it alive," Davis confirmed.[87]

Riding high on his horse, Theodore squinted down the valley. "The whole line, tired of waiting and eager to close with the enemy, was straining to go forward," Theodore remembered the sene. "And it seems that different parts slipped the leash at almost the same moment."[88]

It had only taken one man to start it, and when he did, 2,522 men exploded up the Heights at once.[89]

The advance was slow, the artillery guns fortified on the opposing hill sputtered violently. "Still we ran a few feet," trooper Cosby recalled, "fell flat, jumped up, ran, fell flat again. On the runs, a man would double up as though squeezed like an accordion—then he would pitch forward—often with no more than a grunt. Still we moved onwards and upwards."[90]

The guidon bearer of the 3rd cavalry the white regiment, was shot. A black soldier from the 10th cavalry picked up the regimental colors and ran on.[91]

Charging next to Theodore was Henry Bardshar, Sergeant Campbell, Dudley Dean, and a number of the Arizona men. Theodore looked to the hillside and saw the Spanish retreating from the ranch houses, running parallel across the Heights towards San Juan Hill.[92] Watching the combatants run, he shouted something, and then his world goes blurry. His glasses fell off, he was absolutely blinded. He fumbled through his breast pocket and found another pair.[93]

Forty yards from the top of the hill, Roosevelt was stopped by a six-foot tall barbed wire entanglement that cut horizontally across the hillside. He jumped off his horse and turned the animal loose. A bullet snapped into his forearm. He looked at the blood on his sleeve.

"I've got it, boys! I've got it!!" he shouted loudly.[94]

As bullets flew overhead, Theodore ordered Henry Bardshar to cut the fence with nippers, and sent orders down the fence line to do the same. "I think we can do better than that," Bardshar shouts. Gathering three troopers, he pulled the post straight out of the ground. The troopers followed Bardshar's lead and the entire ensnarement was uprooted and laid down in a matter of seconds.[95]

Theodore crouched again, ready to charge the last forty yards. He saw a wounded volunteer, lying on the ground, grunting, perhaps dying. "You needn't be so damned proud," he says with a smile.[96]

1:10 p.m.

Bardshar outpaced Theodore, fired at two Spaniards running alongside a trench and killed them both.[97] Theodore continued to run on. Colonel Hamilton was shot, dead before his body hits the earth. Captain Mills was shot through the eye and rendered-blind.[98]

Theodore and Bardshar reached the crest of Kettle Hill and took shelter behind a large iron caldron.[99] To Theodore's left was an expansive view of the Spanish blockhouse on San Juan Hill. Four hundred yards away, across an open valley, there was a pond in the middle. It was a now a race to the blockhouse. The U.S. 1st brigade was storming the hill from the bottom, the Spanish soldiers were fleeting the rifle pits of Kettle Hill, running along the ridge to fortify San Juan Hill.[100]

Above the din of battle the unmistakable drumming of machine gun fire began.

chunk—chunk—chunk—chunk—chunk—chunk—chunk— chunk—chunk—chunk

"The Spanish machine guns!" a man next to Theodore cried out, certain that death would follow. Crouched behind the iron kettle a cryptic thought arrested all: had the Spanish drawn the Americans into the open to slaughter them with machine guns? Theodore turned his head down, listening.

chunk—chunk—chunk—chunk—chunk—chunk—chunk— chunk—chunk—chunk

The automatic fire was coming from the flat ground to the left, from the Americans.

"It's the Gatlings, men, our Gatlings!" Theodore shouted.[101] The exposed Americans on the face of Kettle Hill erupted into loud cheers.

For nine minutes, Lieutenant John Parker shelled out a lead screen of 3,600 rounds per minute.[102] The Americans had cover fire for the first time in the battle.

Theodore rushed the rest of the way up Kettle Hill. A disorientated and frightened Spanish bugle boy, perhaps only twelve years old, bolted from the bunkhouse right into Theodore's arms.[103] No other Spanish soldier was on the hill. All enemy combatants had fled into the trails on the way to Santiago or were charging across the hillside towards the San Juan Hill bunkhouse.

Kettle Hill was his.

1:28 p.m.

General Parker called for a cease fire, afraid he may shoot the advancing Americans.[104]

Theodore saw Frank Hughes, blood pouring profusely into his eyes and mouth. "Didn't I order you back?" Theodore shouted, referring to his order at the bottom of the hill that Hughes go to the field hospital.

Fred Bugbee, also wounded and fighting alongside Hughes, shouted at Roosevelt, "You go to hell! We are not going back!"[105]

Theodore smiled and stormed off another thirty feet up the hill, shouting for his officers to assemble.

Theodore hastily called together the surviving captains and lieutenants who were trying to manage the troops into columns, to make structure of the varied men from the different units.

Almost all of them were soaked with sweat and exhausted; many were bloodied.

"What is going on here? What are you trying to do?" Roosevelt bellowed to an officer.

"I am trying to restore troop formation," someone responded.

"Let the formation take care of itself . . . the main thing is to win the fight!"

Theodore relayed the plan to charge towards San Juan Hill, pointing to the fortification, only slightly higher in elevation, four hundred yards along the same ridgeline. Everyone stood in silence. They had already taken Kettle Hill, an officer reminded Theodore, and they should wait for further orders to advance.

Theodore could have sat on Kettle Hill and been the hero of the war; the charge he had started up the Heights was heroic and brave. But he had to finish the job. This whole thing—leaving his family and his post as assistant secretary of the navy to go fight in Cuba—was not about political gain or popularity. It was personal, and deeply intrinsic. He had to prove to himself, to the world, that the Roosevelts were fighters.

When reflecting on the order, a trooper flatly stated, "If the Colonel was looking out for a prospective governorship, it must have been in Hades, for no one courted death more."[106]

"I, very much elated, ordered another charge on my own hook," Theodore confirmed later.[107]

"Forward to the charge! Charge the hill ahead!" Theodore shouted before dashing through the open ravine across the hillside towards San Juan Hill, not up the hill as legend holds, but across.[108]

Theodore lept over a wire entanglement and sprinted for a hundred yards, diving into what little cover he found in the ravine. Bullets ripped the grass all around him.

Theodore looked back and was mortified. Only five soldiers have followed him. He waved his arm forward to the rest of the men on Kettle Hill, "Come on! Come on! Come on!"[109]

"For God's sakes follow the colonel!" Oliver Norton, one of the five troopers who had followed Theodore, shouted back to the Rough Riders. "For God's sakes follow . . ." The words still stuck in Norton's mouth as a bullet passed through his head, killing him instantly.[110]

In the seconds that followed, two of the five that had trailed Theodore into the ravine were shot dead, and one other, Winslow Clark, a Harvard man, was badly wounded. Theodore, uninjured, handed Clark a canteen, and sprinted back to Kettle Hill—back across the open ravine, back over the wire fence, back over the crest of the hill a full hundred yards away.[111]

In a berserk rage Theodore unloaded on his men. "We must advance!" His arms flailed, his teeth clenched, his face a maroon color.

In the upheaval of battle, the original command went unheard. A trooper recalled a lump in his throat the size of a walnut, feeling as if "my mother had accused me of striking her."

"We didn't hear you. We didn't see you go, colonel. Lead on now; we'll sure follow you."[112]

Theodore turned back toward San Juan Hill and saw the Spaniards.

"Come on boys! There they go; damn them!"[113]

And then he charged again, for the third time that day. This time the entire dismounted cavalry went with him.

The sight of the Americans charging up the hill, and now across the ravine, sent the Spanish soldiers running from the trenches and blockhouses off the hillside towards Santiago.

Just moments later, Theodore was standing at the main entrenchment along San Juan Hill, perhaps no more than fifty yards from the main blockhouse. Looking down in the trench he saw a pile of "dead bodies in the light blue and white uniform of the Spanish regular army."[114]

Lieutenant Milton Davis and Henry Bardshar were standing next to Theodore when two Spanish soldiers rose from among the dead in the trench, not more than ten yards away. Both Spaniards fired their guns at the three Americans. Remarkably, not one bullet connected. Theodore threw up his revolver and fired twice, missing the first and killing the second.[115]

What if the Spaniards had hit their mark, just a mere ten yards away? How would have history remembered Theodore Roosevelt? Would his name be synonymous with Daniel Boone and Davy Crocket and not Abraham Lincoln and Franklin Roosevelt? Would the world have ever known Franklin or Eleanor Roosevelt? Perhaps Theodore would have been remembered as a tortured soul, dying an impulsive death? Perhaps he would have been the most heroic frontiersman in American history? Perhaps his name would have been one that history forgets?

Theodore looked into the trench for more living soldiers, and finding none, he charged the rest of the way to San Juan Hill.

"Holy Godfrey, what fun!" a trooper heard Theodore shout, as the last Spaniard disappeared over the hill in retreat.[116]

At the crest of the ridge, Theodore looked to the west. The city of Santiago was beneath him.

2:00 p.m.

"There was very great confusion at this time," Theodore remembers, "the different regiments being completely intermingled— white regulars, colored regulars, and Rough Riders."[117]

Everyone was waiting for leadership. Who is the officer in command, troopers asked aloud? Who is in charge here? Do we pursue or entrench?

The highest ranking officer on the hill at that moment was Theodore Roosevelt, but he did not wait to find that out. He began to shout commands, ordering the men to fortify along the ridge facing the city of Santiago—the last line of Spanish fortification just 700 yards below. Soldiers were ordered to fan out and lie on their stomachs, propped up by their elbows. General Parker's Gatlings are rolled into position, facing the port city.

"Hold the hill at all hazards," Theodore ordered.[118]

The Spaniards began firing from a trench line below. Several Americans were killed.

"Hold the hill at all hazards," Theodore commanded.

A few moments passed before General Parker's guns began to pop again.

4:15 p.m.

General Lawton's division finally took the town of El Caney, eight hours later than expected.[119]

5:15 p.m.

Fragments of four cavalry regiments fanned out on San Juan Hill. "They were seldom more than a company at any one spot, and there were bare spaces from 100 to 200 yards apart held by only a dozen men," Richard Harding Davis wrote. "The position was painfully reminiscent of Humpty-Dumpty on the wall."[120]

The Stars and Stripes were driven into the ground above the trenches. A hearty cheer resonated from the top of the hill. As night approached, everyone realized, as Harding confirms, that the Americans were "clinging to the ridge by their fingernails."[121]

6:00 p.m.

General Wheeler rode to the front and pulled Theodore aside. Shafter, still bedridden, was concerned about a counter attack and was considering a retreat.[122] Benjamin Colbert, a native from Tishomingo, Oklahoma, serving as Theodore's secretary on the hill, looked square at his boss, awaiting his reaction. "It is a disgrace for the American army to retreat at any time, and especially three days prior to the anniversary of the Signing of the Declaration of Independence," Theodore retorted, full of patriotic bravado. "Is it compulsory to obey oral orders? If not, I will remain to die by this American flag."

Fighting Joe Wheeler paused for a moment. "I will see that there is no falling back," he replies.[123]

Theodore quickly issued a casualty report to ascertain whether his patriotic bravado had outreached his reason. There were portions of four cavalry regiments on the hill, he was told, of the six that had started the day. He had gone into battle with nearly four hundred men under his command, and eighty-nine Rough Riders had either been wounded or killed. In the battle for El Caney and the San Juan Heights, 200 Americans lost their lives and another 1,100 were wounded.[124]

The officers had been hit the hardest. He was told, "of the eight troops, two were now commanded by captains, three by first lieutenants, two by second lieutenants, and one by a sergeant."[125]

"The proportion of loss in killed and wounded was considerably greater among the officers than among the troopers," Theodore wrote later, "and this was exactly as it should be."[126]

7:00 p.m.

The shooting, though raging fitfully at intervals, had gradually died down.[127]

The men had been without food for fourteen hours. Theodore sent a detail back to Kettle Hill to rummage the blockhouse. They found a Spanish officer's mess, his dinner still simmering: three big iron pots of beef, rice, and peas, as well as loaves of bread. The food was brought to the front and divided equally amongst the men, regardless of rank or color. It did not provide very much to eat, but according to Theodore, "it freshened us all."[128]

Warren Crockett—the thin IRS officer from Georgia—discovered several pounds of Spanish coffee in another bunkhouse. Theodore ordered it to be brewed on the camp fire and delivered to the men in the trenches. A soldier sprinted between trenches with the coffee pail in his hand.[129] The deliveries went on throughout the night.

8:00 p.m.

As the sun began to set, Roosevelt ordered every able-bodied man to continue to dig trenches in a zig-zag formation across the ravine. One company shoveled at a time, the other lay back a few yards in support. Shifts changed every half hour. Roosevelt personally superintended the digging, moving back and forth from his headquarters to the front, a distance of four hundred yards.

Theodore barked the order for a shift change. "The relieving party would come up from the lower side of the hill and would make a dash over the top and tumble into our trenches, as we would tumble out and make a dash for the rear," Frank Knox, a northeasterner, recounted."[130]

"I ran across that hill so fast and down the grade so hard that I tripped and pitched headlong right at Colonel Roosevelt's feet," Knox remembered.

"Are you hit?" Theodore asked.

"No sir, I stumbled."

Theodore smiled. "Go back to headquarters and tell the cook I said to give you something to eat."[131]

Frank Knox went to the headquarters tent and got himself something to eat. A few years later, Knox went on to become a famous newspaper editor and then the Republican vice-presidential candidate in 1936. After World War II broke out, he became the secretary of navy under the other Roosevelt president.

11:55 p.m.

Digging was called to a halt. The exhausted troopers climbed into the trenches, free to sleep where they stood, if their nerves allowed. The tropical night was crisp.

Theodore, in the bunkhouse, laid down, exhausted and fulfilled. He grabbed his diary.

Rose at four.
Big Battle.
Commanded regiment.
At extreme front of firing line.[132]

22. THE SIEGE

———————————————◇

TWO DAYS LATER, PHOTOGRAPHER WILLIAM DINWIDDIE SET UP a tripod on top of San Juan Hill, and naturally Theodore gravitated to the middle of the picture. The backdrop was a splendid American flag which, like the men, was ragged and war-torn. Theodore's head is cocked to the side in self-assurance, his right hand resting on his revolver. Behind him, and to his immediate left and right, stood a few of the Rough Riders, their expressions gritty and resilient.

To the far left and to the far right stood the 3rd and 10th cavalries, fanned out in a semi-circle. There were roughly a hundred men who stood for the picture; most would be left out of history. Magazines and newspapers would choose to publish a second shot, one that zoomed in on Roosevelt, the flag, and the handful of Rough Riders. The cropped photo would instantly become iconic; exemplifying a new world order with America as its supreme power.

The original, wider image with its swell of Americanism—not the cropped photo—should be the most famous image of the war, the most famous picture of Theodore Roosevelt's life. The wider image shows several soldiers not ready, facing the wrong way; a trench cuts across the foreground looking like an unhealed scar; a forgotten African-American soldier, close to the camera, stares forward with a stern detached gaze; a second American flag, off to the right, hangs lifelessly. It looks as if the second flag is held by the 10th cavalry—perhaps even by Sgt. George Berry himself.[1] The wider picture and the second flag symbolize another America, a still segregated America, a still imperfect America. The wider image shows the variety of men on the hill, the melting pot of characters from the four corners of the country, men from every walk of life. The wider picture illustrates the genius of the American experiment, the beauty of unified diversity. The wider picture also illustrates the genius of Theodore Roosevelt's leadership. He had united the men, and when he did, he united a country.

The man in the middle of the zoomed-in photo would get all the credit for the charge. He would become the next president of the United States.

Shortly after the picture was taken, Theodore walks off the hill towards his headquarters tent, passing a journalist from *Leslie's Weekly*. Theodore smiles broadly, "Oh, didn't we have a bully fight back there on the hill!" he shouts.[2]

At the headquarters tent, Theodore took out a pen and paper and wrote a letter to Henry Cabot Lodge. ". . . I am quite content to go now and to leave my children at least an honorable name."[3]

From the late afternoon of July 1st until Spain's official surrender on July 17th, the Rough Riders would not partake in another military conflict. The on-ground fighting was over, but nobody knew it yet.

The 4th of July on San Juan Heights was "probably the quietest any of us ever saw," a Rough Rider recalled. "It was as silent as an empty church . . . there were neither fire-crackers nor fire-works. We had no picnics, no lemonade, no ice cream. A few shots were fired far in our rear at guerrillas."[4]

As America celebrated its one hundred and twenty-second year of independence, its citizens read about the feats of Theodore Roosevelt.

The *Journal* triumphantly announced:

Roosevelt: the American Soldier. No finer picture of young American manhood in war has ever been presented than that of Theodore Roosevelt at the head of his Rough Riders and the colored cavalry storming the blockhouse at San Juan.

The Spaniards were entrenched at the crest of a hill up which, under the pitiless storm of Mauser bullets, the assailants were forced to advance. Men fell fast, but the ranks closed up mechanically and pressed on, firing rapidly. Roosevelt rode a hundred feet of the line, waving his sword and "yelling like a Sioux" . . .

We think that Mr. Roosevelt's military career affords a fine illustration of the possibilities inherent in American character. Born to the walks of peace, equipped with every facility for living a purposeless and idle existence, Roosevelt, after creditable essays in political life, manifests the very highest qualities which go to make up the successful soldier.[5]

Life magazine touted:

Without a doubt the military man who has made the biggest renown is Mr. Theodore Roosevelt. He stormed the heights of glory with the eagerness of a milk-fed puppy rushing to his first piece of meat. To think of him is like thinking of a comet with a tail all exclamation points.[6]

The *San Francisco Chronicle* included a hand drawing and claimed that "Theodore Roosevelt led the charge with great bravery . . ."[7]

On the 4th, while the country was ablaze with patriotism, Theodore sent two official statements to Washington D.C. which, in short order, were released by the War Department to the public. The first statement is an action-packed account of the movements of battle, the gallantry of the campaign. The second statement mentions, by name, over thirty troopers who "distinguished themselves by their bravery." Theodore gives full credit to his men, naming almost a full ten percent of them in his report before declaring that any "attempt to give a list of the men who showed signal valor would necessitate sending in an almost complete roster of the regiment."[8] Theodore fastidiously praises his men, signaling them out for honor, bestowing upon them the glory he thought they earned. The words he uses to describe his troopers are noteworthy:

> "courage, great hardihood, soldierly conduct, self-reliant, self-sufficient, eagerness, devotion, bravery, boldness, enterprising natures, resolution, intelligence, gallantry, and fortitude."[9]

Journalist Ralph Paine used an interesting analogy to explain how Roosevelt talked about his men: "You may have heard a father talk like that when the boy has scored the winning touch-down in a big football game."[10]

Again this was genuine, but purposeful. Theodore loved speaking about his regiment and promoting the ideal of frontiersmanship. But he also knew that his followers delighted in the glory of recognition. He intentionally put his men on a pedestal, leveraging the bonding power of praise. For his part, Theodore would spend the rest of his life redirecting the acclaim of his legendary charge. "The American press has given me credit for leading the charge up San Juan Hill," Theodore stated sincerely in a speech. "But I did not lead the charge! I simply gave the command and had to run as fast as I could to keep up."[11]

In the early 1920s several surviving Rough Riders were asked to explain how Theodore led, what he said, what he did, how he became so respected amongst the men who originally were unimpressed with him in San Antonio. The surviving stories are not profound on their own, but when they are collectively pieced together, a portrait of Theodore Roosevelt's leadership style emerges.

There is a story of compassion.

Roosevelt may have been quick to wrath but he was none the less ready to make allowances for frailties, I know that personally. I preferred charges against a private for some infraction of duty while we were in camp near [El] Caney after the surrender. At lunch at the mess that day Colonel Roosevelt told me that he had seen the charges and had dismissed them, whereupon I, with very regrettable lack of courtesy and discipline announced that thereafter I would not bother to prefer any charges.

He fixed me . . . and coldly announced that . . . he would take such measures as might be necessary.

I lapsed into sulky silence and at the conclusion of the meal retired to my hammock under a mango tree at the rear of the regimental hospital. About an hour later he sent for me but my Hospital Steward went to him and reported that I had a temperature of 104 and a very bad chill. In a few minutes I heard Roosevelt's voice asking where I was and the next thing I knew the Colonel had both arms around my shoulder and was saying, "My *dear* boy, I am *so sorry*, I might have known at lunch that you were sick; please forgive me, will you?"

That sort of treatment from your "K.O." rather gets under your skin.[12]

There is a story of simple understanding.

. . . Roosevelt came upon Captain Llewellyn just beneath the ridge looking unhappy and swearing profusely.

"Excuse my French, Colonel," said Llewellyn [well aware of Theodore's strict policy that no officer could use profanity] "but I am damn hungry."

Roosevelt grinned. "Why don't you forage something?"

Llewellyn grunted, and made off, returning half an hour later with two cans of tomatoes, some bacon and some sugar. They managed to contrive to open the can of tomatoes but they had no fire to fry the bacon by and no coffee to put the sugar in. Llewellyn's profanity became more eloquent than before.

"Excuse my French," he interrupted at intervals, [embarrassed that he lost it again] "excuse my French."

"It's all right Captain, it's all right," said Roosevelt, "I know it helps."

There is an account of selflessness.

... small wonder the entire regiment loved and admired Leonard Wood and Theodore Roosevelt, ever their first thought was for the care and comfort of their men without admonition, although we were well disciplined without fuss or worry, and without that most miserable feeling of apprehension and fear of the guard house and court martial which obtains in the regular army, they would see to it before they thought for themselves, that the Rough Riders were under cover, fed and cared for so far as in their power lay. If we went without food they did also, if for us no shelter, likewise for them; they ever led, we followed naturally.

There is a story of presence.

One day after the surrender of Santiago, I was acting as Roosevelt's orderly. One of the boys in my troop asked me to buy him a couple of bottles of Jamaican rum if I had the chance. I got the two bottles . . . and rolled them up in a pancho [sic] and tied them on the back of my saddle. While going through El Caney, the saddle strings became loosened and the bottles began to rattle. I was riding about twenty feet behind Colonel Roosevelt. He heard the noise and stopped. He said, "Fred, what is that noise?"

I told him, "I don't know, I haven't heard anything."

I had no chance to tighten the saddle strings and he went on. The bottles began to rattle again.

"Fred, I don't like that noise. Tighten up those bottles," Theodore said. "At the turn of the road there is a tree with large soft leaves. I wish you would stuff some of them into that nose bag," adding with a smile, "some of those—er—purchases might smash. And you never can tell whom we might meet."

At the tree the nose bag was packed with leaves, the sound deadened. Five minutes later a General was met on the road, and Col. Roosevelt's foresight was gloriously vindicated.[13]

There is a story of mentoring.

On an occasion or two I sat there with him and swapped stories of adventure. He saw that mine had been rather a purposeless life—haunting the danger spots for the mere sake of excitement—and he advised me to settle down, capitalize my energy and ingenuity, and do something worthwhile . . . when I pressed the point, he repeated the old adage: "He who has no plan is bound to hesitate and he who hesitates is lost"; and went on to say: "Have a plan! I've had a plan for many years and everything that comes to me either does, or does not fit my plan. If it fits, I'm for it. If it don't, I'm against it. As to persons—I trust largely to my intuition. Men are either real or false; and the false ones are not usually great enough actors to deceive unblunted [sic] intuitions."

There is a story of kindness.

[At the makeshift hospital] I found Colonel Roosevelt visiting the disabled boys, shaking hands, commiserating with the warmest words of praise and approbation. He cheered the suffer[ing] up wonderfully. It seemed marvelous to see an officer who could be absolutely reckless in a fight and lead his men into carnage and in the next moment bend in pitying compassionate tenderness over the wounded men, almost with tears trying to assuage their sufferings.

There is an account of praise.

Roosevelt had to a marked degree that happy faculty of extending generous approbation and withholding censure. He was quick to spot men who were manifestly doing Yeoman service to the best ability, and instantly to shout his words of approbation and cheer. With his marvelous and accurate memory he seemed not only to know the men's names but their leading characteristics and it would make some of those hard-boiled old plainsmen or cowboys redden with pleasure when the Colonel would address them by name and compliment them.

There is an account of selflessness.

We all got mighty hungry . . . but you never heard anyone complain, and the Colonel was always jollying with the bunch, and we could stand it if he could, for by this time we would have gone through Hell and high water for him.

There is a story of humility.

. . . Roosevelt found a wide gap [while on night patrol] in the line of Cossack posts and sent a hurry call for a detail. The orderly awakened me and brought the order. I awakened Sergeant McGehey and together we awakened the ten men wanted. . . . I personally led them by a short cut that saved nearly two-thirds of the distance.

When nearly at the place where they were wanted, I returned to the troop camp and found Colonel Roosevelt there angrily inquiring for the first sergeant of G troop. I replied that I was the sergeant and got the most thorough "bawling" out of my life. He [Roosevelt] had come by the long way around and missed the detail and I tried to tell him so but it seemed impossible to make headway against his volcanic language until I lost my own temper and yelled as loudly as he did with language as sulphuric [sic] as his own. When he understood, he wheeled his horse and galloped off madly with his staff clattering on behind.

I slept no more that night and got more and more angry and humiliated as the scene came back and back again, and was fully determined to have it out with him the next day.

Dawn came. . . . [W]hile I was inspecting arms at roll call, I noticed that the men stiffened into attention and I knew some superior officer was near but I was past caring.

I then heard Roosevelt's voice saying: "Your men came up in fine shape last night, sergeant." He had waited until the troop was at roll call and in line to acknowledge it.

It was this fairness and fine manhood that made the men love him. Few army officers will acknowledge their injustice in the case of enlisted men.

There is a story of equivalence.

. . . I got by the fellows to my left [in the trenches] and went back to a sheltered place to get out, and started back about where our regiment met the 10th. . . . I was pretty hungry, having had nothing all night and day. . . . [I saw a] man making some coffee and some grub, and I thought it was one of the 10th and asked him for a cup of coffee.

It happened to be regimental headquarters again, and Colonel Roosevelt came out, and with his hearty, "Hello Smith," he grabbed a cup and told. . .[someone] to get me something to eat. He himself [Roosevelt] poured the coffee.

And then there is a simple story about blankets. A modest anecdote that epitomizes Theodore Roosevelt's outlook on leadership.

On a rainy afternoon . . . a weary a bedraggled trooper joined me at my tent. He claimed he was from New York City, but didn't look like it, as his uniform was rather ragged. . . .

I noticed he had half an army blanket, and as blankets were a scarce article in the camp I wondered where he had got it. After inquiry, he divulged the fact that Colonel Roosevelt had donated it to him, so I told him that I was troop commander. I had a small supply of blankets and I would issue him one from my stock and return this one to the Colonel, as the Colonel was undoubtedly depriving himself.

So I took the blanket and went to the Colonel's wicky-up and just held out the blanket towards him. He said, "I am glad to see you, Mr. Hayes, with the blanket, because I have been putting in some stormy nights here." I then said,

"Colonel, I draw extra blankets from the brigade quartermaster, by reason of my old friendship with him, and I don't think in the future that you need deprive yourself of your clothing or your blankets to supply the men."

"Well," he said. "Bully for you, Mr. Hayes, but I can't see the boys suffer, *and I realize it is really what I am here for!*"

The official surrender ceremony took place in Santiago de Cuba on July 17th, full of pomp and chivalry. On San Juan Heights overlooking Santiago, the soldiers who had fought to make the surrender a reality were in deplorable condition. "It was a pitiful column of men that started toward Caney from the San Juan battle site," an account tells, ". . . nothing about them justified the nickname of Rough Riders, so far as the human eye could see."[14] The culprit was yellow fever, which, combined with a lack of food, meant that half of the Rough Riders were now, according to Theodore, "dead or disabled by wounds and sickness."[15] The yellow fever meant fever, internal bleeding, liver failure, blood in the vomit.[16]

The fear that yellow fever could wipe out the entire army was on everyone's mind when a panicky general gave orders to burn the hospital in Siboney to the ground and to quarantine the affected troopers to outposts and blockhouses. Trooper John Avery McIlhenny—the son of the man who invented Tabasco Sauce, Edmund McIlhenny—had taken ill with a fever and went to Siboney, passing two troopers lying in the mud and dying of disease. According McIlhenny he ran to Shafter's headquarters and began waving for assistance, "Come help me move these sick men," he shouted. To his horror McIlhenny was met with armed guards, who, with raised rifles, told him that the men in the road were infected, and since he had touched them, he could infect the whole camp. At gunpoint McIlhenny was turned away from the perimeter and told to retreat to Siboney.

"All this happened in front of Shafter's headquarters," McIlhenny recounts, "and Shafter himself was lying in his pajamas in a hammock being fanned." By the afternoon, both men that McIlhenny had tried to help were dead. Their corpses lay face down in the mud, just outside of headquarters.[17]

The authorities in Washington, receiving cabled updates from the terrified generals, became panic-stricken and balked at bringing the army home.

It was not until July 31st that General Shafter summoned a council of officers to the Governor's Palace at Santiago to discuss the disease destroying the men. From Washington Secretary Alger had indicating that he desired to keep the army in Cuba through the sick season, which lasted until October.[18] Shafter knew this meant certain death for thousands of soldiers and he devised a plan "to wake up the Washington authorities to the actual condition of things."[19] But the general also did not want to call out Alger and McKinley and risk sacrificing his career. He decided that Theodore Roosevelt should do it.

The plan was that Theodore should hold a press conference with the journalists in Cuba, and openly discuss the deplorable conditions. The press would print the news and force Secretary Alger's hand. Leonard Wood, thinking politically, intervened and suggested that a statement should be put down in writing and signed by *all* officers.[20] Theodore, never one to shirk from the task of going to the public, volunteered to author the statement, the Round Robin letter as it became known. At Wood's suggestion, Theodore's report would include the signatures of all U.S. field commanders.

That night Theodore poured into the report and, when finished, he summoned Henry Bardshar.

"I have a letter here I want you to type for me if you can."

Bardshar read the letter and was disappointed. "If you send that in to the War Department, they will have you shot at sunrise," Bardshar retorted.

"What's the matter? Isn't it all true?" Theodore rebutted.

"It certainly is true, but you are criticizing your own government and that is something they will not stand for in the army," Bardshar responded, taken aback by Theodore's harsh language and accusations.[21]

Theodore pocketed the letter and slept on it.

The next morning finds him storming into the make-shift correspondents club in Santiago where American journalists had congregated to count the days until they could go home.

"Colonel Roosevelt came striding into the club . . . with a mien even more earnest and intense than usual," journalist Ralph D. Paine recounted. "I think there were five of us in the group, and [he] pulled a sheet of paper from his pocket. It was the rough draft of a letter to the Secretary of War . . . shown to the group in the club . . . in confidence of friends and gentlemen."

"What do you boys think of it? Have you any changes to suggest?"

"This was always Theodore Roosevelt's way with the newspaper men. He trusted and respected them then, as he did later in the White House," Paine recounted.

The journalist's sat silent as the letter was read. Paine got his courage up and told Roosevelt in no uncertain terms that the letter, as it stood, was not ready for publication.

"What do you suggest?" Theodore inquired.

The five correspondents then spent the next two hours drafting a new more diplomatic and appropriate letter.

Theodore then took the new letter, and with a correspondent of the Associated Press in tow, charged over to Shafter's headquarters. The politically explosive message was too much for Shafter, and the general in charge waved the back of his hand. "I don't want to take it; do whatever you wish with it."[22]

"I, however insisted on handing it to him," Theodore wrote later, "whereupon he shoved it toward the correspondent of the Associated Press, who took hold of it, and I released my hold. . . . [L]ater I was much amused when General Shafter stated that he could not imagine how my letter and the round robin got out!"[23]

The exchange between the two men was indicative of their leadership style. One man authored and put his name on an extraordinary politically sensitive matter for mass publication throughout the country. The other did not want to touch it, literally.

President William McKinley and Secretary of War Alger received the news of the Round Robin letter the same way the American people did: in the morning papers. Alger was furious, his pride wounded. "It would be impossible to exaggerate the mischievous and wicked effect of the 'Round Robin,'" he wrote, "It affected the country with a plague of anguish and apprehension."[24] Several newspapers saw it as a publicity stunt; again Theodore was putting himself above the government. "Irresistible self-assertion and egotism," the *Journal* stated. "[I]ntense indignation" claimed the *Philadelphia Press*.[25]

On the contrary, Ralph Paine explains, "the country learned that the Army, after a victorious campaign, was perishing of stupidity and neglect, and in no uncertain voice it demanded that the troops come out of Cuba."[26] The Round Robin letter was viewed by the public the same way Rough Rider W. J. McCann viewed it: "He [Theodore] felt that his duty was to stand by his own men and *make* the War Department understand the real and desperate plight of the American troops."[27] The man who instigated the war and the man who led the defining battle in victory, was also the same man who put his career on the line to get the surviving soldiers home.

The first Round Robin letter that Theodore himself drafted was not made public. Henry Bardshar tore up his copy and threw it away, admitting twenty years later that "Roosevelt criticized the whole campaign severely" and wrote frankly of "Shafter's incompetence."[28] One wonders what would have happened if Theodore had not learned how to counter his impetuous nature, and had not chosen to get diplomatic assistance from journalists on a document of such significance. General Shafter, after all, never read the letter before it was published in the newspapers.

The Round Robin worked. Just three days after it hit the papers, the army was ordered to set sail for Montauk on Long Island, New York.[29] The northern port city was believed to have the right climate to kill off the tropical diseases and mend the troops back to health.

Though Theodore's defiant Round Robin letter got the army home, it cost him personally. As he had done as a New York State assemblyman and on the Civil Service Commission, he attached himself to a public report that insinuated that those in charge were incompetent, unfit to lead. Secretary Alger, enraged, considered court martialing Roosevelt. Aides talked Alger out of it. How could the secretary of war court martial the hero of the war?

Alger never forgave Theodore and declined to endorse him for the Medal of Honor—the nation's highest military award, even though several military men including Wheeler, Wood, Sumner, Young, and Howze all wrote testimonies on behalf of Theodore's heroics. In all, some twenty-eight participants of the Santiago campaign received the Medal of Honor for gallantry in action. But the man who started the charge up the fortified hill that won the war, evidently, was not heroic enough for the War Department.[30]

Edith would claim that Theodore's failure to receive the award was "one of the bitterest disappointments of his life."[31] Theodore wanted the medal more than anything, writing to Henry Cabot Lodge, "if I didn't earn it, then no commissioned officer can ever earn it. . . . I don't ask this as a favor—I ask it as a right."[32]

Forty-six years later, a Roosevelt would receive the nation's highest military award when Theodore Junior was given the blue neck sash and gold crested eagle for his actions at Normandy, France on June 6th, 1944. It was awarded posthumously, Ted Junior having died of a heart attack just one month after the D-Day invasion.

On January 16th, 2001—one hundred and three years after the charge—President William Jefferson Clinton awarded Theodore Roosevelt the Medal of Honor at a small ceremony in the Roosevelt Room of the White House. Only one other father-son duo—Arthur MacArthur in the U.S. Civil War and son Douglas MacArthur in World War II—have both held the distinction.

"T.R. was a larger-than-life figure, who gave our nation a larger-than-life vision of our place in the world," President Clinton said at the ceremony. "Part of that vision was formed on San Juan Hill. . . . This led to the Spanish surrender and opened the era of America as a global power."[33]

Theodore would never get over the fact that the Medal of Honor was withheld from him. It was a colossal injustice, just plain wrong. In his *Autobiography,* published in 1913, he included seventeen accounts of bravery that had been submitted on his behalf to the Brevet Board that decided the Medal of Honor recipients.

Roosevelt published the letters so that the public could decide whether or not he deserved the award. It is important to note that he did this after he had spent eight years as a widely successful president of the United States and was already viewed by the world as the most famous politician of a generation.

Theodore coveted the award his entire life. After all, the Medal of Honor would have been the crowning achievement for a boy born of such a sickly beginning, the ultimate triumph in a pursuit from weak to strong.

On the morning of August 8th, the steamer *Miami* set sail for Montauk, New York, carrying the last of the American troops. The trip home had fair winds and following seas, and the cool ocean breeze rippled across the open deck, refreshing the men. Heading north, all appreciated that war was over, their glory earned. The men, even at that time, realized that the event they had just engaged in had changed the world.

And as Cuba slipped smaller onto the horizon the lore of the Rough Rider's charge up San Juan Heights would grow larger and loftier. Long forgotten to history are the struggles of an amateur army fighting a war that it was wholly unprepared to wage. John Hay would famously write that the entire engagement was just "a splendid little war; begun with the highest motives, carried on with magnificent intelligence and spirit, favored by that fortune which loves the brave."[34] Hay's description of the "splendid little war" stuck.

The truth of the campaign, complete with its warts and ineptness, is much more compelling. America had been exposed, her military and its leadership was not ready take care of her soldiers, not ready to lead globally. The logistical problems, the outdated artillery, the antiquated supplies, the poor management, were responsible for far more casualties than the Spanish Mausers. The battle at Cuba was a wake-up call to a country that had the resources, the citizens, and the economy to lead the world into the twentieth century, but not the military, not the foreign policy leadership, not the Big Stick.

During the summer of 1898, for the first time since it had been conceived, America broke away from isolationism. This choice, and its imperialistic repercussions, is still debated to this day, an unending dispute of America's place in world affairs. But it was America's profound lack of preparation which instigated the proverbial pendulum swing towards a government aware of the requirement to have a strong standing military; a government aware of its place on the world stage. Troubling questions arise: Absent the lessons learned in the Spanish-American War, would America have been prepared to intervene in World War I? Would America have stopped Hitler's tyrannical conquests in World War II?

How different would our world look today had the U.S. not seized the torch of leadership on the eve of the twentieth century? This question should probably still be debated.

The *Miami* docked into the pier at Montauk Point, New York, around 11 a.m. on August 15th, 1898. "With the first glimpse of Roosevelt on the bridge of the ship, the crowd on shore went mad," a correspondent wrote. "When 'Teddy and his teeth' came down the gangplank, the last ultimate climax of the possibility of cheering was reached. He was bronzed by the Cuban sun, and his uniform was worn out, and stained by the trials of the campaign. But he was happier than Theodore Roosevelt ever had been before, or probably ever will be again."[35]

"How are you, Colonel Roosevelt?" Someone shouted to the man waving his campaign hat.

"I am feeling disgracefully well!" Theodore boomed, before looking down at this uniform, "I feel positively ashamed of my appearance." Lifting his head back up, he scans the crowd and then pauses for what seemed like a minute—an actor's trick. "Oh! But we had a bully fight!" he booms. The crowd burst into a roar.[36]

Almost as if on cue, Fighting Joe Wheeler charges up and takes Roosevelt by the arm. "Hurrah for Fighting Joe!" the crowd shouts, "Hurrah! Hurrah!" The two men walk arm and arm down the gangplank together.[37] It was a dandy of an image, the old confederate general who had traded in his southern loyalties to fight for all of America, standing next to the young government reformer who represented both the Badlands cowboy and the New York aristocrat. One man embodied unity from South to the North, the other from East to the West.

Roosevelt's eye catches a few Rough Riders walking down the gangplank. "There go three well-known athletes and college men—Bull of Harvard and Wrenn and Larned, the tennis champions," Theodore shouts pointing at the men. "If any man can tell them from any cowpuncher in the whole outfit, he's a dandy!"[38]

"Will you be the next Governor?" a reporter shouts, cutting to the chase.

"None of that," he snaps, "All I'll talk about is the regiment. It's the finest regiment that ever was, and I'm proud to command it."[39]

Roosevelt, now swarmed by reporters, seemed to be the only one on the ship that was healthy. "My God," a witness demurred, watching the troopers hobble ashore, "there are not half of the men there that left."[40] The troopers, ordered by the War Department, were confined to detention in an effort to quarantine the yellow fever. "They are a worn and tired lot," the *New York Sun* reported, "and it will take lots of good air, good food, and absolute rest to bring them back to the health and strength that made them the finest regiment of volunteer cavalry that ever went forth to war."[41]

Both during and after quarantine, Theodore still worked to occupy the men's time, to distract them from causing trouble. He demanded that mounted drills take place, but with no war, drilling seemed odd and he quickly changed mounted drills to exhibitions where soldiers competed in various rodeo tricks.[42]

On September 3rd President McKinley arrived to pay his gratitude and bask in the bright glow of patriotic accord. A twenty-one gun salute marked the arrival of the presidential entourage at 8:45 in the morning, and the motorcade, a column of horse drawn carriages, made its first stop at the headquarters tent a short time later.

General Shafter was in his cot.

"Don't get up, General," McKinley said "You are entitled to a rest. How are you?"

"A little achy," Shafter replied, "but otherwise all right."[43]

Rather distinctively, Roosevelt greeted the president with what was described as "the ease of a cowboy."

> The President held out his hand [a reporter recounted]; Col. Roosevelt struggled to pull off his right glove. He yanked at it desperately and finally inserted the ends of his fingers in his teeth and gave a mighty tug. Off came the glove and a beatific smile came over the Colonel's face as he grasped the President's hand. The crowd which had watched the performance tittered audibly.[44]

Roosevelt then leaned into the President. "Come visit my boys," he bellowed enthusiastically.[45]

Rough Rider Happy Jack—the fugitive from Arizona—had set up a game of craps and was standing on a box overlooking the crowd.

"Stand back, soldiers—stand back! The Commander in Chief is coming. President McKinley is going to throw four-bits," Happy Jack shouted as the presidential entourage, which included the vice president and the secretary of war neared his table.

McKinley laughed, put his hand in his pocket, took out a few coins and threw them on the table. Picking up the dice, the president rolled the bones: snake eyes.

Happy Jack laughed heartily.

"The President craps! The President craps! Who is the next lucky guy?" he hollered, waving the leader of the free world on with the swipe of his hand. "Move on, Mr. President, get going. *The President craps, the President craps, the President craps!*"

President McKinley laughed sheepishly, bowed and passed on.

Happy Jack, like all of the Rough Riders, appreciated that the man before him had the most formal authoritative title in world: President of the United States. McKinley was the leader of the country, the commander in chief, the head honcho. But that did not mean much to the fellow from the frontier. Nobody in the regiment would dare yell "Roosevelt craps, Roosevelt craps!" The Colonel had proven he could lead. McKinley just had a fancy title.[46]

Several days later, and while the men were nursing back to health, a few Rough Riders charged Theodore's tent and asked for permission to enter. Theodore was documenting military paperwork and hearing the row outside, and half expecting that a fight had broken out, rushed outside. Throwing open the flap to the tent, and squinting through his glasses in the bright sun, he is stunned. Before him is the entire regiment of 1,090 soldiers, all standing in salute. A crude pine table was placed in the forefront, a large horse-blanket covering a lump of something.

Theodore smiles and then straightens his face. A breathless silence reigned. Theodore "stood awkwardly," an account recalls, "not knowing what to do."[47]

William S. Murphy, a judge from the Indian Territory, steps forward. "As lieutenant-colonel of our regiment," he stammered, "you first made us respect you; as our colonel you have taught us to love you deeply, as men love men."[48]

Murphy finishes his speech and pulls away the blanket, revealing a large statue of a bronco buster statue by Fredric Remington. The men erupt into cheers, hats waving.

When the men quieted down several sobs were heard in the square. *It was a strange thing,* a reporter for the *Journal* thought to himself, *to see such strong men, who endured hardship without any emotion, all of a sudden overcome with such sentiment that they simply could not contain their feelings.*[49]

Theodore puts his hand on the statue. "Now, boys," he concluded after a short and emotional speech, "I wish to take each of you by the hand, as a special privilege, and say good-by to you individually; this is to be our farewell in camp; I hope that it will not be our farewell in civil life."[50]

The men lined up by company, and passed in a single file, each shaking the Colonel's hand. "I felt a handshake was but poor expression," a Rough Rider claimed, "I wanted to hug him."[51] For the next several hours, Roosevelt said good bye to each individual, shaking the hand of the mountain man, the Ivy Leaguer, the athlete, the scholar, the fugitive, the cowpuncher. For each he had a nickname or a joke; he knew who they were, where they were from, what they stood for. And they knew him.[52]

From formation to disbandment the Rough Rider regiment lasted 133 days.[53]

Theodore Roosevelt took just two days off. The regiment mustered out on September 15th, 1898 and on September 17th he announced that he was throwing his hat into the ring for Governor of New York.[54] On Election Day, November 8th, less than two months later, Theodore the war hero was elected.

As Governor he led admirably, both a visionary idealist and a practical politician, simultaneously inspiring the public and managing the political machinery.

"All I ask is a square deal for every man," Theodore urged everyone, "give him a fair chance."[55]

Eleven months after Roosevelt took the oath of office as Governor of New York, Vice President Garret Hobart died suddenly of complications from heart failure. The nation turned its patriotic eyes to Theodore Roosevelt. William McKinley, seeking reelection to the White House consented with the public.

On the cloudy morning of March 4th, 1901, the first presidential inauguration of the twentieth century took place exactly one hundred years to the day that Thomas Jefferson took the oath of office. The swearing-in ceremony was swift and stoic. The stark contrast of the old President McKinley standing next to the vigorous Vice President Roosevelt propelled a McKinley aide to quip that the President "has a man of destiny behind him."[56] The man of destiny was the vice president, the man who had captured the soul of the country, the man who embodied everything American at the turn of the century. The leader who was bursting with energy and ideas, the one ready to put vigor in the executive; the one ready to shape world events, not just lead the country.

Theodore did not see it that way. A short time after the ceremony ended, his deep rooted melancholy flared. In a letter to Leonard Wood, Theodore confided in guarded pessimism that his political fortunes had peaked. He would study law, he told Wood, "with a view to seeing if I cannot go into practice as a lawyer when my term as Vice-President ends."[57]

23. MIDNIGHT RIDE

———————————————————◇

THEODORE ROOSEVELT'S OFFICIAL DUTIES PRESIDING OVER THE Senate lasted just four days, from March 4th to March 8th, 1901.[1] When the Senate adjourned until December, Theodore was greeted with what he termed a "time of slack water."[2] The vice presidency was exactly what he feared. "The man who occupies it may at any moment be everything," he told a friend, "but meanwhile he is practically nothing."[3] During the spring of 1901, Theodore spent an enormous amount of time at Oyster Bay, claiming that he was "just living out in the country, doing nothing but ride and row with Mrs. Roosevelt, and walk and play with the children; chop trees in the afternoon and read books by a wood fire in the evening."[4]

To stave off boredom, he went to New York and then to Harvard to give speeches. In July, and again in August, he went west to hunt, stopping over in Colorado to speak at the twenty-five-year commemorative of its statehood.

On the afternoon of September 4th, 1901, Theodore arrived in Rutland, Vermont to give a speech on conservation. From there, the Roosevelt family would leave for a camping trip in the Adirondack Mountains. On the same day, William McKinley's train charged toward Buffalo, New York taking the President to the grand Pan-American Exposition.

4:00 p.m. September 6th, 1901, Buffalo New York

On an unusually hot day, President McKinley arrived in an open carriage outside of the Temple of Music auditorium to the cheers of thousands of people who had arrived for the opportunity to shake his hand. The previous day at the World's Fair had been

"President's Day" and an astonishing crowd of 50,000 had turned out to hear McKinley give a dandy of a speech on America's "unexampled prosperity."[5]

On the horizon of the 350-acre fair grounds stood the exposition's most crowning attraction, the radiant Electric Tower, a fitting monument to the progress of electricity. Adorned with 44,000 light bulbs, the Tower shot a powerful beacon heavenward, a grand signal to the promise of the new century ahead.[6]

The receiving line to meet McKinley had swelled since dawn. By four o'clock in the afternoon some twenty-thousand had filled the corridors of the Temple of Music building, chocking off the gallery above and spilling into the streets below. The energy inside the Hall was nothing short of electric when the president and his entourage entered the pavilion. The massive pipe organ above bellowed Schumann's *Träumerei*.[7]

President McKinley took his position at the reception area between two security agents. Behind him were several potted palm trees and an enormous American flag that draped down from a pole some ten feet high.[8] George B. Cortelyou, McKinley's secretary, had been worried about the president's safety all week in Buffalo and had tripled the personal security detail. There were now three agents specifically in charge of the president's safety. Exposition guards and local policemen stood at the doorways and along the aisles.[9]

The receiving line was scheduled to last just ten minutes.[10]

At 4:05, Cortelyou pulled out his pocket watch, anxious to signal to the security team to close the doors. The organist began playing Bach. The Hall, on sheer account of the humanity, was a swelter of heat. Many fanned themselves with handkerchiefs.

The president's face lit up when twelve-year-old Myrtle Ledger, accompanied by her mother, stepped forward and asked for his flower. McKinley smiled and took off the red carnation that he wore on his lapel and handed it to the girl. He had worn a red carnation—his lucky flower, it was called—ever since he was an unknown politician from Ohio.[11] The little girl smiled, thanked the president and walked on, enchanted by the lucky omen.

Two minutes later, at 4:07 p.m., anarchist Leon Czolgosz, concealing a .32-caliber Iver Johnson under a handkerchief, stepped forward from the receiving line and shot the president twice at point blank range.

McKinley straightened up before staggering back into a potted plant and collapsing. The crowd swept into pandemonium; shrieks and cries turned into a rapid riot of violence as policemen and agents tackled the shooter to the ground. "Don't let them hurt him," McKinley mumbled.[12]

The twelve-year-old holding the lucky flower knew something had gone terribly wrong. "People were shouting to each other everywhere," Myrtle Ledger remembered sadly. "Then there was an announcement, very loud. . . . through a megaphone."

"It said that the president had been shot."[13]

4:30 p.m., September 6th, 1901, Isle La Motte, Lake Champlain, Vermont

Theodore Roosevelt had just given a speech to the Vermont Fish and Game League on the lawn of the sprawling estate of former Governor Nelson W. Fisk. The late afternoon luncheon was a relaxed event, the merry crowd on the lakeshore was happy to eat and drink and shake hands with the most famous man in America.

Theodore was standing on the veranda when a phone rang inside.

Governor Fisk took the call, a relay from the New England Telephone Company alerting the vice president of the wire bulletin coming out of Buffalo.[14]

FIRST
4.10 p.m.-7-Collect, D.P.R- President McKinley shot.
SECOND
4.15 p.m.-22-Collect, D.P.R- Shot twice at the Temple of Music in the stomach by a stranger.[15]

Fisk walked outside, found Roosevelt and beckoned him into the house without a word. The weight of the message showed heavily on Fisk's face, the crowd knew something terrible had happened. In a hushed agonized whisper, an awful question swept through those standing on the sunny lawn: had something just happened to the president?[16]

Theodore was ushered into the house and the door to the mansion shut behind him and locked.[17] Roosevelt picked up the receiver. The president has been shot, perhaps dead, the shooter in custody, more details to follow.

Theodore stood in "stunned amazement."[18] A few seconds pass before he speaks.

"Gentlemen, I am afraid that there is little ground for hope that the report is untrue," Theodore tersely told those in the room with him. ". . .[I]t appears to be authentic."[19]

Theodore left the home at once on a boat owned by a railroad trustee, crossing the channel to Burlington where a special train was waiting to take him to Buffalo.[20] An aide made a remark that Theodore should stay clear of the Pan-American Exposition and await word on McKinley's condition, "given the delicate matter of succession."[21] Theodore responded that he would rather do the "natural thing" and raced to his friend's bedside.[22]

The next morning—Saturday, September 7th—doctors were encouraged that McKinley would survive. Theodore was told that the first bullet had hit a belt buckle or a button and deflected away harmlessly, but that the second bullet had slammed through the president's stomach before lodging somewhere in his back. Though the doctors could not find the bullet and feared infection, it seemed that the president would survive.

After four days in Buffalo, it was decided that Theodore should continue on to the Adirondacks where his family was waiting for their planned camping trip. The physicians believed that McKinley was going to survive, and the president, for all he had been through, was in good spirits and humorous. Besides, the departure of the vice president would assure the nation that the crisis was over.

"Thank Heaven," Theodore wrote in a letter on September 10th, "the President is now out of danger."[23] That afternoon he boarded a train headed for Mount Marcy, the highest peak in the state of New York.

Pre-dawn, Friday September 13th, 1901, Mount Marcy, New York

Theodore rises before the sun at a cottage near Lake Colden, a remote area dozens of miles from the nearest civilization. The day before, Theodore, Edith, and a few of the children had hiked up to an elevation of 3,500 feet and canoed across the lake to the cottage on the western embankment.[24] The night before, by the crackling of the fire, Theodore had no doubt let his mind wander to the momentous event that was avoided. So many nights, by the somber light of a campfire, he had found strength in solitude.

Theodore had been forlorn the entire week. The significant emotions born of the assassination attempt weighed heavily on his mind. Had he been ready for the burden of the office he undoubtedly pondered? Only he knew. The one glimpse we have into his state of mind is found in a letter to Jacob Riis where he indicates "that a shadow had fallen across his path, be-tween him and those youthful days, through which he would never cross again the same man."[25] What this actually meant, only Theodore knew.

The weather the morning of the thirteenth was cold and gray, a dense fog had blanketed off the mountain above. On account of the treacherous condition, it was decided that Edith and the children would travel with a guide back down the mountain to the Tahawus base camp. Theodore, naturally, could not resist the challenge to climb to the top of the mountain.[26]

As the vice president and his hiking party began their ascension up Mount Marcy, the president began to die.

11:50 a.m.

After a several-hour hike, Roosevelt and his party reached the summit of Mount Marcy. For a brief moment the clouds part and beautiful rays of sunlight empty onto the vast expanse below. "Beautiful country! Beautiful country!" the vice president repeats.[27] At 5,344 feet he was standing at the highest point for several hundred miles. It felt natural to him.

A few minutes after summiting, a dark threatening sky rolls in beneath the hiking party, turning the ridgeline below into a sea of grey. It was as if they were standing atop a lighthouse, looking down at the vast obscure ocean; heavy, dark, deep. A thick fog again seized the summit; a light rain began to fall.

At about the same time, McKinley began slipping in and out of consciousness, his breathing heavily strained, his heart failing.

A special train was sent for Mark Hanna and the president's closest confidants, who, like Theodore, had left Buffalo believing McKinley would survive.

"Nearer, My God, to Thee," McKinley murmured, his eyes half open, his body ravaged from the inside by infection. It was time only for prayer, the president mumbled to no one in particular.[28]

George Cortelyou dispatched an urgent telegram to William Loeb, Roosevelt's personal secretary. Loeb immediately took a train to the Adirondack station at North Creek—the closest train stop to Mount Marcy, still a full thirty-five miles from Theodore.[29] A single-wire circuit telephone line had recently been installed connecting the North Creek Depot to the Tahawus Club, the Roosevelt's base camp on Mount Marcy. Loeb relayed the terrible message to Harrison Hall, a local guide.

Harrison copies down the momentous dispatch before charging out into the misty wild to track down the vice president. In his hand was the most awful of messages:

Buffalo, N.Y
Hon. T. Roosevelt

The President appears to be dying and members of the Cabinet in Buffalo think you should lose no time in coming.[30]

Loeb stayed at the station to procure a train and clear the tracks to rush Theodore to Buffalo. But no one knew when, or if, the message would reach the vice president deep in the wild.

Shortly after Harrison Hall embarked for the woods, Mark Hanna reaches the bedside of his dying friend. Hanna was distraught. "Mr. President, Mr. President?" he said in vain, before dropping decorum: "William! William! Don't you know me?"[31]

1:55 p.m.

Roosevelt descends a few miles to a clearing at Lake Tear of the Clouds. He sits on a flat rock, surrounded by a damp grassy clearing. With a sandwich in one hand, he squints down the wet misty trail and sees a guide running through the fog toward the party, a yellow piece of paper clenched in his hand.

Theodore "instinctively knew" what the message held.[32]

Guide Harrison Hall hands Theodore the summons.

"He said nothing," Hall recounted, "but calmly turned and finished his lunch."[33]

5:15 p.m.

Theodore reaches the Upper Tahawus Club—a twelve mile hike from Lake Tear of the Clouds—to discover that no solid developments had been sent from Buffalo. Soaked and muddy, he removes his clothes and eats a hearty meal. The conflicting reports were unsettling; nobody seemed to know if McKinley was dying or if Cortelyou had overreacted. "I'm not going unless I am really needed," Theodore told Edith, "I am going to wait here."[34]

It starts to thunder. Moments later large sporadic bursts of lightening explode across the mountain range. One of the children begins to cry, afraid that since his father might become president, he too would be killed by an assassin.[35] Strain arrests the cabin. Every noise heard outside was thought to be a messenger or worse. The unspoken question still remained: was McKinley's assassin really just a lone wolf or a part of a larger anarchist cell?

Theodore paces the hall like a caged lion—calm, collected, lost in his own mind.

10:00 p.m.

An affirmative message finally reaches Roosevelt. The president is all but dead.[36]

Preparations were made at once for the thirty-five mile trip to the North Creek train station, beginning at dawn. Theodore tells the men that he is leaving now. The roads cutting across the mountain range were steep and treacherous, the locals replied. A midnight ride was all but impossible, potentially fatal. Theodore threatens to take a lantern and go alone if no driver steps forward immediately.[37]

The nighttime journey was hastily planned by the guides who knew the area. With nothing but obscure muddy roads for miles, it was decided that a three part relay was required to get the vice president to the awaiting train.

Theodore ate a quick meal and packed a small rucksack. A 1,400-pound bay was harnessed to a buckboard; a lantern tied to the rear axle for light. Theodore Roosevelt and a single guide, David Hunter, set out for the town of Lower Works, ten miles away.

"He took a most terrifying ride in the middle of the night," Edith recalled.[38]

The world was pitch-black. The thunderstorm had just ended. The sodden trees that lined the narrow roadway passed by invisible, though just inches away. Two men, the driver and the next president, journeyed into the dead of the night.

The ride was "full of mud holes and corduroy," Hunter remembers. "The road was in terrible shape. So we started out down through the mud—*plunk, plunk, plunk.*"[39]

Theodore stares out into the black, not knowing what lies ahead.

"Faster! Faster!" he shouts.[40]

12:35 a.m., September 14th, 1901

Theodore reaches Lower Works, the first ten miles of the trip completed. Orrin Kellogg, driver of the next relay, had seen the light of the approaching lantern about two miles away, his signal to hitch up his bays to a two-seat wagon. Theodore steps into the Lower Tahawus Club to use the telephone and drink a cup of coffee. He was there but five minutes. The Tahawus Club Climbing Register still has his signature, with the words: "Went up Mt. Marcy."[41]

He walks outside and gets into the awaiting second wagon; nine miles to go until the next relay. It begins to rain again. Orrin Kellogg gives Theodore an old coat to protect the next president from the mud splashing up from the wheels.[42]

"He talked but little," Kellogg recalled of his portion of the relay. "He wasn't any afraid."[43]

After several minutes, Theodore, unprompted, gives only one cruel glimpse into his thoughts: "I think if it had been I who had been shot, he wouldn't have got away so easily," he tells Kellogg. "I think I'd have guzzled him first."[44]

Theodore's face tightens, he stares into the dark night, he says nothing more.

2:15 a.m.

President McKinley dies. For the next thirteen hours the country is without a president.[45]

3:00 a.m.[46]

Theodore Roosevelt reaches the town of Aiden Lair. He leaps out of the carriage, and speaking in a quiet tone he does not waste his words. "Any news?" he asks.

Mike Cronin, the third and final driver, had received a call from William Loeb and knew that McKinley had just died.

"No," Cronin responds, lying. Cronin decides not to tell Theodore Roosevelt that he was the president of the United States, and had been for a little under an hour. Cronin later explains that he wished to save his traveling companion from the "added anxiety on the weary journey."[47]

As the carriage pulled away from Aiden Lair someone questioned where to put the lantern.

"Here, give it to me!" Theodore said, grabbing the light, holding it out in front.[48]

Sixteen more miles of dark wet terrain stood between Aiden Lair and the train depot.

"It was the darkest night I ever saw," Cronin recalled, "I could not even see my horses except for spots where the flickering lantern light fell on them."[49]

Theodore was in "deep thought and very sad," Cronin recounted. Only a few times did he speak: "Push Along! Hurry up! Go faster!"[50]

A mile from the train station dawn starts to slowly lift the dark veil on the woods. In the grey twilight Theodore sees the awaiting train, idling on the track, ready to take him to the presidency.[51] He asks Cronin to halt the carriage.

Theodore gets out, takes a few steps, straightens his tie and wipes his mud-spackled suit. To Mike Cronin it was a "treasured pause." Through the morning fog he watches the next president of the United States collect his thoughts and "spruce up"; taking a moment to ready himself for the monumental challenge that lay ahead.[52]

"Three-o'clock-in-the-morning courage is the most desirable kind," Theodore would claim as a maxim.[53]

Now, more than ever, Theodore had to look as if he was ready to lead. His life would change the minute he got out of the woods. The American people needed him to be composed and poised, ready to lead.

Several minutes pass before Theodore gets back into the carriage.

The final dramatic dash into the station took just a few moments. At the depot a few dozen locals stood on the platform, having stayed up the night before to witness history. As the two-seater rumbled into town a local begins to shout. "There he comes!"[54]

4:46 a.m.[55]

Roosevelt and Cronin finally arrive at the North Creek Station. Theodore had travelled thirty-five miles by horse in just over six hours, through the dead of a rainy night. Mayne Reid could not have penned a more fabled story of a frontiersman charging from the wilderness on a midnight ride to ascend to the highest office in the land.

"President Roosevelt jumped out of the wagon," an eye witness recounted. ". . . [H]e was swift, no sign of fatigue. He turned and rushed up the platform steps two at a time. . . ."[56]

William Loeb hands Theodore a telegram from Secretary of State John Hay—Thee's old friend. By the flickering light of a kerosene lamp, Theodore reads that he is president.

Buffalo, N.Y., Sept. 14, 1901
Hon. Theodore Roosevelt
North Creek, New York

The President died at 2:15 this morning.

John Hay
Secretary of State

Theodore pockets the paper and bounds across the damp platform. A nine-year-old boy who witnessed the event recalled that the train was moving before the door was shut.[57]

7:00 a.m.

On a flat near Stony Creek the locomotive brakes squeal, sending its passengers lurching forward. A loud crash shakes the entire train.

Roosevelt charges to the front to see what happened. The train had hammered a handcar on the track, he was told. Two men on the handcar were badly shaken, having all but died.

"The President's train was tearing along and the fog was still close to the ground," the *Albany Evening Journal* retold, "The men on the handcar saw the engine just in time. They jumped and a minute later their car went hurtling into a ditch. There was a stiff jar, and the President, the superintendent and the President's secretary hurried to the platform."[58] The train came to a stop, the conductor and crew jumped off to examine the damage. A few minutes later, finding no injury, the train started again for Albany.[59]

Everyone on board was left to wonder what would have happened had that been a boxcar, not a handcar.

7:54 a.m. Albany, New York

Roosevelt arrives in Albany, New York. Stopping for just eight minutes the train engineers—rather symbolically—replace the old engine car with a new engine car. The new engine is the fastest and most powerful engine in the Delaware & Hudson Railroad fleet, probably the fastest train engine in the entire country.[60]

Along the tracks, police and plain-clothes detectives keep a close watch on the growing crowd gathered at the depot. A currier runs towards the train to deliver a shirt that Loeb had arranged to replace the muddy one that the frontiersman wore.

Off in the distance, in the morning light, the granite façade of the Capitol building was aglow. It had been nineteen years earlier that Theodore had charged into its corridors, full of patrician arrogance armed with only an ambiguous desire to honor his father's memory and to do something in the name of good government.

At 8:02, the train rocked from the station, the new engine car in the lead. "Nearly a thousand people saw the train leave Albany," recounted the *World*, "but it quickly disappeared from their view . . . and the new President flew across the country at the record rate of a mile a minute."[61]

1:34 p.m., Buffalo, New York

Theodore finally arrives in Buffalo, New York. The four-hundred-and-forty-mile adventure from Lake Tear of the Clouds consisted of twelve miles on foot, thirty-five miles in three carriages, five horses, three drivers, two train engines, and just over twenty-four hours of time.

The nervous conductor does not properly stop the train at the station. Theodore is forced to jump from the platform onto the terrace below.[62] Several hundred onlookers line the track. When they see Theodore they raise their hats in unison, a show of solidarity and respect for the tumult that lay ahead. Theodore nods his head in acknowledgement.

Theodore is immediately ushered into an automobile surrounded by twenty mounted officers. One policeman charges towards him. "Mr. Roosevelt," he says, "will you shake hands with me?"

"Why, hello Tony," Theodore says to Anthony Gavin, a former Rough Rider and now Buffalo policeman. "I'm glad to see you."[63]

Theodore is taken to the home of lawyer Ansley Wilcox, a man that Roosevelt had worked with on Grover Cleveland's Civil Service Commission in the early 1880s.

1:45 p.m.

Theodore arrives at the Wilcox home. Ansley Wilcox, roughly the same size as Roosevelt, lends the next president a frock coat, a waistcoat and trousers.[64] A neighbor, John Scatchard, runs home to fetch Theodore a black silk hat. After a brief shower and a quick meal, Roosevelt hastily wipes the mud off his boots, polishing away the only visible trace of his extraordinary midnight ride.

He emerges from the home somber of countenance and is immediately ushered back into the automobile.[65] A detail of the Fourth Signal Corps now surrounds the next president.

2:38 p.m.

Theodore arrives at the Milburn House, hat in hand, to pay his final respects to McKinley's family. The two large American flags on both sides of the entrance had been draped in black, the patriotic badge of mourning.[66] For the second time in his life he is next to the body of a dead president. Thirty-six years earlier, Teedie and his brother Elliott had watched the coffin of Abraham Lincoln advance into Union Square from the window of their grandfather's mansion.

3:15 p.m.

Theodore arrives back at the Wilcox home. Several cabinet members and Federal Judge John Raymond Hazel had already arrived. No one had remembered to bring a Bible.

Theodore is ushered into the small library of the home, a picturesque den with heavy oak trimmings and a massive bookcase. He peers outside a small bay window; the room is silent. A bird lands on the windowsill, catching Theodore's eye. He looks at it for a long moment. The bird chirps and flutters its wings. Another moment passes, then another. The bird flies away.[67]

With a strong face, Roosevelt clears his throat and quietly speaks, "I shall take the oath at once."[68]

3:30 p.m.

Theodore Roosevelt recites the oath and then bows his head in prayer. His brow begins to bead sweat, his jaw is locked. The room is filled with an excruciating silence, "a death-like hush," it was described later.[69] Someone begins to sob.

Two minutes pass before Theodore moves. He raises his head and opens his eyes for the first time as president. He was forty-two years old.

As flags were lowered to half-staff and citizens wept for the assassinated William McKinley, a calloused but appropriate question was put forth in every courthouse and post office, tavern and church, from North to South, New York to Montana.

Was Theodore Roosevelt ready to lead as president of the United States?

Epilogue

────────────────────────────◇

NO ONE HAS HAD AS MUCH FUN BEING PRESIDENT AS DID THE-odore Roosevelt. He loved the power, he loved the ability to get action, he loved the attention. The presidency was the perfect "Bully Pulpit," as he called it. Moving into the White House on what would have been Thee's seventieth birthday, Theodore vowed to "continue absolutely unbroken the policies of President McKinley."[1] When the restraints of the tragedy had parted, just enough, he began to amass an incredible array of accomplishments on his own terms, in his own unique way.

Within his first month in office Theodore invited Booker T. Washington to dine with him and his family at the White House—the first African-American ever to receive such an invitation. At the same time, Theodore's first significant appointment in the Deep South was the very capable U.S. District Judge Thomas G. Jones, a Democrat who fought under Stonewall Jackson in the Confederate Army. For the same reason both fringe elements of the country erupted in anger. The middle of America applauded.[2]

As president, Theodore Roosevelt was noisy, imaginative, vibrant, and visionary in ways that captivated the country. The press covered him in color, which was not hard to do. The elders in his party—the Old Guard—worried about his every move, bothered about what he might do next. For the common American it was his force of personality and demand for action that inspired. If the president could not sit still, then could America afford to sit still? Progress, equity, growth, competition, and world power were the themes of the man, which became the theme of the country, a theme that has lasted for over a century.

In 1901, America rallied around the idea of a strong executive—the epicenter of world power—which could have shifted from England to Russia or Japan or Germany. It was Theodore Roosevelt who permeated the idea that the American president should lead in the foreign theater. In so doing, he forever changed the office of the executive and became the prototype for all future presidents.

Then, as it is now, his admirers loved him and his critics could not stand him. He "was the greatest executive of his generation," according to Gifford Pinchot, and was "a Superman if there ever was one" for Sir Arthur Conan Doyle.[3] To Woodrow Wilson, Theodore Roosevelt was "the most dangerous man of the age," to Poultney Bigelow, "an excellent specimen of the genus Americanus egotisticus."[4] Thomas Edison thought Roosevelt was "the most striking figure in American life."[5] Mark Twain thought Roosevelt was "clearly insane."[6]

Theodore Roosevelt was, if one thing, a massive contradiction.

He was not born to lead. He was the sickly aristocratic city-kid, Harvard educated, who became the champion of the common man. He had deep ancestral roots to the South on his mother's side, while his father's family was entirely northeastern; yet he viewed himself as most in touch with the westerner. He exuded vitality, but was keenly aware of his fragile health. He had an enthusiasm the like never before seen in the White House, but often quietly and suddenly, he would succumb to what his daughter would call "a melancholic streak."[7] He wanted to be famous, but he never feared failure. He coveted the stage—the man wanted everyone to talk about him, and only him—but led in a way that was intensely selfless, always putting the welfare of others at the forefront. He was egotistical and self-deprecating; he kept favorable newspaper clippings for his scrapbook and laughed the hardest at those who poked fun at him. He always wanted to be president, more than anything in the world, but at a young age he refused to enter into the inner-circle of kingpins that would have made his path to the White House that much more certain. He was the loving and wonderful father, who never spoke of his first wife to his first daughter; Alice Lee Roosevelt never seems to have existed. For all of his achievements, he never became a great speaker, he never could quite master the sheer flow of words that tumbled from his mouth. But today, there is no president who is more quoted, with more concise and memorable catch phrases.

Theodore obviously inherited his father's wealth of character. But the genius of the second Theodore Roosevelt lay in the way he interpreted the contradictions in his life. It was how he understood his inconsistencies, his tragedies, his experiences, that crystallized his ability to see the world through the eyes of others. His personal contradictions illustrated clearly to him that the world was a place of commonalities; people were not all that different. He led by downplaying differences, focusing on inclusiveness—focusing on the greater good for all Americans. This made him genuine to the masses. He would fight for anyone, so long as that person worked hard, did their part, had character. "He had the virtues we like to call American, and he had the faults," a friend recalled. "He knew us and we knew him."[8]

A newspaperman would state that Roosevelt's greatness came from "that peculiar trait about him of being able to sit down on the ground and eat with a cowpuncher, a prospector, and in the same breath turn around and address a crowned head, if one should be present, never losing his dignity and always holding the respect of his men."[9] This greatness was not given; Theodore made the courageous decision to live and enjoy fellowship with those outside his own social status. As a young assemblyman, he went to the tenement housing to see how the poor survived, the challenges they faced. And when he lived and worked and laughed and cried with the frontiersmen of the West—the likes of the Merrifelds, the Langs, the Sewalls—he was able to understand their outlook on life, their struggles, their hopes, their visions.[10] "He was quick to find the real man in very simple men," Bill Sewall claimed. "He didn't look for a brilliant man when he found me; he valued me for what I was worth."[11]

Theodore Roosevelt's vast understanding of the ramifications of the social scale was authentic; he never pandered. He tried to get to know people, to learn about them so he could take them to his new frontier. An old friend once asked Theodore how he "felt the pulse" of the country. "I don't know the way the people do feel," he responded. "I simply made up my mind what they ought to think, and then did my best to get them to think it."[12]

The rich and poor, the easterner and the westerner, the young and the old, all felt they had a friend, and a fighter, as their president. At a ceremony on the White House lawn on January 1st, 1907, Theodore shook the hands of 8,513 people, just because he wanted to. It became a *Guinness World Record* which stood for almost seventy years, until a publicity stunt in 1977.[13] Back in 1907, people stood for hours in a line several miles long, just for the chance to look the man in the eye and shake his hand. He enjoyed it more than they did.

The great lesson from the life of Theodore Roosevelt is that he was a man who embraced contradiction—his own, as well as society's. He understood the expansive humanity at play in every great leadership challenge, and in that humanity he found opportunity. Roosevelt focused on uniting values inherent in disparate groups; centering the attention on the collective work required to own the future. While leading, he never accentuated the differences amongst people, the margins where hatred can easily manifest. And it was because of Roosevelt's authenticity that Americans from all different walks of life followed him. They knew he was genuine, that his aim was to bond the common American. Theodore's words on authentic leadership are as severely poignant today as they were a century ago: "We need leaders of inspired idealism, leaders to whom are granted great visions, who dream greatly and strive to make their dreams come true; who can kindle the people with the fire from their own burning souls."[14]

Roosevelt's authentic leadership was a product of a life-long odyssey. With a goal of pure government, he set out to live life as if he was a character in a grand novel with the title something like: *The New Frontiersman, The New Century, The New America, starring Theodore Roosevelt.* He spent his whole life auditioning for the part.

The problem with Theodore Roosevelt is that history sees the result of his life's work and believes it to be destined, when in fact, the journey is the story. And to those who knew him prior to his ascension to the White House, the president's accomplishments were not original. He had done them before—the stage had only been smaller, the cast of characters only slightly different.

As he did with Jay Gould, Judge Westbrook, Stockman Fred Willard, and Post Office General John Wanamaker, Theodore went after a kingpin to prove a point. Within six months of taking

office he struck down James Pierpont Morgan, the mighty financier whose massive monopolistic holdings were said to "command
resources worth more than all the gold and silver in the United
States Treasury, almost 10 times what the federal government spent
each year."[15] Roosevelt felt that one man had too much power and
slapped Morgan's holdings of the Northern Securities with the
first ever corporate antitrust suit, citing "an illegal combination in
restraint of trade."[16] Stunned, the world's most powerful man went
to the White House to inquire if the president had lost his mind.
J. P. Morgan had had a seat at *every* large business and economic
decision in Washington; he was the centrifugal figure in which the
power elite, the inner-circle, orbited around. No president had
done anything like this before, Morgan shouted. Why had Theodore not asked him for advice; they could have worked something
out in advance, like the inner-circle of power had always done.

"Warning you was just what we did not want to do," Theodore
told the tycoon, before standing up and walking to the door.[17]
Morgan insinuated that Roosevelt's career was over, his presidency
a destined failure. Theodore had heard a version of that line
before. The President saw the tycoon into the hallway, closed the
door, and then proceeded to bust up the trusts, forever altering
the relationship between business and government in America.

In everything he did, Theodore promoted his idea of the
America Dream. His economic policies, the Square Deal as it was
called, had three tenets: conservation of natural resources, control of corporations, and protection for the common American.
He had seen enough as an assemblyman and governor, as well as
on his night prowls as police commissioner, to know that the poor
needed a strong executive fighting for them.

When the coal strike of 1902 threatened to cripple the country, Theodore acted like no president had ever done before
him. Coal was essential to the economy, it heated homes, it
powered factories. The strike flirted with violence, anarchy,
and revolution. On one hand, he had rich tycoons, not willing
to meet the workers meager demands; on the other, he had
laborers who were threatening mob rule. Theodore detested
both equally.

To settle the matter he called the mine owners and the labor
representatives to the White House and discovered that the

owners were not leading, instead acting "intransigent and brutal and stupid."[18] Assessing the lack of leadership from the coal owners, the president took action.

He placed the mines under his control, protected the area with the U.S. Army, and reemployed the striking miners back to work. His swift action won over public support. A Republican congressman was baffled. "What about the Constitution of the United States?" he asked the president. "The Constitution was made for the people," Roosevelt replied, "not the people for the Constitution."[19] The coal tycoons, fearing federal takeover, consented to the workers' demands. Theodore had tied the hands of the powerful with the bindings born of public support—just as he had done to President Benjamin Harrison as a Civil Service Commissioner and then later John D. Long as the assistant secretary of the navy.

The boy who found strength in the outdoors, and the man who witnessed the environmental catastrophe of the "Great Cattle Die Up" in Medora, North Dakota, became America's greatest conservationist. As president, he increased the area of federal protection to almost 230 million acres or 360,000 square miles—an area equivalent to Ohio, Virginia, Tennessee, Kentucky, Indiana, Maine, South Carolina, West Virginia, Maryland, Hawaii, Massachusetts, Vermont, New Hampshire, New Jersey, Connecticut, Delaware, and Rhode Island *combined.* He also established the United States Forest Service, five national parks, eighteen national monuments, four national game preserves, one hundred and fifty national forests and fifty-one federal bird sanctuaries. He placed the Grand Canyon under federal protection.[20]

The young child who adored his mother's naval stories of the cavalier Bulloch uncles built a Navy the likes the world had never seen before. He then sent the Great White Fleet to the four corners of the earth, to promote peace, with a Big Stick.

The college chap who wrote the *Naval War of 1812* and then spent a lifetime brooding over naval tactics and the importance of strategic waterways led the charge to acquire the Panama Canal. The Rough Rider, who suffered through the morass of governmental red tape, would take charge as a strong executive. "I took the Canal Zone and let Congress debate," Theodore would boast, "and while the debate goes on, the canal does also."[21]

The lessons that the upstart young man took from his Civil Service days lead to the modernization of the entire civil service machinery in the U.S. government. He was the first executive to break the back of the spoils system, setting the now common-sense precedent that government officials in America should be hired on merit.

Learning from his failure on the Sunday Excise Law as the New York police commissioner, Theodore learned to embrace the thorny issue of political negotiation, the ability to find common ground and compromise. He became the first American to win the Nobel Peace Prize for brokering an armistice between Russia and Japan, ending the Russo-Japanese War.

Theodore was the youngest man to become president, but he was probably as well prepared as any executive, before or since. From New York state assemblyman, to Badlands rancher, to civil service commissioner, to police commissioner of New York City, to assistant secretary of the navy, to colonel of the Rough Riders, to governor of New York, and to vice president of the United States; at each station stop he learned and improved, consistently molding his leadership character. And through it all, he never stopped writing about history, making him the president with the greatest appreciation for the past, which gave him strength to fight for posterity.

In March of 1905, Theodore was inaugurated in his own right, crushing his Democrat opponent Alton B. Parker in one of the largest landslide victories in U.S. presidential history. At this swearing ceremony, unlike the first time he recited the oath in Buffalo, a bible was present. Theodore chose to open up the scripture and place is hand on James 1:22–23: "be ye doers of the world, not hearers only."[22] One could almost hear Thee in the background, telling his son to get action, to seize the moment. Of the inauguration, Theodore would write tenderly, "how I wish Father could have lived to see it."[23]

On election night Theodore told a group of reporters that "under no circumstances will I be a candidate for or accept another nomination," claiming to honor "the two-term tradition set by George Washington." It was said that Edith, who had heard her husband make the proclamation, simply "flinched."[24] She knew better.

Leaving the White House in 1909 after eight years as president, Theodore quickly became disgruntled about his hand-picked successor's lack of accomplishments. In 1912, he decided to return to the White House and run against William Taft in the first ever Republican Party primary election. Theodore overwhelmingly beat the incumbent president, winning nine out of thirteen states, eight by a landslide. But at the 1912 Republican National Convention, Taft supporters and the Republican Party machinery united, stripping Roosevelt of his primary delegate votes and re-nominating the sitting president. The people had wanted Theodore; the machine wanted Taft.

Believing that the nomination had been stolen from him, Theodore quickly joined the Progressive Party movement, nicknamed the "Bull Moose Party," and became its candidate for president. At a campaign stop in Milwaukee on October 14th, 1912—at about eight o'clock in the evening—Roosevelt left the Hotel Gilpatrick and entered his motorcade to take him to the Milwaukee Auditorium where nine thousand people waited to hear him speak. He stepped into his open-top car and stood to wave to the throng of people trying to get a glimpse of him. A deranged madcap, who had been stalking the colonel for three weeks across nine different cities, charged towards the motorcade and fired a shot from a .38-caliber Colt into Roosevelt's chest.[25] The force of the bullet knocked Theodore backward. A. O. Girard, the president's bodyguard and former Rough Rider, jumped on the gunman and struggled to take away the revolver.[26]

"He pinked me," Theodore roared before jumping down from the car amidst the chaos.

"I want to look at him," he demanded.

The assailant, now apprehended by several police and body guards, was stood upright. The mob was frenzied, shouting "Kill him, kill him!"

Roosevelt charged the gunman.[27] "Why did you do it? What was your reason?" Theodore barked coldly, teeth clenched, leaning forward. He stared his would-be assassin in the eye for several tense moments.

There was no response. Theodore turned to look at the revolver. "A 38-Colt has an ugly drive,"[28] he said before turning to a security agent. "Take charge of him and see that there is not violence done to him."[29]

"He has shot you," the aide screamed after seeing the small hole in Theodore's overcoat.

"I know it," Theodore responded before opening up his overcoat and exposing a white linen shirt saturated with blood. Then he coughed into his hand, and seeing that no blood came up, the experienced hunter knew that the bullet had not punctured his lungs.[30]

"I know I am good now; I don't know how long I may be," Theodore said. "This may be my last talk in this cause to our people, and while I am good I am going to drive to the hall and deliver my speech."[31]

The aide stared in disbelief.

"Get me to that speech!" Roosevelt boomed.

At the auditorium doctors urged Theodore to go to the hospital immediately. The gunshot wound was potentially fatal, he was told. Theodore went on stage.

The audience of nine thousand at the auditorium was stunned when he opened his overcoat and showed them his blood soaked shirt. "It takes more than one bullet to kill a Bull Moose!" he said to start his speech, ending it eighty minutes later, having almost passed out on two separate occasions.[32]

Directly from the podium Theodore went to the hospital where an X-ray determined that the bullet rested less than one inch from his heart, having ripped through the fifty page speech that he had folded in his breast pocket. The hefty papers, along with a metal glasses case, absorbed the brunt of the bullet and spared him of death. The bullet remained in him the rest of his life.[33]

Of his speech and the ordeal, he would downplay it. It was no different, really, from the time he was bucked off his horse and broke his ribs on the round-up in the Badlands and had to continue the day's work.

On Election Day 1912, Theodore received more votes than Taft, and the most votes for any third party presidential candidate in U.S. history. But the Republican Party split opened the door for Democrat Woodrow Wilson to take the presidency with forty-two percent of the vote.

The following year, in 1913, Theodore, then fifty-five years old, decided on a new adventure and embarked on a journey to explore and map Brazil's River of Doubt—a treacherous tributary deep into the uncharted Amazon rain forest. Contracting a bacterial infection from a flesh wound, he almost died.

In 1917, after eight years out of office, Theodore delivered his verdict, claiming that he was "having a horrid, unimportant time."[33] He wanted action, to be important again. During the debate on American intervention in World War I, he wrote a letter to Woodrow Wilson on May 18th, 1917 seeking permission to immediately "raise two divisions for immediate service at the front." President Wilson denied the request; Theodore was fifty-nine years old.[34]

Undeterred, the colonel gritted his teeth and set his sights on the 1920 presidential election—it was his to win.

Throughout his life the only thing that could keep Roosevelt's mind entirely occupied was a book. Often he read two of them a day. A ferocious writer, he also penned over 150,000 letters and completed over thirty books, often working on several at one time.[35] Considering the enormous amount of time required to accomplish such a literary feat, one must appreciate that the man spent years—literally years—of his life devoted to reading and writing. This time was spent alone, thinking, brooding; time spent arrested in introspection. Everything he read and wrote became a part of him, but some things never changed. The last letter he penned, just like his first letter written in his childhood scrawl, was about birds.[36]

Shortly after his sixtieth birthday, on the evening of January 5th, 1919, Theodore complained of a headache and went to bed at his home at Sagamore Hill. Around four in the morning, he had a coronary embolism and died. Upon hearing the news, Vice President Thomas Marshall, shook his head, "Death had to take him sleeping, for if Roosevelt had been awake, there would have been a fight."[37]

Perhaps the most poignant eulogy of Roosevelt was given by Edith Wharton, who had known Theodore since childhood: "he was so alive at all points, and so gifted with the rare faculty of living intensely and entirely in every moment as it passed. . . ."[38]

A New York City Policeman remarked, "It was not only that he was a great man, but, oh, there was so much fun in being led by him."[39]

Secretary of State Elihu Root, who like most political men of the day oscillated between a Roosevelt adversary and ally, put the death into historical perspective:

> Review the roster of the few great men of history, our own history, the history of the world; and when you have finished the review, you will find that Theodore Roosevelt was the greatest teacher of the essentials of popular self-government the world has ever known. . . .

> The future of our country will depend upon having men, real men of sincerity and truth, of unshakable conviction, of power, of personality, with the spirit of Justice and the fighting spirit through all the generations; and the mightiest service that can be seen today to accomplish that for our country is to make it impossible that Theodore Roosevelt, his teaching and his personality shall be forgotten.[40]

Theodore Roosevelt was laid to the earth in a simple ceremony at a simple cemetery, just down the road from Sagamore Hill at Oyster Bay. The death was a shock to most Americans, those certain that he was destined to retake the presidency in 1921. Old friend and cowboy Jack Willis was not surprised upon hearing the news of the Old Lion's death. By the dying embers of a campfire in the Badlands, some thirty-five years prior, Theodore had told Jack that the one challenge of his life was to stay alive.

"When I was 21, I promised myself that I would live my life up to the hilt until I was 60," the young Theodore Roosevelt told the cowpuncher, "and to be prepared for anything that happened after that."[41]

Theodore Roosevelt exceeded his own challenge by two months and one week.[42]

Author's Note

⎯⎯⎯⎯⎯⎯⎯⎯⎯⎯⎯⎯⎯⎯⎯⎯◇

I MET THEODORE ROOSEVELT WHEN I WAS ALMOST 8 YEARS old. I was lying on a stack of firewood by the side of my house reading a book on the twenty-sixth president [I think it may have been the children's book, *Don't You Dare Shoot That Bear!*]. On that hot summer afternoon, time was not of the essence; the auburn sun slipped over the horizon unnoticeable to me. The greatest phenomenon that the planet had ever known was in my hands. All existence faded into the tale of Theodore Roosevelt. He was Davy Crocket, John Wayne, Natty Bumpo, Chief Joseph, Huckleberry Finn, The Lone Ranger, my father, Abraham Lincoln, Clark and Lewis all wrapped into one. He said "Bully" wherever he went. He charged a hill and won a war. He was a hunter. He was an author. He started a museum. He was a policeman. He was a vice president. He was a president. He dug a canal. He was the manual of patriotism.

He would never shoot a bear unless it was fair game. He was born with a disability but overcame it. This inspired me because I was born with profound hearing loss. It seemed that Roosevelt always had with him a big stick. I decided to carry a stick around for the next few days. I told anyone that would listen that Theodore was much better than his younger brother Franklin, my proclamation more advanced than my facts.

As I got older I became less enthralled with Roosevelt. My boyhood curiosity waned as I had other things to think about. But when I was twenty-eight years old I left my home in Bozeman, Montana for graduate school in the Northeast. I think leaving the majesty of Big Sky country for the eastern seaboard made me rethink Theodore. Was this guy even a leader? Or was he insane, like Mark Twain believed?

There were two catalysts to the creation of this book. The first took place when I stumbled upon the Houghton Library at Harvard and discovered the unpublished first-hand accounts from Theodore Roosevelt's contemporaries. The documents were direct insights into how Theodore became a leader. The second catalyst took place when, at that the same time I found the documents, I was also a part of a study group with Charlie Gibson, the longtime host of *Good Morning America* and the anchor of *ABC World News*. The Gibson Group, as we called ourselves, was researching the causation of incivility, vitriol, and intransigence so profoundly malignant in U.S. politics of today. How could we overcome this partisanship, the group wondered?

The titanic divide between my two research projects was just sad. My first project looked at the turn of the twentieth century, a model of inclusive leadership that focused on embracing commonality and leading diverse peoples into a new frontier, together. The other endeavor with The Gibson Group focused on the twenty-first century, and was ripe with divisive characters and politicians trying to gain power through dividing the electorate. Why is it that in politics today we have an overwhelming desire to delineate a human being down to a single thing: elitist, black, immigrant, Latino, white, small business owner, gay, liberal, middle class, conservative, blue-collar, Asian, progressive, woman, you name it—as if a single label could encompass all there is to know about someone? What if we led as one thing: Americans? What if we sought out the next frontier together? What if, when we looked to solve the most challenging problems in the world, we leveraged our diversity and patriotism and national values and character?

This book was written for the future. I realized that when I was standing at Theodore Roosevelt's gravesite. My wife had scheduled an outing at Oyster Bay—the Roosevelt home and nearby cemetery. She knew that I was dithering over whether or not I should write the book. She wanted to provide some inspiration.

As I stood at the tomb, I realized that beneath the earth's floor was a dead man whose life could still teach future generations about leadership. With me was my one-month-old daughter Avary, in the dawn of her youth, full of life. At that moment, I knew why Theodore Roosevelt's leadership journey must be told.

What began as a boyhood curiosity on a stack of firewood eventually led to this book. My hope is that one day it will inspire my daughters and the next generation of American leaders.

My parents deserve thanks first. My mother, JoAnn, for always making it seem that I could accomplish absolutely anything I set my mind to do—so long as I worked hard and never gave up. My father, Alan, for his wit and wisdom, and for providing a model of leadership that every son should be so fortunate enough to follow. I am privileged to call you my parents.

Rachel, Drew, Cade and Siena, you are loved dearly. As mom always reminds us: "There is nothing more important than family." Rachel, you have always been an inspiration to me.

My editor, Alexandra Hess: your expert guidance as this story took shape was monumental and your killer humor made this project that much more enjoyable. The Skyhorse Publishing team, from end-to-end, was entirely effective and proficient.

The Luminoso family: if you did not open up your hearts and home to Avary, Meghan and me, this book would not have been written. Gerry, Melanie, Elizabeth, Thomas and Christina, thank you so much for your benevolence and support.

There are several people whose teachings, research, and guidance assisted me immensely: Roger Porter, John McConnell, David Gergen, Heather Cole, Wallace Finley Dailey.

Betsy Winslow deserves special thanks. When I went to her office to discuss my far-fetched idea to write a modern business case on the twenty-sixth President, she not only agreed immediately but provided guidance—over the course of several months—that made me see Roosevelt in a new way.

I started this project as a student at The Tuck School of Business at Dartmouth. My classmates and the faculty rallied around the idea of this book in a very meaningful way. The Tuck Community exemplifies leadership: community minded professionals who seek diversity and promote stewardship and sustainability. That recipe is the past and future of leadership.

Much of the research and the majority of the book was written during my time at the Harvard Kennedy School. My friends at Kennedy challenged and inspired me in ways I did not think possible. The commitment to advancing the public interest is the most noble of callings.

To the Montana State family: Bobcat Nation is strong and leading all across the world. It is interesting to appreciate that Roosevelt was a man who led at the intersection of Mountains & Minds.

Lauren and Dayna DeLaney: thank you so much for the Rough Rider weekend in Tampa.

My grandparents Henry and Jean Naegeli taught me a lot about values and character; which I believe permeated this book. Marjorie and Eugene Knokey brought a sense of wonderment into my life when I was a child. My grandfather, Eugene, had a substantial influence on this book. When I was a boy, no more than seven or eight years old, he began asking me questions like: "What would America look like today if Beauregard would have just charged into Washington after beating the Union Army at the First Battle of Bull Run?" or "Did Woodrow Wilson's stroke lead to WWII?" or "What if Kennedy does not get shot in Dallas? Do we go to war with Vietnam?" I had no idea what he was talking about then and I do not have answers to his questions now. But my grandfather's stories made history fun and intriguing, a theater of perpetual mystery. His version of history had ghosts that came to life, ghosts that entertained the oversized imagination of a boy.

My final thank you is for my immediate family. Avary and Quinn, this book was written for you two girls. You are darlings that have decorated your parent's life beyond which words are able to describe. Neither of you had any regard for my attempt at becoming an author. Avary, you would just barge into the room and begin to tell me about your day at school or show me a new dance move you just learned or you would just push aside the laptop and hug me with muddy hands because you were digging a hole in the back yard. Quinn, you would come into my office, smile that smile of yours, and then steal one of the books that had been laid across the table. I will never forget the multiple times you ran out of the room, giggling, wearing nothing but a diaper, book in hands. Both of you are lovely reminders of what really matters. The honor of my life is to be your Dad.

Meghan Knokey you are, to me, perfect. My love for you is immeasurable. I started writing this book four weeks after you gave birth to Avary. Of my long hours and sleepless nights, as well as days so caught up in Theodore's life that I forgot to shower, you never complained. Instead you inspired and encouraged and edited and loved and motivated and laughed and did that thing where you just start randomly dancing and I was forced to have a brighter outlook on the day, as well as hug you. I am humbled to call you my soul mate, my rock. Your quiet grace is inexplicably hard to define, but easy to be grateful for. The night we got married in Pray, Montana—and threw peaches at the horse barn alone at midnight—I knew I had just done something very special. I just did not know then how special you would continue to become.

—Jak

Endnotes

Preface:
1. "Lincoln's Funeral," *Life Magazine*, April 24th, 1950, 12.
2. James MacGregor Burns and Susan Dunn, *The Three Roosevelts* (New York: Atlantic Monthly Press, 2001), 1.
3. "Lincoln's Funeral," 12.
4. Burns and Dunn, *The Three Roosevelts*, 1.
5. Ibid., 2.
6. "Lincoln's Funeral," 12.
7. A. F. Cosby, *A Rough Rider Looks Back* (MS Am 1515), Houghton Library, Harvard University.
8. Richard Harding Davis, *Notes of a War Correspondent* (New York: Harper & Brothers, 1911), 96.
9. Virgil Carrington Jones, *Roosevelt's Rough Riders* (New York: Doubleday & Company, 1971), 183.
10. Hermann Hagedorn: *The Rough Riders–Research Notes* (MS Am 2995), Theodore Roosevelt Collection, Houghton Library, Harvard University.
11. Jones, *Roosevelt's Rough Riders*, 181.
12. Hagedorn: The Rough Riders–Research Notes.
13. Evan Thomas, *The War Lovers* (New York: Little, Brown and Company, 2010), 321.
14. Ibid., 323.
15. Ibid., 324.
16. Ibid.
17. Edward Renehan Jr. *The Lion's Pride: Theodore Roosevelt and His Family in Peace and War* (New York: Oxford University Press, 1998). 74.
18. Cosby: *A Rough Rider Looks Back*.
19. Peggy Samuels and Harold Samuels, *Teddy Roosevelt at San Juan Hill: The Making of a President* (College Station: University of Texas Press, 1997), 238.
20. Kathleen Dalton, *Theodore Roosevelt: A Strenuous Life* (New York: Vintage Books, 2002), 9.
21. James Strock, *Theodore Roosevelt on Leadership: Executive Lessons from the Bully Pulpit* (California: Prima, 2001), 194.

Chapter 1:

1.   Corinne Roosevelt Robinson, *My Brother Theodore Roosevelt* (New York: Charles Scribner's Sons, 1921), 3.
2.   Carleton Putnam, *Theodore Roosevelt: The Formative Years, 1858–1886* (New York: Charles Scribner's Sons, 1958), 4.
3.   Nathan Miller, *Theodore Roosevelt: A Life* (New York: William Morrow and Company, 1992), 25.
4.   Putnam, *Theodore Roosevelt: The Formative Years*, 5.
5.   David McCullough, *Mornings on Horseback* (New York: Simon & Schuster, 2001), 24.
6.   Ibid.
7.   Ibid.
8.   Ibid., 27, and "Old Bullion's Team," *Time* (Jan. 28, 1935).
9.   Ibid.
10.   McCullough, *Mornings on Horseback*, 27.
11.   Ibid., 26.
12.   Paul Grondahl, *I Rose Like a Rocket* (New York: Free Press, 2004), 14.
13.   Ibid.
14.   Ibid., 20.
15.   Ibid., 18.
16.   H. W. Brands, *T.R.: The Last Romantic* (New York: Basic Books, 1997), 4.
17.   Stephen O'Connor, *Orphan Trains: The Story of Charles Loring Brace and the Children He Saved* (New York: Houghton Mifflin, 2001), 78.
18.   "American Notes for General Circulation," *Athenæum: A Journal of English and Foreign Literature, Science, the Fine Arts*, vol. 2 (London: Chapman and Hall, 1842), 901.
19.   Putnam, *Theodore Roosevelt: The Formative Years*, 43; Grondahl, *I Rose Like a Rocket*, 25.
20.   Miller, *Theodore Roosevelt: A Life*, 32.
21.   McCullough, *Mornings on Horseback*, 31.
22.   Ibid., 32.
23.   Ibid., 28.
24.   Putnam, *Theodore Roosevelt: The Formative Years*, 43.
25.   McCullough, *Mornings on Horseback*, 29.
26.   Grondahl, *I Rose Like a Rocket*, 25.
27.   Robinson, *My Brother Theodore Roosevelt*, 5.
28.   Ibid.
29.   Ibid.
30.   Ibid.
31.   Ibid.
32.   McCullough, *Mornings on Horseback*, 29.
33.   Putnam, *Theodore Roosevelt: The Formative Years*, 33.
34.   Dalton, *Theodore Roosevelt: A Strenuous Life*, 26.

35. Putnam, *Theodore Roosevelt: The Formative Years,* 6.
36. Miller, *Theodore Roosevelt: A Life,* 25; and Putnam, *Theodore Roosevelt: The Formative Years,* 7.
37. McCullough, *Mornings on Horseback,* 43.
38. Edmund Morris, *The Rise of Theodore Roosevelt* (New York: Coward, McCann & Geoghegan, 1979), 796.
39. Putnam, *Theodore Roosevelt: The Formative Years,* 3.
40. Ibid.
41. Ibid.
42. Robinson, *My Brother Theodore Roosevelt,* 16.
43. Dalton, *Theodore Roosevelt: A Strenuous Life,* 24.
44. Ibid., 23.
45. Morris, *The Rise of Theodore Roosevelt,* 37.
46. Ibid., 520.
47. Ibid.
48. Ibid.
49. Ibid.
50. Margaret Mitchell, *Gone with the Wind* (New York: Macmillan Company, 1936), 550.
51. McCullough, *Mornings on Horseback,* 25.
52. Jeff Wallenfeldt, *The American Civil War and Reconstruction* (New York: Britannica, 2010), 26.
53. Harold Holzer, *The Lincoln-Douglas Debates: The First Complete, Unexpurgated Text* (New York: Fordham University Press, 2004), 43.
54. Hagedorn, *The Boys' Life of Theodore Roosevelt* (New York: Harper & Brothers, 1922), 6.
55. Jean Edward Smith, *Grant* (New York: Touchstone, 2001), 90 and Hagedorn, *The Boys' Life of Theodore Roosevelt,* 7

Chapter 2:

1. Morris, *The Rise of Theodore Roosevelt,* 38.
2. Betty Boyd Caroli, *The Roosevelt Women* (New York: Basic Books, 1998), 45.
3. McCullough, *Mornings on Horseback,* 55.
4. Putnam, *Theodore Roosevelt: The Formative Years,* 47.
5. Morris, *The Rise of Theodore Roosevelt,* 38.
6. Ellis Coulter, *The Confederate States of America, 1861–1865* (Texas: University of Texas Press, 1978), 62. Note: three were half-brothers-in-law, three half-sisters-in-law were wives of Confederate soldiers.
7. Robinson, *My Brother Theodore Roosevelt,* 29.
8. Dalton, *Theodore Roosevelt: A Strenuous Life,* 26.
9. Grondahl, *I Rose Like a Rocket,* 31.
10. Ibid.
11. McCullough, *Mornings on Horseback,* 57.

12. Miller, *Theodore Roosevelt: A Life,* 33.
13. Putnam, *Theodore Roosevelt: The Formative Years,* 49.
14. Dalton, *Theodore Roosevelt: A Strenuous Life,* 61.
15. Morris, *The Rise of Theodore Roosevelt,* 39.
16. Ibid.
17. Robinson, *My Brother Theodore Roosevelt,* 20.
18. McCullough, *Mornings on Horseback,* 59.
19. Ibid.
20. Robinson, *My Brother Theodore Roosevelt,* 28.
21. McCullough, *Mornings on Horseback,* 60.
22. Robinson, *My Brother Theodore Roosevelt,* 9.
23. Ibid.
24. Ibid.
25. Ibid.
26. Ibid.
27. McCullough, *Mornings on Horseback,* 62.
28. Warren Zimmerman, *First Great Triumph* (New York: Farrar, Straus, and Giroux, 2002), 192.
29. McCullough, *Mornings on Horseback,* 74.
30. Ibid.
31. Ibid., 75.
32. Ibid.
33. Ibid.
34. Ibid.
35. Ibid.
36. Ibid., 73.
37. Theodore Roosevelt, *Autobiography of Theodore Roosevelt* (New York: Charles Scribner's Sons, 1927), 13.
38. McCullough, *Mornings on Horseback,* 74.
39. Ibid., 44.
40. Robinson, *My Brother Theodore Roosevelt,* 36.
41. Ibid., 35.
42. Ibid., 37.
43. Hagedorn, *The Boys' Life of Theodore Roosevelt,* 34.
44. Dalton, *Theodore Roosevelt: A Strenuous Life,* 20.
45. Roosevelt, *Autobiography of Theodore Roosevelt,* 27.
46. Theodore Roosevelt speech on October 19th, 1905 in Roswell, Georgia.
47. Robinson, *My Brother Theodore Roosevelt,* 38.
48. Morris, *The Rise of Theodore Roosevelt,* 40.

Chapter 3:

1. Grondahl, *I Rose Like a Rocket,* 8.
2. McCullough, *Mornings on Horseback,* 95.

3. Ibid.
4. Ibid.
5. Dalton, *Theodore Roosevelt: A Strenuous Life*, 36.
6. Ibid.
7. Brands. *T.R.: The Last Romantic*, 23.
8. McCullough, *Mornings on Horseback*, 96.
9. Dalton, *Theodore Roosevelt: A Strenuous Life*, 37.
10. Ibid.
11. Ibid.
12. Ibid.
13. Ibid.
14. Ibid., 35.
15. McCullough, *Mornings on Horseback*, 95.
16. Ibid., 105.
17. Ibid.
18. Miller, *Theodore Roosevelt: A Life*, 31.
19. Grondahl, *I Rose Like a Rocket*, 11.
20. Dalton, *Theodore Roosevelt: A Strenuous Life*, 46.
21. Ibid.
22. McCullough, *Mornings on Horseback*, 107.
23. Roger L. Di Silvestro, *Theodore Roosevelt in the Badlands: A Young Politician's Quest for Recovery in the American West* (New York: Walker, 2011), 67.
24. Miller, *Theodore Roosevelt: A Life*, 36.
25. Strock, *Theodore Roosevelt on Leadership*, 195.
26. Putnam, *Theodore Roosevelt: The Formative Years*, 27.
27. Dalton, *Theodore Roosevelt: A Strenuous Life*, 41.
28. Grondahl, *I Rose Like a Rocket*, 20.
29. Morris, *The Rise of Theodore Roosevelt*, 45.
30. Grondahl, *I Rose Like a Rocket*, 20.
31. Hagedorn, *The Boys' Life of Theodore Roosevelt*, 23.
32. Ibid., 24.
33. Ibid., 27.
34. Ibid., 39.
35. Ibid.
36. Roosevelt, *Autobiography of Theodore Roosevelt*, 25.
37. Ibid.
38. Ibid., 16.
39. McCullough, *Mornings on Horseback*, 115.
40. Ibid. The quote is from the beginning of *Scalp Hunters*.
41. Dalton, *Theodore Roosevelt: A Strenuous Life*, 43.
42. Ibid.; McCullough, *Mornings on Horseback*, 11.
43. McCullough, *Mornings on Horseback*, 116.
44. Roosevelt, *Autobiography of Theodore Roosevelt*, 14.

45. Ibid.
46. Ibid.
47. McCullough, *Mornings on Horseback,* 114.
48. Ibid., 30.
49. Grondahl, *I Rose Like a Rocket,* 17.
50. Dalton, *Theodore Roosevelt: A Strenuous Life,* 41.
51. Andrew Vietze, *Becoming Teddy Roosevelt: How a Maine Guide Inspired America's 26th President* (Maine: Down East, 2010), 26.
52. "American History Museum Annual Report," accessed August 2nd, 2014, http://www.amnh.org/about-us/annual-report/online-annual-report-2012–2013.
53. Dalton, *Theodore Roosevelt: A Strenuous Life,* 38, and McCullough, *Mornings on Horseback,* 35.
54. McCullough, *Mornings on Horseback,* 35.
55. Dalton, *Theodore Roosevelt: A Strenuous Life,* 45.
56. Ibid.
57. Ibid.
58. Joseph Bucklin Bishop, *Theodore Roosevelt and His Time Shown in His Own Letters,* vol. 1 (New York: Hodder and Stoughton, 1920), 2.

Chapter 4:
1.   Hagedorn, *The Boys' Life of Theodore Roosevelt,* 39.
2.   Ibid.
3.   Putnam, *Theodore Roosevelt: The Formative Years,* 71.
4.   Robinson, *My Brother Theodore Roosevelt,* 50.
5.   Ibid.
6.   Putnam, *Theodore Roosevelt: The Formative Years,* 72.
7.   Robinson, *My Brother Theodore Roosevelt,* 50.
8.   McCullough, *Mornings on Horseback,* 112.
9.   Putnam, *Theodore Roosevelt: The Formative Years,* 72.
10. McCullough, *Mornings on Horseback,* 112.
11. Roosevelt, *Autobiography of Theodore Roosevelt,* 28.
12. Ibid.
13. Putnam, *Roosevelt: The Formative Years,* 75, This analogy is from a historian who interviewed TR's sisters.
14. Roosevelt, *Autobiography of Theodore Roosevelt,* 21.
15. Putnam, *Theodore Roosevelt: The Formative Years,* 76.
16. Roosevelt, *Autobiography of Theodore Roosevelt,* 28.
17. Ibid.
18. Ibid.
19. Ibid.
20. Ibid.
21. Ibid., 27.

22. Putnam, *Theodore Roosevelt: The Formative Years*, 77.
23. Hagedorn, *The Boys' Life of Theodore Roosevelt*, 40.
24. Ibid.
25. Morris, *The Rise of Theodore Roosevelt*, 63.
26. Strock, *Theodore Roosevelt on Leadership*, 213.
27. Ibid., 214.
28. McCullough, *Mornings on Horseback*, 118.
29. Ibid.
30. Dalton, *Theodore Roosevelt: A Strenuous Life*, 53.
31. Roosevelt, *Autobiography of Theodore Roosevelt*, 18.
32. Ibid.
33. McCullough, *Mornings on Horseback*, 118.
34. Ibid.
35. Ibid., 126.
36. Brands. *T.R.: The Last Romantic*, 33.
37. Ibid., 37.
38. Morris, *The Rise of Theodore Roosevelt*, 73.
39. Ibid., 74.

Chapter 5:
1. Putnam, *Theodore Roosevelt: The Formative Years*, 130.
2. Hagedorn, Research Notes.
3. McCullough, *Mornings on Horseback*, 197.
4. Putnam, *Theodore Roosevelt: The Formative Years*, 129.
5. McCullough, *Mornings on Horseback*, 197.
6. Putnam, *Theodore Roosevelt: The Formative Years*, 129.
7. Hagedorn, Research Notes
8. Putnam, *Theodore Roosevelt: The Formative Years*, 130
9. *Harvard Advocate* 5, December 8th, 1871.
10. Putnam, *Theodore Roosevelt: The Formative Years*, 134.
11. Mark J. Chiusano, "When They Were Young, From Crimson editors to rowers, Harvardian presidents first made their marks on campus," *Harvard Crimson*, February 18th, 2009.
12. Morris, *The Rise of Theodore Roosevelt*, 86.
13. Burns and Dunn, *The Three Roosevelts*, 9.
14. Ibid., 9.
15. Ibid., 9.
16. Hagedorn, Research Notes.
17. Burns and Dunn, *The Three Roosevelts*, 9.
18. McCullough, *Mornings on Horseback*, 167.
19. Hagedorn, Research Notes.
20. Ibid.
21. Letter to Anna (Oct 13 1879).

22. Morris, *The Rise of Theodore Roosevelt*, 83.
23. Hagedorn, Research Notes.
24. Putnam, *Theodore Roosevelt: The Formative Years*, 135.
25. McCullough, *Mornings on Horseback*, 206; and Clarence Long, *Wages and Earnings in the United States 1860–1890* (New Jersey: Princeton University Press, 1960), 42.
26. McCullough, *Mornings on Horseback*, 206, and Clarence Long, *Wages and Earnings in the United States 1860–1890* (New Jersey: Princeton University Press, 1960), 42.
27. Putnam, *Theodore Roosevelt: The Formative Years*, 136.
28. Hagedorn, Research Notes.
29. Ibid.
30. Morris, *The Rise of Theodore Roosevelt*, 83.
31. Ibid., 81.
32. Ibid.
33. Ibid.
34. Ibid., 82.
35. Hagedorn, Research Notes.
36. Putnam, *Theodore Roosevelt: The Formative Years*, 131.
37. Ibid.
38. Phillip Boffey, "Theodore Roosevelt at Harvard," *Harvard Crimson*, December 12th, 1957.
39. Morris, *The Rise of Theodore Roosevelt*, 83.
40. Hagedorn, Research Notes.
41. Burns and Dunn, *The Three Roosevelts*, 9.
42. Stefan Lorant, *The Life and Times of Theodore Roosevelt* (New York: Doubleday & Company, 1959), 151.
43. Ibid.
44. Hagedorn, Research Notes Interview with Owen Wister, 1882 graduate.
45. Ibid.
46. Putnam, *Theodore Roosevelt: The Formative Years*, 138.
47. Ibid.
48. Donald Wilhelm, *Theodore Roosevelt as an Undergraduate* (Boston: J. W. Luce & Co., 1910), 41.
49. Hagedorn, Research Notes.
50. Ibid.
51. Ibid.
52. Ibid.
53. Ibid.
54. Ibid.
55. Putnam, *Theodore Roosevelt: The Formative Years*, 141.
56. Ibid., 142.

57. Lorant, *The Life and Times of Theodore Roosevelt*, 161.
58. Putnam, *Theodore Roosevelt: The Formative Years*, 144.
59. Hagedorn, *The Boys' Life of Theodore Roosevelt*, 58.
60. Ibid., 57.
61. Lorant, *The Life and Times of Theodore Roosevelt*, 155.
62. Morris, *The Rise of Theodore Roosevelt*, 87.
63. Ibid., 91.
64. Roosevelt, *Autobiography of Theodore Roosevelt*, 24.
65. Ibid.
66. McCullough, *Mornings on Horseback*, 170.
67. Ibid., 171.
68. Ibid., 170.
69. Putnam, *Theodore Roosevelt: The Formative Years*, 147.
70. McCullough, *Mornings on Horseback*, 177.
71. Dalton, *Theodore Roosevelt: A Strenuous Life*, 65.
72. McCullough, *Mornings on Horseback*, 179.
73. Morris, *The Rise of Theodore Roosevelt*, 93.
74. Ibid.
75. Ibid., 94.
76. Putnam, *Theodore Roosevelt: The Formative Years*, 146; and Morris, *The Rise of Theodore Roosevelt*, 93.
77. Brands. *T.R.: The Last Romantic*, 79.
78. Putnam, *Theodore Roosevelt: The Formative Years*, 147.
79. Morris, *The Rise of Theodore Roosevelt*, 94.
80. Putnam, *Theodore Roosevelt: The Formative Years*, 148.
81. Ibid., 148.
82. Hagedorn, Research Notes.
83. Morris, *The Rise of Theodore Roosevelt*, 95.
84. Ibid., 95.
85. Dalton, *Theodore Roosevelt: A Strenuous Life*, 68.
86. Putnam, *Theodore Roosevelt: The Formative Years*, 149. Carleton Putnam is credited with finding these quotes.
87. Dalton, *Theodore Roosevelt: A Strenuous Life*, 69.
88. Ibid., 68.
89. Putnam, *Theodore Roosevelt: The Formative Years*, 151.
90. Morris, *The Rise of Theodore Roosevelt*, 96.
91. Robinson, *My Brother Theodore Roosevelt*, 93.
92. Ibid.
93. Ibid., 106.
94. McCullough, *Mornings on Horseback*, 364.
95. Ibid., 365.
96. Ibid., 165.
97. Ibid.

98. Morris, *The Rise of Theodore Roosevelt*, 97.
99. McCullough, *Mornings on Horseback*, 189.
100. Ibid.
101. Morris, *The Rise of Theodore Roosevelt*, 98.
102. Miller, *Theodore Roosevelt: A Life*, 83.
103. Ibid.
104. Putnam, *Theodore Roosevelt: The Formative Years*, 153.
105. Ibid., 154.
106. Ibid., 155.
107. Ibid.
108. Ibid. 156.
109. Hagedorn, *The Boys' Life of Theodore Roosevelt*, 61.
110. Theodore Roosevelt, *My Debt to Maine* (Maine: Maine Writers Research Club, 1919), 19.
111. Putnam, *Theodore Roosevelt: The Formative Years*, 164.
112. Ibid, 159.
113. Lorant, *The Life and Times of Theodore Roosevelt*, 157.
114. Ibid.
115. Di Silvestro, *Theodore Roosevelt in the Badlands*, 12.
116. Theodore Roosevelt Diary, January 16th, 1879.
117. McCullough, *Mornings on Horseback*, 205.
118. Ibid., 205, Note: David McCullough gets credit for making this great comparison.
119. Di Silvestro, *Theodore Roosevelt in the Badlands*, 16.
120. McCullough, *Mornings on Horseback*, 220.
121. Ibid., 220.
122. Di Silvestro, *Theodore Roosevelt in the Badlands*, 12.
123. Hagedorn, Research Notes.
124. Di Silvestro, *Theodore Roosevelt in the Badlands*, 19.
125. Morris, *The Rise of Theodore Roosevelt*, 115.
126. Di Silvestro, *Theodore Roosevelt in the Badlands*, 18.
127. Ibid.
128. Hagedorn, Research Notes.
129. Di Silvestro, *Theodore Roosevelt in the Badlands*, 19.
130. McCullough, *Mornings on Horseback*, 226.
131. Hagedorn, Research Notes.
132. Ibid.
133. Wilhelm, *Theodore Roosevelt as an Undergraduate*, 28.
134. Hagedorn, Research Notes.
135. Ibid.
136. Ibid.
137. Ibid.
138. Ibid.

139. McCullough, *Mornings on Horseback*, 215.
140. Hagedorn, *The Boys' Life of Theodore Roosevelt*, 53.
141. Hagedorn, Research Notes.
142. Ibid.
143. Dalton, *Theodore Roosevelt: A Strenuous Life*, 84.
144. Hagedorn, Research Notes.
145. Hagedorn, *The Boys' Life of Theodore Roosevelt*, 64.
146. Morris, *The Rise of Theodore Roosevelt*, 129.
147. William Roscoe Thayer, *Theodore Roosevelt: An Intimate Biography* (New York: Grosset & Dunlap, 1919), 21.
148. Ibid.

Chapter 6:
1. Morris, *The Rise of Theodore Roosevelt*, 135.
2. Ibid., 136.
3. Lorant, *The Life and Times of Theodore Roosevelt*, 161.
4. Putnam, *Theodore Roosevelt: The Formative Years*, 208.
5. Ibid., 209.
6. Ibid., 211.
7. Morris, *The Rise of Theodore Roosevelt*, 136.
8. Putnam, *Theodore Roosevelt: The Formative Years*, 201.
9. Morris, *The Rise of Theodore Roosevelt*, 141.
10. Hagedorn, Research Notes.
11. Morris, *The Rise of Theodore Roosevelt*, 137.
12. Putnam, *Theodore Roosevelt: The Formative Years*, 219.
13. Grondahl, *I Rose Like a Rocket*, 60.
14. Roosevelt, *Autobiography of Theodore Roosevelt*, 22.
15. Morris, *The Rise of Theodore Roosevelt*, 140.
16. Putnam, *Theodore Roosevelt: The Formative Years*, 224.
17. Ibid., 225.
18. Ibid.
19. Ibid., 224.
20. Roosevelt, *Autobiography of Theodore Roosevelt*, 56.
21. Putnam, *Theodore Roosevelt: The Formative Years*, 217.
22. Roosevelt, *Autobiography of Theodore Roosevelt*, 56.
23. Thayer, *Theodore Roosevelt: An Intimate Biography*, 27.
24. Roosevelt, *Autobiography of Theodore Roosevelt*, 56.
25. Ibid.
26. Hagedorn, Research Notes.
27. Ibid.
28. Roosevelt, *Autobiography of Theodore Roosevelt*, 56; McCullough, *Mornings on Horseback*, 254.
29. Roosevelt, *Autobiography of Theodore Roosevelt*, 57.

30. McCullough, *Mornings on Horseback*, 252.
31. Ibid.
32. Hagedorn, Research Notes.
33. Morris, *The Rise of Theodore Roosevelt*, 146.
34. Putnam, *Theodore Roosevelt: The Formative Years*, 231.
35. W.C. Madden, *Tecumseh's Curse* (Xlibris Publishing, 2011), 119. Note: The Baltimore and Potomac Railroad station was located on the southwest corner of present-day Sixth Street N.W. and Constitution Avenue in Washington, D.C.
36. Putnam, *Theodore Roosevelt: The Formative Years*, 231.
37. Ibid., 232.
38. Ibid., 237.
39. Morris, *The Rise of Theodore Roosevelt*, 149.
40. Roosevelt, *Autobiography of Theodore Roosevelt*, 54.
41. Ibid.
42. Albert Baird, *Public Discussion and Debate* (Boston: Ginn, 1928), 29.
43. Morris, *The Rise of Theodore Roosevelt*, 144.
44. Putnam, *Theodore Roosevelt: The Formative Years*, 241.
45. Grondahl, *I Rose Like a Rocket*, 60.
46. Roosevelt, *Autobiography of Theodore Roosevelt*, 59; Morris, *The Rise of Theodore Roosevelt*, 150.
47. Morris, *The Rise of Theodore Roosevelt*, 150; Putnam, *Theodore Roosevelt: The Formative Years*, 242.
48. Hagedorn, Research Notes.
49. Ibid. The original transcript misspells Trimble as Trimball. The author uses the correct spelling throughout.
50. Hagedorn, Research Notes.
51. Putnam, *Theodore Roosevelt: The Formative Years*, 240–241.
52. Roosevelt, *Autobiography of Theodore Roosevelt*, 57.
53. Hagedorn, Research Notes.
54. Morris, *The Rise of Theodore Roosevelt*, 151.
55. Ibid.
56. Ibid.
57. McCullough, *Mornings on Horseback*, 252.
58. Roosevelt, *Autobiography of Theodore Roosevelt*, 56.
59. Hagedorn, Research Notes.
60. Morris, *The Rise of Theodore Roosevelt*, 37.
61. McCullough, *Mornings on Horseback*, 270.
62. Morris, *The Rise of Theodore Roosevelt*, 180.
63. Hagedorn, Research Notes.
64. Ibid.
65. Ibid.
66. Roosevelt, *Autobiography of Theodore Roosevelt*, 60.

67. Putnam, *Theodore Roosevelt: The Formative Years,* 247.
68. McCullough, *Mornings on Horseback,* 252.
69. Hagedorn, Research Notes.
70. Morris, *The Rise of Theodore Roosevelt,* 153.
71. Putnam, *Theodore Roosevelt: The Formative Years,* 248.

Chapter 7:
1. Putnam, *Theodore Roosevelt: The Formative Years,* 249.
2. Morris, *The Rise of Theodore Roosevelt,* 161.
3. Hagedorn, Research Notes.
4. Ibid.
5. Morris, *The Rise of Theodore Roosevelt,* 161.
6. Ibid.
7. Miller, *Theodore Roosevelt: A Life,* 123.
8. Hagedorn, Research Notes.
9. Ibid.
10. Ibid.
11. Putnam, *Theodore Roosevelt: The Formative Years,* 250.
12. Morris, *The Rise of Theodore Roosevelt,* 162; Putnam, *Theodore Roosevelt: The Formative Years,* 250.
13. Putnam, *Theodore Roosevelt: The Formative Years,* 251.
14. Ibid.
15. Grondahl, *I Rose Like a Rocket,* 74.
16. Roosevelt, *Autobiography of Theodore Roosevelt,* 70.
17. Putnam, *Theodore Roosevelt: The Formative Years,* 252.
18. Morris, *The Rise of Theodore Roosevelt,* 181.
19. Ibid., 163.
20. Ibid., 162.
21. Putnam, *Theodore Roosevelt: The Formative Years,* 252.
22. Hagedorn, Research Notes.
23. Ibid.
24. Ibid.
25. Ibid.
26. George Grant, *The Courage and Character of Theodore Roosevelt* (Tennessee: Cumberland House, 2005), 74.
27. Hagedorn, Research Notes, as told by George Spinney.
28. Grondahl, *I Rose Like a Rocket,* 79.
29. Ibid., 79.
30. Hagedorn, Research Notes.
31. Ibid.
32. Ibid.
33. Ibid.
34. Ibid.

35. Hagedorn, Research Notes.
36. Grondahl, *I Rose Like a Rocket*, 2.
37. Hagedorn, Research Notes.
38. Morris, *The Rise of Theodore Roosevelt*, 166.
39. Ibid.; Putnam, *Theodore Roosevelt: The Formative Years*, 274.
40. Morris, *The Rise of Theodore Roosevelt*, 166.
41. Ibid.
42. Hagedorn, Research Notes. Evening Telegram, January 28/23, State Assembly Record for 1884 shows "'rookie' fought political foes even then."
43. Roosevelt, *Autobiography of Theodore Roosevelt*, 85.
44. Lorant, *The Life and Times of Theodore Roosevelt*, 183.
45. Morris, *The Rise of Theodore Roosevelt*, 170.
46. Putnam, *Theodore Roosevelt: The Formative Years*, 254.
47. Morris, *The Rise of Theodore Roosevelt*, 170.
48. Hagedorn, Research Notes.
49. Ibid.
50. McCullough, *Mornings on Horseback*, 256.
51. Hagedorn, Research Notes.
52. Roosevelt, *Autobiography of Theodore Roosevelt*, 62.
53. Hagedorn, Research Notes. Memorandum of Conversation between Hagedorn, Hunt, and Spinney, September 20th, 1923 at Harvard Club.
54. Putnam, *Theodore Roosevelt: The Formative Years*, 254.
55. Roosevelt, *Autobiography of Theodore Roosevelt*, 79.
56. Ibid., 79.
57. Ibid.
58. Ibid., 80.
59. Ibid.
60. Ibid., 81.
61. Ibid.
62. Grant, *The Courage and Character of Theodore Roosevelt*, 112.
63. Roosevelt, *Autobiography of Theodore Roosevelt*, 71.
64. Morris, *The Rise of Theodore Roosevelt*, 173.
65. Ibid.
66. Ibid.
67. McCullough, *Mornings on Horseback*, 263.
68. Ibid., 262.
69. Ibid., 263.
70. Ibid.
71. Steve Hargreaves, "The Richest Americans in History." Cable News Network. June 2nd, 2014. Accessed January 15th, 2015, http://money.cnn.com/gallery/luxury/2014/06/01/richest-americans-in-history/
72. McCullough, *Mornings on Horseback*, 261.

73. Ibid., 263.
74. Morris, *The Rise of Theodore Roosevelt,* 174.
75. Hagedorn, Research Notes.
76. Putnam, *Theodore Roosevelt: The Formative Years,* 265.
77. Ibid.
78. Morris, *The Rise of Theodore Roosevelt,* 177.
79. Putnam, *Theodore Roosevelt: The Formative Years,* 266.
80. Ibid., 269.
81. Ibid., 267.
82. Hagedorn, Research Notes.
83. Ibid.
84. Morris, *The Rise of Theodore Roosevelt,* 177.
85. Roosevelt, *Autobiography of Theodore Roosevelt,* 84.
86. Ibid., 77.
87. Ibid.
88. McCullough, *Mornings on Horseback,* 265.
89. Di Silvestro, *Theodore Roosevelt in the Badlands,* 24.
90. Putnam, *Theodore Roosevelt: The Formative Years,* 267.
91. Ibid., 267.
92. Putnam, *Theodore Roosevelt: The Formative Years,* 272.
93. McCullough, *Mornings on Horseback,* 265; Brands. *T.R.: The Last Romantic,* 140.
94. McCullough, *Mornings on Horseback,* 266.
95. Henry Pringle, *Theodore Roosevelt: A Biography* (New York: Harvest/ HBJ, 1984), 52.
96. McCullough, *Mornings on Horseback,* 266.
97. Ibid.
98. Morris, *The Rise of Theodore Roosevelt,* 191.
99. Grondahl, *I Rose Like a Rocket,* 106.
100. McCullough, *Mornings on Horseback,* 268.
101. Morris, *The Rise of Theodore Roosevelt,* 191.
102. Grondahl, *I Rose Like a Rocket,* 107.
103. Ibid.
104. Putnam, *Theodore Roosevelt: The Formative Years,* 289.
105. Grondahl, *I Rose Like a Rocket,* 107.
106. Hagedorn, Research Notes.
107. McCullough, *Mornings on Horseback,* 271.
108. Roosevelt, *Autobiography of Theodore Roosevelt,* 85.
109. Putnam, *Theodore Roosevelt: The Formative Years,* 284.
110. Miller, *Theodore Roosevelt: A Life,* 147.
111. Hagedorn, Research Notes.
112. Putnam, *Theodore Roosevelt: The Formative Years,* 286.
113. Ibid.

114. Morris, *The Rise of Theodore Roosevelt*, 194.
115. McCullough, *Mornings on Horseback*, 270; Morris, *The Rise of Theodore Roosevelt*, 191.
116. McCullough, *Mornings on Horseback*, 270; Morris, *The Rise of Theodore Roosevelt*, 191.
117. McCullough, *Mornings on Horseback*, 270.
118. Morris, *The Rise of Theodore Roosevelt*, 191.
119. Hagedorn, Research Notes.
120. Putnam, *Theodore Roosevelt: The Formative Years*, 305.
121. McCullough, *Mornings on Horseback*, 271. McCullough suggests that this took place in 1883. See Putnam, *Theodore Roosevelt: The Formative Years*, 305.
122. Putnam, *Theodore Roosevelt: The Formative Years*, 305.
123. Ibid.
124. Ibid., 290.
125. McCullough, *Mornings on Horseback*, 276.
126. Putnam, *Theodore Roosevelt: The Formative Years*, 290.

Chapter 8:

1. Putnam, *Theodore Roosevelt: The Formative Years*, 384. Putnam gets credit for finding the weather report.
2. Morris, *The Rise of Theodore Roosevelt*, 189.
3. Putnam, *Theodore Roosevelt: The Formative Years*, 384. See also *New York Times*, February 12th, 1884.
4. Putnam, *Theodore Roosevelt: The Formative Years*, 384. See also *New York Times*, February 12th, 1884.
5. Hagedorn, Research Notes.
6. Ibid.
7. Morris, *The Rise of Theodore Roosevelt*, 241. See also *New York Times*, February 14th, 1884.
8. Morris, *The Rise of Theodore Roosevelt*, 241.
9. Putnam, *Theodore Roosevelt: The Formative Years*, 386.
10. Morris, *The Rise of Theodore Roosevelt*, 241.
11. Grondahl, *I Rose Like a Rocket*, 130.
12. Morris, *The Rise of Theodore Roosevelt*, 241.
13. Ibid.
14. McCullough, *Mornings on Horseback*, 287.
15. Putnam, *Theodore Roosevelt: The Formative Years*, 387.
16. Ibid.
17. Ibid.
18. Ibid.
19. Ibid.
20. Ibid., 387.

21. McCullough, *Mornings on Horseback*, 285.
22. Ibid., 284.
23. Putnam, *Theodore Roosevelt: The Formative Years*, 390.
24. Morris, *The Rise of Theodore Roosevelt*, 244.
25. Candice Millard, *The River of Doubt* (New York: Double Day, 2005), 343.
26. Strock, *Theodore Roosevelt on Leadership*, 82.
27. Putnam, *Theodore Roosevelt: The Formative Years*, 390.
28. Ibid.
29. Hagedorn, Research Notes.
30. Morris, *The Rise of Theodore Roosevelt*, 248.
31. McCullough, *Mornings on Horseback*, 286.
32. Morris, *The Rise of Theodore Roosevelt*, 258.
33. Hagedorn, Research Notes.
34. McCullough, *Mornings on Horseback*, 366.

Chapter 9:
1. McCullough, *Mornings on Horseback*, 292.
2. Ibid.
3. Mark Summers, *Rum, Romanism & Rebellion: The Making of a President, 1884* (North Carolina: University of North Carolina Press, 2000), 62.
4. McCullough, *Mornings on Horseback*, 293.
5. Putnam, *Theodore Roosevelt: The Formative Years*, 416.
6. Grondahl, *I Rose Like a Rocket*, 136.
7. Putnam, *Theodore Roosevelt: The Formative Years*, 416.
8. McCullough, *Mornings on Horseback*, 294.
9. Putnam, *Theodore Roosevelt: The Formative Years*, 429.
10. Ibid.
11. Hagedorn, Research Notes.
12. McCullough, *Mornings on Horseback*, 289.
13. Ibid., 296.
14. Ibid., 295.
15. Ibid.
16. Ibid., 296.
17. Ibid., 297.
18. Morris, *The Rise of Theodore Roosevelt*, 264.
19. McCullough, *Mornings on Horseback*, 300.
20. Republican National Party, *Proceedings of the Eighth Republican National Convention Held at Chicago, Illinois* (Illinois: Rand, McNally & Co., 1884), 10.
21. Ibid.
22. McCullough, *Mornings on Horseback*, 300, and Morris *The Rise of Theodore Roosevelt*, 264.
23. McCullough, *Mornings on Horseback*, 300.

24. Ibid., 304.
25. Morris, *The Rise of Theodore Roosevelt*, 265.
26. McCullough, *Mornings on Horseback*, 304.
27. Morris, *The Rise of Theodore Roosevelt*, 267.
28. McCullough, *Mornings on Horseback*, 305.
29. Ibid.
30. Morris, *The Rise of Theodore Roosevelt*, 267.
31. Ibid.
32. Ibid.
33. McCullough, *Mornings on Horseback*, 307.
34. Ibid., 306.

Chapter 10:
1. Hagedorn, Research Notes.
2. Morris, *The Rise of Theodore Roosevelt*, 277.
3. Hagedorn, Research Notes.
4. Hagedorn, Research Notes; Di Silvestro, *Theodore Roosevelt in the Badlands*, 84.
5. Di Silvestro, *Theodore Roosevelt in the Badlands*, 84.
6. Ibid., 161.
7. Ibid., 97.
8. McCullough, *Mornings on Horseback*, 330.
9. Morris, *The Rise of Theodore Roosevelt*, 211.
10. Ibid., 213.
11. Ibid., 270.
12. Ibid., 272.
13. Theodore Roosevelt, *Hunting Trips of a Ranchman and the Wilderness Hunter* (New York: Modern Library, 1996), 216.
14. McCullough, *Mornings on Horseback*, 309.
15. Ibid., 307.
16. Putnam, *Theodore Roosevelt: The Formative Years*, 467.
17. Ibid.
18. McCullough, *Mornings on Horseback*, 313.
19. Ibid.
20. Ibid., 312.
21. Putnam, *Theodore Roosevelt: The Formative Years*, 502.
22. Ibid., 504.
23. Hazell Price, *Hazell's Annual Cyclopedia*, (London: Hazell, Watson & Viney, 1888).
24. Hagedorn, Research Notes.
25. Ibid.
26. Putnam, *Theodore Roosevelt: The Formative Years*, 474.
27. Jack Willis, *Roosevelt in the Rough* (New York: Washburn, 1931), 55.

28. Di Silvestro, *Theodore Roosevelt in the Badlands,* 115.
29. Ibid.
30. Putnam, *Theodore Roosevelt: The Formative Years,* 475.
31. Hagedorn, Research Notes.
32. Ibid. Merrifield interview, his responses paraphrased.
33. Ibid.
34. Ibid.
35. Ibid.
36. Ibid.
37. Putnam, *Theodore Roosevelt: The Formative Years,* 481.
38. Ibid., 485.
39. Ibid.
40. Ibid.
41. Roosevelt, *Autobiography of Theodore Roosevelt,* 52.
42. Hagedorn, Research Notes. J. C. Fisher interview.
43. McCullough, *Mornings on Horseback,* 320.
44. Dale Walker, *The Boys of '98: Theodore Roosevelt and the Rough Riders* (New York: Tom Doherty Associates, 1998), 67.
45. Di Silvestro, *Theodore Roosevelt in the Badlands,* 167.
46. Hagedorn, Research Notes.
47. Di Silvestro, *Theodore Roosevelt in the Badlands,* 171.
48. Hagedorn, Research Notes.
49. Ibid.
50. Ibid.
51. Roosevelt, *Autobiography of Theodore Roosevelt,* 119.
52. Lincoln Lang, *Ranching with Roosevelt* (New York: J. B. Lippincott Co., 1926), 185.
53. Elting L. Morison and Theodore Roosevelt, *The Letters of Theodore Roosevelt,* vol. 1: *The Years of Preparation* (Cambridge, Mass.: Harvard University Press, 1951), 91.
54. Hagedorn, *Roosevelt in the Bad Lands* (Boston: Houghton Mifflin Co., 1921), 398.
55. Putnam, *Theodore Roosevelt: The Formative Years,* 526.
56. Hagedorn, Research Notes.
57. Putnam, *Theodore Roosevelt: The Formative Years,* 526.
58. Ibid., 527.
59. Ibid. Off in the distance, a gruff cowboy, in an effort to stay awake and comfort the cattle, could be heard singing a cowboy song, soft and low: "Roll on, roll on; roll on little dogies, roll on, roll on."
60. Hagedorn, Research Notes.
61. Putnam, *Theodore Roosevelt: The Formative Years,* 528.
62. Hagedorn, Research Notes.
63. Hagedorn, Research Notes; Hagedorn, *Roosevelt in the Bad Lands,* 417.

64. Hagedorn, Research Notes.
65. Hagedorn, Research Notes. Newspaper account, clipping, no date or title, probably from a local paper.
66. "Theodore Roosevelt-Cowboy and Ranchman," *Harper's Weekly* 48 (August 6th, 1904): 121.
67. Hagedorn, Research Notes.
68. Hagedorn, *Roosevelt in the Bad Lands*, 226.
69. Hagedorn, Research Notes.
70. Ibid.
71. William Thompson Dantz, "Tales of The Roosevelt Country," *McClure's Magazine* (May 1925).
72. Ibid.
73. Hagedorn, Research Notes.
74. Hagedorn, *Roosevelt in the Bad Lands*, 291.
75. Roosevelt, *Autobiography of Theodore Roosevelt*, 106.
76. Hagedorn, *Roosevelt in the Bad Lands*, 291.
77. Hagedorn, Research Notes.
78. Lang, *Ranching with Roosevelt*, 308.
79. Ibid., 154.
80. Ibid.
81. Ibid.
82. Hagedorn, Research Notes.
83. Ibid.
84. Putnam, *Theodore Roosevelt: The Formative Years*, 562.
85. Morris, *The Rise of Theodore Roosevelt*, 323.
86. Merrill E. Lewis, "History as Melodrama: Theodore Roosevelt's *The Winning of the West*," in *The American West: An Appraisal*, ed. R. G. Ferris (Santa Fe: Museum of New Mexico Press, 1963), 201–10 and 249–51
87. Morris, *The Rise of Theodore Roosevelt*, 323.
88. Hagedorn, *Roosevelt in the Bad Lands*, 291.
89. Morris, *The Rise of Theodore Roosevelt*, 324.
90. "Sheriff's Work on a Ranch," *Century Illustrated Monthly Magazine* 36 (1888): 44.
91. Theodore Roosevelt and Frederic Remington, *Ranch Life and the Hunting Trail* (New York: Dover Publications, 2009), 120.
92. Hagedorn, *Roosevelt in the Bad Lands*, 375.
93. Ibid., 377.
94. Roosevelt, *Ranch Life and the Hunting Trail*, 120.
95. Morris, *The Rise of Theodore Roosevelt*, 327.
96. "Sheriff's Work on a Ranch," 44.
97. Ibid., 47.
98. Morris, *The Rise of Theodore Roosevelt*, 328.
99. Roosevelt, *Ranch Life and the Hunting Trail*, 128.
100. McCullough, *Mornings on Horseback*, 348.

101. Hagedorn, Research Notes. How Roosevelt the Sheriff Outwitted the Thieves, Victor Hugo Stickney, M.D.

102. Samuels, *Teddy Roosevelt at San Juan Hill,* 52.

103. McCullough, *Mornings on Horseback,* 316.

104. Ibid.

105. Hagedorn, Research Notes. *Tribune,* July 28th, 1884.

106. Hagedorn, Research Notes.

107. "The American Experience: T.R. The Story of Theodore Roosevelt," Public Broadcasting Service (Aired October 6th and 7th, 1996).

108. Di Silvestro, *Theodore Roosevelt in the Badlands,* 217.

109. Morris, *The Rise of Theodore Roosevelt,* 348.

110. Ibid., 350.

111. Ibid.

112. Ibid., 348.

113. Ibid., 352.

114. Roosevelt Letter to Lodge, October 12th, 1886.

115. Morris, *The Rise of Theodore Roosevelt,* 349.

116. Ibid., 356.

117. Ibid., 357.

118. Ibid., 357.

119. Ibid., 358.

120. Morris, *The Rise of Theodore Roosevelt,* 365; Hagedorn, *Roosevelt in the Bad Lands,* 436.

121. Morris, *The Rise of Theodore Roosevelt,* 364.

122. Hagedorn, *Roosevelt in the Bad Lands,* 436.

123. Ibid., 436.

124. Morris, *The Rise of Theodore Roosevelt,* 65; Brands. *T.R.: The Last Romantic,* 225.

125. McCullough, *Mornings on Horseback,* 345.

126. Bush, George. "Remarks at an Environmental Agreement Signing Ceremony at the Grand Canyon, Arizona," September 18th, 1991.

127. Di Silvestro, *Theodore Roosevelt in the Badlands,* 175.

128. Putnam, *Theodore Roosevelt: The Formative Years,* 530.

129. Ibid., 529.

130. John Hamilton, *Theodore Roosevelt National Park* (Minnesota: ABDO Publishing Co, 2008), 5.

131. Theodore Roosevelt and William E. Leuchtenburg, *The New Nationalism* (New Jersey: Prentice-Hall, 1961), 106.

132. Hagedorn, Research Notes.

133. Morris, *The Rise of Theodore Roosevelt,* 15.

134. Di Silvestro, *Theodore Roosevelt in the Badlands,* 256.

135. Willis, *Roosevelt in the Rough,* 86.

136. Ibid., 87.

Chapter 11:
1. Di Silvestro, *Theodore Roosevelt in the Badlands*, 238
2. Hagedorn, Research Notes, McCullough, *Mornings on Horseback*, 278.
3. Morris, *The Rise of Theodore Roosevelt*, 372.
4. Dalton, *Theodore Roosevelt: A Strenuous Life*, 123.
5. Ibid.
6. Morris, *The Rise of Theodore Roosevelt*, 374.
7. Ibid., 375.
8. Lewis, *History as Melodrama*, 202; Morris, *The Rise of Theodore Roosevelt*, 388.
9. Zimmerman, *First Great Triumph*, 217.
10. Theodore Roosevelt, *The Winning of the West* (Nebraska: Bison Book, 1995), 207.
11. Roosevelt, *Winning of the West*, 374.
12. Dalton, *Theodore Roosevelt: A Strenuous Life*, 117
13. "Roosevelt's *The Winning of the West*," *Atlantic Monthly* 64 (1889): 694.
14. Theodore Roosevelt, *Literary Essays, National Edition* (New York: Charles Scribner's Sons, 1926), 247.
15. Daniel Ruddy, *Theodore Roosevelt's History of the United States: His Own Words, By Theodore Roosevelt* (New York: Smithsonian Books, 2010), xii.

Chapter 12:
1. Marion Miller, *Great Debates in American History: Revenue: the Tariff and Taxation, United States. Congress, Great Britain. Parliament* (Current Literature Publishing, 1913), 224.
2. Brands, *T.R.: The Last Romantic*, 219.
3. Ibid., 225.
4. Brands, *T.R.: The Last Romantic*, 224.
5. Ibid., 225.
6. Morris, *The Rise of Theodore Roosevelt*, 392.
7. Ibid.
8. Ibid.
9. Brands, *T.R.: The Last Romantic*, 219.
10. Ibid., 221.
11. Ibid.
12. Morris, *The Rise of Theodore Roosevelt*, 393.
13. Pringle, *Theodore Roosevelt: A Biography*, 85.
14. Morris, *The Rise of Theodore Roosevelt*, 401.
15. Ibid., 402.
16. Ibid.
17. Brands, *T.R.: The Last Romantic*, 223.
18. Ibid.
19. Morris, *The Rise of Theodore Roosevelt*, 402.

20. Brands, *T.R.: The Last Romantic*, 323.
21. Ibid., 224.
22. Pringle, *Theodore Roosevelt: A Biography*, 87.
23. Ibid.
24. Morris, *The Rise of Theodore Roosevelt*, 434.
25. Ibid.
26. Ibid.
27. Ibid., 435.
28. "The Whitewash in Baltimore: Maryland Reformers Will Try to Undo Wanamaker's Work," *The New York Times*, April 13th, 1892.
29. Ibid.
30. Morris, *The Rise of Theodore Roosevelt*, 435.
31. Ibid., 403.
32. Grondahl, *I Rose Like a Rocket*, 195.
33. Brands, *T.R.: The Last Romantic*, 224.
34. Grondahl, *I Rose Like a Rocket*, 195.
35. Pringle, *Theodore Roosevelt: A Biography*, 86.
36. Morris, *The Rise of Theodore Roosevelt*, 435.
37. Ibid., 443.
38. Ibid., 452.
39. Ibid., 453.
40. Brands, *T.R.: The Last Romantic*, 253.
41. Ibid.
42. Dalton, *Theodore Roosevelt: A Strenuous Life*, 133.
43. Ibid., 139.
44. Ibid.
45. Brands. *T.R.: The Last Romantic*, 227.
46. Pringle, *Theodore Roosevelt: A Biography*, 90.
47. Brands, *T.R.: The Last Romantic*, 230.
48. Zimmerman, *First Great Triumph*, 102.
49. Ibid.
50. Morris, *The Rise of Theodore Roosevelt*, 424.
51. Dalton, *Theodore Roosevelt: A Strenuous Life*, 84.
52. Morris, *The Rise of Theodore Roosevelt*, 424.
53. Brands, *T.R.: The Last Romantic*, 236.
54. Ibid.
55. Morris, *The Rise of Theodore Roosevelt*, 473.
56. Brands. *T.R.: The Last Romantic*, 266.
57. Morris, *The Rise of Theodore Roosevelt*, 473.
58. Ibid., 475.
59. Dalton, *Theodore Roosevelt: A Strenuous Life*, 147.
60. Morris, *The Rise of Theodore Roosevelt*, 475.
61. Dalton, *Theodore Roosevelt: A Strenuous Life*, 148.

62. Morris, *The Rise of Theodore Roosevelt*, 475.

63. Ibid.

64. Morison, *The Letters of Theodore Roosevelt*.

65. Ibid.

66. Paul Jeffers, *Commissioner Roosevelt: The Story of Theodore Roosevelt and the New York City Police, 1895–1897* (New York: John Wiley & Sons, 1994), 54.

67. Ibid.

68. Ibid., 50.

69. Ibid., 54.

70. Ibid., 63.

71. Ibid., 60.

72. Morris, *The Rise of Theodore Roosevelt*, 477.

73. Ibid., 478.

74. *The Civil Service Chronicle* 2 (1895): 223.

75. Morris, *The Rise of Theodore Roosevelt*, 820.

76. Richard White, *Theodore Roosevelt as Civil Service Commissioner: Linking the Influence and Development of a Modern Administrative President* (Administrative Theory & Praxis, 2000 — JSTOR) and Morris, *The Rise of Theodore Roosevelt*, 478.

77. "Our Mission, Role & History, Theodore Roosevelt," accessed September 20th, 2013, http://www.opm.gov/about-us/our-mission-role-history/theodore-roosevelt/

78. Morris, *The Rise of Theodore Roosevelt*, 423.

Chapter 13:

1. Jeffers, *Commissioner Roosevelt*, 73.

2. Morris, *The Rise of Theodore Roosevelt*, 485.

3. Ibid., 481.

4. Jeffers, *Commissioner Roosevelt*, 67.

5. Morris, *The Rise of Theodore Roosevelt*, 483. *New York Evening Post*, May 6th, 1895.

6. Morris, *The Rise of Theodore Roosevelt*, 483.

7. Burns, *The Three Roosevelts*, 41.

8. Jeffers, *Commissioner Roosevelt*, 71.

9. Morris, *The Rise of Theodore Roosevelt*, 481.

10. H. W. Brands, *The Selected Letters of Theodore Roosevelt* (New York: Cooper Square Press, 2001), 104; Morris, *The Rise of Theodore Roosevelt*, 491.

11. Morris, *The Rise of Theodore Roosevelt*, 482.

12. Jeffers, *Commissioner Roosevelt*, 99.

13. Roosevelt, *Autobiography of Theodore Roosevelt*, 171.

14. Morris, *The Rise of Theodore Roosevelt*, 487.

15. Jeffers, *Commissioner Roosevelt*, 72.

16. Dalton, *Theodore Roosevelt: A Strenuous Life*, 149.
17. Pringle, *Theodore Roosevelt: A Biography*, 96.
18. Jeffers, *Commissioner Roosevelt*, 82.
19. Ibid., 82.
20. Ibid., 83.
21. Ibid., 84.
22. Ibid., 93.
23. Ibid.
24. Morris, *The Rise of Theodore Roosevelt*, 492.
25. Ibid.
26. Ibid.
27. Ibid.
28. Jeffers, *Commissioner Roosevelt*, 69.
29. Lorant, *The Life and Times of Theodore Roosevelt*, 269.
30. Morris, *The Rise of Theodore Roosevelt*, 492.
31. Ibid., 493.
32. Ibid.
33. Ibid.
34. Richard Zacks, *Island of Vice: Theodore Roosevelt's Quest to Clean up Sin-loving New York* (New York: Anchor, 2012), 96.
35. Ibid., 97.
36. Ibid.
37. Burns and Dunn, *The Three Roosevelts*, 42.
38. Morris, *The Rise of Theodore Roosevelt*, 493.
39. Ibid., 494.
40. Morris, *The Rise of Theodore Roosevelt*, 494.
41. Morris, *The Rise of Theodore Roosevelt*, 494.
42. Burns and Dunn, *The Three Roosevelts*, 42.
43. Brands, *T.R.: The Last Romantic*, 280.
44. Samuels, *Teddy Roosevelt at San Juan Hill*, 93.
45. Hagedorn, *The Boys' Life of Theodore Roosevelt*, 173.
46. Zacks, *Island of Vice*, 157.
47. Noel Busch, *T.R.: The Story of Theodore Roosevelt and His Influence on Our Times* (New York: Reynal & Company, 1963), 99.
48. Morris, *The Rise of Theodore Roosevelt*, 511.
49. Pringle, *Theodore Roosevelt: A Biography*, 94; Jeffers, *Commissioner Roosevelt*, 41.
50. Roosevelt, *Autobiography of Theodore Roosevelt*, 194.
51. Ibid., 172.
52. Dalton, *Theodore Roosevelt: A Strenuous Life*, 152.
53. Burns and Dunn, *The Three Roosevelts*, 44.
54. Roosevelt, *Autobiography of Theodore Roosevelt*, 177.
55. Burns and Dunn, *The Three Roosevelts*, 41.

56. Ibid.; Jeffers, *Commissioner Roosevelt*, 71.
57. Dalton, *Theodore Roosevelt: A Strenuous Life*, 152.
58. Roosevelt, *Autobiography of Theodore Roosevelt*, 186.
59. Ibid., 187.
60. Hagedorn, Research Notes.
61. Grondahl, *I Rose Like a Rocket*, 233, and Pringle, *Theodore Roosevelt: A Biography*, 98.
62. Grondahl, *I Rose Like a Rocket*, 215.
63. Burns and Dunn, *The Three Roosevelts*, 44.
64. Jeffers, *Commissioner Roosevelt*, 129.
65. Grondahl, *I Rose Like a Rocket*, 224.
66. Burns and Dunn, *The Three Roosevelts*, 44.
67. Morris, *The Rise of Theodore Roosevelt*, 511.
68. Ibid., 512.
69. Ibid.
70. Hagedorn, *The Boys' Life of Theodore Roosevelt*, 171.
71. Pringle, *Theodore Roosevelt: A Biography*, 100.
72. Morris, *The Rise of Theodore Roosevelt*, 513.
73. Ibid., 512.
74. Ibid., 497.
75. Roosevelt, *Autobiography of Theodore Roosevelt*, 189.
76. Ibid., 191.
77. Dalton, *Theodore Roosevelt: A Strenuous Life*, 153.
78. Roosevelt, *Autobiography of Theodore Roosevelt*, 191.
79. Morris, *The Rise of Theodore Roosevelt*, 513.
80. Ibid., 530.
81. Ibid., 522.
82. Ibid.
83. Ibid., 526.
84. Busch, *The Story of Theodore Roosevelt and His Influence on Our Times*, 106.
85. Ibid., 106.
86. Pringle, *Theodore Roosevelt: A Biography*, 102.
87. Ibid.
88. Ibid.
89. Morris, *The Rise of Theodore Roosevelt*, 529.
90. Ibid., 527.
91. Ibid., 514.
92. Zimmerman, *First Great Triumph*, 228.
93. Burns and Dunn, *The Three Roosevelts*, 45.
94. Ibid., 46.
95. Morris, *The Rise of Theodore Roosevelt*, 552.
96. Ibid., 553.

97. Morris, *The Rise of Theodore Roosevelt*, 540. Morris discovered Theodore's naval actions.

98. Busch, *The Story of Theodore Roosevelt*, 111.

99. Burns and Dunn, *The Three Roosevelts*, 42.

100. Theodore Roosevelt *The Works of Theodore Roosevelt: American Ideals, with a Biographical Sketch by F. V. Greene. Administration–Civil Service* (New York: P. F. Collier, 1897), 54.

101. Morris, *The Rise of Theodore Roosevelt*, 514.

Chapter 14:

1. Pringle, *Theodore Roosevelt: A Biography*, 115.

2. John Lawrence Tone, *War and Genocide in Cuba, 1895–1898* (North Carolina: University of North Carolina Press, 2006), 209.

3. H. W. Brands, *The Reckless Decade: America in the 1890s* (New York: St. Martin's, 1995), 316.

4. Roosevelt, *Autobiography of Theodore Roosevelt*, 209.

5. Dalton, *Theodore Roosevelt: A Strenuous Life*, 165.

6. Zimmerman, *First Great Triumph*, 25.

7. Ibid.

8. Ibid.

9. This phenomenon is pointed out in Hargreaves, "The Richest Americans in History," and Zimmerman, *First Great Triumph*, 25

10. Zimmerman, *First Great Triumph*, 25.

11. Grondahl, *I Rose Like a Rocket*, 244.

12. Brands, *The Selected Letters of Theodore Roosevelt*, 126. Letter to Anna Roosevelt Cowles, January 2nd, 1897, Oyster Bay.

13. William McKinley Inaugural Address, March 4th, 1887.

14. Zimmerman, *First Great Triumph*, 252.

15. Ibid., 253.

16. Brands, *T.R.: The Last Romantic*, 304.

17. Morris, *The Rise of Theodore Roosevelt*, 555.

18. Brands, *T.R.: The Last Romantic*, 304.

19. Morris, *The Rise of Theodore Roosevelt*, 556.

20. Lorant, *The Life and Times of Theodore Roosevelt*, 284.

21. Ibid.

22. Paul Jeffers, *Colonel Roosevelt: Theodore Roosevelt Goes to War, 1897–1898* (New York: John Wiley & Sons, 1996), 31; Morris, *The Rise of Theodore Roosevelt*, 560.

23. Jeffers, *Colonel Roosevelt*, 31.

24. Morris, *The Rise of Theodore Roosevelt*, 560; Lorant, *The Life and Times of Theodore Roosevelt*, 284.

25. Ibid., 560.

26. Bishop, *Theodore Roosevelt and His Time Shown in His Own Letters*, 73.

27. Morris, *The Rise of Theodore Roosevelt*, 566.
28. Walker, *The Boys of '98*, 76.
29. Jeffers, *Colonel Roosevelt*, 31.
30. Brands, *The Selected Letters of Theodore Roosevelt*, 129.
31. Thomas, *The War Lovers*, 170; "About the Club," accessed August 2nd, 2014, http://www.metroclub.com/About-The-Club.aspx
32. Jeffers, *Colonel Roosevelt*, 3.
33. Ibid., 33.
34. Ibid., 34.
35. G. J. A. O'Toole, *The Spanish War: An American Epic 1898* (New York: W. W. Norton & Company, 1984), 97.
36. Charles West Stewart, *John Paul Jones: Commemoration at Annapolis* (Washington: Government Printing Office, 1907).
37. Thomas, *The War Lovers*, 172.
38. Theodore Roosevelt, War College Speech, June 2nd, 1897.
39. George Washington's First Annual Message to Congress, January 8th, 1790.
40. Zimmerman, *First Great Triumph*, 239.
41. Bishop, *Theodore Roosevelt and His Time Shown in His Own Letters*, 77.
42. Ibid.
43. Ibid.
44. Morris, *The Rise of Theodore Roosevelt*, 571.
45. Ibid.
46. Theodore Roosevelt, War College Speech, June 2nd, 1897.
47. Thomas, *The War Lovers*, 173.
48. Jeffers, *Colonel Roosevelt*, 33.
49. Ibid.
50. Dalton, *Theodore Roosevelt: A Strenuous Life*, 165.
51. Jeffers, *Colonel Roosevelt*, 40.
52. Morris, *The Rise of Theodore Roosevelt*, 575.
53. Ibid., 580.
54. Jeffers, *Colonel Roosevelt*, 38.
55. Ibid. Jeffers made this connection.
56. Morris, *The Rise of Theodore Roosevelt*, 579.
57. Jeffers, *Colonel Roosevelt*, 42.
58. Thomas, *The War Lovers*, 175.
59. Jeffers, *Colonel Roosevelt*, 42. This quote is from TR's first visit aboard the Iowa, earlier that summer.
60. Thomas, *The War Lovers*, 149.
61. Jeffers, *Colonel Roosevelt*, 45.
62. Thomas, *The War Lovers*, 176.
63. Jeffers, *Colonel Roosevelt*, 49.
64. Morris, *The Rise of Theodore Roosevelt*, 586.

65. Michael Golay, *The Spanish-American War* (New York: Facts on File, 1995), 32.
66. Jeffers, *Colonel Roosevelt*, 58.
67. Morris, *The Rise of Theodore Roosevelt*, 587.
68. Ibid.
69. Ibid.
70. Ibid.
71. Roosevelt, *Autobiography of Theodore Roosevelt*, 212.
72. Morris, *The Rise of Theodore Roosevelt*, 587.
73. Roosevelt, *Autobiography of Theodore Roosevelt*, 211.
74. Burns and Dunn, *The Three Roosevelts*, 47.
75. Gerald R. Anderson, *Subic Bay: From Magellan to Mt. Pinatubo: The History of the U.S. Naval Station, Subic Bay* (Dagupan City: Lazer, 1991), 192.
76. Morris, *The Rise of Theodore Roosevelt*, 589.
77. Thomas, *The War Lovers*, 153.
78. Ibid., 93.
79. Ibid., 94.
80. Ibid., 96.
81. Ibid., 97.
82. Jeffers, *Colonel Roosevelt*, 83.
83. Thomas, *The War Lovers*, 180.
84. John Britton, *Cables, Crises, and the Press: The Geopolitics of the New Information System in the Americas, 1866–1903* (New Mexico: University of New Mexico, 2013), 195.
85. Thomas, *The War Lovers*, 180.
86. Ibid., 180.
87. Ibid., 180.
88. Ibid., 181.
89. Brands, *T.R.: The Last Romantic*, 324.
90. Hagedorn, Research Notes.
91. Dalton, *Theodore Roosevelt: A Strenuous Life*, 169.
92. Thomas, *The War Lovers*, 197.
93. Ibid., 197.
94. Morris, *The Rise of Theodore Roosevelt*, 594.
95. Ibid.; John D. Long, Journal, January 13th, 1898.
96. Thomas, *The War Lovers*, 24. John D. Long, Journal, January 13th, 1898.
97. John D. Long, Journal, January 13th, 1898.
98. Samuels, *Teddy Roosevelt at San Juan Hill*, 115.
99. John C. Reilly and Robert L. Scheina, *American Battleships 1886—1923: Predreadnought Design and Construction* (Maryland: Naval Institute Press, 1980), 26–28, 37.; Army Corps of Engineers, *Final Report on Removing Wreck of Battleship "Maine" from Harbor of Habana, Cuba* (Washington, D.C.: U.S. Government Printing Office, 1914), 1.

100. Pringle, *Theodore Roosevelt: A Biography*, 123.
101. Morris, *The Rise of Theodore Roosevelt*, 596.
102. Ibid.
103. Ibid.
104. Thomas, *The War Lovers*, 199.
105. Pringle, *Theodore Roosevelt: A Biography*, 122.
106. Thomas, *The War Lovers*, 204.
107. O'Toole, *The Spanish War*, 34.

Chapter 15:
1.   Surgeon General of the United States Navy, *Annual Report 1898*, 173.
2.   O'Toole, *The Spanish War*, 21.
3.   Ibid., 29.
4.   Ibid., 28.
5.   Ibid., 30.
6.   Jeffers, *Colonel Roosevelt*, 108.
7.   Ibid.
8.   Thomas, *The War Lovers*, 207.
9.   Jeffers, *Colonel Roosevelt*, 108.
10. O'Toole, *The Spanish American War*, 30.
11. *Annual Report 1898*, Surgeon General of the United States Navy: 173
12. Jeffers, *Colonel Roosevelt*, 103.
13. O'Toole, *The Spanish American War*, 31.
14. Ibid., 34.
15. Ibid.
16. Ibid.
17. Morris, *The Rise of Theodore Roosevelt*, 599.
18. O'Toole, *The Spanish War*, 33.
19. Jeffers, *Colonel Roosevelt*, 112.
20. Pringle, *Theodore Roosevelt: A Biography*, 124.
21. Ibid.
22. Thomas, *The War Lovers*, 209.
23. Ibid., 210.
24. Ibid., 209.
25. O'Toole, *The Spanish American War*, 125.
26. Pringle, *Theodore Roosevelt: A Biography*, 124.
27. Thomas, *The War Lovers*, 20, via *Washington Star*, February 16th, 1898.
28. O'Toole, *The Spanish War*, 129.
29. Thomas, *The War Lovers*, 216.
30. Morris, *The Rise of Theodore Roosevelt*, 602.
31. Jeffers, *Colonel Roosevelt*, 121.
32. Harvey C. Mansfield, *Manliness* (Connecticut: Yale University Press, 2006), 97.
33. Zimmerman, *First Great Triumph*, 243.

34. Ibid., 244.
35. Ibid.
36. Jeffers, *Colonel Roosevelt*, 122.
37. Lorant, *The Life and Times of Theodore Roosevelt*, 290.
38. Morris, *The Rise of Theodore Roosevelt*, 603.
39. Jeffers, *Colonel Roosevelt*, 122.
40. Ibid.
41. Thomas, *The War Lovers*, 219. Surgery was on March 5th, 1898.
42. Dalton, *Theodore Roosevelt: A Strenuous Life*, 170.
43. Charles Sigsbee and Thomas Watson Ball, *The "Maine": An Account of Her Destruction in Havana Harbor* (New York: The Century Co., 1899.
44. Ibid.
45. Morris, *The Rise of Theodore Roosevelt*, 608.
46. O'Toole, *The Spanish War*, 169.
47. Ibid., 171.
48. Morris, *The Rise of Theodore Roosevelt*, 612.
49. Jeffers, *Colonel Roosevelt*, 141.
50. Jeffers, *Colonel Roosevelt*, 142; Zimmerman, *First Great Triumph*, 269.
51. Jeffers, *Colonel Roosevelt*, 142.
52. Samuel Etinde Crompton, *The Sinking of the USS Maine: Declaring War Against Spain* (New York: Chelsea House, 2009), 63.
53. Zimmerman, *First Great Triumph*, 270.
54. Ibid.
55. Morris, *The Rise of Theodore Roosevelt*, 613.
56. Ibid.
57. Roosevelt, *Autobiography of Theodore Roosevelt*, 218.
58. Ibid.
59. Ibid.
60. Ibid.
61. Lorant, *The Life and Times of Theodore Roosevelt*, 294.
62. O'Toole, *The Spanish War*, 195; Lorant, *The Life and Times of Theodore Roosevelt*, 293.
63. Lorant, *The Life and Times of Theodore Roosevelt*, 294.
64. Hagedorn, Research Notes.

Chapter 16:
1. Edward Marshall, *The Story of the Rough Riders* (New York: G. W. Dillingham Co., 1899), xi.
2. Ibid., xi.
3. Walker, *The Boys of '98*, 88.
4. Jones, *Roosevelt's Rough Riders*, 20.
5. Theodore Roosevelt, *The Rough Riders* (New York: The Library of America, 2004), 15.
6. Marshall, *The Story of the Rough Riders*, 22.

7. Ibid.

8. Hagedorn, Research Notes.

9. Samuels, *Teddy Roosevelt at San Juan Hill,* 14.

10. David Key, "Theodore Roosevelt, The Rough Riders, and the Alteration of Myth," *Journal of the West* 37, no. 2 (April 1998): 71.

11. Ibid., 71.

12. Ibid., 72.

13. C. M. Barnes, *Report of the Governor of Oklahoma to the Secretary of the Interior for the Fiscal Year Ended June 30th, 1898.* (Washington: Government Printing Office, 1898).

14. Ibid.

15. Clifford Westermeier, *Who Rush to Glory* (Idaho: Caxton Printers, 1958), 54.

16. *Bureau of the Census Report. Arizona Population of Counties by Decennial Census: 1900 to 1990.* Compiled and edited by Richard Forstall Population Division (Washington: US Bureau of the Census, 1996).

17. Jeffers, *Colonel Roosevelt,* 136.

18. Walker, *The Boys of '98,* 98.

19. O'Toole, *The Spanish War,* 196.

20. Walker, *The Boys of '98,* 98.

21. Jones, *Roosevelt's Rough Riders,* 18.

22. Ibid., 18.

23. O'Toole, *The Spanish War,* 196.

24. *New York Sun,* May 8th, 1898.

25. David King, *New Orleans* (Connecticut: Twenty-First Century, 1998), 63.

26. Roosevelt, *The Rough Riders,* 31.

27. Ibid., 25.

28. O'Toole, *The Spanish War,* 197.

29. Ibid.

30. Lorant, *The Life and Times of Theodore Roosevelt,* 292; Roosevelt, *Autobiography of Theodore Roosevelt,* 204.

31. Roosevelt, *The Rough Riders,* 18.

32. Samuels, *Teddy Roosevelt at San Juan Hill,* 14.

33. Tom Hall, *The Fun and Fighting of the Rough Riders* (New York: Stokes Co., 1899), 9.

34. Walker, *The Boys of '98,* 108.

35. Ibid.; Samuels, *Teddy Roosevelt at San Juan Hill,* 15.

36. Samuels, *Teddy Roosevelt at San Juan Hill,* 15.

37. Ibid.

38. Jones, *Roosevelt's Rough Riders,* 21.

39. Marshall, *The Story of the Rough Riders,* 20.

40. Samuels, *Teddy Roosevelt at San Juan Hill,* 15.

41. Jeffers, *Colonel Roosevelt,* 164.

42. Hagedorn, Research Notes.

43. Walker, *The Boys of '98*, 101.

44. Mitchell Newton-Matza, *Disasters and Tragic Events: An Encyclopedia of Catastrophes in American History* (California: ABC-CLIO, 2014), 40.

45. Jim Donovan, *The Blood of Heroes: The 13-day Struggle for the Alamo–and the Sacrifice That Forged a Nation* (New York: Little, Brown, 2012), 318.

46. Philip Haythornthwaite, *The Alamo and the War of Texan Independence 1835–36* (London: Osprey, 1986), 22.

47. Jones, *Roosevelt's Rough Riders*, 30.

48. Jones, *Roosevelt's Rough Riders*, 23; Marshall, *The Story of the Rough Riders*, 23.

49. Walker, *The Boys of '98*, 92.

50. Ibid.

51. Jones, *Roosevelt's Rough Riders*, 24; Hagedorn, Research Notes.

52. Jones, *Roosevelt's Rough Riders*, 24.

53. Key, *Theodore Roosevelt, The Rough Riders, and the Alteration of Myth*, 70-79

54. Jones, *Roosevelt's Rough Riders*, 24; Dale Walker, *Death Was the Black Horse: The Story of Rough Rider Buckey O'Neill* (Texas: Madrona, 1975), 113.

55. Marshall, *The Story of the Rough Riders*, 23.

56. Walker, *The Boys of '98*, 92.

57. Marshall, *The Story of the Rough Riders*, 23.

58. Westermeier, *Who Rush to Glory*, 57.

59. Hagedorn, Research Notes.

60. Westermeier, *Who Rush to Glory*, 57.

61. Ibid., 60.

62. Jones, *Roosevelt's Rough Riders*, 26.

63. Ibid.; Allen P. Bristow, *Whispering Smith: His Life and Misadventures* (New Mexico: Sunstone, 2007), 51.

64. Jeffers, *Colonel Roosevelt*, 166.

65. Jones, *Roosevelt's Rough Riders*, 26.

66. Ibid., 21.

67. Ibid.

68. Walker, *The Boys of '98*, 93.

69. Westermeier, *Who Rush to Glory*, 58. The newspaper article is about Oklahoma Troopers but the Indian Troopers who arrived on May 17th were equally subdued in their departure.

70. Roosevelt, *The Rough Riders*, 24.

71. Ibid.

72. Ibid., 26.

73. Jones, *Roosevelt's Rough Riders*, 27.

74. Samuels, *Teddy Roosevelt at San Juan Hill*, 18.

75. Jones, *Roosevelt's Rough Riders*, 28.

76. O'Toole, *The Spanish War*, 195.
77. Walker, *The Boys of '98*, 109.
78. Jones, *Roosevelt's Rough Riders*, 62; Marshall, *The Story of the Rough Riders*, 29.
79. Jones, *Roosevelt's Rough Riders*, 27, 62; Marshall, *The Story of the Rough Riders*, 28, 44; Walker, *The Boys of '98*, 109.
80. Jones, *Roosevelt's Rough Riders*, 27, 62; Marshall, *The Story of the Rough Riders*, 28; Walker, *The Boys of '98*, 109; Hall, *The Fun and Fighting of the Rough Riders*, 74.
81. Jones, *Roosevelt's Rough Riders*, 27.
82. Roosevelt, *The Rough Riders*, 18.
83. Jeffers, *Colonel Roosevelt*, 152; Samuels, *Teddy Roosevelt at San Juan Hill*, 19.
84. Samuels, *Teddy Roosevelt at San Juan Hill*, 19.
85. Jones, *Roosevelt's Rough Riders*, 29.
86. Hall, *The Fun and Fighting of the Rough Riders*, 9.
87. Jeffers, *Colonel Roosevelt*, 156.
88. Ibid.
89. Ibid., 157.
90. Marshall, *The Story of the Rough Riders*, 27.
91. Jeffers, *Colonel Roosevelt*, 147; Walker, *The Boys of '98*, 102.
92. Jeffers, *Colonel Roosevelt*, 151.
93. Roosevelt, *The Rough Riders*, 20.
94. Walker, *The Boys of '98*, 103.
95. Samuels, *Teddy Roosevelt at San Juan Hill*, 23.
96. Allyn Capron and the Indian contingent had not arrived until the 17th; however, several Native Americans from the other territories had already arrived.
97. Stephen Hess, *America's Political Dynasties from Adams to Kennedy* (New York: Doubleday, 1966), 83.
98. Hagedorn, Research Notes.
99. Ibid.
100. Jones, *Roosevelt's Rough Riders*, 39; Roosevelt, *The Rough Riders*, 28, Mr. Smith comes from Roosevelt, *The Rough Riders*, 41.
101. Jones, *Roosevelt's Rough Riders*, 342; Hagedorn, Research Notes.
102. Walker, *The Boys of '98*, 119.
103. Hagedorn, Research Notes.
104. Walker, *The Boys of '98*, 119.
105. Roosevelt, *The Rough Riders*, 25; Walker, *The Boys of '98*, 111; Hagedorn, Research Notes; Jones, *Roosevelt's Rough Riders*, 27, 39; Hall, *The Fun and Fighting of the Rough Riders*, 32; Morris, *The Rise of Theodore Roosevelt*, 674.
106. Hall, *The Fun and Fighting of the Rough Riders*, 32.
107. Roosevelt, *The Rough Riders*, 170; Hagedorn, Research Notes.
108. Jones, *Roosevelt's Rough Riders*, 8.

109. Hagedorn, Research Notes.
110. Ibid.
111. Samuels, *Teddy Roosevelt at San Juan Hill,* 36.
112. Ibid., 34.
113. Hagedorn, Research Notes.
114. Samuels, *Teddy Roosevelt at San Juan Hill,* 20.
115. Hagedorn, Research Notes.
116. Ibid.
117. Ibid.
118. Samuels, *Teddy Roosevelt at San Juan Hill,* 31.
119. Hagedorn, Research Notes.
120. Walker, *The Boys of '98,* 118.
121. Theodore Roosevelt Letter to Ted, White House, Oct. 4, 1903.

Chapter 17:
1. Samuels, *Teddy Roosevelt at San Juan Hill,* 33.
2. Jones, *Roosevelt's Rough Riders,* 35.
3. Hagedorn, Research Notes.
4. Samuels, *Teddy Roosevelt at San Juan Hill,* 35.
5. Hagedorn, Research Notes.
6. Samuels, *Teddy Roosevelt at San Juan Hill,* 35.
7. Hagedorn, Research Notes.
8. Ibid.
9. Walker, *The Boys of '98,* 127.
10. Roosevelt, *The Rough Riders,* 33.
11. Hagedorn, Research Notes.
12. Ibid.
13. Hall, *The Fun and Fighting of the Rough Riders,* 16.
14. Hagedorn, Research Notes.
15. Morris, *The Rise of Theodore Roosevelt,* 620–622.
16. Hagedorn, Research Notes.
17. Hagedorn, Research Notes; Morris, *The Rise of Theodore Roosevelt,* 622.
18. Morris, *The Rise of Theodore Roosevelt,* 622.
19. Hall, *The Fun and Fighting of the Rough Riders,* 19.
20. Hagedorn, Research Notes.
21. Walker, *The Boys of '98,* 123.
22. Hall, *The Fun and Fighting of the Rough Riders, 19.*
23. *New York Times,* October 7th, 1898.
24. Hagedorn, Research Notes.
25. Ibid.
26. Jones, *Roosevelt's Rough Riders,* 40.
27. Samuels, *Teddy Roosevelt at San Juan Hill,* 37.
28. Marshall, *The Story of the Rough Riders,* 35.

29. Jeffers, *Colonel Roosevelt*, 174.
30. Jones, *Roosevelt's Rough Riders*, 40.
31. Roosevelt, *The Rough Riders*, 34.
32. Hagedorn, Research Notes.
33. Ibid. The 'first encounter' actually was the war games but the quote is included here during the mounting stage.
34. Hagedorn, Research Notes.
35. Ibid.
36. Ibid.
37. Ibid.
38. Ibid.
39. Ibid.
40. Ibid., *New York Times*, November 11th, 1899.
41. Ibid., *New York Times*, November 11th, 1899.
42. Ibid.
43. Ibid.
44. Ibid.
45. Ibid.
46. Ibid.
47. Walker, *The Boys of '98*, 113.
48. Hagedorn, Research Notes.
49. Ibid.
50. Ibid.
51. Ibid.
52. Jones, *Roosevelt's Rough Riders*, 35.
53. Ibid., 34.
54. Hagedorn, Research Notes.
55. Ibid.
56. Marshall, *The Story of the Rough Riders*, 56.
57. Hagedorn, Research Notes.
58. Walker, *The Boys of '98*, 131.
59. Jeffers, *Colonel Roosevelt*, 198.
60. Hagedorn, Research Notes. This event takes place on May 17th.
61. Ibid.
62. Ibid.
63. Ibid.
64. Ibid.
65. Ibid.
66. Samuels, *Teddy Roosevelt at San Juan Hill*, 39.
67. Ibid., 39.
68. Hagedorn, Research Notes.
69. Ibid.
70. Jeffers, *Colonel Roosevelt*, 164–165; Brands, *T.R.: The Last Romantic*, 341; Morris, *The Rise of Theodore Roosevelt*, 624.

71. Roosevelt, The Rough Riders, 182.
72. Ibid., 37.
73. Hagedorn, Research Notes. *New York Times,* November 11th, 1899.
74. Ibid.
75. Marshall, *The Story of the Rough Riders,* 44.
76. Hagedorn, Research Notes.
77. Marshall, *The Story of the Rough Riders,* 44.
78. Ibid.
79. Ibid.
80. Samuels, *Teddy Roosevelt at San Juan Hill,* 38.
81. Westermeier, *Who Rush to Glory,* 77.
82. Marshall, *The Story of the Rough Riders,* 47.
83. Westermeier, *Who Rush to Glory,* 77.
84. Marshall, *The Story of the Rough Riders,* 47.
85. Walker, *The Boys of '98,* 128.
86. Jones, *Roosevelt's Rough Riders,* 42.
87. Ibid., 42.
88. Walker, *The Boys of '98,* 129.
89. Samuels, *Teddy Roosevelt at San Juan Hill,* 46.
90. Jones, *Roosevelt's Rough Riders,* 43.
91. Ibid., 43.
92. Ibid., 45.
93. Roosevelt gave this speech on May 28th, 1898.
94. Hagedorn, Research Notes.
95. Jones, *Roosevelt's Rough Riders,* 43.
96. Jeffers, *Colonel Roosevelt,* 183.
97. Ibid.
98. Jones, *Roosevelt's Rough Riders,* 44; Hagedorn, Research Notes.
99. Samuels, *Teddy Roosevelt at San Juan Hill,* 58.
100. Walker, *The Boys of '98,* 131.

Chapter 18:
1.   Hagedorn, Research Notes, Note: newspaper clippings.
2.   Samuels, *Teddy Roosevelt at San Juan Hill,* 59.
3.   Hagedorn, Research Notes, Note: Frank Hayes interview.
4.   Ibid.
5.   Ibid.
6.   Ibid.
7.   Ibid.
8.   Samuels, *Teddy Roosevelt at San Juan Hill,* 60.
9.   Hagedorn, Research Notes.
10. Ibid.
11. Cosby, *A Rough Rider Looks Back,* 47.
12. Jones, *Roosevelt's Rough Riders,* 50.

13. Ibid., 50.
14. Ibid., 51.
15. Walker, *The Boys of '98*, 97.
16. Walker, *The Boys of '98*, 98; Jones, *Roosevelt's Rough Riders*, 22; Hagedorn, Research Notes.
17. Samuels, *Teddy Roosevelt at San Juan Hill*, 56.
18. Ibid.
19. Roosevelt, *The Rough Riders*, 47.
20. Westermeier, *Who Rush to Glory*, 171.
21. Morris, *The Rise of Theodore Roosevelt*, 627.
22. Roosevelt, *The Rough Riders*, 47.
23. Cosby, *A Rough Rider Looks Back*, 50.
24. Hall, *The Fun and Fighting of the Rough Riders*, 83.
25. Hagedorn, Research Notes. *New York Sun* account of Rough Riders in camp.
26. Samuels, *Teddy Roosevelt at San Juan Hill*, 65.
27. Roosevelt, *The Rough Riders*, 48.
28. Walker, *The Boys of '98*, 136.
29. Cosby, *A Rough Rider Looks Back*, 53.
30. Samuels, *Teddy Roosevelt at San Juan Hill*, 66.
31. Ibid.
32. Hagedorn, Research Notes.
33. Jones, *Roosevelt's Rough Riders*, 65.
34. Ibid. Shafter's reply is actually in the same message. It is broken up for the sake of the story.
35. Roosevelt, *The Rough Riders*, 48.
36. Cosby, *A Rough Rider Looks Back*.
37. Roosevelt, *The Rough Riders*, 48.
38. Morris, *The Rise of Theodore Roosevelt*, 628.
39. Ibid.
40. Roosevelt, *The Rough Riders*, 50.
41. Jones, *Roosevelt's Rough Riders*, 64.
42. Ibid.
43. Roosevelt, *The Rough Riders*, 50.
44. Cosby, *A Rough Rider Looks Back*.
45. Samuels, *Teddy Roosevelt at San Juan Hill*, 79.
46. Thomas, *The War Lovers*, 282.
47. Roosevelt, *The Rough Riders*, 52.
48. Ibid.
49. Marshall, *The Story of the Rough Riders*, 56.
50. Hagedorn, Research Notes.
51. Jones, *Roosevelt's Rough Riders*, 68.
52. Samuels, *Teddy Roosevelt at San Juan Hill*, 75.

53. Roosevelt, *The Rough Riders,* 52.

54. Ibid.

55. Jones, *Roosevelt's Rough Riders,*70.

56. Hagedorn, Research Notes.

57. Jones, *Roosevelt's Rough Riders,* 71.

58. Ibid.

59. Greenville Dodge, et al. *Report of the Commission Appointed by the President to Investigate the Conduct of the War Department in the War with Spain,* vols. 5, 7 and 8 (Washington: Government Printing Office, 1900), 3403.

60. Samuels, *Teddy Roosevelt at San Juan Hill,* 80.

61. Hagedorn, Research Notes.

62. Jones, *Roosevelt's Rough Riders,*78.

63. French Chadwick, *The Relations of the United States and Spain: The Spanish-American War* (New York: Charles Scribner's Sons, 1911), 20.

64. Jones, *Roosevelt's Rough Riders,* 78, 73; Walker, *The Boys of '98,* 150; Chadwick, *The Relations of the United States and Spain,* 20. The original list is from the military tables, and is therefore not quoted.

65. Jones, *Roosevelt's Rough Riders,* 74.

66. Ibid.

67. Ibid.

68. Ibid., 75.

69. Walker, *The Boys of '98,* 149.

70. Roosevelt, *The Rough Riders,* 54.

71. Cosby, *A Rough Rider Looks Back,* 63; Marshall, *The Story of the Rough Riders,* 57.

72. Marshall, *The Story of the Rough Riders,* 57.

73. Roosevelt, *The Rough Riders,* 55.

74. Jones, *Roosevelt's Rough Riders,* 76.

75. Roosevelt, *The Rough Riders,* 54.

76. Samuels, *Teddy Roosevelt at San Juan Hill,* 86; Hagedorn, Research Notes.

77. Ibid.

78. Samuels, *Teddy Roosevelt at San Juan Hill,* 85.

79. Hagedorn, Research Notes.

80. Troopers made a dollar a day and meals were three dollars.

81. Hagedorn, Research Notes.

82. Ibid., 78.

83. Roosevelt, *Autobiography of Theodore Roosevelt,* 250.

84. Ibid., 251.

85. Jones, *Roosevelt's Rough Riders,* 78.

86. Ibid., 78.

Chapter 19:

1. Walker, *The Boys of '98,* 156.
2. Jeffers, *Colonel Roosevelt,* 197.
3. They arrived on the 20th and spent a day drifting.
4. Samuels, *Teddy Roosevelt at San Juan Hill,* 100.
5. Hagedorn, Research Notes.
6. Samuels, *Teddy Roosevelt at San Juan Hill,* 100.
7. Jones, *Roosevelt's Rough Riders,* 92.
8. Ibid.; Hagedorn, Research Notes.
9. Jones, *Roosevelt's Rough Riders,* 92.
10. Morris, *The Rise of Theodore Roosevelt,* 636.
11. Jones, *Roosevelt's Rough Riders,* 91.
12. Samuels, *Teddy Roosevelt at San Juan Hill,* 103.
13. Jones, *Roosevelt's Rough Riders,* 97.
14. Ibid., 98.
15. Samuels, *Teddy Roosevelt at San Juan Hill,* 102.
16. Morris, *The Rise of Theodore Roosevelt,* 637; Samuels, *Teddy Roosevelt at San Juan Hill,* 105.
17. Walker, *The Boys of '98,* 160.
18. Morris, *The Rise of Theodore Roosevelt,* 639.
19. Jeffers, *Colonel Roosevelt,* 206.
20. Morris, *The Rise of Theodore Roosevelt,* 638.
21. Cosby, *A Rough Rider Looks Back,* 76.
22. Samuels, *Teddy Roosevelt at San Juan Hill,* 105.
23. Jeffers, *Colonel Roosevelt,* 205.
24. Morris, *The Rise of Theodore Roosevelt,* 638.
25. Roosevelt, *The Rough Riders,* 65.
26. Marshall, *The Story of the Rough Riders,* 72.
27. Jones, *Roosevelt's Rough Riders,* 102.
28. Marshall, *The Story of the Rough Riders,* 69.
29. Walker, *The Boys of '98,* 164.
30. Marshall, *The Story of the Rough Riders,* 69.
31. Jones, *Roosevelt's Rough Riders,* 106.
32. Hagedorn, Research Notes.
33. Ibid.
34. Ibid.
35. Morris, *The Rise of Theodore Roosevelt,* 640.
36. Jones, *Roosevelt's Rough Riders,* 114.
37. Ibid.
38. Morris, *The Rise of Theodore Roosevelt,* 641.
39. Angus Konstam, *San Juan Hill 1898: America's Emergence as a World Power* (London: Praeger, 2004), 27.
40. Morris, *The Rise of Theodore Roosevelt,* 640.

Chapter 20:
1.   Morris, *The Rise of Theodore Roosevelt*, 642.
2.   Jones, *Roosevelt's Rough Riders*, 120.
3.   Hagedorn, Research Notes.
4.   Marshall, *The Story of the Rough Riders*, 91.
5.   Jones, *Roosevelt's Rough Riders*, 121.
6.   Roosevelt, *The Rough Riders*, 73.
7.   Morris, *The Rise of Theodore Roosevelt*, 642.
8.   Hall, *The Fun and Fighting of the Rough Riders*, 135.
9.   Hagedorn, Research Notes.
10. Roosevelt, *The Rough Riders*, 73.
11. Konstam, *San Juan Hill 1898*, 27.
12. Roosevelt, *The Rough Riders*, 73.
13. Hagedorn, Research Notes.
14. Marshall, *The Story of the Rough Riders*, 96.
15. Ibid., 99.
16. Marshall, *The Story of the Rough Riders;* Hagedorn, Research Notes.
17. Marshall, *The Story of the Rough Riders*, 100.
18. Ibid.
19. Walker, *The Boys of '98*, 174.
20. Roosevelt, *The Rough Riders*, 75.
21. Ibid.; Hagedorn, Research Notes.
22. Marshall, *The Story of the Rough Riders*, 105.
23. Ibid., 110.
24. Ibid., 119, 112.
25. O'Toole, *The Spanish War*, 275.
26. Young, 183; Morris, *The Rise of Theodore Roosevelt*, 643.
27. Morris, *The Rise of Theodore Roosevelt*, 643.
28. Roosevelt, *Autobiography of Theodore Roosevelt*, 236.
29. Ibid., 237–238.
30. Marshall, *The Story of the Rough Riders*, 104.
31. Roosevelt, *Autobiography of Theodore Roosevelt*, 236; Marshall, *The Story of the Rough Riders*, 104.
32. Marshall, *The Story of the Rough Riders*, 104.
33. Ibid.
34. Samuels, *Teddy Roosevelt at San Juan Hill*, 151.
35. Ibid., 152.
36. Hagedorn, Research Notes.
37. Roosevelt, *Autobiography of Theodore Roosevelt*, 237.
38. Morris, *The Rise of Theodore Roosevelt*, 644.
39. Ibid.
40. Roosevelt, *The Rough Riders*, 76.
41. Morris, *The Rise of Theodore Roosevelt*, 645; Roosevelt, *The Rough Riders*, 76.

42. Roosevelt, *Autobiography of Theodore Roosevelt*, 237.
43. Morris, *The Rise of Theodore Roosevelt*, 645.
44. Ibid.
45. Thomas, *The War Lovers*, 306.
46. Walker, *The Boys of '98*, 184.
47. Hagedorn, Research Notes.
48. Thomas, *The War Lovers*, 306.
49. Jeffers, *Colonel Roosevelt*, 219.
50. Ibid.
51. Marshall, *The Story of the Rough Riders*, 164.
52. Hagedorn, Research Notes.
53. Ibid.
54. Roosevelt, *Autobiography of Theodore Roosevelt*, 252.
55. Ibid.
56. Morris, *The Rise of Theodore Roosevelt*, 647.
57. Hagedorn, Research Notes.
58. Dodge, *Report of the Commission Appointed by the President*, 2263.
59. Hagedorn, Research Notes.
60. Ibid.
61. Ibid.
62. Ibid.
63. Ibid.
64. Ibid.
65. Ibid.
66. Morris, *The Rise of Theodore Roosevelt*, 648.
67. Hagedorn, Research Notes.
68. Konstam, *San Juan Hill 1898*, 37.
69. Ibid., 78.
70. Walker, *The Boys of '98*, 199.
71. Ibid., 198.
72. Konstam, *San Juan Hill 1898*, 39.
73. Walker, *The Boys of '98*, 199.
74. Morris, *The Rise of Theodore Roosevelt*, 649.
75. O'Toole, *The Spanish War*, 293.
76. Morris, *The Rise of Theodore Roosevelt*, 649.

Chapter 21:
1. Morris, *The Rise of Theodore Roosevelt*, 650.
2. Hall, *The Fun and Fighting of the Rough Riders*, 179.
3. Thomas, *The War Lovers*, 314.
4. Hagedorn, Research Notes.
5. Jones, *Roosevelt's Rough Riders*, 163.
6. A. M. Quesada and Stephen Walsh, *Roosevelt's Rough Riders* (Oxford: Osprey Pub, 2009), 22.

7. Jones, *Roosevelt's Rough Riders*, 168.
8. Samuels, *Teddy Roosevelt at San Juan Hill*, 215.
9. Roosevelt, *The Rough Riders*, 97.
10. O'Toole, *The Spanish War*, 300.
11. Ibid.
12. Ibid., 301.
13. Konstam, *San Juan Hill 1898*, 61; O'Toole, *The Spanish War*, 302.
14. Konstam, *San Juan Hill 1898*, 61.
15. Hall, *The Fun and Fighting of the Rough Riders*, 181.
16. O'Toole, *The Spanish War*, 303.
17. Ibid.
18. Roosevelt, *The Rough Riders*, 98.
19. Ibid.
20. Samuels, *Teddy Roosevelt at San Juan Hill*, 218.
21. Roosevelt, *Autobiography of Theodore Roosevelt*, 241.
22. Roosevelt, *The Rough Riders*, 98.
23. Ibid., 218.
24. O'Toole, *The Spanish War*, 305.
25. Hagedorn, Research Notes.
26. Morris, *The Rise of Theodore Roosevelt*, 653.
27. Konstam, *San Juan Hill 1898*, 62; O'Toole, *The Spanish War*, 310.
28. Marshall, *The Story of the Rough Riders*, 179.
29. Jeffers, *Colonel Roosevelt*, 229.
30. Marshall, *The Story of the Rough Riders*, 180.
31. Konstam, *San Juan Hill 1898*, 61.
32. Bruce, *History of Milwaukee*, 609.
33. O'Toole, *The Spanish War*, 308.
34. Roosevelt, *The Rough Riders*, 98.
35. O'Toole, *The Spanish War*, 308.
36. Hagedorn, Research Notes.
37. Marshall, *The Story of the Rough Riders*, 180.
38. Konstam, *San Juan Hill 1898*, 62.
39. Samuels, *Teddy Roosevelt at San Juan Hill*, 223.
40. Ibid.
41. O'Toole, *The Spanish War*, 311.
42. Cosby, *A Rough Rider Looks Back*.
43. Hagedorn, Research Notes.
44. Jones, *Roosevelt's Rough Riders*, 175.
45. Haywood actually died on July 2nd, not instantly.
46. O'Toole, *The Spanish War*, 310.
47. Ibid.
48. Ibid., 313.
49. Ibid.
50. Ibid., 311.

51. Morris, *The Rise of Theodore Roosevelt*, 652.
52. O'Toole, *The Spanish War*, 314. O'Toole says this took place at 1 p.m. a Rough Rider eyewitness account has Captain Lee at Bloody Ford at noon, so the author approximates that Captain Lee left by 11:30 a.m. Morris, *The Rise of Theodore Roosevelt*, 653.
53. Cosby, *A Rough Rider Looks Back.*
54. Samuels, *Teddy Roosevelt at San Juan Hill*, 233.
55. Roosevelt, *The Rough Riders*, 102.
56. Ibid.
57. Walker, *The Boys of '98*, 211.
58. O'Toole, *The Spanish War*, 315.
59. Roosevelt, *The Rough Riders*, 102. This is a rough quote as TR was writing about the incident in his autobiography.
60. Ibid., 102. This quote is derived from TR's writings.
61. Konstam, *San Juan Hill 1898*, 66.
62. Roosevelt, *The Rough Riders*, 102.
63. Samuels, *Teddy Roosevelt at San Juan Hill*, 250.
64. O'Toole, *The Spanish War*, 313.
65. Hagedorn, Research Notes.
66. O'Toole, *The Spanish War*, 313.
67. Ibid. Worth was wounded.
68. Ibid., 313.
69. Samuels, *Teddy Roosevelt at San Juan Hill*, 229.
70. Roosevelt, *The Rough Riders*, 107.
71. Konstam, *San Juan Hill 1898*, 61.
72. O'Toole, *The Spanish War*, 315.
73. Thomas, *The War Lovers*, 332
74. Roosevelt, *The Rough Riders*, 103.
75. Ibid.
76. Hagedorn, Research Notes.
77. Jones, *Roosevelt's Rough Riders*, 183.
78. Roosevelt, *The Rough Riders*, 104.
79. Roosevelt, *The Rough Riders*, 106; Samuels, *Teddy Roosevelt at San Juan Hill*, 253.
80. Hagedorn, Research Notes.
81. Jones, *Roosevelt's Rough Riders*, 181.
82. Hagedorn, Research Notes.
83. Thomas, *The War Lovers*, 323.
84. Ibid., 324.
85. Ibid.
86. Thomas Handford, *Theodore Roosevelt: The Pride of the Rough Riders: An Ideal American* (Chicago: Donohue, Henneberry, 1899), 125.
87. Hagedorn, Research Notes.
88. Renehan, *The Lion's Pride: Theodore Roosevelt and His Family in Peace and War.*

89. Strock, *Theodore Roosevelt on Leadership*, 55.
90. Walker, *The Boys of '98*, 215.
91. Ibid., 216.
92. Cosby, *A Rough Rider Looks Back*.
93. Konstam, *San Juan Hill 1898*, 66.
94. Roosevelt, *The Rough Riders*, 107.
95. Samuels, *Teddy Roosevelt at San Juan Hill*, 254.
96. Marshall, *The Story of the Rough Riders*, 195.
97. Hagedorn, Research Notes.
98. Marshall, *The Story of the Rough Riders*, 196.
99. Roosevelt, *The Rough Riders*, 108.
100. Ibid., 110.
101. Ibid., 108.
102. Ibid., 110.
103. Jones, *Roosevelt's Rough Riders*, 185.
104. Walker, *The Boys of '98*, 219.
105. Samuels, *Teddy Roosevelt at San Juan Hill*, 259.
106. Konstam, *San Juan Hill 1898*, 69; Jones, *Roosevelt's Rough Riders*, 185.
107. Hagedorn, Research Notes.
108. Jones, *Roosevelt's Rough Riders*, 183.
109. Roosevelt, *Autobiography of Theodore Roosevelt*, 243.
110. Samuels, *Teddy Roosevelt at San Juan Hill*, 267.
111. Roosevelt, *The Rough Riders*, 111.
112. Ibid., 235.
113. Ibid., 111.
114. Hagedorn, Research Notes.
115. Ibid.
116. Roosevelt, *The Rough Riders*, 112.
117. Ibid., 112.
118. Hagedorn, Research Notes.
119. Roosevelt, *The Rough Riders*, 112.
120. Jeffers, *Colonel Roosevelt*, 239.
121. O'Toole, *The Spanish War*, 321.
122. Konstam, *San Juan Hill 1898*, 76.
123. Jeffers, *Colonel Roosevelt*, 249.
124. Hagedorn, Research Notes. From Edward Livermore Burlingame, *Scribner's Magazine* 24, p. 650.
125. Roosevelt, *Autobiography of Theodore Roosevelt*, 244.
126. Thomas, *The War Lovers*, 338; Konstam, *San Juan Hill 1898*, 76.
127. Jones, *Roosevelt's Rough Riders*, 192.
128. Roosevelt, *The Rough Riders*, 144.
129. O'Toole, *The Spanish War*, 323.
130. Roosevelt, *The Rough Riders*, 120.
131. Hagedorn, Research Notes; Jones, *Roosevelt's Rough Riders*, 193.

132. Hagedorn, Research Notes.
133. Ibid.
134. Jones, *Roosevelt's Rough Riders*, 193.

Chapter 22:
1.   Berry is the one who picked up the 3rd cavalry's colors, per Trask.
2.   Hagedorn, Research Notes.
3.   Morris, *The Rise of Theodore Roosevelt*, 661.
4.   Hall, *The Fun and Fighting of the Rough Riders*, 220.
5.   Samuels, *Teddy Roosevelt at San Juan Hill*, 293.
6.   Ibid.
7.   "Spanish Troops Routed by American Cavalry," *San Francisco Call*, June 25th, 1898. This was a telling of the Las Guasimas Charge.
8.   Dodge, *Report of the Commission Appointed by the President*, 470.
9.   Walker, *The Boys of '98*, 273. Walker gets credit for identifying the words found in TR's book, *The Rough Riders*.
10. Hagedorn, Research Notes.
11. Ibid.
12. Ibid. Some of these accounts have been slightly edited for grammar and content; the context has remained intact.
13. Marshall, *The Story of the Rough Riders*, 247.
14. Jones, *Roosevelt's Rough Riders*, 249.
15. Morris, *The Rise of Theodore Roosevelt*, 658.
16. Walker, *The Boys of '98*, 253.
17. Hagedorn, Research Notes.
18. Jones, *Roosevelt's Rough Riders*, 256.
19. Roosevelt, *The Rough Riders*, 162.
20. Jones, *Roosevelt's Rough Riders*, 257.
21. Hagedorn, Research Notes
22. Roosevelt, *Autobiography of Theodore Roosevelt*, 247.
23. Ibid.
24. Ralph Paine, *Roads of Adventure* (New York: Houghton Mifflin, 1922), 271.
25. Morris, *The Rise of Theodore Roosevelt*, 660.
26. Hagedorn, Research Notes.
27. Ibid.
28. Ibid.
29. Morris, *The Rise of Theodore Roosevelt*, 660.
30. National Archives and Records Service, *Prologue: Selected Articles*, 30, no. 1 (Spring 1998): 17 Accessed: January 2015.
31. Jeffers, *Colonel Roosevelt*, 270.
32. Morison, *The Letters of Theodore Roosevelt*, 1093–1098.
33. Bill Clinton, *Public Papers of the Presidents of the United States, William J. Clinton* (District of Columbia: Office of the Federal Register, National Archives and Records Administration, 1994), 2922.

34. John Taliaferro, *All the Great Prizes: The Life of John Hay, from Lincoln to Roosevelt* (New York: Simon & Schuster, 2013), 330.
35. Marshall, *The Story of the Rough Riders*, 240.
36. Morris, *The Rise of Theodore Roosevelt*, 664.
37. Marshall, *The Story of the Rough Riders*, 24; Morris, *The Rise of Theodore Roosevelt*, 664.
38. Jones, *Roosevelt's Rough Riders*, 267.
39. Morris, *The Rise of Theodore Roosevelt*, 664.
40. Ibid.
41. Jones, *Roosevelt's Rough Riders*, 267.
42. Roosevelt, *The Rough Riders*, 175; Hagedorn, Research Notes.
43. Jones, *Roosevelt's Rough Riders*, 272.
44. Morris, *The Rise of Theodore Roosevelt*, 672.
45. Jones, *Roosevelt's Rough Riders*, 272.
46. Hagedorn, Research Notes.
47. Ibid.
48. Jones, *Roosevelt's Rough Riders*, 277.
49. Marshall, *The Story of the Rough Riders*, 251.
50. Ibid.
51. Morris, *The Rise of Theodore Roosevelt*, 674.
52. Ibid.
53. Ibid., 672.
54. Jones, *Roosevelt's Rough Riders*, 281; Morris, *The Rise of Theodore Roosevelt*, 67.
55. Edward Lewis, *Order Number Ten: Being Cursory Comments on Some of the Effects of the Great American Fraud Order* (Missouri: University City, 1911). Quote is from the time when TR was president; his policies as governor were a precursor to his square deal policies as president.
56. Morris, *The Rise of Theodore Roosevelt*, 732.
57. Miller, *Theodore Roosevelt: A Life*, 346.

Chapter 23:
1. Morris, *The Rise of Theodore Roosevelt*, 737.
2. Brands, *T.R.: The Last Romantic*, 411.
3. Ibid.
4. Ibid., 407.
5. Antoine Wilson, *The Assassination of William McKinley* (New York: Rosen, 2002), 8.
6. Douglas Wayne Houck, *Energy & Light in Nineteenth-Century Western New York: Natural Gas, Petroleum & Electricity* (South Carolina: History Press, 2014), 139.
7. Charles Bishop, *The Lion and the Journalist: The Unlikely Friendship of Theodore Roosevelt and Joseph Bucklin Bishop* (Connecticut: Lyons, 2012), 119.

8.   Wilson, *The Assassination of William McKinley*, 8.
9.   Shawn Reese, *The U.S. Secret Service: An Examination and Analysis of Its History and Missions* (District of Columbia: Congressional Research Service, 2009), 7.
10. Wilson, *The Assassination of William McKinley*, 8.
11. "Luck Ran Out With a Carnation When McKinley Gave It Away," *Evening Independent*, September 7th, 1984.
12. Morris, *The Rise of Theodore Roosevelt*, 738.
13. Luck Ran Out With a Carnation When McKinley Gave It Away," *Evening Independent*, September 7th, 1984.
14. A. M. Dyer, *Notice: Bell Telephone Company* (Buffalo Commercial, Associated Newspapers of Buffalo, September 9th, 1901); Grondahl, *I Rose Like a Rocket*, 367.
15. A. M. Dyer, *Notice: Bell Telephone Company*.
16. Morris, *The Rise of Theodore Roosevelt*, 738.
17. Ibid.
18. Brands, *T.R.: The Last Romantic*, 411.
19. Morris, *The Rise of Theodore Roosevelt*, 738.
20. Grondahl, *I Rose Like a Rocket*, 368.
21. Ibid.
22. Brands, *T.R.: The Last Romantic*, 412.
23. Grondahl, *I Rose Like a Rocket*, 371.
24. Morris, *The Rise of Theodore Roosevelt*, 739; Grondahl, *I Rose Like a Rocket*, 373.
25. Jacob A. Riis, *Theodore Roosevelt, the Citizen* (New York: Outlook, 1904), 76.
26. Morris, *The Rise of Theodore Roosevelt*, 739.
27. Eloise Cronin Murphy, *Theodore Roosevelt's Night Ride to the Presidency* (New York: Adirondack Museum, 1977), 15.
28. Miller, *Theodore Roosevelt: A Life*, 349.
29. Grondahl, *I Rose Like a Rocket*, 375; Murphy, *Theodore Roosevelt's Night Ride to the Presidency*, 14.
30. Murphy, *Theodore Roosevelt's Night Ride to the Presidency*, 16.
31. Miller, *Theodore Roosevelt: A Life*, 349.
32. Ibid., 350.
33. Murphy, *Theodore Roosevelt's Night Ride to the Presidency*, 17.
34. Miller, *Theodore Roosevelt: A Life*, 350.
35. Ibid.
36. Ibid.
37. Grondahl, *I Rose Like a Rocket*, 377.
38. Ibid.
39. Murphy, *Theodore Roosevelt's Night Ride to the Presidency*, 21.
40. Grondahl, *I Rose Like a Rocket*, 378.

41. Ibid.
42. Murphy, *Theodore Roosevelt's Night Ride to the Presidency*, 21.
43. Ibid., 22.
44. Ibid., 21.
45. Murat Halstead, Chauncey Depew, and A. J. Munson, *Life and Distinguished Services of William McKinley: Our Martyr President* (Chicago: Memorial Association, 1901), 512.
46. Murphy, *Theodore Roosevelt's Night Ride to the Presidency*, 25.
47. Ibid., 29.
48. Ibid., 23.
49. Ibid., 25.
50. Ibid.
51. Grondahl, *I Rose Like a Rocket*, 379.
52. Murphy, *Theodore Roosevelt's Night Ride to the Presidency*, 25.
53. Roosevelt, *Autobiography of Theodore Roosevelt*, 244.
54. Edmund Morris, *Theodore Rex* (New York: Random House, 2001), 7.
55. Murphy, *Theodore Roosevelt's Night Ride to the Presidency*, 29; Grondahl, *I Rose Like a Rocket*, 380.
56. Murphy, *Theodore Roosevelt's Night Ride to the Presidency*, 26.
57. Ibid., 28.
58. Grondahl, *I Rose Like a Rocket*, 381, and Morris, *Theodore Rex*, 8.
59. Grondahl, *I Rose Like a Rocket*, 381.
60. Ibid., 383.
61. Ibid., 384.
62. "The New President," *Washington Post*, September 15th, 1901.
63. Miller, *Theodore Roosevelt: A Life*, 351.
64. Morris, *Theodore Rex*, 13.
65. "The New President," *Washington Post*, September 15th, 1901.
66. Ibid.
67. Miller, *Theodore Roosevelt: A Life*, 352.
68. "The New President," *Washington Post*, September 15th, 1901.
69. "Roosevelt Takes Oath of Office," *San Francisco Chronicle*, September 15th, 1901.

Epilogue:
1. Thomas Guthrie Marquis, *Presidents of the United States from Pierce to McKinley* (London: Linscott Pub., 1907), 468.
2. Wallace Chessman, *Theodore Roosevelt and the Politics of Power* (Massachusetts: G. K. Hall & Co., 1969), 118.
3. McCullough, *Mornings on Horseback*, 363; Dalton, *Theodore Roosevelt: A Strenuous Life*, 520.
4. McCullough, *Mornings on Horseback*, 363.
5. Ibid.

6. Dalton, *Theodore Roosevelt: A Strenuous Life*, 9.
7. Strock, *Theodore Roosevelt on Leadership*, 171.
8. Hagedorn, *The Boys' Life of Theodore Roosevelt, 3.*
9. Hagedorn, Research Notes.
10. Putnam, *Theodore Roosevelt: The Formative Years*, 602.
11. Strock, *Theodore Roosevelt on Leadership*, 136.
12. Bishop, *The Lion and the Journalist*, 414; Putnam, *Theodore Roosevelt: The Formative Years*, 601.
13. Norris McWhirter, Stan Greenberg, David Boehm, and Steven Morgenstern, *Guinness Sports Record Book: 1979–1980* (New York: Bantam, 1980), 464.
14. Strock, *Theodore Roosevelt on Leadership*, 166.
15. "The American Experience: T.R. The Story of Theodore Roosevelt," *Public Broadcasting Service* (Aired October 6th and 7th, 1996).
16. Ibid.
17. Ibid.
18. Ibid.
19. Ibid.
20. McCullough, *Mornings on Horseback*, 364; United States Census Bureau, "State Area Measurements and Internal Point Coordinates," accessed April 2015, https://www.census.gov/geo/reference/state-area.html
21. Edmund Morris, *Colonel Roosevelt* (New York: Random House, 2010), 134.
22. Michael Kazin, Rebecca Edwards, and Adam Rothman, *The Princeton Encyclopedia of American Political History* (New Jersey: Princeton University Press, 2010), 420.
23. McCullough, *Mornings on Horseback*, 365.
24. "The American Experience: T.R. The Story of Theodore Roosevelt," *Public Broadcasting Service.*
25. Willard Oliver and Nancy Marion, *Killing the President: Assassinations, Attempts, and Rumored Attempts on U.S. Commanders-in-Chief* (California: Praeger, 2010), 74.
26. Oliver Remey, Henry Cochems, and Wheeler Bloodgood, *The Attempted Assassination of Ex-President Theodore Roosevelt,* (Wisconsin: R.H. Hunt, 1978), 15.
27. Oliver, Cochems, and Bloodgood, *Killing the President*, 76.
28. William Bruce, *History of Milwaukee, City and County*, vol. 1 (Milwaukee: S. J. Clarke Publishing Co., 1922), 608.
29. Oliver, Cochems, and Bloodgood, *Killing the President*, 76.
30. Bruce, *History of Milwaukee*, 608.
31. Oliver, Cochems, and Bloodgood, *Killing the President*, 76.
32. Oliver, Cochems, and Bloodgood, *The Attempted Assassination of Ex-President Theodore Roosevelt*, 15.

33. Patricia O'Toole, *When Trumpets Call: Theodore Roosevelt After the White House* (New York: Simon & Schuster, 2005), 323.
34. Theodore Roosevelt letter to Woodrow Wilson, May 18th, 1917.
35. McCullough, *Mornings on Horseback*, 366–367.
36. Ibid., 367.
37. Renehan, *The Lion's Pride: Theodore Roosevelt and His Family in Peace and War*, 22.
38. McCullough, *Mornings on Horseback*, 368.
39. Strok, *Theodore Roosevelt on Leadership*, 237.
40. Rick Marschall, *Bully! The Life and Times of Theodore Roosevelt* (District of Columbia: Regnery, 2011), 391.
41. Willis, *Roosevelt in the Rough*, 237.
42. It was two months and ten days.

Bibliography

Primary Sources

Cosby, A. F. A Rough Rider Looks Back (MS Am 1515), Houghton Library, Harvard University.

Hagedorn, Hermann. The Rough Riders–research notes (MS Am 2995), Theodore Roosevelt Collection, Houghton Library, Harvard University.

Books

Anderson, Gerald R. *Subic Bay: From Magellan to Mt. Pinatubo: The History of the U.S. Naval Station.* Dagupan City: Lazer, 1991.

Auchincloss, Louis. *Theodore Roosevelt.* New York: Times Book, 2001.

Baird, Albert. *Public Discussion and Debate.* Boston: Ginn, 1928.

Bishop, Charles. *The Lion and the Journalist: The Unlikely Friendship of Theodore Roosevelt and Joseph Bucklin Bishop.* Connecticut: Lyons, 2012.

Bishop, Joseph. *Theodore Roosevelt and His Time Shown in His Own Letters,* vol. 1. New York: Hodder and Stoughton, 1920.

Brands, H. W. *The Reckless Decade: America in the 1890s.* New York: St. Martin's, 1995.

Brands, H. W. *T.R.: The Last Romantic.* New York: Basic Books, 1997.

Brands, H. W. *The Selected Letters of Theodore Roosevelt.* New York: Cooper Square Press, 2001.

Bristow, Allen P. *Whispering Smith: His Life and Misadventures.* New Mexico: Sunstone, 2007.

Britton, John. *Cables, Crises, and the Press: The Geopolitics of the New Information System in the Americas, 1866–1903.* New Mexico: University of New Mexico, 2013.

Bruce, William. *History of Milwaukee, City and County,* vol. 1. Milwaukee: S. J. Clarke Publishing Co., 1922.

Burns, James MacGregor and Susan Dunn. *The Three Roosevelts.* New York: Atlantic Monthly Press, 2001.

Busch, Noel. *T.R.: The Story of Theodore Roosevelt and His Influence on Our Times.* New York: Reynal & Company, 1963.

Caroli, Betty Boyd. *The Roosevelt Women.* New York: Basic Books, 1998.

Chadwick, French. *The Relations of the United States and Spain: The Spanish-American War.* New York: Charles Scribner's Sons, 1911.

Chessman, Wallace. *Theodore Roosevelt and the Politics of Power.* Massachusetts: G. K. Hall & Co., 1969.

Clinton, Bill. *Public Papers of the Presidents of the United States, William J. Clinton.* District of Columbia: Office of the Federal Register, National Archives and Records Administration, 1994.

Coulter, Ellis. *The Confederate States of America, 1861–1865.* Texas: University of Texas Press, 1978.

Crompton, Samuel Etinde. *The Sinking of the USS Maine: Declaring War against Spain.* New York: Chelsea House, 2009.

Dalton, Kathleen. *Theodore Roosevelt: A Strenuous Life.* New York: Vintage Books, 2002.

Davis, Richard Harding. *Notes of a War Correspondent.* New York: Harper & Brothers, 1911.

Di Silvestro, Roger. *Theodore Roosevelt in the Badlands: A Young Politician's Quest for Recovery in the American West.* New York: Walker, 2011.

Donald, Aida. *Lion in the White House: A Life of Theodore Roosevelt.* New York: Basic Books, 2007.

Donovan, Jim. *The Blood of Heroes: The 13-Day Struggle for the Alamo—and the Sacrifice That Forged a Nation.* New York: Little, Brown, 2012.

Golay, Michael. *The Spanish-American War.* New York: Facts on File, 1995.

Grant, George. *The Courage and Character of Theodore Roosevelt.* Tennessee: Cumberland House, 2005.

Grondahl, Paul. *I Rose Like a Rocket.* New York: Free Press, 2004.

Hagedorn, Hermann. *The Boys' Life of Theodore Roosevelt.* New York: Harper & Brothers, 1922.

Hagedorn, Hermann. *Roosevelt in the Bad Lands.* Boston: Houghton Mifflin Co., 1921.

Hall, Tom. *The Fun and Fighting of the Rough Riders.* New York: Stokes Co., 1899.

Halstead, Murat, Chauncey Depew, and A. J. Munson. *Life and Distinguished Services of William McKinley: Our Martyr President.* Chicago: Memorial Association, 1901.

Hamilton, John. *Theodore Roosevelt National Park.* Minnesota: ABDO Publishing Co, 2008.

Handford, Thomas W. *Theodore Roosevelt: The Pride of the Rough Riders, An Ideal American: An Example and an Inspiration to Young Men.* Chicago: Donohue, Henneberry, 1899.

Haythornthwaite, Philip. *The Alamo and the War of Texan Independence 1835–36.* London: Osprey, 1986.

Hess, Stephen. *America's Political Dynasties from Adams to Kennedy.* New York: Doubleday, 1966.

Holzer, Harold. *The Lincoln-Douglas Debates: The First Complete, Unexpurgated Text.* New York: Fordham University Press, 2004.

Houck, Douglas Wayne. *Energy & Light in Nineteenth-Century Western New York: Natural Gas, Petroleum & Electricity.* South Carolina: History Press, 2014.

Jeffers, Paul. *Colonel Roosevelt: Theodore Roosevelt Goes to War, 1897–1898.* New York: John Wiley & Sons, 1996.

Jeffers, Paul. *Commissioner Roosevelt: The Story of Theodore Roosevelt and the New York City Police, 1895–1897.* New York: John Wiley & Sons, 1994.

Jones, Virgil Carrington. *Roosevelt's Rough Riders.* New York: Doubleday & Company, 1971.

Kazin, Michael, Rebecca Edwards, and Adam Rothman. *The Princeton Encyclopedia of American Political History.* New Jersey: Princeton University Press, 2010.

King, David. *New Orleans.* Connecticut: Twenty-First Century, 1998.

Konstam, Angus. *San Juan Hill 1898: America's Emergence as a World Power.* London: Praeger, 2004.

Lang, Lincoln. *Ranching with Roosevelt.* New York: J. B. Lippincott Co., 1926.

Lewis, Edward. *Order Number Ten: Being Cursory Comments on Some of the Effects of the Great American Fraud Order.* Missouri: University City, 1911.

Lorant, Stefan. *The Life and Times of Theodore Roosevelt.* New York: Doubleday & Company, 1959.

Madden, W. C. *Tecumseh's Curse.* Xlibris Publishing, 2011.

Mansfield, Harvey C. *Manliness.* Connecticut: Yale University Press, 2006.

Marquis, Thomas Guthrie. *Presidents of the United States from Pierce to McKinley.* London: Linscott Pub., 1907.

Marschall, Rick. *Bully! The Life and Times of Theodore Roosevelt.* District of Columbia: Regnery, 2011.

Marshall, Edward. *The Story of the Rough Riders.* New York: G. W. Dillingham Co., 1899.

McCullough, David. *Mornings on Horseback.* New York: Simon & Schuster, 2001.

McWhirter, Norris, Stan Greenberg, David Boehm, and Steven Morgenstern. *Guinness Sports Record Book: 1979–1980.* New York: Bantam, 1980.

Millard, Candice. *The River of Doubt.* New York: Double Day, 2005.

Miller, Marion. *Great Debates in American History: Revenue: The Tariff and Taxation, United States. Congress, Great Britain. Parliament.* Current Literature Publishing, 1913.

Miller, Nathan. *Theodore Roosevelt: A Life.* New York: William Morrow and Company, 1992.

Morison, Elting and Theodore Roosevelt. *The Letters of Theodore Roosevelt, The Years of Preparation,* vol. 1. Massachusetts: Harvard University Press, 1951.

Morris, Edmund. *Colonel Roosevelt.* New York: Random House, 2010.

Morris, Edmund. *The Rise of Theodore Roosevelt.* New York: Coward, McCann & Geoghegan, 1979.

Morris, Edmund. *Theodore Rex.* New York: Random House, 2001.

Murphy, Eloise Cronin. *Theodore Roosevelt's Night Ride to the Presidency.* New York: Adirondack Museum, 1977.

Newton-Matza, Mitchell. *Disasters and Tragic Events: An Encyclopedia of Catastrophes in American History.* California: ABC-CLIO, 2014.

O'Connor, Stephen. *Orphan Trains: The Story of Charles Loring Brace and the Children He Saved.* New York: Houghton Mifflin, 2001.

Oliver, Willard and Nancy Marion. *Killing the President: Assassinations, Attempts, and Rumored Attempts on U.S. Commanders-in-Chief.* California: Praeger, 2010.

O'Toole, G. J. A. *The Spanish War: An American Epic 1898.* New York: W. W. Norton & Company, 1984.

O'Toole, Patricia. *When Trumpets Call: Theodore Roosevelt After the White House.* New York: Simon & Schuster, 2005.

Paine, Ralph. *Roads of Adventure.* Boston and New York: Houghton Mifflin, 1922.

Pine, Joslyn. *Wit and Wisdom of the American Presidents: A Book of Quotations.* New York: Dover Publications, 2001.

Putnam, Carleton. *Theodore Roosevelt: The Formative Years, 1858–1886.* New York: Charles Scribner's Sons, 1958.

Pringle, Henry. *Theodore Roosevelt: A Biography*. New York: Harvest/HBJ, 1984.

Riis, Jacob A. *Theodore Roosevelt, the Citizen*. New York: Outlook, 1904.

Remey, Oliver, Henry Cochems, and Wheeler Bloodgood. *The Attempted Assassination of Ex-President Theodore Roosevelt*. Wisconsin: R. H. Hunt, 1978.

Renehan, Edward, Jr. *The Lion's Pride: Theodore Roosevelt and His Family in Peace and War*. New York: Oxford University Press, 1998.

Republican National Party. *Proceedings of the Eighth Republican National Convention Held at Chicago, Illinois*. Illinois: Rand, McNally & Co., 1884.

Robinson, Corinne Roosevelt. *My Brother Theodore Roosevelt*. New York: Charles Scribner's Sons, 1921.

Roosevelt, Theodore. *Autobiography of Theodore Roosevelt*. New York: Charles Scribner's Sons, 1927.

Roosevelt, Theodore. *Hunting Trips of a Ranchman and the Wilderness Hunter*. New York: Modern Library, 1996.

Roosevelt, Theodore. *Literary Essays, National Edition*. New York: Charles Scribner's Sons, 1926.

Roosevelt, Theodore. *My Debt to Maine*. Maine: Maine Writers Research Club, 1919.

Roosevelt, Theodore. *The Rough Riders*. New York: The Library of America, 2004.

Roosevelt, Theodore. *Winning of the West*, vol. 2. Nebraska: Bison Book, 1995.

Roosevelt, Theodore, and Frederic Remington. *Ranch Life and the Hunting Trail*. New York: Dover Publications, 2009.

Roosevelt, Theodore, and F. V. Greene. *American Ideals, with a Biographical Sketch by Gen. Francis Vinton Greene; Administration–Civil Service*. New York: Collier, 1897.

Roosevelt, Theodore, and William E. Leuchtenburg. *The New Nationalism*. New Jersey: Prentice-Hall, 1961.

Ruddy, Daniel. *Theodore Roosevelt's History of the United States: His Own Words, By Theodore Roosevelt.* New York: Smithsonian Books, 2010.

Samuels, Peggy, and Harold Samuels. *Teddy Roosevelt at San Juan Hill: The Making of a President.* College Station: University of Texas Press, 1997.

Sigsbee, Charles and Thomas Watson Ball. *The "Maine": An Account of Her Destruction in Havana Harbor.* New York: The Century, Co., 1899.

Smith, Jean Edward. *Grant.* New York: Touchstone, 2001.

Stewart, Charles West. *John Paul Jones Commemoration at Annapolis, April 24th, 1906.* Washington: Government Printing Office, 1907.

Strock, James. *Theodore Roosevelt on Leadership: Executive Lessons from the Bully Pulpit.* California: Prima, 2001.

Summers, Mark. *Rum, Romanism & Rebellion: The Making of a President, 1884.* North Carolina: University of North Carolina Press, 2000.

Taliaferro, John. *All the Great Prizes: The Life of John Hay, from Lincoln to Roosevelt.* New York: Simon & Schuster, 2013.

Thayer, William Roscoe. *Theodore Roosevelt: An Intimate Biography.* New York: Grosset & Dunlap, 1919.

Thomas, Evans. *The War Lovers.* New York: Little, Brown and Company, 2010.

Tone, John Lawrence. *War and Genocide in Cuba, 1895–1898.* North Carolina: University of North Carolina Press, 2006.

Trask, David F. *The War with Spain in 1898.* Connecticut: Easton, 2002.

Vietze, Andrew. *Becoming Teddy Roosevelt: How a Maine Guide Inspired America's 26th President.* Maine: Down East, 2010.

Walker, Dale. *Death Was the Black Horse: The Story of Rough Rider Buckey O'Neill.* Texas: Madrona, 1975.

Walker, Dale. *The Boys of '98: Theodore Roosevelt and the Rough Riders.* New York: Tom Doherty Associates, 1998.

Wallenfeldt, Jeff. *The American Civil War and Reconstruction.* New York: Britannica, 2010.

Willis, Jack. *Roosevelt in the Rough.* New York: Washburn, 1931.

Westermeier, Clifford. *Who Rush to Glory.* Idaho: Caxton Printers, 1958.

Wilhelm, Donald. *Theodore Roosevelt as an Undergraduate.* Boston: J. W. Luce & Co., 1910

Wilson, Antoine. *The Assassination of William McKinley.* New York: Rosen, 2002.

Wilson, Walter and Gary McKay, edited by Edmund Cody Burnett. *James D. Bulloch: Secret Agent and Mastermind of the Confederate Navy.* Letters of members of the Continental Congress, 520.

Young, James and Joseph Hampton Moore. *Reminiscences and Thrilling Stories of the War by Returned Heroes: Containing Vivid Accounts of Personal Experiences by Officers and Men.* California: J. Dewing, 1899.

Zacks, Richard. *Island of Vice: Theodore Roosevelt's Quest to Clean up Sin-loving New York.* New York: Anchor, 2012.

Zimmerman, Warren. *First Great Triumph.* New York: Farrar, Straus and Giroux, 2002.

Articles, Reports and Television

American History Museum Annual Report 2014, 4, 7.

Army Corps of Engineers. *Final Report on Removing Wreck of Battleship "Maine" from Harbor of Havana.* Washington, D.C.: U.S. Government Printing Office, 1914.

Athenæum: A Journal of English and Foreign Literature, Science, the Fine Arts. American Notes for General Circulation. vol. 2. London: Chapman and Hall (1842): 901.

Barnes, C. M. *Report of the Governor of Oklahoma to the Secretary of the Interior for the Fiscal Year Ended June 30th, 1898.* Washington: Government Printing Office, 1898.

Boffey, Phillip. "Theodore Roosevelt at Harvard." *The Harvard Crimson* (December 12th, 1957).

Buffalo Commercial. *Notice: Bell Telephone Company.* A. M. Dyer, Associated Newspapers of Buffalo, September 9th, 1901.

Bush, George. "Remarks at an Environmental Agreement Signing Ceremony at the Grand Canyon, Arizona." September 18th, 1991.

Census Report. *Arizona Population of Counties by Decennial Census: 1900 to 1990.* Compiled and edited by Richard Forstall Population Division. Washington: US Bureau of the Census. Bureau of the Census Report, 1996.

Civil Service Chronicle 2 (1893): 223.

Dantz, William Thompson. "Tales of The Roosevelt Country." *McClure's Magazine* (May 1925).

Dodge, Greenville, et al. *Report of the Commission Appointed by the President to Investigate the Conduct of the War Department in the War with Spain.* vols. 5, 7, and 8 (1900). Washington: Government Printing Office.

Hargreaves, Steve A. "The Richest Americans in History." Cable News Network. June 2nd, 2014. Retrieved: January 2015.

Harper's Weekly 48 (1904): 121.

Key, David. "Theodore Roosevelt, The Rough Riders, and the Alteration of Myth." *Journal of the West* 37, no. 2 (April 1998): 71.

Lewis, Merrill E. "History as Melodrama: Theodore Roosevelt's 'The Winning of the West'." *The American West, An Appraisal.* Ed. R. G. Ferris. Santa Fe: Museum of New Mexico Press, 1963.

Life (April 24th, 1950): 12.

Long, Clarence. *Wages and Earnings in the United States 1860–1890.* New Jersey: Princeton University Press, 1960.

"Luck Ran Out with a Carnation When McKinley Gave It Away." *The Evening Independent,* September 7th, 1984.

National Archives and Records Service. *Prologue: Selected Articles.* National Archives and Records Administration 30, no. 1 (Spring 1998). Retrieved online: January 2015.

"The New President: Mr. Roosevelt Takes the Oath of Office at Buffalo: A Deeply Emotional Scene." *Washington Post*, September 15th, 1901.

"Old Bullion's Team." *Time*, January 28th, 1935.

"Our Mission, Role & History: Theodore Roosevelt." Office of Personnel Management, accessed September 20th, 2013, http://www.opm.gov/about-us/our-mission-role-history/theodore-roosevelt/

Price, Hazell. *Hazell's Annual Cyclopaedia 1888*. London: Hazell, Watson & Viney, 1888.

Public Broadcasting Service. *T.R.: The Story of Theodore Roosevelt*. The American Experience: Season 9, Episode 1. Release date: 6 Oct. 1996.

Reese, Shawn. *The U.S. Secret Service: An Examination and Analysis of Its History and Missions*. District of Columbia: Congressional Research Service, 2009.

Reilly, John and Robert Scheina. *American Battleships 1886–1923: Predreadnought Design and Construction*. Maryland: Naval Institute Press (1980): 26-28, 37.

"Roosevelt Takes Oath of Office: Solemn Scene as the Vice-President Becomes the Nation's Chief." *San Francisco Chronicle*, September 15th, 1901.

"Roosevelt's *The Winning of the West*," *Atlantic Monthly*, 64 (1889): 694.

"Sergt Ledwidge to the Boys: Talks of Cuban Battles at the East Side House Settlement: 'The Goose' Gets Excited." *The New York Times*, October 7th, 1898.

"Sheriff's Work on a Ranch." *Century Illustrated Monthly Magazine* 36 (1888): 44.

"Spanish Troops Routed by American Cavalry." *San Francisco Call* 84, no. 25 (June 25th, 1898).

Surgeon General of the United States Navy. *Annual Report 1898* (1898): 173.

United States Census Bureau. "State Area Measurements and Internal Point Coordinates." Retrieved April 2015.

White, Richard. *Theodore Roosevelt as Civil Service Commissioner: Linking the Influence and Development of a Modern Administrative President*. Administrative Theory & Praxis—JSTOR, 2000, Page 696.

"The Whitewash in Baltimore: Maryland Reformers Will Try to Undo Wanamaker's Work." *The New York Times*, April 13th, 1892.